NUCLEAR
WEAPONS
AFTER THE
COLD WAR

NUCLEAR WEAPONS AFTER THE COLD WAR

Guidelines for
U.S. Policy

Edited by **Michèle A. Flournoy**
Center for Science and International Affairs
John F. Kennedy School of Government
Harvard University

With a Foreword by Ashton B. Carter

HarperCollins*CollegePublishers*

Executive Editor: Lauren Silverman
Project Editor: Thomas R. Farrell
Design Supervisor and Cover Design: Kay Petronio
Production Manager/Assistant: Willie Lane/Sunaina Sehwani
Compositor: ComCom Division of Haddon Craftsmen
Printer and Binder: R.R. Donnelley & Sons Company
Cover Printer: Lynn Art Offset Corporation

Nuclear Weapons After the Cold War: Guidelines for U.S. Policy

Library of Congress Cataloging-in-Publication Data

Nuclear weapons after the Cold War : guidelines for U.S. policy /
    edited by Michele A. Flournoy : with a foreword by Ashton B. Carter.
        p.   cm.
    Includes bibliographical references and index.
    ISBN 0-06-501128-7
    1. United States—Military policy.   2. Nuclear weapons—United
States.   I. Flournoy, Michele A.
UA23.N793   1992
355'.0335'73—dc20   92-18633
                                                                    CIP

92 93 94 95   9 8 7 6 5 4 3 2 1

To Scott

Contents

Foreword

The world is moving, as the authors of this book contend, into a second nuclear age. In some respects the second nuclear age exhibits features longed for during the first nuclear age, notably the absence of fierce, all-out competition between the United States and the former Soviet Union. In other respects the new age poses unsettling problems, notably the inexorable spread of nuclear know-how to parties that have not yet demonstrated their willingness to live by the norms of nuclear nonuse that have evolved among the great powers during the half-century since Nagasaki.

No doubt to much of the public the end of the first nuclear age spells a welcome relief from nuclear fear and from news reports chronicling a seemingly endless minuet of superpower summits, crises, negotiations, and debate. But for public policy as a whole, now is not the time to abandon the effort to control nuclear weapons, though the approach must be revised thoroughly. For though the political mood between the superpowers has warmed, 40 years of Cold War tension is still "hard-wired" into the nuclear arsenals, their command systems, and the policy conceptions that define their purposes. Organizations as large and complex as those that grew up over half a century of Cold War to build and operate nuclear weapons do not change all by themselves when the times change: A deliberate effort must be made to reshape them so that they come to embody the new attitudes that have emerged in political relations.

Another reason, even more important, should compel public policymakers to press on with efforts to control nuclear weapons even when the political climate seems to demand it least. The United States and the former Soviet Union, and the other nuclear nations that have struggled for several decades to manage this powerfully destructive technology, need to set the right example of respect and care for nuclear weapons—an example to other nations that come into possession of nuclear weapons, and an example to all the generations of humanity yet unborn that will unavoidably possess the knowledge and capacity to make nuclear weapons.

In this book, a group of scholars at the Center for Science and International Affairs has risen to the challenge of prescribing for U.S. nuclear policy-makers the first steps over the threshold of the second nuclear age. Their treatment is wide-ranging, covering strategic and nonstrategic nuclear weapons, offenses and defenses, modernization and arms control, forces and command and control, policy substance, and policy process. They develop a comprehensive, internally consistent, and persuasive set of policy recommendations in all these areas. The analysis is completely up-to-date, including assessment of the consequences of the disintegration of the former Soviet Union. Moreover, this book gets to the fundamentals and basic dilemmas of living in the nuclear age, and will thus be a reliable compass in the years ahead, which are sure to be filled with continued change. Few readers will not find something to disagree with in this volume, but none will find an important option or argument neglected. The result is a volume of great value to policy-makers as well as to scholars and students of the nuclear dilemma.

To many, nuclear policy must seem completely adrift, cast loose from its Cold War moorings and tossed by the waves of revolution in the former Soviet Union, inexorable proliferation of destructive technology around the world, and global shifts in political and economic influence. Through the efforts of this talented group of scholars, readers will discover that an intellectual anchor exists after all—though the storm is not nearly over.

ASHTON B. CARTER
Director
Center for Science and International Affairs
John F. Kennedy School of Government
Harvard University

Preface

Dramatic changes in the international security environment have rendered U.S. nuclear weapons policy ripe for review and revision. This book undertakes precisely such a review, developing a comprehensive and coherent set of guidelines for U.S. nuclear strategy, force planning, and arms control efforts over the next decade.

The product of a year-long study conducted under my direction by the Nuclear Arms Working Group at Harvard's Center for Science and International Affairs, this volume brings the expertise of a diverse group of scholars and practitioners to bear on one of the most salient policy issues of our time. Members of the working group were Michael Brower, Kurt Campbell, Albert Carnesale, Ashton Carter, Paul Doty, Mark Goodman, George Lewis, Susanne Peters, Michael Stafford, Larry Stewart, Nina Tannenwald, Cindy Williams, Joel Wit, Michael Yaffe, Charles Zraket, and myself. Over the course of the 1990–1991 academic year, the group met biweekly to discuss key issues, build consensus, and edit draft chapters.

Unlike most edited volumes, this is an integrated treatise rather than a collection of independent chapters. Each chapter, although written by an individual, is the product of extended group study; each has been commented upon by many members of the group; and each builds on those that precede it and lays the foundation for those that follow. Given the range of views represented in the group, not all members of the working group agree on all of the book's conclusions and recommendations. Nevertheless, these reflect a general, if imperfect, consensus. Ultimately, however, the responsibility for each chapter lies with its author.

This book offers a vision of our nuclear future and a blueprint for getting there. In so doing, it provides a potential tool for policy-makers, experts, journalists, congressional staff, public interest groups, and members of the military. But it also constructs a broader framework for thinking about nuclear weapons issues in the post–Cold War world, identifying central questions and analyzing alternative answers. As such, it is a resource for scholars, teachers, and students of international security.

In addition to thanking all of the members of the Nuclear Arms Working Group, I would like to thank Robert J. Einhorn of the Policy Planning Staff at the State Department and Brigadier General C. Jerome Jones, USAF, of the Joint Staff at the Pentagon for their constructive criticism of the project in its formative stages. I would also like to express my deepest appreciation to all those who commented on draft chapters or contributed ideas to the project, including Paul Bernstein, George Bing, Alfred Buckles, McGeorge Bundy, George Bunn, Matthew Bunn, Marie Chevrier, Steven Dudley, Kenneth Ford, Lawrence Freedman, Charles Glaser, Wayne Glass, Sidney Graybeal, Lisbeth Gronlund, David Hafemeister, Robert Herman, Ted Jarvis, Terry Joos, Richard Ned Lebow, Dunbar Lockwood, Jack Mendelsohn, Matthew Meselson, Joseph Nye, Michael O'Hanlon, Cmdr. Mike Pocalyko, Ted Postol, Thomas Risse-Kappen, Stan Riveles, Amy Sands, Jeffrey Starr, John Steinbruner, Tobyanne Suyemoto, Robert Toth, Carl Triebs, Robert Veale, Jenonne Walker, Ted Warner, Gen. Larry Welch, Dean Wilkening, and David Wright. Thanks also to the reviewers of the manuscript: Larry Elowitz, Georgia College; Lynn H. Miller, Temple University; Edward Rhodes, Rutgers University; and B. Thomas Trout, University of New Hampshire. Finally, I am very grateful to Albert Carnesale, the Center for Science and International Affairs at Harvard's John F. Kennedy School of Government, and the Carnegie Corporation's Avoiding Nuclear War Project for their financial support.

MICHÈLE A. FLOURNOY

Contributors

MICHAEL C. BROWER is a senior analyst for the Union of Concerned Scientists. In his four years at UCS, he has published numerous articles on nuclear arms policy, including analyses of the B-2 Stealth bomber and the future of strategic defenses. Dr. Brower received his B.S. from the Massachusetts Institute of Technology and his Ph.D. in Physics from Harvard University.

MICHÈLE A. FLOURNOY is a research fellow, coordinator of the Nuclear Arms Working Group, and coordinator of the Avoiding Nuclear War Project at the Center for Science and International Affairs. Before joining the Center, she spent five years as a senior policy analyst in Washington, D.C., most recently at the Arms Control Association. Ms. Flournoy received her B.A. in Social Studies from Radcliffe College, Harvard University, and a master's degree in International Relations and Strategic Studies from Balliol College, Oxford University, where she was a Newton-Tatum scholar. She has published several dozen articles and book chapters on arms control and national security issues.

MARK W. GOODMAN is a research fellow at the Center for Science and International Affairs and recipient of a MacArthur fellowship in International Peace and Security. Prior to coming to Harvard, he received a Ph.D. in theoretical physics from Princeton University and held postdoctoral research positions in physics at the University of California at Santa Barbara and Rutgers University. His current research focuses on military space policy.

GEORGE N. LEWIS is a postdoctoral fellow in the Defense and Arms Control Studies Program at the Massachusetts Institute of Technology. After receiving his Ph.D. in experimental solid state physics from Cornell University in 1983, he spent five years as a research associate in Cornell's Department of Applied Physics. Prior to coming to MIT, Dr. Lewis was a fellow in the Peace Studies program at Cornell and at the Center for International Security and Arms Control at Stanford University. He has published several articles on arms control issues.

MICHAEL F. STAFFORD is the executive director of the Center for Science and International Affairs. Before coming to Harvard, he served in the State Department as a special assistant to Ambassador Paul H. Nitze (who was then Special Advisor to the President and Secretary of State on Arms Control Matters) and in the Defense Department as a program analyst in the Office of the Assistant Secretary of Defense for Program Analysis and Evaluation. He gained negotiating experience as a member of the U.S. Delegation to the U.S.-Soviet INF talks and operational experience as an army officer in a nuclear missile battalion. Mr. Stafford received a B.S. in engineering from the U.S. Military Academy at West Point and a masters in public policy from the John F. Kennedy School of Government.

NINA TANNENWALD is a doctoral candidate in International Relations and the Peace Studies Program at Cornell University and a fellow at the Center for International Security and Arms Control at Stanford University. She was previously a fellow at Harvard's Center for Science and International Affairs. She is writing a dissertation on the historical evolution of norms against the use of nuclear weapons. Ms. Tannenwald received a B.A. from Dartmouth College and an M.A. in International Affairs from Columbia University.

CINDY WILLIAMS is head of the Strategic Air Command Systems department at The MITRE Corporation. Before joining MITRE, Dr. Williams directed the Strategic Offensive Forces Division of the Defense Secretary's Office of Program Analysis and Evaluation and worked at the Rand Corporation. She holds a B.A. from the University of Oklahoma and a Ph.D. in mathematics from the University of California at Irvine.

JOEL S. WIT is a Council on Foreign Relations International Affairs fellow and a resident associate at the Carnegie Endowment for International Peace. He is currently on leave from the State Department, where he has served in the Bureau of Politico-Military Affairs and the Bureau of Intelligence and Research. Mr. Wit received his B.A. from Bucknell University and an M.A. in International Affairs from Columbia University. He has published numerous articles on arms control policy.

Introduction

Michèle A. Flournoy

*T*he end of the Cold War has shaken the very foundations on which U.S. security policy has rested for more than 40 years. The legendary Soviet threat has crumbled, the division of Europe has ended, and the Soviet Union itself has undergone a profound political transformation.[1] In light of these changed realities, U.S. nuclear weapons policy—the ultimate guarantor of U.S. security during the Cold War—demands reassessment. What is the relevance of nuclear weapons in the post–Cold War world? What roles should nuclear weapons play in providing for U.S. security in the future? What should U.S. nuclear strategy be? How many and what type of nuclear weapons should the United States field? And what type of arms control and modernization policies should it pursue? At present, there is little consensus on the answers to these questions or on how the United States should arrive at them.

Nor is it self-evident that these questions—and a book that addresses them—are still important, particularly in the wake of the failed Soviet coup of August 1991 and the unilateral nuclear initiatives announced by Presidents Bush and Gorbachev shortly thereafter. However, we believe they are, for several reasons.

The continued existence of thousands of nuclear weapons remains an inescapable fact of life and an unavoidable focus of U.S. policy. Nuclear weapons present three distinct but related challenges for the United States after the Cold War. The first is reducing the risk of the accidental

---

[1]Throughout this book, the terms "Soviet Union," "USSR," and "former Soviet Union" refer to the national entities emerging on what used to be Soviet territory.

or unauthorized use of nuclear weapons. Of particular concern are those weapons based in an increasingly chaotic Soviet Union. The second is slowing, stopping, or managing the spread of nuclear weapons to other countries or subnational groups. The third is dealing with the mammoth nuclear legacy—the set of policies, practices, weapons, and habits of mind—the United States accumulated during more than 40 years of Cold War.

While taking the first two challenges into account, this book focuses on the third. Transforming the U.S. nuclear legacy into a set of policies more appropriate to the world we now live in will take time and considerable effort. It will also require a wholesale reexamination of the first principles upon which U.S. nuclear policies are based. Although piecemeal policy changes may move the United States in the right direction, they cannot substitute for a back-to-basics reevaluation of U.S. nuclear needs. Failing to undertake such a review could leave the United States with nuclear policies and practices that are no longer rooted in reality.

This book is among the first efforts to examine in detail the impact of the changing security environment on U.S. nuclear weapons policy.[2] As such, it seeks to devise a comprehensive and coherent set of guidelines for U.S. nuclear weapons policy for the next 10 years. This is a significant departure from the norm: Most analyses focus on a single, narrow aspect of nuclear policy in isolation from all others. Consequently, recommendations are often made without due consideration of their impact on or degree of consistency with other aspects of U.S. nuclear policy. The results are at best disjointed and at worst conflicting. Given the opportunities at stake in the post–Cold War world and the severe budget constraints on policy, the United States can no longer afford anything less than coherence in the nuclear realm.

This volume seeks to integrate all the pieces of the nuclear puzzle into a cohesive whole: the roles of nuclear weapons, strategy, targeting, nonstrategic forces, strategic forces, modernization, arms control, defenses, and command and control. By treating these subjects as distinct but interwoven threads of the policy fabric, we seek to ensure that our recommendations are mutually consistent, if not mutually reenforcing.

In addition, this book departs from past practice by rigorously and systematically assessing America's nuclear needs. Too often in the past,

---

[2]See, for example, Leon Sloss, *Reexamining Nuclear Policy in a Changing World* (Los Alamos: Center for National Security Studies, 1990); and National Academy of Sciences, *The Future of the U.S.-Soviet Nuclear Relationship* (Washington, D.C.: National Academy Press, 1991). In addition, the papers from several conferences on the future of nuclear weapons have been published in edited volumes or paper series. See, for example, Rose E. Gottemoeller, ed., *Strategic Arms Control in the Post-START Era* (London: Brassey's 1991); Sybil Francis, et al., *The Role of Nuclear Weapons in the Year 2000: Summary of the Workshop Proceedings* (Livermore, Calif.: Center for Technical Studies on Security, Energy and Arms Control, January 25, 1991); and David Goldfischer and Thomas W. Graham, eds., *Nuclear Deterrence and Global Security in Transition* (Boulder, Colo.: Westview Press, 1991).

technological developments, weapons procurement decisions, bureaucratic and congressional politics, and infeasible objectives have driven U.S. nuclear weapons policy. Indeed, logic has made only cameo appearances in the policy-making process. This book, by contrast, follows a compelling logic of inquiry that deduces specific nuclear weapons requirements from an in-depth analysis of the contribution nuclear weapons can and cannot make to U.S. security in the post–Cold War world. In so doing, it provides not only specific conclusions and recommendations, but also a broader framework for thinking through the key issues. Particular emphasis is placed on clarifying decision points, options, and trade-offs so that the reader can reach his or her own conclusions.

OVERVIEW

This book is comprised of nine highly interdependent chapters, several of which form conceptual clusters. For example, Chapter 2 (on the roles of nuclear weapons) provides an intellectual foundation for Chapter 3 (on strategy), Chapter 4 (on nonstrategic forces), and Chapter 5 (on strategic forces). Similarly, the strategic force posture recommended in Chapter 5 is a direct outgrowth of the targeting doctrine advocated in Chapter 3. In addition, Chapters 5 and 6 (on strategic forces) form an integrated pair: The first defines a vision for U.S. strategic forces and the second details an arms control and modernization blueprint for realizing that vision. Finally, Chapters 7, 8, and 9 flesh out the implications of earlier chapters for defenses, C³I, and the arms control process respectively.

As the world proceeds beyond the Cold War era, what lies ahead is not yet clear. The future of the former Soviet Union, which still possesses a formidable nuclear arsenal, is highly uncertain. Europe, although free from Soviet domination and the threat of general war, remains vulnerable to ethnic conflict, economic hardship, and social unrest. Regional conflicts, such as those in the Middle East, continue to flare. And the spread of nuclear weapons stalks regions, like the Middle East and East Asia, where the United States has vital interests and key allies whom it is committed to defend. In this context, the military and political relevance of nuclear weapons, particularly U.S. nuclear weapons, requires reappraisal. Are nuclear weapons more or less relevant to U.S. security in the post–Cold War world? The first chapter of this volume seeks to answer this question, focusing on threats to U.S. security in areas of greatest past importance or potentially growing future importance to U.S. nuclear weapons policy— namely, the Soviet Union, Europe, the Middle East, and East Asia. It argues that the military and political relevance of nuclear weapons is declining in the first two areas, but is more difficult to gauge in the second two due to the risk of further nuclear proliferation. This chapter also evaluates the changing economic and political constraints within which U.S. security policy in general and U.S. nuclear policy in particular must operate, both at home and abroad. In short, it sets the scene for all of the chapters that follow.

Given the profound changes in the security environment, the United States must reexamine the roles nuclear weapons should and should not play in providing for its security, now and in the future. Should the United States rely on nuclear weapons to do more than deter nuclear attack on its homeland? What is the future of extended deterrence in Europe and other parts of the world? And what role will nuclear weapons play in safeguarding U.S. security against threats from new adversaries wielding weapons of mass destruction? Chapter 2 addresses these and related questions, taking a "top-down" approach, which evaluates nuclear policy as a means of achieving broader U.S. foreign and security policy goals. It attempts to discern what past experience reveals about the utility of nuclear weapons and identifies several factors that should be considered in assessing future roles. It then systematically evaluates the roles the United States has assigned to nuclear weapons in the past and asks, in light of the changing security environment, whether and how these roles should change in the future. This chapter argues that the only legitimate roles for U.S. nuclear weapons in the post–Cold War world are to deter or respond to *nuclear* attack on the U.S. homeland, U.S. troops, or allies. The United States should not rely on nuclear weapons to deter the use of conventional, chemical, or biological weapons against its territory, forces, or friends. Furthermore, while deterring the use of nuclear weapons by a new nuclear state may be a valid role for U.S. nuclear weapons in the future, deterrence may prove unreliable in such circumstances; and, in the event that deterrence fails, it may be in the U.S. interest to respond with conventional rather than nuclear means. This chapter concludes with a set of specific recommendations and lays a foundation for the chapters that follow.

Throughout the Cold War, U.S. nuclear strategy was shaped by two primary roles for nuclear weapons: deterring Soviet nuclear attack on the U.S. homeland (basic deterrence) and deterring a Soviet conventional or nuclear attack on U.S. NATO allies (extended deterrence). Of the two, the latter had far more influence on U.S. planning for nuclear war. Now that the threat of a Soviet-led invasion of Western Europe has all but disappeared, what should U.S. nuclear strategy be in the 1990s and beyond? Chapter 3 argues that to the extent that the United States need no longer rely on nuclear weapons to deter conventional conflict with the Soviet Union or any other potential adversary, it can safely adopt a deterrent posture at substantially lower levels of forces, both strategic and nonstrategic. At the same time, however, the U.S. nuclear posture must be robust against new threats that could arise in the future. Building on an analysis of the evolution of U.S. nuclear strategy, this chapter evaluates the future objectives of strategy and the future directions of targeting policy and response policy. In so doing, it seeks to design a new U.S. nuclear strategy that reflects lasting changes in the security environment, is consistent with the larger goals of U.S. security policy, and makes sense in the context of declining defense budgets. Specifically, this chapter argues that U.S. targeting doctrine should be fundamentally refocused. The current emphasis on Soviet strategic forces, strategic command and control, and leadership should be replaced by an emphasis on those conventional forces, command and control assets, and industrial facilities that would be essential to the former Soviet Union's ability to project power in a sustained fashion beyond its borders. The chapter offers a notional target set in an effort to illustrate how this new philosophy might translate into practice. Based on this target set, it concludes that the United States would need to hold at risk no more than 1,100–1,900 targets in the former Soviet Union. Similarly, the chapter argues for a new U.S. response policy, one that places greater emphasis on flexible and strictly limited attack options and the ability to "ride out" a substantial nuclear attack before ordering retaliation.

Relative to topics such as strategic targeting doctrine and response policy, nonstrategic nuclear forces (NSNF) have been a much neglected subject in the literature on nuclear weapons. Yet the changing security environment has affected these weapons more profoundly than perhaps any other aspect of U.S. nuclear policy, as evidenced by the Bush and Gorbachev initiatives of September–October 1991. Indeed, developments in the Soviet Union, Europe, and East Asia have called into question the *raison d'être* of U.S. NSNF. No longer is there a clear need for these weapons to bolster allied conventional forces in the face of numerically superior forces of adversaries like the Soviet Union, the Warsaw Pact, and North Korea. Meanwhile, advances in conventional weapons technologies have produced precision-guided "smart" munitions that can perform many if not all of the missions traditionally assigned to NSNF, and the process of substituting such conventional weapons for nonstrategic nuclear weapons (NSNWs) is well underway. Furthermore, the distinction between strategic and nonstrategic forces has eroded. These trends suggest that the military utility of NSNF has declined sharply. At the same time, many if not all of the obstacles that once blocked progress on limiting or reducing NSNF have been removed. In light of these trends, Chapter 4 considers whether or not the United States needs to retain a force of NSNWs and, if so, what form this force should take. Building on an analysis of NSNF history and of the Bush-Gorbachev initiatives, it argues for the eventual elimination of most or all remaining U.S. and Soviet NSNWs and the immediate implementation of several measures to enhance the security of Soviet nuclear weapons. More specifically, it makes the case for destroying all naval NSNWs, withdrawing all air-delivered NSNWs to a small number of highly secure storage sites, and possibly denuclearizing significant portions of the U.S. and Soviet tactical air forces and integrating remaining U.S. air-delivered NSNWs and nuclear-capable aircraft into the strategic bomber force. The chapter also recommends that the United States and the former Soviet Union halt production of fissile materials for weapons, reduce their fissile materials stockpiles by at least 50 percent, and consider destroying the warheads from eliminated weapons in a cooperative, verifiable manner.

Strategic offensive forces are also destined to be reshaped by the changing security environment. Although the primary objective of these forces will remain the same—to deter deliberate nuclear attack on the United States while avoiding the accidental, inadvertent, or unauthorized use of nuclear weapons—the end of the Cold War presents an opportunity to rethink the numbers and types of weapons needed to meet these objectives. There are two basic approaches to determining how many strategic nuclear weapons the United States should field. Most analysts outside government take a rather "intuitive" approach, arriving at desired force levels by starting with a baseline of existing or anticipated forces and arbitrarily reducing it by some percentage. A less common, more "analytical" approach calculates the level of forces required from a specific set of targets, taking into account estimated measures of weapons performance. Building on Chapter 3's strategy and targeting recommendations, Chapter 5 takes an analytical approach to determining "how much is enough" in the context of negotiated arms reductions beyond a Strategic Arms Reduction (START) Treaty. It seeks to design a notional U.S. strategic force that fulfills the roles and meets the requirements designated in earlier chapters at the lowest possible force level consistent with stability and within anticipated constraints. This chapter recommends, as a next step, that the United States reduce its strategic nuclear forces to approximately 3,600 deployed warheads and restructure these forces along specified guidelines. In the interest of reducing the risk and consequences of inadvertent or unauthorized nuclear weapons use, it also urges the United States to abandon the option of launching its ICBMs on warning, install permissive action links (PALs) on all its SLBM warheads, and research and develop command destruct mechanisms for all its strategic missiles.

Modernization and arms control are the primary tools for shaping U.S. strategic forces and maintaining their effectiveness as a deterrent. Modernization ensures that new systems come on line as older systems reach obsolescence and that the overall capability of U.S. strategic forces is maintained, if not enhanced, over time. At the same time, arms control enables the United States to constrain the threat posed by Soviet strategic forces. In theory, arms control and modernization go hand in hand as complementary, even synergistic means of reaching and maintaining a desired force structure. They should also be firmly grounded in a thoughtful assessment of U.S. needs, available resources, applicable constraints, and the requirements of stability. In practice, however, this has rarely been the case. Too often, modernization and arms control have followed uncoordinated and divergent paths. As a result, each has created problems for the other. Chapter 6 breaks from past practice by seeking to devise a *coherent* agenda of strategic modernization and arms control measures to reach the force posture proposed in Chapter 5. Placing a premium on maintaining both synergy and stability, this chapter assesses a comprehensive menu of modernization and arms control options and makes specific recommendations for each leg of the triad and for future negotiations on strategic offensive arms. For example, it advises the United States to download Minuteman III missiles, refurbish Minuteman II missiles, disable submarine missile tubes, and procure no more than 15 B-2 bombers to achieve the force goals outlined in Chapter 5. It also proposes that the United States conduct research and development on a number of additional programs—such as a low-MIRV SLBM, a small sub, and road-mobile and carry-hard basing for a small ICBM—as a hedge against threats to survivability that could arise in the future. It also delineates aggregate limits, sublimits, and other provisions for a follow-on agreement to START I.

Any assessment of the future of offensive nuclear weapons would be incomplete without a companion assessment of defenses. The desirability of defenses against nuclear weapons has been a subject of recurring and often rancorous debate in the United States. In the 1960s, the focus was antiballistic missile (ABM) defenses; in the 1980s, it was President Reagan's Strategic Defense Initiative (SDI); and in the 1990s, it is a more modest version of SDI, the Global Protection Against Limited Strikes (GPALS) system. The demise of the Cold War has, however, changed some of the familiar arguments for and against defenses and has potentially shifted the balance between them. At the same time, the continued proliferation of ballistic missiles and weapons of mass destruction and the much publicized use of the Patriot air defense system against Iraqi Scud missiles during the Persian Gulf War have given the issue of defenses renewed prominence. Chapter 7 examines the desirability of defenses against nuclear weapons in light of the new security environment and the goals and policies outlined elsewhere in the book. It evaluates how changes in the world have affected the balance of arguments for and against defenses, delineates criteria that should govern U.S. decisions in this area, and applies these criteria to three cases: long-range missile defenses, short-range missile defenses, and air defenses. Based on this analysis, the chapter recommends that the United States continue to abide by the traditional interpretation of the Anti-Ballistic Missile (ABM) Treaty and enter into negotiations with the former Soviet Union to clarify ambiguous treaty terms by establishing verifiable threshold limits on specific ABM technologies. In addition, in an effort to avoid the costs of premature development and testing and to facilitate compliance with the ABM Treaty, it proposes that the SDI program be divided into three parts: antitactical ballistic missile (ATBM) defenses, fixed ground-based ABM defenses, and other ABM technologies. Finally, it encourages the United States to place greater emphasis on research and development of ABM countermeasures and to maintain vigorous efforts to limit, prevent, and even reverse the proliferation of weapons of mass destruction and advanced delivery vehicles.

The changing security environment has important implications not only for U.S. nuclear forces and defenses, but also for strategic command, control, communications, and intelligence (C³I)—the collection of systems and procedures the United States relies on to control its strategic forces and operations. For example, the emergence of new nuclear weapons states may, in the long term, present a new challenge to C³I: identifying the source of a nuclear attack on the United States. Whereas the Soviet Union would have been the presumed culprit during the Cold War, it may be only one of many suspects, and perhaps among the least likely, in years to come. In addition, strategic forces may be called upon to perform new missions in the post–Cold War world that may place new demands on C³I. Furthermore, the changes advocated for U.S. strategic forces in Chapters 5 and 6 would require changes in the existing C³I architecture. Meeting these new challenges will, however, not be easy. Defense budget constraints can be expected to limit the degree of C³I restructuring and modernization, create pressures to streamline wherever possible, and require choosing between competing C³I priorities. Chapter 8 examines the future needs and directions of C³I in this context, making specific recommendations for future priorities and streamlining efforts. In short, it argues that U.S. C³I priorities for the post–Cold War world should be: (1) to maintain effective peacetime control and management of its strategic forces; (2) to improve the flexibility of intelligence, planning, and C³ systems to accommodate changing potential enemies and new roles and missions for strategic forces; and (3) to enhance the ability of C³I to ride out any nuclear attack. It also urges the United States to make every effort to streamline C³I operations wherever possible and to adopt acquisition approaches that reduce overall investment and operations costs.

As outlined in several chapters, a broad range of nuclear arms control initiatives will be both possible and central to achieving U.S. national security objectives in the coming decade. To take full advantage of the opportunities that may arise, the United States must be able to rely on a well-oiled, smoothly functioning arms control process. This process consists not only of negotiations with the former Soviet Union but also extensive consultations and bargaining within the United States—between the White House, key bureaucratic players, and Congress—and with important U.S. allies to build domestic and international coalitions in support of U.S. arms control positions. Historically, this process has proven time consuming, arduous, and sometimes unresponsive to opportunities for progress. Treaties have generally taken years to negotiate, arms control and defense planning have sometimes been out of step, and the process has been prone to paralysis due to bureaucratic in-fighting. Clearly, the arms control process, as it stands today, is in need of basic institutional reform. Chapter 9 examines how this process can be improved—how it can be made more flexible, effective, and responsive to opportunities for progress—in the context of changing domestic and international circumstances. The chapter diagnoses problems plaguing the current process, analyzes potential implications of the post–Cold War environment for the process in the future, and recommends measures to remedy existing problems and bypass new ones. Specifically, it calls on the United States to adopt a system of strong central management for arms control policy, integrate defense and arms control policy-making, and rely on more diverse sources for technical advice on arms control matters. In addition, it urges the executive branch to seek closer arms control consultations with Congress and to change the way it consults with its European allies as European security structures evolve. This chapter also recommends that the United States make use of multiple forms of agreement and negotiation in pursuing its arms control objectives with the former Soviet Union and that it reform the means by which compliance and implementation policies are made and managed within the U.S. bureaucracy.

The United States will confront many difficult choices and challenges as it seeks to adjust its nuclear weapons policies to the realities of the post–Cold War world. This volume offers a coherent set of guidelines for this process. With analyses of the roles of nuclear weapons, strategy and targeting doctrine, nonstrategic forces, strategic offensive forces, defenses, C³I, and the arms control process, it provides a comprehensive vision and blueprint for U.S. nuclear weapons policy as the twenty-first century approaches.

Chapter
1

Nuclear Weapons and the Changing Security Environment

Michèle A. Flournoy

The end of the Cold War has ushered in an era of profound change for U.S. security policy. Developments in the Soviet Union, Eastern Europe, and elsewhere have shifted the foundations on which this policy has rested for the past 45 years. Containing Soviet expansionism and countering Soviet influence around the globe no longer drive U.S. foreign policy and military planning. What lies beyond containment, however, is not yet clear. In this context, the relevance of nuclear weapons, both military and political, demands reevaluation. Are nuclear weapons more or less relevant to U.S. security in the post–Cold War world?

The changing security environment can be understood from a variety of related but distinct perspectives, each of which has a unique emphasis. One can, for example, focus on the shifting nature and distribution of power in the international system in an effort to discern whether the world has moved toward greater multipolarity, unipolarity, or something else altogether.[1] Or, one can attempt to redefine America's national interests, foreign policy objectives, and grand strategy in the post–Cold War world, weighing the advantages and disadvantages of alternatives ranging

---

[1]See, for example, Paul M. Kennedy, *The Rise and Fall of Great Powers: Economic Change and Military Conflict from 1500 to 2000* (New York: Random House, 1987); Joseph S. Nye, *Bound to Lead: The Changing Nature of American Power* (New York: Basic, 1990); Josef Joffe, "Entangled Forever," *The National Interest*, No. 21 (Fall 1990), pp. 35–44; Aaron L. Friedberg, "Is the United States Capable of Acting Strategically?," *The Washington Quarterly* (Winter 1991); Charles Krauthammer, "The Unipolar Moment," *Foreign Affairs*, America and the World 1991 Issue, pp. 23–33; and John Lewis Gaddis, "Toward the Post–Cold War World," *Foreign Affairs*, Vol. 70, No. 2 (Spring 1991), pp. 102–122.

from isolationism to internationalism.[2] This chapter, however, views the evolving environment through the prism of past, present, and potential threats to U.S. security.[3] Although fairly narrow in focus, this approach is appropriate in a book about the future of U.S. nuclear weapons policy, as the relevance of U.S. nuclear weapons in the new world hinges on the presence and nature of serious threats to U.S. security. This chapter also assumes that U.S. foreign policy will continue to have an internationalist orientation for the foreseeable future, defining U.S. interests in global terms.

It begins with an assessment of such threats in the changing environment, paying particular attention to the relevance of nuclear weapons in each case and to the questions raised for U.S. nuclear weapons policy. It then examines the changing economic and political constraints within which U.S. security policy in general and nuclear weapons policy in particular must operate, both at home and abroad. The chapter concludes with an evaluation of the political and military relevance of nuclear weapons in the post–Cold War world.

CHANGING THREATS TO U.S. SECURITY

In order for a particular adversary or action to be considered a serious threat to U.S. security, it must endanger U.S. vital interests. Although any list of such interests is necessarily subjective and its application to real-world situations highly political, one can identify a core set of vital interests around which there is widespread consensus: national survival, territorial integrity, and the survival and territorial integrity of key allies. Beyond these few, there is considerable dissension and debate about what else should be on America's list of vital interests. For example, many would add stopping the spread of nuclear weapons and other weapons of mass

[2]See, for example, Stephen Van Evera, "Why Europe Matters, Why the Third World Doesn't: American Grand Strategy After the Cold War," *The Journal of Strategic Studies*, Vol. 13, No. 2 (June 1990), pp. 1–51; Samuel P. Huntington, "America's Changing Strategic Interests," *Survival*, Vol. XXXIII, No. 1 (January/February 1991), pp. 3–17; Ted Galen Carpenter, "The New World Disorder," *Foreign Policy*, No. 84 (Fall 1991), pp. 24–39; Earl Ravenal, "The Case for Adjustment," *Foreign Policy*, No. 81 (Winter 1990–91), pp. 3–19; Robert J. Art, "A Defensible Defense: America's Grand Strategy After the Cold War," *International Security*, Vol. 15, No. 4 (Spring 1991), pp. 5–53; and Alan Tonelson, "What is the National Interest?" *The Atlantic*, Vol. 268, No. 1 (July 1991), pp. 35–52.

[3]Throughout this chapter, the word "security" refers to the ability of the United States to protect its homeland and vital interests from attack, invasion, conquest, or destruction. This is an essentially military use of the term. Although broader definitions of security—encompassing threats ranging from economic competition to environmental degradation—now pervade the literature, this narrow definition is best suited to our focus on nuclear weapons. For a thoughtful discussion of a broader notion of security, see Jessica Tuchman Matthews, "Redefining Security," *Foreign Affairs*, Vol. 68, No. 2 (Spring 1989), pp. 162–177.

destruction. Other candidates include: a healthy U.S. economy based on international economic openness; U.S. access to key resources (such as oil) and markets; the growth of human freedom, democratic institutions, and free market economies throughout the world; the safety of U.S. citizens and assets at home and abroad; the protection of the sovereignty of nations from external aggression; and, in the wake of the Cold War, a new world order.[4] This chapter focuses primarily on the core interests just defined.

Any assessment of a particular threat must take into account both the intentions and the capabilities of a potential adversary. Allies and adversaries alike may harbor intentions that conflict with U.S. interests, broadly defined. What separates a competitive friend from a clear foe is the nature of the interests at stake. Only an adversary has intentions that threaten one's core interests. If an adversary also possesses the capabilities to act on its intentions, the threat it poses is more serious. If it does not possess the necessary capabilities but is actively seeking to acquire them, it poses a potential future threat, one that should be assessed based on the likelihood and consequences of its fruition. Perhaps the most difficult case to evaluate is a country that has the means to harm U.S. vital interests but whose desire to do so remains unclear. Because intentions can change quickly and unexpectedly, a country's past actions and perceived interests must guide U.S. policy between the poles of dangerous inaction and costly overreaction.

Too often, however, threat assessment slips into worst-case analysis. One assumption underlying planning for the worst case is that it is also preparation for anything less than the worst. For example, during the Cold War, threats other than a Warsaw Pact invasion of Western Europe were considered "lesser included cases." However, worst-case analysis can lead to myopia, if not blindness: In focusing on the worst case, one often neglects or ignores lesser but more likely or immediate threats, threats that may require a very different response than the worst case to which one's capabilities have been tailored.

Worst-case planning is particularly ill-suited to the post–Cold War world, as there is no longer any predictable and plausible worst case. As the Soviet threat recedes, the lesser threats it has long overshadowed or obscured are gradually coming into focus. At present, none of these potential threats to U.S. security is as large or as demanding as the former Warsaw Pact threat to Western Europe. Collectively, however, they are far more unpredictable in nature and may, as a result, pose novel challenges to U.S. interests, as Iraq's 1990 invasion of Kuwait so aptly demonstrated.

---

[4]In his January 29, 1991, State of the Union Address, President Bush argued that what was at stake in the war against Iraq was not only Kuwait's sovereignty but also "a new world order—where diverse nations are drawn together in common cause, to achieve the universal aspirations of mankind: peace and security, freedom, and the rule of law." As quoted in "Documentation," *Survival*, Vol. XXXIII, No. 2 (March/April 1991), p. 183.

As an alternative to worst-case analysis, this chapter focuses on potential threats in two types of areas: areas that have been of greatest importance to U.S. nuclear weapons policy in the past (the Soviet Union and Europe); and areas of potentially growing importance to U.S. nuclear weapons policy in the future, due to the strength of the U.S. commitment to defend key allies and the spread of nuclear weapons and other weapons of mass destruction (currently, the Middle East and the Far East).[5] In short, we consider only threats to which nuclear weapons may be relevant, either as instruments of threat or as instruments of response. For each of these areas, the following questions are posed: (1) What has changed? (2) What has not changed? (3) How does the changing security environment affect the military and political relevance of nuclear weapons in this area?[6] and (4) What questions or issues does this area raise for U.S. nuclear weapons policy in the future?

The Soviet Union

The degree and nature of change in the Soviet Union since Mikhail Gorbachev came to power in 1985 are of historic proportions. Indeed, it is far beyond the scope of this chapter to catalogue them here. It is, however, both possible and useful to note some of the more significant changes that have affected or are likely to affect the Soviet Union's relations with the outside world in general and the United States in particular.

Under Gorbachev, the Soviet Union redirected its energies from expansionism and competition abroad to reform and restructuring at home. This turning inward to grapple with immense domestic problems precipitated a fundamental reorientation of Soviet foreign and military policies toward cooperative diplomacy and the prevention of war—what President Gorbachev called "new political thinking."[7]

On the foreign policy front, a number of palpable—and in some cases dramatic—changes have occurred. First and foremost, the Soviet Union peacefully disengaged from its former satellites in Eastern Europe as well

---

[5]Three caveats are in order here. First, the spread of nuclear weapons is a concern in other regions as well, particularly South Asia, but the United States lacks comparable alliance relationships and defense commitments there. Second, it is possible that in the future, as in the not too distant past, other regions could fall into this category. Finally, the challenge to U.S. security posed by the spread of nuclear weapons is not new; it is only more visible now that the Soviet threat no longer dominates the U.S. security agenda and the extent of Iraq's nuclear weapons program has come to light in the wake of the Gulf War.

[6]This chapter addresses whether the relevance of nuclear weapons is increasing or decreasing in particular contexts. It is left to the next chapter to address the specific roles of U.S. nuclear weapons.

[7]One premise of Gorbachev's new political thinking was that in the nuclear age and in an era of global interdependence, adversaries must recognize and pursue their common interests to ensure their survival. See Mikhail Gorbachev, *Perestroika: New Thinking for Our Country and the World* (New York: Harper & Row, 1987).

as several other former areas of influence, from Afghanistan to Angola. The impact of its disengagement from Eastern Europe in particular cannot be overestimated. The replacement of the Brezhnev Doctrine, which had long justified Soviet military intervention to support neighboring communist governments, with what Soviet Foreign Ministry spokesman Gennadi Gerasimov called the "Sinatra" or "I Did It My Way" Doctrine,[8] in which each country is free to choose its own path to political and economic development, paved the way for the largely peaceful democratic revolutions that swept across Eastern Europe in 1989.

At the same time, the Soviet Union displayed a new interest in finding diplomatic solutions to regional conflicts and a greater willingness to cooperate with the West in confronting international problems. Indeed, without the Soviet Union's assent the allied coalition against Iraq would not have been able to operate with the blessing of the United Nations.

The Soviet Union also sought to become a more active member of the international community via greater participation in the United Nations and membership in institutions such as the General Agreement on Tariffs and Trade and the International Monetary Fund. In addition, it sought assistance from the West to underwrite its transition to a market economy and a more democratic society.

On the military front, Moscow made some equally significant changes in its doctrine, force posture, and operations. At the twenty-seventh Congress of the Soviet Communist Party in March 1986, Gorbachev announced that henceforth the Soviet military posture would be defensively oriented and force levels would be determined by the principle of "reasonable sufficiency."[9] This doctrinal shift was echoed in a 1987 announcement by the Warsaw Pact of a new military doctrine of "defensive sufficiency" for its conventional armed forces in Europe. The same year, Moscow agreed to asymmetric cuts in its nuclear forces and on-site inspection at its military facilities under the Intermediate-range Nuclear Forces (INF) Treaty. This was followed by a unilateral Soviet withdrawal of 500,000 troops and tens of thousands of weapons from Eastern Europe in 1989, the negotiation in 1990 of timetables for the withdrawal of all Soviet forces from Central and Eastern Europe, the signing of the Conventional Forces in Europe (CFE) Treaty mandating further reductions in Soviet military equipment and establishing a conventional balance in the region from the Atlantic Ocean to the Ural Mountains, and the dissolution of the Warsaw Pact in 1991. In addition, Admiral William J. Crowe, then chairman of the Joint Chiefs of Staff, and General Mikhail A. Moiseyev, chief of the Soviet General Staff, signed the Dangerous Military Activities Agreement in June 1989, establishing procedures to avert accidental U.S.-

---

[8]Gerasimov on "Good Morning America," October 25, 1989.

[9]Gloria Duffy and Jennifer Lee, "The Soviet Debate on 'Reasonable Sufficiency,'" *Arms Control Today*, Vol. 18, No. 8 (October 1988), pp. 19–24.

Soviet military encounters or contain them before they escalate into full-fledged confrontations.

These shifts in Soviet foreign and military policies profoundly altered the security environment, particularly in Europe. As former Assistant Secretary of Defense Richard Perle put it in early 1990, "the canonical threat against which a defensive NATO alliance has long been poised is no longer credible."[10] Indeed, with the dissolution of the Warsaw Pact, the threat of a Soviet-led Pact invasion of Western Europe evaporated. Similarly, once withdrawn Soviet troops and NATO forces were separated by hundreds of miles of territory and several independent states, an effective *Soviet* surprise conventional attack on Western Europe also became impossible. As these scenarios faded, so too did a dangerous East-West face-off and one of the most likely paths to nuclear war. Even before the Soviet Union began to disintegrate into its constituent republics, these changed realities were essentially irreversible, as any such aggression would require years of observable preparation and would encounter substantial obstacles.[11]

But perhaps the most profound change has been the disintegration of the Soviet Union and the devolution of power from the center to the republics. This process began with the Baltic states' declarations of independence, was fueled by subsequent negotiations between Gorbachev and republican leaders, and was greatly accelerated by the failure of the August 1991 coup and the collapse of the Communist Party. As of this writing, the future of the Soviet Union remains highly uncertain.

Nevertheless, one can discern several issues that will help determine this future. The first is the nature of the states that ultimately succeed the USSR. Will some form of a central government survive? Will the republics ultimately emphasize independence or interdependence in their relations with one another? And will these relations be friendly or hostile? The centrifugal and centripetal forces at work in the Soviet Union could produce any number of outcomes, most of which would be variations on one or more of the following themes: The center collapses entirely and 15 republics rise from its ashes as fully independent states; some form of central government survives, weakened and reconstituted, providing the

---

[10]Testimony before the Senate Armed Services Committee, January 24, 1990. Similarly, the House Armed Services Committee's Defense Policy Panel concluded that, "The Soviet conventional threat is becoming an empty threat. Large-scale Soviet military interventions outside of Soviet territories seem beyond the Red Army's powers, no matter who rules in Moscow." See Defense Policy Panel of the House Committee on Armed Services, *The Fading Threat: Soviet Conventional Military Power in Decline*, 101st Congress, 2nd session (Washington, D.C.: U.S. Government Printing Office, 1990).

[11]For example, Fred Ikle, undersecretary of defense for policy in the Reagan administration, argues that "Since 1989, NATO's warning time is to be measured neither in fourteen days, nor in thirty-seven days, but in years—the years it would take to re-Stalinize Europe." Fred Ikle, "The Ghost in the Pentagon," *The National Interest*, Vol. 19 (Spring 1990), p. 15.

basis for a loose federation of largely independent states; or the republics split and move in different directions, with some forming a federation clustered around Russia and others going it alone.

The second key issue is the nature of whatever transition occurs. It is clear that any such transition will take time and be fraught with confusion and difficulty. Less clear is whether it will be peaceful or violent, planned or piecemeal, complete or only partial. In any case, the character of the process will undoubtedly have a powerful impact on the results.

Third, the future of the Soviet Union and its republics will obviously be affected by the disposition of the governing bodies that emerge. Will they be democratic or authoritarian, liberal or conservative, reform-minded or repressive, tolerant or intolerant of minorities? Or will they be the product of compromises between these extremes?

The fourth issue relates to the relations that the republics ultimately establish, collectively or individually, with the outside world. It is easy to imagine foreign policies that are paid relatively little attention due to preoccupation with internal affairs. To the extent that active policy agendas exist, they could conceivably be cooperative, competitive, or openly hostile to the West.

Finally, the fate of Soviet nuclear weapons—under whose control they fall, at whom they are aimed, and how they are managed in the transition—will play a significant role in how the United States responds to the entity or entities that emerge.

Which brings us to what has *not* changed. The former Soviet Union still has roughly 27,000 nuclear weapons in its possession. About 12,000 of these are strategic offensive weapons capable of reaching the United States. Most are based on Russian soil, and about a quarter are based in the Ukraine, Kazakhstan, and Byelorussia. If these four republics ultimately abide by the START Treaty, the number of deployed strategic weapons will decline to about 7,000.[12] If they comply with the unilateral reductions announced by Gorbachev in October 1991, this number will drop still further to approximately 5,000.

The Soviet Union also possesses about 3,000 nuclear warheads for its air and missile defenses and about 12,000 nonstrategic or tactical nuclear weapons, which are dispersed far more widely among the republics. Indeed, every Soviet republic except Kirghizia has at one time been home to tactical nuclear weapons. Although Gorbachev's October 1991 initiative calls for many of these weapons to be eliminated, there remain substantial political and physical obstacles to its implementation.

In this context, and in the context of increasing turmoil in the Soviet Union, the greatest danger is that the central government might lose control over some portion of its vast nuclear arsenal or some facilities in

---

[12]As of this writing, both the Russian republic and the Ukrainian republic have affirmed their intentions to abide by the terms of START.

its vast nuclear weapons production complex.[13] This would increase the risk that nuclear weapons and materials might be stolen, used in an unauthorized manner, or fall into the hands of third parties.

There are essentially four distinct scenarios here. Although none of them would be likely to pose an immediate threat to U.S. security, all would be cause for grave concern.

The first is proliferation within the Soviet Union. In this scenario, new nuclear weapons states would emerge as newly independent republics take control of the nuclear weapons deployed or stored on their territory. Although most of the republics, other than Russia, have proclaimed their intentions to be nuclear-free states, many of them have also insisted on having some authority over the nuclear weapons on their soil and have refused to return these weapons to Russia. If this scenario were to materialize, it would not only strain relations between republics, but could also cause a number of states in Eastern, Central, and Western Europe to rethink their decisions not to pursue a nuclear option.

The second scenario is proliferation beyond Soviet borders, in which Soviet nuclear weapons, material, or know-how would be obtained by outside countries or subnational groups. This could result from the theft of Soviet nuclear weapons or materials, from their sale on the international black market, or from the hiring of disaffected Soviet nuclear scientists and technicians. Given mounting pressures on the people and the system that ensure the security of Soviet nuclear weapons, widespread hunger for hard currency, and the rise of powerful black marketeers in various republics, this scenario must be taken seriously.

In the third scenario, Soviet nuclear weapons would be seized by military units no longer loyal to Moscow, raising the specter of unauthorized nuclear use. In a fourth and somewhat similar scenario, nuclear weapons or materials could be stolen and perhaps used by political groups or terrorists. Although a variety of procedural and physical safeguards exist to prevent both of these eventualities, they are not foolproof, particularly when challenged by people familiar with their details and vulnerabilities.[14] Nor can these safeguards, however robust under normal

---

[13]For contrasting views on the seriousness of this problem, see Gabriel Schoenfeld, "Loose Cannon," *The New Republic*, March 11, 1991, pp. 16–18; David C. Morrison, "Loose Soviet Nukes: A Mountain or a Molehill?" *Arms Control Today*, Vol. 21, No. 3 (April 1991), pp. 15–19; Mark Kramer, "Warheads and Chaos: The Soviet Threat in Perspective," *The National Interest*, No. 25 (Fall 1991), pp. 94–97; and Kurt M. Campbell, Ashton B. Carter, Steven E. Miller, and Charles A. Zraket, *Soviet Nuclear Fission: Control of the Nuclear Arsenal in a Disintegrating Soviet Union*, CSIA Studies in International Security, No. 1 (Cambridge, Mass.: Center for Science and International Affairs, November 1991).

[14]For a discussion of the procedural and physical safeguards that would have to be overcome in order for different types of Soviet nuclear weapons to be used in an unauthorized manner, see Campbell, Carter, Miller, and Zraket, *op. cit.*; Bruce G. Blair and Henry W. Kendall, "Accidental Nuclear War," *Scientific American*, Vol. 263, No. 6 (December 1990), p. 56; and Stephen M. Meyer, "Soviet Nuclear Operations," in Ashton B. Carter, John D. Steinbruner,

circumstances, be counted on to withstand the stresses created by the disintegration of a country's social fabric.

The possibility that the Soviet Union could lose control over its nuclear weapons also raises the larger question of inadvertent or accidental nuclear war. Have changes in the Soviet Union and East-West relations reduced the risk of a nuclear war begun by miscalculation or misperception? To the extent that superpower crises, the assumed context for any such war, have become less likely, the risk of inadvertent war has declined. However, to the extent that nuclear operations remain vulnerable to accident, human or technical error, and unauthorized use, this risk remains.[15] Indeed, as these scenarios suggest, the risk of unauthorized use under some circumstances may well increase.

In sum, there is ample evidence of profound change in the Soviet threat—in both intentions and capabilities. The most feared scenario of the Cold War—a Soviet-led Warsaw Pact invasion of NATO—is no longer imaginable. Any reconstitution of the Soviet conventional military threat to Europe would require years of effort and would be fraught with new difficulties in the wake of Eastern Europe's political reorientation and the withdrawal of Soviet forces from Central and Eastern Europe.

What is the relevance of nuclear weapons in this altered U.S.-Soviet context? During the Cold War, nuclear weapons stood at the center of U.S.-Soviet relations. Each side's nuclear deployments had a powerful effect on the other's threat perceptions, strategies, and behavior. At the same time, nuclear arms control negotiations provided the primary vehicle for superpower dialogue and cooperation. Indeed, they were perhaps the greatest symbol of political detente. However, with the end of the Cold War, U.S.-Soviet relations are likely to expand and diversify, and other areas, such as economic cooperation and diplomatic coordination, can be expected to displace nuclear concerns at the top of the U.S.-Soviet agenda.

Nevertheless, because Soviet nuclear capabilities remain formidable and are likely to be reduced over a period of years, nuclear weapons will continue to be a factor in the U.S.-Soviet equation, at least in the near term. Indeed, nuclear deterrence will remain an aspect of the U.S.-Soviet relationship as long as each side's nuclear arsenal threatens the other's homeland and as long as each side views the other as a potential, if unlikely, adversary. For the United States, nuclear weapons will provide the ultimate insurance against the uncertain future of its Cold War adversary. For the Soviet central government, if it survives, nuclear weapons will

---

and Charles A. Zraket, eds., *Managing Nuclear Operations* (Washington, D.C.: The Brookings Institution, 1987), p. 521.

[15]For more on accidental nuclear war, see Blair and Kendall, *op. cit.*; Kurt Gottfried and Bruce G. Blair, eds., *Crisis Stability and Nuclear War* (New York: Oxford University Press, 1988), and Bruce G. Blair, *The Effects of Warning on Strategic Stability* (Washington, D.C.: The Brookings Institution, 1991).

continue to serve as the much-valued (and perhaps only) currency of superpowerdom. For those republics with some portion of the Soviet nuclear arsenal on their soil, nuclear weapons may be seen as an unnecessary burden, as bargaining chips in negotiations for independence, or, worse, as the coveted trappings of great power status.

Militarily, however, nuclear weapons are likely to be largely if not wholly irrelevant to the U.S.-Soviet relationship if current trends continue: Nuclear threats are unlikely to be made and even less likely to be carried out between the two countries. The use of nuclear weapons based on miscalculation in a crisis is also less likely than before, but the possible loss of control over Soviet nuclear weapons and facilities remains cause for considerable concern.

The changing relevance of nuclear weapons in the U.S.-Soviet relationship raises several questions for U.S. nuclear policy. What are the requirements of nuclear deterrence in the post–Cold War world? What strategy, force levels, and types of nuclear weapons are needed to underwrite U.S. security in the next decade? What type of arms control measures should be pursued to reach the nuclear force desired? And what can be done to further reduce the risk of accidental, inadvertent, or unauthorized nuclear weapons use? These and other questions will be addressed in the chapters that follow.

Europe

The end of Soviet domination of Eastern Europe and the dissolution of the Warsaw Pact have all but freed Europe from the threat of general war. Nevertheless, long-seething but silenced ethnic tensions have found new expression in the more open societies of several Eastern European countries. Under the pressure of economic or other hardship, these sparks of conflict could ignite, as in the case of Yugoslavia, and possibly spread to involve other countries in Europe, as happened in World War I. Other possible but remote scenarios include conflicts stemming from German attempts to establish itself as a regional hegemon (perhaps acquiring its own nuclear weapons) or from Russian-German competition for influence in Eastern Europe or the Balkans.

Several factors will be instrumental in determining the extent to which Europe remains peaceful in the next decade or so. The first of these is the political and economic evolution of Eastern Europe.[16] To the extent that Eastern European nations can protect the rights of minorities as they build democracies, make the transition to market economies without se-

---

[16]For more on the future of Eastern and Central European security, see Charles Gati, "East-Central Europe: The Morning After," *Foreign Affairs*, Vol. 69, No. 5 (Winter 1990/91), pp. 129–145; Curt Gasteyger, "The Remaking of Eastern Europe's Security," *Survival*, Vol. XXXIII, No. 2 (March/April 1991), pp. 111–124; and Jiri Dienstbier, "Central European Security," *Foreign Policy*, No. 83 (Summer 1991), pp. 119–127.

vere and lasting economic dislocation, and be integrated into the European community and European institutions, large-scale intrastate and interstate conflict will be less likely.

The second factor is Germany's future role in Europe. In the highly unlikely event that Germany chose to "go it alone," either economically or militarily, the risk of conflict would be greater than if it continued to pursue its interests through broader European economic and security structures. Of particular concern would be a German decision to acquire its own nuclear weapons. This might well send ripples of anxiety throughout Europe, not to mention the Soviet republics. Such a decision would, however, be highly unlikely as long as Germany remains firmly integrated into European alliances and organizations, the German government continues to see its leadership in European institutions and its economic performance as the best means of exercising and augmenting its power, the German public remains opposed to a nuclear option, and the United States is willing to provide Germany with adequate security guarantees.

Third, the extent of conflict in Europe will depend on the future security structures established to guarantee borders, deter and respond to aggression, and limit military activities and deployments in the region. These structures are likely to evolve from some combination of existing frameworks, including NATO, the Conference on Security and Cooperation in Europe (CSCE), the Western European Union, the European Community, and bilateral accords between various European states. The likelihood of conflict will also depend on the success or failure of efforts to cultivate European economic interdependence, particularly the European Community's efforts to create a single unified European market by 1992 and future efforts to integrate the economies of Eastern and Central Europe.

Finally, the degree of conflict in Europe will be influenced by future U.S. and Soviet (or Russian) involvement on the continent. The U.S. military presence in Europe is generally viewed as a guarantor of stability during a time of transition and is expected to continue for the foreseeable future. How long it should remain, what form it should take, whether it should continue to have an in-theater nuclear component, and the specifics of burden-sharing are, however, hotly debated. In contrast, the Soviet Union is not expected to maintain a military presence in Central Europe after the mid-1990s. But beyond that, the future of Soviet (or Russian) involvement in Europe is open to question. On one hand, the Soviet Union under Gorbachev actively sought acceptance as a European power, as evidenced by Moscow's behavior in the multilateral "Two-Plus-Four" talks on Germany's future, its cultivation of a special friendship with Germany, and Gorbachev's notion of a "common European home." Similarly, the Russian Republic, as well as others, has thus far appeared to be similarly disposed, seeking to cultivate warm relations with European nations, particularly those that might provide economic assistance and markets. On the other hand, many European countries, particularly those formerly dominated by the Soviet Union and still struggling to become part of the European family themselves, remain wary of welcoming Russia and the other republics with open arms. Thus, if there is a seed of conflict in future Soviet or Russian behavior toward Europe, it is no longer aggression toward NATO but the potential for economic and political competition with European rivals and intimidation of weaker European neighbors.

In this context, what relevance do nuclear weapons have? Militarily, as the prospect of a Soviet-led invasion of Western Europe has vanished, so too has the main rationale for NATO's nuclear deterrent. In addition, the withdrawal of Soviet troops from Eastern Europe and the political reorientation of the countries that once hosted them have eliminated the targets at which most U.S. nuclear weapons on the continent were aimed. President Bush's unilateral withdrawal of all U.S. land-based tactical nuclear weapons from Europe and NATO's follow-on decision to reduce sharply the number of nuclear weapons for tactical aircraft in Europe reflect these changes.[17] Thus, barring the remote possibility of further proliferation on the continent (as discussed in the following), the military relevance of nuclear weapons in Europe is likely to decline.

But can the same be said for their political relevance? The ultimate answer to this question lies in the nature and outcome of Europe's transition to new economic relationships, political institutions, and security structures. In the meantime, nuclear weapons may retain a degree of political relevance disproportionate to their military utility as long as key allies need to be reassured of the U.S. commitment to their defense and as long as uncertainty—with regard to the Soviet Union's future and to the nature of potential "Nth country" threats to Europe—looms large on the horizon. In any case, the role of U.S. nuclear weapons in Europe is changing (as will be discussed in detail in Chapters 2, 3, and 4).

Similarly, the military relevance of British and French nuclear weapons is also in decline. Like their U.S. counterparts, British and French short-range nuclear weapons now lack meaningful targets, but their long-range systems (i.e., those that can reach Soviet territory) are likely to retain some deterrent value as long as the Soviet Union (or whatever replaces it) retains a sizeable nuclear arsenal and is viewed as a potential (if unlikely) adversary. Politically, the relevance of British and French nuclear forces could conceivably rise if they were to replace U.S. nuclear forces as the backbone of Europe's nuclear deterrent in the future.

Finally, the prospects for nuclear proliferation in Europe must also be considered. In order for the spread of nuclear weapons on the continent to be at all likely in the post–Cold War environment, the perceived relevance of nuclear weapons would have to increase substantially. Some

---

[17]"Remarks by President on Reducing U.S. and Soviet Nuclear Weapons," *New York Times*, September 28, 1991, p. 4; R. Jeffrey Smith, "NATO Approves 50% Cut in Tactical A-Bombs," *Washington Post*, October 18, 1991, p. A28.

combination of the following would have to occur: the emergence of a serious Soviet (or other) security threat, the proliferation of nuclear weapons among the Soviet republics, the folding of the American nuclear umbrella, the failure of a European nuclear deterrent (perhaps based on British and/or French forces) to take its place, the wholesale failure or disintegration of existing and emerging European security structures, or a failure to integrate Eastern and Central European nations into strong security structures. It is unlikely that any one of these factors alone would tip the scales in favor of nuclear weapons acquisition for any European power, but two or more might do so.

This discussion raises a number of questions for U.S. nuclear weapons policy. What role should U.S. nuclear weapons play in providing for European security in the future? Should the United States continue to extend a nuclear guarantee to Europe? If so, what kind of nuclear forces should it rely on to uphold this commitment? Need it deploy nuclear weapons in the European theater? Are there viable military rationales for in-theater deployments? And if not, would political rationales be sufficient to sustain them and their credibility? Finally, should the United States extend its nuclear umbrella to Central Europe? These and other questions will be considered in Chapters 2, 3, and 4.

The Spread of Nuclear Weapons

Before turning to an assessment of potential threats to U.S. security in the Middle East and East Asia, it is important to evaluate why the spread of nuclear weapons to these regions is of concern to the United States.[18] Kenneth Waltz, for one, argues that "the measured spread of nuclear weapons is more to be welcomed than feared."[19] Waltz believes that the gradual spread of nuclear weapons will promote peace and reinforce international stability because nuclear weapons induce caution between adversaries who possess them. In short, "more may be better."[20]

But the conventional wisdom holds that more is definitely worse: The spread of nuclear weapons increases the likelihood that nuclear weapons will actually be used. The more countries that possess nuclear arsenals, the

---

[18]For an excellent survey of the extent to which nuclear weapons technology has spread, see Leonard S. Spector's series of books on nuclear proliferation, including (with Jacqueline R. Smith), *Nuclear Ambitions: The Spread of Nuclear Weapons 1989–1990* (Boulder, Colo.: Westview, 1990).

[19]Kenneth N. Waltz, *The Spread of Nuclear Weapons: More May Be Better*, Adelphi Paper No. 171 (London: International Institute for Strategic Studies, 1981), p. 30. For a similar view, see Bruce Bueno de Mesquita and William H. Riker, "An Assessment of the Merits of Selective Nuclear Proliferation," *Journal of Conflict Resolution*, Vol. 26, No. 2 (June 1982), pp. 283–306.

[20]Waltz, *op. cit.*

greater the risk of nuclear war. Several arguments support this view.[21] Because of their relatively small size and the improbability of their being deployed in truly survivable basing modes, newly acquired nuclear forces are likely to be more vulnerable to destruction than those of long-standing nuclear powers. As a result, these forces are more likely to be used early in a crisis to escape preemption and/or to execute a preemptive attack on the similarly vulnerable forces of an adversary. In addition, security and command and control arrangements for new nuclear forces are likely to be primitive compared to those for U.S. and Soviet nuclear weapons. Consequently, there is a greater risk that they could be stolen, used without authorization, or launched by accident. Furthermore, many of the nations that are seeking a nuclear weapons capability have experienced internal strife and their governments remain vulnerable to political instability. This raises the unsettling prospect of "nuclear inheritance," the transfer of nuclear weapons or related nuclear assets from one regime to another as the result of war, revolution, or a coup d'état.[22] Finally, many of these countries are also parties to ongoing and seemingly intractable regional conflicts that could ultimately threaten their vital interests, including their national survival. As a result, they might not exercise the degree of nuclear restraint that their nuclear predecessors have.

For what purpose would a so-called "Nth country" actually use its nuclear weapons in war? In any number of ways, including: to dictate the terms of a settlement (i.e., blackmail); to force the intervention of an outside power on its side; to paralyze a conflict or stop the intervention of an outside power on an adversary's side; to destroy and disperse an adversary's military forces, stop or slow their advance, and interrupt their supply lines; or to terrorize an adversary's cities and population.

Thus, the spread of nuclear weapons is to be more feared than welcomed. But does it pose a serious threat to U.S. security? In the near term, the use of nuclear weapons by an Nth country is unlikely to endanger U.S. territory, as no such country possesses both long-range nuclear-capable delivery vehicles *and* intentions or reason to harm the United States.[23] Indeed, some have argued that even if the spread of nuclear weapons

---

[21]These arguments are summarized in Art, *op. cit.*, pp. 24–25. For a more detailed discussion of these arguments, see Lewis A. Dunn, *Controlling the Bomb: Nuclear Proliferation in the 1980s* (New Haven: Yale University Press, 1982), pp. 69–95.

[22]This term is from Leonard S. Spector, *Going Nuclear* (Cambridge, Mass.: Ballinger, 1987), p. 17.

[23]However, the risk of nuclear terrorism is another matter. See Art, *op. cit.*, pp. 9, 24–27; Thomas C. Schelling, "Thinking about Nuclear Terrorism," *International Security*, Vol. 6, No. 4 (Spring 1982), pp. 61–77; Paul Leventhal and Yonah Alexander, eds., *Nuclear Terrorism: Defining the Threat* (Washington, D.C.: Pergamon-Brassey's, 1986); and International Task Force on the Prevention of Nuclear Terrorism, *Preventing Nuclear Terrorism* (Lexington, Mass.: Lexington Books, 1987).

makes nuclear wars more likely, the United States need not be drawn into them.[24] While this might be true in the context of an isolationist foreign policy or in regions where the United States lacks vital interests, it is less likely to be true in the context of the internationalist foreign policy of the past four decades and in regions where the United States has standing defense commitments to key allies. Indeed, nuclear proliferation in such regions poses a serious potential threat to U.S. security, as will be discussed in the following. Furthermore, any actual use of nuclear weapons—even if it were not directed at U.S. territory, troops, or allies—would be of grave concern as it would break the international norm of nuclear nonuse, set a bad precedent for future conflicts and adversaries, and potentially heighten the risk of escalation.

The proliferation of chemical weapons, biological weapons, ballistic missiles, and high-tech conventional weapons poses another potential threat to U.S. security.[25] Although estimates vary, at least 20 countries are believed capable of producing chemical weapons.[26] Although these weapons are of questionable military utility against a protected adversary, they

---

[24]Robert W. Tucker, *A New Isolationism: Threat or Promise?* (New York: Universe Books, 1972), pp. 39–54.

[25]For an overview of the first three, see Aspen Strategy Group, *New Threats: Responding to the Proliferation of Nuclear, Chemical, and Delivery Capabilities in the Third World* (Lanham, Md.: University Press of America, 1990); and Steve Fetter, "Ballistic Missiles and Weapons of Mass Destruction: What is the Threat? What Should Be Done?" *International Security*, Vol. 16, No. 1 (Summer 1991), pp. 5–42. For more on the transfer of conventional weapons to developing countries, see Ian Anthony, et al., "The Trade in Major Conventional Weapons," *SIPRI Yearbook 1991: World Armaments and Disarmament* (Oxford: Oxford University Press: 1991), pp. 197–231; Richard F. Grimmett, *Trends in Conventional Arms Transfers to the Third World by Major Suppliers, 1982–1989* (Washington, D.C.: Congressional Research Service, June 1990); U.S. Arms Control and Disarmament Agency, *World Military Expenditures and Arms Transfers 1989* (Washington, D.C.: U.S. Government Printing Office, October 1990); Office of Technology Assessment, *Global Arms Trade* (Washington, D.C.: U.S. Government Printing Office, June 1991).

[26]Even official estimates vary. Only one developing country (Iraq) is known, without doubt, to possess chemical weapons; 11 others are reported by U.S. government officials, on the record, as developing, producing, or possessing chemical weapons; 11 more are reported by various Western government officials as seeking to acquire chemical weapons or as suspected of possessing them. See Elisa D. Harris, "Chemical Weapons Proliferation: Current Capabilities and Prospects for Control," in Aspen Strategy Group, *op. cit.*, pp. 67–87. Rear Admiral Thomas A. Brooks, director of Naval Intelligence, recently told a congressional subcommittee that the following countries outside NATO and the former Warsaw Pact "probably possess" offensive CW capabilities: Burma, China, Egypt, India, Iran, Iraq, Israel, Libya, North Korea, Pakistan, South Korea, Syria, Taiwan, and Vietnam. In addition, Indonesia, Saudi Arabia, South Africa, and Thailand "may possess" offensive CW capabilities. See Statement of Rear Admiral Thomas A. Brooks before the Seapower, Strategic, and Critical Materials Subcommittee of the House Armed Services Committee on Intelligence Issues, March 7, 1991. For a review of the development and use of chemical weapons, see Stockholm International Peace Research Institute, *The Problem of Chemical and Biological Warfare*, Vol I: *The Rise of CB Weapons* (New York: Humanities Press, 1971); and Victor A. Utgoff, *The Challenge of Chemical Weapons: An American Perspective* (London: Macmillan, 1990).

can be horribly effective against unprotected troops and civilian popula-tions. Thus, the United States and 39 other nations are currently negotiat-ing a chemical weapons convention that would ultimately ban the produc-tion, stockpiling, and use of chemical weapons worldwide. As for biological weapons, at least 10 countries are believed to be working to produce them in violation of the Biological Weapons Convention, but progress has gener-ally been slow.[27] Although potentially more lethal than chemical agents, biological agents may be less attractive as weapons due to the difficulty of controlling their effects and the greater risk the user runs of infecting its own forces (and population, if near the battlefield). Finally, the spread of ballistic missiles and high-tech weapons in the developing world has the potential to fuel regional arms races and increase the lethality of regional conflicts.[28] It is, however, unclear whether or not these trends will affect the perceived relevance of nuclear weapons or U.S. nuclear weapons policy.[29]

The Middle East

Much has changed in the Middle East since the end of the Cold War and the experience of the Gulf War. One of the most significant changes has been in the nature of Soviet interest and influence in the region. Moscow now appears to favor diplomatic cooperation over military competition with the West in this region. This reorientation has lowered the risk that a Middle East conflict could escalate to a U.S.-Soviet confrontation; indeed, the Gulf War demonstrated that an unprecedented degree of superpower cooperation is possible in devising a collective response to aggression. In addition, the focus of U.S. military planning in the Middle East has shifted from a Soviet invasion of Iran to aggression by one Middle Eastern country against another that threatens the regional balance of power, U.S. interests

---

[27]William H. Webster, director of the CIA, Statement before the Committee on Governmen-tal Affairs, Hearings on the Global Spread of Chemical and Biological Weapons: Assessing the Challenges and Responses, February 9, 1989. For a review of the development and use of biological weapons, see Stockholm International Peace Research Institute, *op. cit.*

[28]Rear Admiral Brooks recently testified that 18 Third World countries may have ballistic missiles by the year 2000. Brooks, *op. cit.* For more on the spread of ballistic missiles, see Steve Fetter, "Ballistic Missiles and Weapons of Mass Destruction: What is the Threat? What Should Be Done?" *International Security*, Vol. 16, No. 1 (Summer 1991), pp. 5–42; Janne E. Nolan, *Trappings of Power: Ballistic Missiles in the Third World* (Washington, D.C.: The Brookings Institution, 1991); W. Seth Carus, *Ballistic Missiles in the Third World* (Westport, Conn.: Praeger, 1990); Aaron Karp, "Ballistic Missile Proliferation," in Stockholm Interna-tional Peace Research Institute, *SIPRI Yearbook 1990: World Armaments and Disarmament* (Oxford: Oxford University Press, 1990); and Robert D. Shuey, Warren W. Lenhart, Rodney A. Snyder, Warren H. Donnelly, James E. Mielke, and John D. Moteff, *Missile Proliferation: Survey of Emerging Missile Forces* (Washington, D.C.: Congressional Research Service, February 9, 1989).

[29]Whether or not they should is a subject for the next chapter.

(such as oil), or key U.S. allies (such as Israel and the moderate Arab states). Furthermore, the decline of U.S.-Soviet competition in the Middle East has paved the way for former client states to pursue more independent foreign policies and to compete more fiercely for regional dominance.

The Gulf War was a watershed in Middle East politics and a detailed analysis of its implications is beyond the scope of this chapter.[30] Nevertheless, a few key developments in the regional security environment are worth noting here. The most obvious, and perhaps the most important, is that the regional distribution of power has changed. Iraq, at least in the near term, is no longer in a position to bid for regional hegemony. Nor is it able to balance Iran's power in the region. Who or what will fill this vacuum remains to be seen. In addition, there is a new dividing line between Arab states. Not only are there rich and poor Arab states, moderate and more radical states, but now there are also states that joined the U.S.-led coalition and states that did not. This distinction appears to have retained its significance in the immediate aftermath of the conflict, but its longevity is open to question. Moreover, the myth that Arab solidarity is somehow immune to power politics and that fraternal differences can be settled intramurally has been shattered.[31] Both the willingness of some Arab states to call on outside powers for direct military intervention and the willingness of the United States and others to respond have been amply demonstrated.

In addition, in the wake of the war, the United States redoubled its efforts to breathe life into an Arab-Israeli peace process. The Bush administration used its political capital as leader of a victorious coalition, its newfound diplomatic partnership with the Soviet Union, and the fact that Israel and some Arab states had shared a common enemy to bring Arabs and Israelis to the negotiating table. It also sought to focus international attention on stopping the flow of arms to the Middle East. In June 1991, for example, President Bush made a sweeping proposal to control missiles, weapons of mass destruction, and conventional weapons in the region.[32] If such efforts are to have any hope of success, they will require an un-

---

[30]For a discussion of the implications of the war for Mideast security, see Shahram Chubin, "Post-war Gulf Security," *Survival*, Vol. XXXIII, No. 2 (March/April 1991), pp. 140–157.

[31]*Ibid.*

[32]The proposal seeks to stymie further militarization of the region by establishing: a conventional-arms suppliers group to regulate weapons sales; a complete ban on chemical weapons (which would affect Syria, Iran, Iraq, Israel, Egypt, Libya, and possibly Saudi Arabia); measures to strengthen the 1972 Biological Weapons Convention; a freeze on the production of nuclear weapons-grade materials (which would affect only Israel) as well as the construction of new facilities capable of producing these materials; and a ban on the acquisition, production, and testing of surface-to-surface missiles (which would affect virtually every country in the region). For a description and critique of the proposal, see Joel S. Wit and Leonard S. Spector, "A Realistic Path to Mideast Arms Control," *The Christian Science Monitor*, June 13, 1991, p. 19.

precedented degree of cooperation among the nations of the Middle East and among supplier states worldwide, parallel progress on divisive political issues, a shared belief that diplomatic accommodation can enhance national security, and a realistic program of incremental steps.[33]

At the same time, many factors in the Middle East have been remarkably resistent to change. Numerous obstacles to the peace process, old and new, persist, making progress in a multilateral Arab-Israeli dialogue extremely difficult. The United States and its allies continue to sell arms to the region in substantial quantities. Some states, particularly the "have-nots," continue to harbor revisionist agendas and hegemonic ambitions. There is widespread and possibly growing discontent with many of the regimes currently in power, particularly the monarchies. And there are no truly effective regional security structures on which to build a stable peace.

What is the relevance of nuclear weapons in this context? Given Soviet disengagement from the region and the thaw in U.S.-Soviet relations, the relevance of U.S. nuclear weapons to the Middle East—both as means of signaling political resolve and as weapons of last resort—appears to have declined. Their future relevance is, however, more difficult to predict. If nuclear proliferation continues in the Middle East, the perceived relevance of U.S. nuclear weapons there could well increase, particularly if the United States chose to make nuclear guarantees to allies in the region, such as Saudi Arabia.

From the perspective of the countries of the Middle East, nuclear weapons have an obvious military and political relevance due to the fact that Israel possesses them. Acquiring nuclear weapons may be more or less attractive to other countries in the region depending on how one interprets the lessons of the Gulf War. Indeed, the war sent a mixed message to potential proliferators.[34] On one hand, if Kuwait had possessed nuclear weapons, Iraq might not have attacked it. Similarly, if Iraq had had nuclear weapons, the U.S.-led coalition might not have intervened. The purported lesson here is that nuclear weapons deter one's adversaries from taking hostile action, be it an invasion of one's homeland or intervention on behalf of one's enemy. Another possible lesson is that, in reality, chemical weapons are not "the poor man's atomic bomb." Although they can be weapons of mass destruction if used against unprotected troops or civilians, chemical weapons do not pack the same deterrent punch as nuclear weapons. Taken together, these lessons, however valid or invalid, could make the acquisition of nuclear weapons appear more attractive.

On the other hand, Iraq's experience in the war suggests that attempting to go nuclear is a dangerous proposition. Having a nuclear weapons

---

[33]Wit and Spector, *op. cit.*

[34]For another view on the lessons of the Gulf War, see McGeorge Bundy, "Nuclear Weapons and the Gulf," *Foreign Affairs*, Vol. 70, No. 4 (Fall 1991), pp. 83–94.

program rendered Iraq a target of preventive strikes. It can also be argued that Iraq's nuclear ambitions caused the coalition to be less restrained in its use of force. A related lesson might be that preventive attacks against a country's nuclear weapons facilities, although more difficult than some may have thought, may also be more acceptable in the eyes of the international community than others may have thought. Israel destroyed Iraq's Osirak nuclear reactor in a peacetime bombing raid in 1981; and the United States appeared to receive more praise than criticism for bombing Iraqi nuclear facilities in the 1991 Gulf War. These lessons would tend to give a potential proliferator pause.

Nations harboring nuclear ambitions might also infer some "how to" lessons from the Iraqi experience in the Gulf War. For example, if a state is going to go nuclear, it should do everything possible to make its nuclear weapons facilities safe from destruction; they should be dispersed, well-hidden, and hardened. Alternatively, it might be inferred that a nation should cross the nuclear threshold as quietly as possible, preferably without creating observable evidence of its efforts. Judging from rumors that they were in the market to buy a nuclear weapon, the Saudis may have taken this lesson to heart.[35] This points to a possible new path of proliferation in the future. Such a path could become increasingly feasible if any of the following circumstances materialized: the nuclear weapons facilities of a declining nuclear power like the Soviet Union became more vulnerable to security breaches, an economically strapped nuclear power like China chose to ignore nonproliferation restrictions in order to gain hard currency, or emerging nuclear weapons states like India or Pakistan became new nuclear suppliers.

Finally, the war had some potential lessons for the United States with regard to nuclear weapons as well. First, stopping the spread of nuclear weapons, particularly in areas where the United States has key allies and vital interests, is of the utmost importance. Second, the United States should be better prepared to manage proliferation—that is, constrain its scope and consequences should efforts to stop it fail. Third, conventional weapons appear to have been highly effective in missions that were once reserved for tactical nuclear weapons.[36] And finally, as mentioned, preventive strikes appear to be both more acceptable and more difficult than many previously thought.

The Middle East raises several difficult questions for U.S. nuclear weapons policy. Given the changing nature of threats in this region, should the nature of our defense commitment to key allies change? Specifically, should the United States explicitly extend a nuclear guarantee to

---

[35]Jack Anderson and Dale Van Atta, "Do Saudis Have Nuclear Weapons?" *Washington Post*, December 12, 1990, p. G15.

[36]The degree to which missions traditionally assigned to nonstrategic nuclear weapons can now be performed by conventional weapons is discussed in Chapters 3 and 4.

its moderate Arab allies in an effort to dissuade them from acquiring their own nuclear arsenals? Should the United States rely on nuclear weapons to deter or respond to the Nth country use of nuclear weapons? Should the United States rely on nuclear weapons to deter or respond to the use of other weapons of mass destruction? These questions will be addressed in the next chapter.

East Asia

The end of the Cold War has transformed relations among the four great powers that dominate East Asia. Never have relations between the United States, the Soviet Union, China, and Japan been better. And nowhere has this change been more evident than on the Korean peninsula.[37] The Soviet Union established diplomatic relations with South Korea in September 1990, China and South Korea agreed the following month to open trade offices in each other's capitals, and Japan and North Korea began talks on normalizing ties in January 1991. Indeed, the four great powers appear to be on the road to full "cross-recognition"—recognition of both Koreas by each of the four.

Although the Cold War has not come to a complete end between the two Koreas, their relations have warmed somewhat with the East-West thaw. Unprecedented talks between North and South began in September 1990 in Seoul, and it is hoped that these ongoing discussions will pave the way for progress on confidence-building measures, regional arms control, and ultimately Korean reunification.[38] Furthermore, in May 1991, North Korea agreed to submit its own application to the United Nations; as a result, both Koreas are now full members.

In short, the threats that have shaped U.S. security policy in East Asia—the Soviet Union, China, and North Korea—appear to be in various stages of retreat. The Pentagon now regards the Soviet Union's military posture in Asia as being primarily defensive.[39] Similarly, China is not seen as posing any serious threat to U.S. interests or allies in the region, with one major exception: the threat posed by its arms exports, particularly its sales of ballistic missiles to developing countries. Although North Korea remains a cause for concern, as will be discussed in greater detail in the following, it has at least begun to take some important steps toward ending its diplomatic isolation and reducing tensions with the South. Finally, were

---

[37]For a description of the relations between the four great powers and Korea from World War II to the mid-1980s, see Ralph N. Clough, *Embattled Korea: The Rivalry for International Support* (Boulder, Colo.: Westview, 1987), especially pp. 207–273.

[38]Peter Polomka, "Towards a 'Pacific House,' " *Survival*, Vol. XXXIII, No. 2 (March/April 1991), p. 173.

[39]Department of Defense, *Soviet Military Power 1990* (Washington, D.C.: U.S. Government Printing Office, September 1990), pp. 18, 96, 98–99.

North Korea to become involved in a conflict, it could no longer count on the intervention or even support of either the Soviet Union or China.

However, many uncertainties remain. For example, the extent to which Soviet-Japanese relations will improve is questionable as long as long-standing territorial disputes remain unresolved. More importantly, the future of relations between the United States and Japan, particularly the nature and degree of their security cooperation, cannot be foretold. Will the United States remain Japan's ultimate security guarantor? Or will Japan pursue a more independent path? In light of Japan's economic success and the United States' fiscal woes, pressure has mounted for Japan to take greater responsibility for its own defense needs. And in the war against Iraq, Japan was criticized for not playing a larger role in the multinational coalition—both for not sending troops in addition to yen and for not sending more yen. Inside Japan, consideration of a more militarily autonomous posture stems from doubts about whether Japan can count on American protection in the future, given the United States' declining defense budgets and its serious domestic problems.[40] However, such pressures should be balanced against careful thinking about what a militarily autonomous Japan would look like, both from a U.S. perspective and from the perspective of its East Asian neighbors. What sort of choices about rearmament, especially nuclear rearmament, would such a Japan make?

Similarly, it is difficult to predict the future direction of China's foreign and security policies. Now that the Soviet Union has reduced and restructured its forces in Asia, China faces no serious external threat. Moreover, due to its modernization efforts, it has powerful incentives to pursue a benign foreign policy in order to keep its relations with the West on an even keel. Nevertheless, China's behavior as an arms supplier remains worrisome and its military potential vast.

Lastly, one must consider the unpredictable nature of future developments on the Korean peninsula. On one hand, the military balance between North and South appears to be shifting toward parity, if not South Korean superiority. Although North Korea maintains quantitative superiority in categories of weapons and equipment,[41] South Korea has gained an important qualitative edge in others, and has an economy that enables it to outspend North Korea on defense, a superior military-industrial base for indigenous weapons production, and access to sophisticated arms from the United States.[42]

On the other hand, a nuclear arms race on the peninsula cannot be

[40]Polomka, *op. cit.*, p. 178.

[41]In some categories—such as tanks, artillery pieces, combat aircraft, and naval combatants—North Korea's forces are roughly twice those of the South. See *The Military Balance* (London: IISS, 1990), pp. 166–169.

[42]Burrus Carnahan, James Tomashoff, and Joseph Yager, *Nuclear Nonproliferation Policy and the Korean Peninsula* (McLean, Va.: Science Applications International Corporation, April 29, 1991), pp. 1-6–1-9.

ruled out. In October 1990, assistant secretary of state for East Asian and Pacific Affairs Richard Solomon stated that the United States views "nuclear proliferation on the Korean peninsula as the number one threat to security in East Asia."[43] Although North Korea signed the Nuclear Non-Proliferation Treaty in 1985 and has negotiated an agreement with the International Atomic Energy Agency (IAEA) that would allow international inspections of all its nuclear installations, including the Yongbyon complex—which the United States believes is part of a project to build nuclear weapons—it has refused to sign the inspections agreement until several conditions are met. Originally, North Korea insisted on the withdrawal of U.S. nuclear weapons from South Korea or a U.S. assurance not to use nuclear weapons against it. However, in the wake of the U.S. pledge in 1991 to withdraw all its nuclear weapons from South Korea, Pyongyang presented new conditions, including a demand that South Korea renounce the U.S. nuclear guarantee entirely and that the United States be prohibited from flying over the Korean peninsula or from making any calls on South Korean ports with vessels carrying nuclear weapons.[44] Whether and how this standoff will be resolved remains to be seen.

But even if North Korea ultimately signs the IAEA safeguards agreement, its nuclear program could still be perceived as highly provocative if it remains on its current course: If North Korea completed a plutonium extraction plant, it would be legally entitled to stockpile weapons-grade plutonium as long as the material were subject to IAEA inspection; this would leave it dangerously close to possessing nuclear weapons.[45] In that case, South Korea might well respond by restarting its own nuclear weapons program, which some estimate could bear fruit in less than 4–6 years.[46] And it is certainly possible that Japan might follow suit.

What, then, is the relevance of nuclear weapons in East Asia? The general decline of the Soviet and Chinese threats that have traditionally been the focus of U.S. security policy in East Asia suggests that U.S. nuclear weapons should be less relevant to the region in the future. Such an assessment undoubtedly figured into the U.S. decision to withdraw all of its nuclear weapons from South Korea.

But from the perspective of other countries, the view may be some-

---

[43] As quoted in Spector and Smith, *op. cit.*, p. 9.

[44] Steven R. Weisman, "North Korea Adds Barriers to A-Plant Inspections," *New York Times*, October 24, 1991, p. A11.

[45] Spector and Smith, *op. cit.*, p. 10.

[46] Carnahan, Tomashoff, and Yager, *op. cit.*, p. 3-3. Although South Korea's foreign minister has stated that his country would not seek nuclear weapons even if North Korea were to obtain them, South Korea has demonstrated a strong interest in acquiring, or at least approaching, a nuclear weapons capability in the past. In the early 1970s, South Korea was engaged in a clandestine effort to develop nuclear weapons. This effort ceased in the mid-1970s after the United States put pressure on Seoul to refrain from taking any further steps toward a nuclear weapons capability. However, some related activities apparently continued through 1989. *Ibid.*, p. 3-8.

what different. Indeed, the future military and political relevance of nuclear weapons in this area depends in large part on the future of the North
Korean nuclear weapons program and the reactions of other countries to
it. As long as nuclear proliferation stalks the Korean peninsula, nuclear
weapons are likely to be perceived as relevant to the security concerns of
several countries in the region. Indeed, one could imagine nuclear weapons gaining relevance in East Asia if North Korea were to move further
toward or cross the nuclear threshold, particularly for South Korea and
Japan. If, on the other hand, the North Korean program stopped, one
would expect the relevance of nuclear weapons in this region to fall.

The changing security environment in East Asia raises several important questions for U.S. nuclear weapons policy. What is the future role of
nuclear weapons in this region? How does the changing Soviet threat
affect the United States' need to rely on nuclear weapons there? Should
U.S. nuclear guarantees to both Japan and South Korea be maintained?
And if so, what sort of deployments should support these commitments?
Finally, what impact will proliferation dynamics on the Korean peninsula
have on U.S. nuclear weapons policy in the region? These and other
questions will be addressed in subsequent chapters.

CHANGING CONSTRAINTS ON U.S. SECURITY POLICY

In facing future threats to its security, the United States will have to
contend with several constraints—domestic and international, economic
and political. First and foremost, in the context of pressures to reduce
overall federal spending, particularly mandated reductions in the federal
budget deficit, military spending has become a prime target for budget
cuts both within the executive branch and on Capitol Hill. The U.S. defense budget was cut in 1990 more deeply than at any time since the end
of the Vietnam War.[47] And over the next five years, defense spending is
projected to be nearly $100 billion less than the administration's original
request.[48] At the same time, public support for military spending at current levels has waned with the end of the Cold War. Thus shrinking
defense budgets are likely to be an inescapable reality for the foreseeable
future. In this context, funding for nuclear weapons programs can be
expected to decline.[49]

---

[47]Defense Budget Project, "Final Congressional Action on the FY1991 Defense Budget:
Authorization and Appropriations," November 7, 1990, p. 1.

[48]These figures indicate outlays agreed at the budget summit between the Bush administra-
tion and the Congress and do not include the cost of Operation Desert Shield and Operation
Desert Storm. They appear in a chart entitled "National Defense Budget" provided by the
Department of Defense comptroller to congressional staffers in the fall of 1990.

[49]How these budgetary constraints may affect U.S. strategic nuclear weapons is discussed in
Chapter 5.

As a result, U.S. military planners will have limited resources as they attempt to tailor American forces to changing threats. As U.S. military spending and forces are reduced over time, the United States may no longer be able to assume a margin of effective military superiority over any and all adversaries, especially those that would place new or different demands on our capabilities. At the same time, the United States can be expected to put a new premium on burden-sharing with its allies, as it did in the Gulf War.

Second, the demise of East-West hostility and the rise of multipolarity have created new international political constraints on the unilateral use of force. The enlarging pattern of U.S.-Soviet cooperation and the reappearance of the United Nations as an important player on the world stage have elevated multilateralism and diplomacy to new heights. In this context, unilateral military action would likely be met with international ambivalence at best and international condemnation at worst. If these trends continue, future U.S. military actions may be severely constrained unless they are firmly supported by an international consensus and rooted in multilateral security structures. These actions are likely to be further constrained by the fact that the end of the Cold War has weakened both the rationale and host-country support for many U.S. forces and bases abroad. These constraints will undoubtedly influence the calculus of intervention.

The political constraints on the use of nuclear weapons are particularly strong. A "nuclear taboo" has evolved since the bombing of Hiroshima and Nagasaki in 1945, and over time it has gained credence as an international norm against the use of nuclear weapons.[50] Any use of nuclear weapons, particularly any first use, would be likely to provoke an international outcry, particularly if nonnuclear alternatives were perceived to exist. Furthermore, any use of nuclear weapons that resulted in the use of nuclear weapons against the U.S. homeland would undoubtedly provoke an even stronger outcry at home. Finally, insofar as a particular use of nuclear weapons demonstrated their utility as instruments of coercion or warfighting, it could also contribute to the further spread of nuclear weapons.

CONCLUSION

The Soviet Union no longer dominates the U.S. security agenda, and many of the scenarios that drove U.S. military planning during the Cold War are no longer credible. While the uncertain future of the Soviet Union is cause for concern, developments in Europe, the Middle East, and East Asia generally offer more cause for hope than despair as we contemplate the

---

[50]This norm is discussed in greater detail in Chapter 2.

post–Cold War security environment. Nevertheless, potential threats to U.S. security, particularly in areas where the United States has key allies and nuclear weapons are spreading, continue to exist. These threats are likely to be both less formidable and less predictable than the perceived Soviet threat of days gone by. Indeed, in the future, the United States will have to contend with a great deal of uncertainty, including the possibility that unanticipated military threats, such as the resurgence of a Soviet threat or the emergence of new and powerful adversaries, may arise.

At the same time, U.S. security policy must operate within a new set of economic and political constraints. Decreases in defense spending, force levels, and overseas bases will challenge the United States' ability to adapt to the new demands that non-Soviet contingencies may place on its military capabilities. In addition, the viability of U.S. military actions may increasingly depend on an ability to elicit multilateral support for and participation in such actions.

As for nuclear weapons, their relevance appears to be declining sharply in the U.S.-Soviet context. But it has not yet vanished. As in the past, nuclear deterrence will continue to play a role in the U.S.-Soviet relationship, at least in the near term. And nuclear weapons will continue to provide both status and insurance for Moscow and Washington. Militarily, however, nuclear weapons will approach irrelevance in the U.S.-Soviet relationship if current trends continue.

In Europe, the military relevance of nuclear weapons is receding in parallel with the Soviet threat. Nevertheless, these weapons are likely to retain some political relevance as symbols of one ally's commitment to another and as insurance against uncertain and remote contingencies, particularly while Europe is in transition. Although the spread of nuclear weapons on the continent cannot be ruled out, conditions would have to change substantially in order for this to be a likely outcome.

In the Middle East, the future relevance of nuclear weapons may well depend on lessons learned from the Gulf War. Individual states may come to see nuclear weapons as powerful deterrents that could safeguard territorial integrity and prevent outside intervention or as inviting targets for preemptive attack and the wrath of the international community. Whatever the lessons learned, the relevance of nuclear weapons in this region will also hinge in large part on the future of the Israeli nuclear arsenal.

In East Asia, nuclear weapons should become less relevant in light of improving relations among the four great powers in the region, but could conceivably become more so if the North Korean nuclear weapons program continues to go unchecked. In that case, the role of nuclear weapons in U.S. security commitments to both South Korea and Japan might increase or these countries might seek to acquire their own nuclear weapons. In sum, beyond the U.S.-Soviet context, the political and military relevance of nuclear weapons will depend in large part on the degree to which nuclear weapons spread.

From a strictly U.S. perspective, the relevance of nuclear weapons in the post–Cold War world will depend on the answers to the following questions: What roles should nuclear weapons play in providing for U.S. security? Is there a credible strategy for their use in the context of changed circumstances? Are there still unique and necessary missions for nuclear weapons? And are there situations in which the benefits of using nuclear weapons would outweigh the costs? These and other questions will be addressed in the chapters that follow.

SUGGESTED READINGS

"America and the World, 1990/91." *Foreign Affairs*, Vol. 70, No. 1 (1991).

Art, Robert J. "A Defensible Defense: America's Grand Strategy After the Cold War." *International Security*, Vol. 15, No. 4 (Spring 1991), pp. 5–53.

Aspen Strategy Group. *New Threats: Responding to the Proliferation of Nuclear, Chemical, and Delivery Capabilities in the Third World*. Lanham, Md.: University Press of America, 1990.

Campbell, Kurt M., Ashton B. Carter, Steven E. Miller, and Charles A. Zraket. *Soviet Nuclear Fission: Control of the Nuclear Arsenal in a Disintegrating Soviet Union*. CSIA Studies in International Security, No. 1. Cambridge, Mass.: Center for Science and International Affairs, November 1991.

Dean, Jonathan and Kurt Gottfried. *Nuclear Security in a Transformed World*. Cambridge, Mass.: Union of Concerned Scientists, September 1991.

Gaddis, John Lewis. "Toward the Post–Cold War World." *Foreign Affairs*, Vol. 70, No. 2 (Spring 1991), pp. 102–122.

Huntington, Samuel P. "America's Changing Strategic Interests." *Survival*, Vol. XXXIII, No. 1 (January/February 1991), pp. 3–17.

Kaysen, Carl, Robert S. McNamara, and George W. Rathjens. "Nuclear Weapons After the Cold War." *Foreign Affairs*, Vol. 70, No. 4 (Fall 1991), pp. 95–110.

Matthews, Jessica Tuchman. "Redefining Security." *Foreign Affairs*, Vol. 68, No. 2 (Spring 1989), pp. 162–177.

National Academy of Sciences. *The Future of the U.S.-Soviet Relationship*. Washington, D.C.: National Academy Press, 1991.

Spector, Leonard S. (with Jacqueline R. Smith). *Nuclear Ambitions: The Spread of Nuclear Weapons 1989–1990*. Boulder, Colo.: Westview, 1990.

Van Evera, Stephen. "Why Europe Matters, Why the Third World Doesn't: American Grand Strategy After the Cold War." *The Journal of Strategic Studies*, Vol. 13, No. 2 (June 1990), pp. 1–51.

Chapter
2

The Changing Role of U.S. Nuclear Weapons

Nina Tannenwald

*I*n the minds of most Americans, nuclear weapons and the Cold War go hand in hand. The heightened ideological competition of the U.S.-Soviet confrontation, in which fundamental values appeared to be at stake, elevated both the perceived threat and the psychological appeal of nuclear weapons as the ultimate security guarantee. This led to enormous nuclear arsenals on both sides. Now, as the Cold War has thawed, the world is left with two nuclear behemoths, like dinosaurs that have survived the Ice Age. The end of the first nuclear era creates an important opportunity to rethink and rationalize nuclear policy in the context of a more complex, multipolar world.

What role should nuclear weapons play in providing for U.S. security in the new world? The disappearance of the Cold War framework that gave nuclear weapons their meaning raises several fundamental questions. Should nuclear weapons be assigned only to deter nuclear attack, or should they still be relied upon to deter large-scale conventional war? What is the role of U.S. nuclear weapons in the new Europe and in other regions currently covered by an American nuclear guarantee? What is their role in dealing with emerging threats in the Third World? Should the United States rely on nuclear deterrence even in situations in which it would probably not use nuclear weapons? Does a superpower need to maintain nuclear weapons in order to prevent others from acquiring them, or does this encourage proliferation?[1]

---

[1] A related question is whether nuclear weapons are essential to superpower status. Answering this would require investigation into the changing nature of power, a topic beyond the scope of this chapter.

This chapter addresses these questions, laying a foundation for the chapters that follow. In theory, and in simplest terms, the United States has these major options: (1) to increase the role of nuclear weapons, (2) to maintain current roles (basic and extended deterrence), (3) to reduce the role of nuclear weapons, and (4) to eliminate the role of nuclear weapons entirely. The middle two options appear the most appropriate and realistic and are the focus of attention here.

This chapter begins by laying out a framework for examining the question of roles. It discusses two conceptual approaches to evaluating future roles, reviews the utility of nuclear weapons in light of past experience, and identifies several factors that should be taken into account in assessing future nuclear roles. It then evaluates systematically the roles U.S. policy has assigned to nuclear weapons in the past. It asks, in light of the changing world described in Chapter 1, whether and how these roles should change in the future. The chapter concludes with a set of recommendations.[2]

TWO APPROACHES TO EVALUATING FUTURE ROLES

There are two ways to approach the future roles of U.S. nuclear weapons. The first—the political or "top-down" approach—sees U.S. nuclear policy as one instrument for achieving broader U.S. foreign and security policy goals. It emphasizes that nuclear weapons are not simply military implements, capabilities, but also important instruments for communicating intent, signaling political resolve, and reflecting perceptions of threat. Over the course of the U.S.-Soviet relationship, for example, the superpowers' nuclear postures have been viewed as important indicators of each side's perception of the threat posed by the other and of broader foreign policy goals and intentions.

In this view, the end of the Cold War presents a dramatic opportunity to reset the agenda and tone of U.S. foreign policy for the next decade, if not longer, a goal that U.S. nuclear policy can help achieve. Indeed such an agenda might involve reducing reliance on nuclear weapons not only because they may have little military utility, but also because it is to the long-term advantage of the United States to establish and emphasize new

---

[2]It is useful to clarify briefly some terms commonly used in discussions of nuclear policy: *use, reliance,* and *role. Use* of nuclear weapons refers to dropping or launching nuclear weapons in all circumstances other than testing. *Reliance* on nuclear weapons refers to a policy determination that nuclear weapons will carry the burden of deterring or responding to aggression. *Role*, the broadest term, includes the tasks prescribed for nuclear weapons as part of military doctrine (e.g. deterrence, use) as well as political effects they may have. That is, by virtue of their enormous destructive capacity, nuclear weapons possess roles only indirectly related to either "use" or "deterrence." These include reassuring an ally or serving as symbols of political status, prestige, or technological and military-industrial prowess.

patterns of interaction in which nuclear weapons play a less central role. That is, in the early 1990s, the political costs of using nuclear weapons may so outweigh the military benefits of their use in all but the most remote circumstances, except in reply to nuclear use, that their military utility becomes almost a secondary consideration.[3]

According to the second "bottom-up" or military approach, the ideological competition and military threat of the Cold War created incentives to rely on nuclear weapons for deterrence while avoiding serious analysis of their military utility. The end of the Cold War, by reducing the threats nuclear weapons were intended to meet, finally permits some long overdue, hard-nosed scrutiny.[4] This approach evaluates the *military* utility of nuclear weapons by systematically assessing post–Cold War contingencies that might require the use of nuclear weapons. After conclusions about the military utility of nuclear weapons in specific scenarios are reached, the analysis proceeds to ask how political and psychological roles for nuclear weapons follow from, or can be reconciled with, intended military use.

Both these approaches are necessary. The bottom-up approach confronts directly the gap between doctrine and credibility by asserting that there must be a genuine military basis for doctrine, or if there is not, this must be made clear. The top-down approach emphasizes that, with the demise of the Cold War, nuclear policy must adapt to reflect a new and more complex array of foreign policy goals.

This chapter, on the general roles and missions of U.S. nuclear weapons, emphasizes the political approach. Chapter 4, on nonstrategic nuclear weapons, highlights changes in technology, the declining military utility of nuclear weapons, and the fading distinction between strategic and nonstrategic weapons. Together, these chapters provide a comprehensive basis for drawing conclusions about the appropriate roles for U.S. nuclear weapons.

THE UTILITY OF NUCLEAR WEAPONS: WHAT ARE THEY GOOD FOR?

Forty-five years into the nuclear era, the utility of nuclear weapons remains a matter of dispute. The question of whether nuclear weapons have made the world more or less secure remains unanswered.[5] From an histor-

---

[3]This is a theme of McGeorge Bundy, *Danger and Survival: Choices About the Bomb in the First Fifty Years* (New York: Random House, 1988), p. 536.

[4]Ashton B. Carter, "Emerging Themes in Nuclear Arms Control," *Daedalus*, Vol. 120, No. 1 (Winter 1991), pp. 233–249.

[5]Robert Jervis explores this question in *The Meaning of the Nuclear Revolution* (Ithaca, N.Y.: Cornell University Press, 1989).

ical perspective, little agreement exists on what role nuclear weapons played in preventing East-West war during the Cold War, the effectiveness of nuclear threats, the significance of the nuclear balance for the outcome of crises, and whether nuclear weapons deter only nuclear war or all war between nuclear adversaries.[6]

This lack of conclusive historical evidence poses problems for rethinking the role of nuclear weapons. Although the primary role of U.S. nuclear weapons has been to deter Soviet aggression, we lack definitive proof that nuclear deterrence works. While nuclear weapons may have helped prevent East-West war, other factors also played a role.[7] Deterrence exists in the mind of the beholder—not the deterrer—and to date we have little understanding of how the Soviet Union and China, the main recipients of American nuclear threats, perceived American nuclear weapons in crises.[8] The rethinking task becomes even more difficult as new regional conflict scenarios—the dynamics of which we understand far less—appear to supplant the now almost reassuringly familiar U.S.-Soviet confrontation. As Chapter 1 suggested, lessons from the Gulf War about the utility of nuclear weapons, for example, will be the subject of continuing debate, not only within the United States but also among decision-makers in the Middle East and elsewhere.[9]

However, while we may lack conclusive knowledge, the historical

---

[6]The literature on this topic is vast. For surveys of the evidence see John Lewis Gaddis, *Nuclear Weapons and International Systemic Stability*, Occasional Paper No. 2 (Cambridge, Mass.: American Academy of Arts and Sciences, January 1990); Richard Betts, *Nuclear Blackmail and Nuclear Balance* (Washington, D.C.: The Brookings Institution, 1987); Bundy, *op.cit.*; Colin Gray, "Nuclear Strategy: What is True, What is False, What is Arguable," *Comparative Strategy*, Vol. 9 (1990), pp. 1–32.

[7]John Lewis Gaddis evaluates some of these other factors in "The Long Peace: Elements of Stability in the Postwar International System," in Gaddis, *The Long Peace: Inquiries into the History of the Cold War* (New York: Oxford University Press, 1987), pp. 215–245. For the extreme but provocative argument that nuclear weapons were irrelevant to the absence of war in the postwar period, see John Mueller, *Retreat from Doomsday: The Obsolescence of Major War* (New York: Basic Books, 1989).

[8]Recent work on the Cuban missile crisis has shed new light on Soviet perceptions of the crisis. See James G. Blight and David A. Welch, *On the Brink: Americans and Soviets Reexamine the Cuban Missile Crisis* (New York: Hill and Wang, 1989); *Proceedings of the Moscow Conference on the Cuban Missile Crisis* (Lanham, Md.: University Press of America, 1991). The best summary of the available information on U.S. nuclear threats is Betts, *op. cit.* For an extended discussion of problems in analyzing deterrence, see Richard Ned Lebow and Janice Gross Stein, *When Does Deterrence Succeed and How Do We Know?*, Occasional Paper No. 8 (Ottawa: Canadian Institute for International Peace and Security, February 1990).

[9]During the Gulf War, Iraq, a nonnuclear state, willingly fought the United States and initiated attacks upon Israel, both nuclear states. It is an interesting counterfactual exercise to speculate how the crisis would have been different if Iraq, Kuwait, or Saudi Arabia had possessed nuclear weapons.

record does give us some hints as to the utility of nuclear weapons. It is generally agreed that nuclear weapons render *basic deterrence*, deterrence of attack on the homeland, a plentiful commodity, in the sense that they make the expected price of such an attack a fearful prospect for any attacker. It is with respect to *extended deterrence*, deterrence of attack on allies and U.S. troops abroad, that the credibility and therefore the effectiveness of nuclear threats has been especially questioned. Most of the agonizing over what nuclear weapons deter has occurred in the context of the United States' commitment to use nuclear weapons to defend its European allies against a Soviet conventional attack.

Fundamentally, the question is whether nuclear weapons can protect a wide range of American interests beyond its borders.[10] Here, one can think of nuclear utility in two ways: the utility in use (or military utility), and the utility in "nonuse."[11] Nuclear weapons have been *used* in war on only one occasion, when the United States demonstrated their effectiveness at Hiroshima and Nagasaki in 1945, compelling Japan to surrender. In this case, nuclear weapons were used primarily as weapons of terror. Starting in the 1950s, tactical nuclear weapons were developed for use on the battlefield. Over the years, as the tremendously destructive physical effects of nuclear weapons became better understood and the superpowers developed large strategic arsenals, it became widely accepted that little meaningful advantage would be gained by using strategic nuclear weapons. Likewise, in crisis after crisis throughout the Cold War, American decision-makers repeatedly failed to find instances when using tactical nuclear weapons would be advantageous to the United States.[12] Nevertheless, both the United States and the Soviet Union envision using nuclear weapons in the event deterrence fails.

However, the fact that nuclear weapons may be of doubtful military utility does not necessarily mean they lack deterrent or political utility. In fact, the utility residing in their "nonuse" has been more important for international and domestic politics than their military utility. Because of their horrifying destructiveness, nuclear weapons may have induced caution and aversion not only to nuclear war but also to conventional armed conflict between the superpowers. There has been no East-West war in Europe, and the United States and the Soviet Union have avoided direct confrontations between their forces elsewhere in the world. This unique "crystal ball effect" of nuclear weapons enables leaders to envision the

---

[10]The corollary is what strategy maximizes their deterrent effectiveness, a topic treated in the following chapter, on nuclear strategy.

[11]The phrase is Bernard Brodie's: "On Nuclear Weapons: Utility in Non-Use," in *War and Politics* (New York: Macmillan, 1973), pp. 375–432.

[12]Examples include the Korean War, crises over the islands of Quemoy and Matsu in 1954–55 and 1958, and the 1961 crisis over Berlin. John Lewis Gaddis, "The Origins of Self-Deterrence: The United States and the Non-Use of Nuclear Weapons, 1945–1958," in Gaddis, *The Long Peace*, pp. 104–146.

devastating outcome of a nuclear war even before hostilities begin and makes them determined to avoid even conventional confrontations.[13]

The post–WWII period has constituted a learning process about the nature of nuclear security. Since the bomb was first employed as a deterrent in the Berlin crisis of 1948,[14] the main policy role for nuclear weapons has been deterrence—dissuading a would-be aggressor from doing something it is not presently doing. This involves influencing the adversary's calculations of advantage through threats of unacceptable cost. Despite some early beliefs that nuclear weapons could deter a wide range of aggression, in practice, if not in doctrine, U.S. policy-makers have come to recognize limits on the deterrent utility of such weapons. Nuclear weapons have not always deterred attacks by nonnuclear states against the forces, and in some cases the homelands, of nuclear states.[15] Similarly, nuclear weapons have not always prevented attacks upon allies of a nuclear-armed state, and two nuclear powers—the Soviet Union and China—skirmished in 1968.

Likewise, leaders have come to recognize limits on the political advantage nuclear weapons confer. Early expectations that American possession of the bomb could be used to compel the Soviet Union to modify its behavior were soon abandoned in the face of Soviet conquest of Eastern Europe when the United States possessed a nuclear monopoly.[16] U.S. leaders quickly came to accept that the bomb would help *defend* rather than *advance* American interests in Europe vis-à-vis the Soviet Union.[17] There is also little evidence that nuclear weapons were helpful in promoting American foreign policy goals outside Europe.[18] For its part, the Soviet Union, after becoming a nuclear power, witnessed the reduction of its

---

[13]Albert Carnesale, et al., *Living With Nuclear Weapons* (Cambridge, Mass.: Harvard University Press, 1983), p. 44. Related implications of the "nuclear revolution" include the replacement of war with crises as tests of will (and then even the increasing rarity of those) and the maintenance of the basic territorial status quo in Europe. Jervis, *op. cit.*, pp. 23–45.

[14]Ironically, the B-29 aircraft sent to England to convey the deterrent threat neither carried nuclear bombs nor were configured to do so.

[15]China attacked U.S. forces during the Korean War, North Vietnamese forces attacked U.S. forces in Vietnam, Egypt attacked Israel in 1973, Argentina attacked British forces over the Falklands in 1982, and most recently, Iraq attacked Israel and U.S. bases in Saudi Arabia in the Gulf War.

[16]Gregg Herken, *The Winning Weapon: The Atomic Bomb in the Cold War: 1945–1950* (New York: Vintage Books, 1982); John Lewis Gaddis, *Strategies of Containment* (New York: Oxford University Press, 1982); McGeorge Bundy, "The Unimpressive Record of Atomic Diplomacy," in Gwyn Prins, ed., *The Nuclear Crisis Reader* (New York: Vintage, 1984), pp. 42–54. The notion of "compellence" is from Thomas A. Schelling, *Arms and Influence* (New Haven: Yale University Press, 1966), pp. 69–78.

[17]Robert A. Levine, *U.S. Interests and Intervention in the Nuclear Age*, RAND report R-3805-CC, (Santa Monica: November 1989), p. vi.

[18]Bundy, "Unimpressive Record," pp. 44–49.

influence in Yugoslavia, Indonesia, and Egypt, and the spectacular failure of its atomic diplomacy against China. More recently, nuclear weapons were largely irrelevant to the collapse of communism and the breakup of the Soviet empire beginning in 1989.[19] With concern over the physical safety and control of Soviet nuclear weapons heightened by the failed coup attempt of August 1991 and ongoing domestic turmoil, the possession of a large nuclear stockpile may now be perceived by the central Soviet and republican governments to be more of a burden than an instrument of national security.

Nuclear weapons do have important political effects, however. In addition to the general caution they have likely instilled, U.S. nuclear weapons have served as political glue for the Atlantic alliance, given the United States ongoing influence and a leadership position in NATO, and provided psychological reassurance of the U.S. commitment to Europe. Similar, though lesser, effects have occurred in other regions. Nuclear weapons have also helped forge a domestic consensus on foreign and defense policy. As McGeorge Bundy has argued, the principal use of U.S. numerical superiority in nuclear weapons during the Kennedy and Johnson administrations was to reassure the American public and ward off demands for still larger forces.[20] At a more instrumental level, the United States has used arms control and nuclear weapons modernization to exert leverage over the shape of the Soviet Union's nuclear arsenal.[21] On the Soviet side, the Soviet nuclear buildup in the 1960s and 1970s may have encouraged calls in the West in the 1980s for a no-first-use policy.[22]

Yet nuclear weapons have also been a source of tension and competition. At times, the pursuit of deterrence as practiced by both superpowers—the attempt to manipulate the risk and consequences of war for political ends—has had counterproductive effects. Khrushchev's 1957–61 threats to produce missiles "like sausages" likely spurred a U.S. military buildup. Similarly, the continued U.S. deployment of intercontinental and submarine-launched ballistic missiles (ICBMs and SLBMs, respectively) after the missile gap "myth" was discovered in 1961 may have prompted Khrushchev, fearing U.S. intentions given its massive superiority, to de-

---

[19]Some argue that possession of nuclear weapons may have helped make the dissolution of the empire "palatable" for Soviet leaders, in that they safeguard its superpower status. Josef Joffe, "What Just Happened: A Lite History," *The New Republic*, August 13, 1990, p. 20. However, this begs the question of why Soviet leaders did not give up the burdens of empire earlier.

[20]McGeorge Bundy, "Strategic Deterrence Thirty Years Later," in Philip Bobbitt, et al., eds., *U.S. Nuclear Strategy* (New York: New York University Press, 1989), p. 457.

[21]For example, NATO's 1979 decision to deploy intermediate-range nuclear weapons in Europe was intended in part to exert pressure on the Soviet Union to negotiate away its comparable SS-20 missiles.

[22]Lawrence Freedman, "I Exist; Therefore I Deter," *International Security*, Vol. 13, No. 1 (Summer 1988), p. 183.

ploy nuclear weapons in Cuba.[23] Within NATO, U.S. nuclear weapons have often been the source of divisiveness. These examples suggest that while nuclear weapons likely contributed to general stability in East-West relations, the pursuit of more and better deterrence may also have fueled tension and instability and at times increased rather than decreased the risk of nuclear war.

On balance, nuclear weapons possess less utility than many believed in the past, but more than extreme critics of nuclear weapons hold now. Nuclear weapons have clearly not prevented certain instances of conventional aggression. Though there is no incontrovertible historical proof, there is consensus on a few points: In a situation where each side possesses a survivable second strike capability, nuclear weapons deter the use of other nuclear weapons, and nuclear adversaries behave cautiously toward each other. How far one can "extend" the deterrent utility of nuclear weapons beyond one's borders remains unknown, but appears to depend on how vital the interests at stake are, whether they are perceived as such by the adversary, and how highly motivated the adversary is to change the status quo.[24]

FUTURE ROLES OF U.S. NUCLEAR WEAPONS

The balance of this chapter systematically evaluates the major roles of nuclear weapons in the past and assesses possible new roles. Such an evaluation should take into account three important and interrelated considerations of the post–Cold War world: U.S. foreign policy goals, the benefits of reducing reliance on nuclear weapons, and the desirability of strengthening the norm of nuclear nonuse.

U.S. foreign policy goals for the post–Cold War world include both longstanding goals—such as avoiding nuclear war, bringing peace and stability to strife-torn regions, and maintaining and strengthening cooperation with other nations—and goals given new prominence by the end of the Cold War. The latter include, among others, developing and strengthening norms against the acquisition and use of weapons of mass destruction, establishing cooperative relationships with the new entities governing former Soviet territory, and building a peaceful new Europe. Although not a foreign policy goal, the United States must also sustain domestic support for its security policies.

A second consideration in evaluating the future roles of nuclear weap-

---

[23]Gaddis, *Nuclear Weapons and International Systemic Stability*, p. 8; Richard Ned Lebow and Janice Stein, *We All Lost the Cold War. Can We Win the Peace?* [forthcoming], Ch. 2.

[24]For more on these points see Janice Gross Stein, "Deterrence and Reassurance," in Philip E. Tetlock, et al., eds., *Behavior, Society and Nuclear War*, Vol. 2 (New York: Oxford University Press, 1991), pp. 8–72.

ons involves the political and security benefits of deemphasizing nuclear weapons and reducing reliance on them. As U.S., Western, and Soviet leaders have increasingly recognized, the end of the East-West confrontation offers a dramatic opportunity to reduce reliance on nuclear deterrence. This would promote U.S. foreign policy goals in a number of ways. First, it would help meet the challenge of devising roles for nuclear weapons that continue to command domestic support but do not dangerously increase the perceived utility of nuclear weapons by other states. While public opinion polls show that Western mass publics continue to support policies of nuclear deterrence, the widespread antinuclear protests of the 1980s, in both Europe and America, revealed substantial public disquiet with the highly aggressive nuclear policies of the Reagan administration.[25] A less prominent role for nuclear weapons in U.S. security policy would likely sustain the domestic support on which deterrence policies in a democratic society crucially depend.

Additionally, reduced reliance on nuclear deterrence could make a potential, if perhaps only marginal, contribution to U.S. nonproliferation efforts, which have taken on greater urgency in light of the alarming Iraqi nuclear program revealed in the aftermath of the Gulf War. Nonnuclear states have argued that it is inconsistent for the nuclear powers to rely on nuclear deterrence themselves but to discourage it in others.[26] In the view of some, the continued reliance of the superpowers on large nuclear arsenals and testing programs continues to legitimate nuclear weapons in the eyes of nonnuclear powers and thus in the long run threatens to undermine the nonproliferation regime.[27] While it is likely that potential proliferators base their decisions on whether to pursue a nuclear capability mostly on perceived regional threats to their security, and not on superpower disarmament practices, superpower behavior helps shape the nor-

---

[25]See Thomas Graham, *American Public Opinion on NATO, Extended Deterrence, and Use of Nuclear Weapons: Future Fission?* CSIA Occasional Paper No. 4 (Cambridge, Mass.: Center for Science and International Affairs, Harvard, 1989); David Yost, "The Delegitimization of Nuclear Deterrence?" *Armed Forces and Society*, Vol. 16, No. 4 (Summer 1990), pp. 487–508; Robert Tucker, *The Nuclear Future: Political and Social Considerations*, CNSS Papers, No. 11 (Los Alamos: Los Alamos National Laboratory, Center for National Security Studies, June 1988).

[26]Lawrence Scheinman, "The Linkage Between Non-Proliferation, Deterrence Policy, Nuclear Testing and the Arms Race," in *Proceedings of the 39th Pugwash Conference on Science and World Affairs* (Cambridge, Mass., July 1989), p. 244.

[27]Article VI of the Non-Proliferation Treaty (NPT) obligates the nuclear-weapon states to "negotiate in good faith" toward a cessation of the nuclear arms race and toward global disarmament, and the NPT preamble recalls nuclear-weapon state commitments in the Preamble to the 1963 Partial Test Ban Treaty to "seek an end to all nuclear test explosions." For further discussion see Charles Van Doren and George Bunn, "Progress and Peril at the 4th NPT Review Conference," *Arms Control Today*, Vol. 20, No. 8 (October 1990), pp. 8–12; Leonard Spector and Jacqueline R. Smith, "Treaty Review: Deadlock Damages Non-Proliferation," *Bulletin of the Atomic Scientists*, Vol. 46, No. 10 (December 1990), pp. 39–44.

mative context in which decisions are made. U.S. action to reduce reliance on nuclear deterrence would set an example and could strengthen the United States' hand in nonproliferation matters. Although U.S. nuclear weapons and guarantees have at times *reduced* incentives to proliferate, as in the case of South Korea, in the future, as the spread of nuclear know-how becomes harder to control, this benefit will increasingly need to be weighed against the fear nuclear guarantees may create in other states, provoking them to seek their own nuclear arsenals.[28]

More specifically, a policy of relying on nuclear weapons to *deter use of nuclear weapons only* would be advantageous for several reasons. In addition to being more in line with public support for deterrence and no first use,[29] it would promote East-West relations by reducing the threat of nuclear use to proportionate levels. Operationally, it would encourage contingency planning based on conventional alternatives. Additionally, as previously suggested, it would be more consistent with, and might help bolster, nonproliferation efforts: It would reinforce the idea that nuclear weapons have little military utility and that acquiring them is illegitimate, and might strengthen the nuclear "taboo."[30]

Finally, a third consideration in evaluating future roles of nuclear weapons is the evolving norm of nonuse. Prior to the outbreak of the Persian Gulf War in January 1991, then Director of Central Intelligence William H. Webster indicated that a U.S. decision to breach the 45-year-old taboo against nuclear weapons use would be seen as so "appalling" that it should not be considered in the crisis.[31] It appears that nuclear use in this war was never seriously contemplated by U.S. leaders. The tradition of nonuse of nuclear weapons, described as "the most important single legacy of the first half century of fission,"[32] has become one of the most

---

[28]For example, North Korea's nuclear ambitions date from the Korean War, when there was open discussion of using American nuclear weapons to end the conflict. The North's fears were subsequently exacerbated by the basing of U.S. nuclear weapons on South Korean soil. David E. Sanger, "Data Raise Fears of Nuclear Moves by North Koreans," *New York Times*, November 10, 1991, p. 6.

[29]Polls suggest there has been little support for U.S. first-use of nuclear weapons since the mid-1950s, although this does not translate into endorsement of a declared no-first-use policy. According to Graham, the U.S. public "consensus" (defined as 60 percent to 70 percent of the people) has not supported "first use of nuclear weapons and only supports second use after nuclear weapons have been used against U.S. troops overseas or against the U.S. homeland." See Graham, *op. cit.*, pp. 5–16, 27–29. For a discussion of the advantages and disadvantages of a no-first-use declaration, see Chapter 3.

[30]Lewis Dunn, Seminar, Center for Science and International Affairs, Harvard, March 13, 1991.

[31]R. Jeffrey Smith and Rick Atkinson, "U.S. Rules Out Gulf Use of Nuclear, Chemical Arms," *Washington Post*, January 7, 1991, pp. A1, A22.

[32]Bundy, *Danger and Survival*, p. 587; Nina Tannenwald, "How Norms Matter in International Relations: The Non-use of Nuclear Weapons," Ph.D. dissertation, Cornell University, in progress.

significant restraints on U.S. nuclear policy. Given the increasing threat from the proliferation of long-range delivery systems and weapons of mass destruction, the United States should make every effort to ensure that this taboo remains upheld.

Past Roles: Are They Still Valid?

In the past, U.S. nuclear weapons have been seen to play four main roles, based on the greatest perceived threats to U.S. interests:

1. deter Soviet nuclear attack on the United States (basic deterrence)
2. deter Soviet conventional or nuclear attack on U.S. allies or troops (extended deterrence)
3. provide political, psychological reassurance to allies
4. fight war (should deterrence fail)

They have also been seen to possess important secondary roles:

5. deter aggression by other states (e.g. China, North Korea) against the United States, its troops or allies
6. deter use of other weapons of mass destruction (chemical, biological)
7. influence Soviet force planning and resource allocation
8. influence the Soviet Union's external behavior (e.g. dictate outcomes of crises primarily in the Third World)
9. provide symbols of prestige, status
10. provide a basis for domestic consensus on security policy, reassurance to domestic public
11. exert influence over Western allies

The following discussion will concentrate on the most important of these for the future: basic and extended deterrence, deterring the use of other weapons of mass destruction, and potential new roles for U.S. nuclear weapons in emerging Third World scenarios. Warfighting in both its senses—as a way to strengthen deterrence and as nuclear use—is addressed in Chapters 3 and 4.

Basic Deterrence—To Deter Nuclear Attack on the U.S. Homeland
The threat to retaliate in response to a nuclear attack on the homeland remains the most credible nuclear deterrent threat, and consequently the role for which there remains the widest support. During the Cold War, basic deterrence was defined largely in terms of deterring the Soviet adversary. Yet with the evaporation of ideological conflict and the breakup of the Soviet Union, the traditional foe has vanished. In its place are struggling, democratizing republics seeking aid and cooperation, rather than confrontation, with the West. While their future remains

uncertain, a fair chance exists that the United States and emerging governments on Soviet territory will be friends rather than foes in the not-too-distant future. This would render deterrence largely superfluous.

Nevertheless, as long as the decentralizing Soviet Union continues to possess a substantial nuclear arsenal, its governments remain unstable and their intentions unclear, the United States will need to uphold deterrence. However, in contrast to the agonized debates over the issue during the Cold War, there is an emerging consensus that deterring the deliberate use of Soviet nuclear weapons may now be one of the United States' easier tasks. As the subsequent chapter suggests—and as leaders on both sides have recognized—this task can likely be carried out at lower than current force levels because of changing views about the requirements of deterrence.

At the same time, ongoing domestic upheaval in the former Soviet Union has raised new concerns about the physical security of Soviet nuclear weapons and fears of their unauthorized acquisition and use. In this context, the United States should continue to seek assurances that government leaders are exercising tight control over Soviet nuclear weapons, and should encourage nonproliferation commitments by any republics that might inherit control of nuclear weapons deployed on their soil.[33]

While for the United States nuclear weapons will provide the ultimate insurance against the uncertain future of the Soviet polity, the greatest challenges for American leaders will probably lie in establishing new political relations with republican governments. It is even conceivable that someday the Soviet nuclear arsenal will provoke no greater concern in the United States than the French and British nuclear arsenals do now.

Extended Deterrence—To Deter Attacks on Allies or U.S. Troops Abroad   The threat to use nuclear weapons on behalf of allies has been a foundation of U.S. security policy in the post–WWII period, both supporting and reflecting a conception of U.S. security defined in global terms. From an initial U.S. commitment in 1949 to defend Western Europe against Soviet conventional attack with nuclear weapons, if necessary, the U.S. nuclear retaliatory threat expanded in the early 1950s to protect both Japan and South Korea following the Korean War. In the 1970s, as oil emerged as a strategic resource, the nuclear umbrella expanded again to include defending the Persian Gulf from Soviet incursion. While ·this extended deterrence policy has relied on both U.S. conventional forces and strategic and nonstrategic (tactical and theater) nuclear forces, the latter—deployed on aircraft, at sea, but especially on the

---

[33]William C. Potter, "Proliferation Threats and Non-Proliferation Opportunities in a Decentralized Soviet Union," unpublished manuscript, Monterey Institute of International Studies, September 1991. Measures to enhance the safety and security of Soviet nuclear weapons are discussed in greater detail in Chapter 4.

ground with U.S. troops—have come to symbolize the U.S. extended deterrence commitment.[34]

Yet ever since the Soviet Union achieved nuclear parity, the credibility of these nuclear guarantees has been problematic for the United States and its allies, at least in the abstract. Leaders and analysts have voiced recurring doubts that the United States would really be willing to "trade Washington for Bonn" or Seoul—that is, to risk Soviet nuclear retaliation against the U.S. homeland in response to a U.S. nuclear strike to protect an ally. Now, with the evaporation of the Soviet threat, the need for such guarantees may be less pressing.

The following analysis evaluates the future role of U.S. nuclear weapons in extended deterrence by examining the role of U.S. nuclear guarantees in three different contexts. The first case looks at the U.S. nuclear guarantee to Europe, the core commitment of traditional U.S. extended deterrence policy. The second case, focusing on the Far East, highlights challenges to U.S. nuclear guarantees in the context of regional nuclear proliferation. The third case evaluates the future role of U.S. nuclear weapons in deterring or responding to regional conventional aggression. Here the geographic focus is the Middle East. In each case, the aim is to draw upon particular features of a given geographical region to illuminate challenges to the future of U.S. nuclear extended deterrence. While President Bush's September 1991 U.S. initiative to withdraw most U.S. tactical nuclear weapons worldwide represented a substantial shift away from traditional extended deterrence policy and changed the form of U.S. nuclear guarantees in ways that will have important political effects, it does not obviate the need for fundamental reexamination of the role of extended nuclear deterrence.

Traditional Extended Deterrence: Europe The problems of, and challenges to, U.S. extended deterrence policy have traditionally been most evident in Europe, where the strategy and politics of relying on nuclear weapons for protection have been inextricably linked. NATO's often turbulent history since the 1960s has reflected the perceived difficulties of establishing a credible extended deterrence policy. European allies' repeated requests for reassurance from their geographically distant nuclear guarantor typically generated controversial plans for new hardware such as the multilateral force, the neutron bomb, or more recently, intermediate-range nuclear forces.[35] The problem of credibility has also

---

[34]On the history and practice of U.S. extended deterrence see Alexander L. George and Richard Smoke, *Deterrence in American Foreign Policy: Theory and Practice* (New York: Columbia University Press, 1974); and Lawrence Freedman, *The Evolution of Nuclear Strategy* (New York: St. Martin's Press, 1989), 2nd ed.

[35]The literature on NATO nuclear strategy and politics is extensive. See, for example, David Schwartz, *NATO's Nuclear Dilemmas* (Washington, D.C.: The Brookings Institution, 1983); Joseph Lepgold, *The Declining Hegemon: The United States and European Defense, 1960-*

been reflected in a lack of agreement among European allies regarding the role of U.S. nuclear weapons.[36]

Despite periodic political turmoil, the United States and its allies have tolerated the ambiguities of extended deterrence.[37] Nevertheless, as European security in the post–Cold War world is redefined, and with it, the U.S. relationship to Europe, the U.S. nuclear umbrella is being transformed.[38] As suggested earlier, the U.S. nuclear guarantee to Europe has fulfilled a variety of political, military, and psychological roles. These include deterring Soviet conventional and nuclear attack, demonstrating U.S. commitment to the security of Europe, facilitating burden-sharing in the alliance, and providing psychological reassurance to European allies. Two issues, often closely linked but nevertheless separate, are central to any assessment of its future: first, whether the United States should continue its nuclear commitment to Europe; and, second, if so, whether U.S. nuclear weapons deployed *in Europe* ("in-theater deterrence") are needed to meet that commitment effectively. Specifically, if there remain no unique military roles for in-theater weapons, as Chapter 4 concludes, are political and psychological rationales sufficient to sustain such deployments?

The dramatic political changes in Europe at least raise the possibility that a U.S. nuclear guarantee to Europe may no longer be needed in the future. Supporters of this view argue that the disappearance of the Soviet threat, high costs to the United States, inherent incredibility of an extended deterrent threat, and increasing capability of Europe to protect itself make a continuing U.S. commitment to Europe's defense unnecessary.[39] Other critics of the U.S. nuclear guarantee have emphasized the

---

1990 (New York: Greenwood Press, 1990); Stephen Cimbala, *Extended Deterrence: The United States and NATO Europe* (Lexington, Mass.: Lexington Books, 1987).

[36]Since De Gaulle's days, France has explicitly rejected the policy of U.S. extended deterrence as lacking credibility, while half of the 16 NATO members prohibit the deployment of U.S. nuclear warheads on their territory. Some European groups have denounced the U.S. nuclear umbrella while others have expressed ambivalence. Beginning in the early 1980s, for example, German opposition parties made it politically difficult for the West German government to support modernization or new deployments.

[37]NATO strategy is discussed more extensively in Chapter 3.

[38]The discussion here focuses on the future role of U.S. nuclear weapons in protecting Europe. For discussion of U.S. involvement in Europe's security more generally, see Stephen Van Evera, "Why Europe Matters, Why the Third World Doesn't: American Grand Strategy After the Cold War," *Journal of Strategic Studies*, Vol. 13, No. 2 (June 1990), pp. 1–51; Robert Art, "A Defensible Defense: America's Grand Strategy After the Cold War," *International Security*, Vol. 15, No. 4 (Spring 1991), pp. 5–53.

[39]See, for recent examples, Earl Ravenal, "The Case for Adjustment," *Foreign Policy*, No. 81 (Winter 90/91), pp. 3–19; Ted Galen Carpenter, "Competing Agendas: America, Europe, and a Troubled NATO Partnership," in Carpenter, ed., *NATO at Forty* (Washington, D.C.: Cato Institute, 1990); Christopher Layne, in "After the Cold War: A Symposium on New Defense Priorities," *Policy Review*, No. 53 (Summer 1990), p. 9.

danger and moral unacceptability of nuclear deterrent threats and advocate instead the long-term pursuit of disarmament and a nonprovocative and primarily conventional defense of Europe.[40]

While these points have some merit, a U.S. nuclear guarantee of Europe remains, at least for the time being, an essential component of Western security for several reasons. As long as those governing Soviet territory retain vast numbers of nuclear weapons, the U.S nuclear guarantee will remain important in providing insurance against any revival of the Soviet threat should leadership and intentions change, demonstrating U.S. commitment to the security of Europe, and deterring use of the Soviet nuclear arsenal. Most policy-makers on both sides of the Atlantic (including Soviet leaders), cognizant of Europe's tragic fate in the first half of the century when America stayed home, continue to see American involvement in European security as playing a stabilizing role in balancing power on the continent.[41] As long as the United States continues to value a secure Europe, and until new European security structures are solidly in place, eliminating the nuclear guarantee appears hasty and unwise. Alternatives such as an independent European nuclear deterrent may someday emerge, but currently are far from reality.[42]

Nevertheless, while the U.S. nuclear guarantee remains important, the form of the guarantee may continue to change. For our purposes here, the key question is whether or not in-theater deterrence remains a necessary element of this commitment. In the past, many held that nuclear weapons deployed in theater crucially enhanced the credibility of the American nuclear guarantee in the eyes of the Soviets. But such weapons also fulfilled a variety of political and psychological functions within the Western alliance. With the threat of Soviet attack unlikely, and a new politics of East-West partnership emerging in Europe, the continuing need for an American nuclear presence has become increasingly open to question.

---

[40]See, for example, the collections of essays in Anders Boserup and Robert Neild, eds., *The Foundations of Defensive Defense* (New York: St. Martin's Press, 1990); and in Michael Randle and Paul Rogers, eds., *Alternatives in European Security* (Aldershot, U.K.: Dartmouth Publishing, 1990).

[41]At the NATO summit in Rome in November 1991, NATO leaders reaffirmed their commitment to the American presence, declaring, in the words of a French spokesman, that "we all support the presence of U.S. forces in Europe." Alan Cowell, "Bush Challenges Partners in NATO Over Role of U.S.," *New York Times*, November 8, 1991, p. A1. For a discussion of the Soviet interest in keeping the United States in Europe, see Jane M. O. Sharp, "Why Discuss U.S. Withdrawal?" in Sharp, ed., *Europe After American Withdrawal: Economic and Military Issues*, SIPRI (New York: Oxford University Press, 1990), pp. 20–23.

[42]See David Yost, "France in the New Europe," *Foreign Affairs*, Vol. 69, No. 5 (Winter 1990/91), pp. 107–128. Even if the United States declared the end of its nuclear guarantee, there would always remain a residual deterrent threat—due to the mere existence of U.S. nuclear weapons. For example, it is difficult to imagine that a Soviet general could contemplate an attack on a U.S. ally and be certain that the United States would *not* respond with nuclear weapons.

It has been widely recognized, even by those most pessimistic about prospects for peaceful change in Europe after the Cold War, that the role of nuclear weapons in NATO must change. The United States acceded to requests from its European allies to cancel modernization of NATO's ground-based missiles—which the new map of Europe left without targets—and NATO moved in a timely fashion in July 1990 to adopt a "no-early-first-use" policy for its nuclear weapons.[43] In September 1991 President Bush announced unilateral withdrawal of most U.S. tactical nuclear weapons worldwide, and NATO followed in October with an announcement of its intention to destroy half the 1,400 U.S. nuclear bombs stockpiled in Europe.[44] Underlying these adjustments, however, is a firm belief that an American nuclear presence will continue to play a unique role in the new Europe. In this view, NATO should continue to rely on the U.S. nuclear presence to deter war in Europe, to "guarantee political order and stability" there,[45] and to alleviate any pressures within Germany to seek a nuclear capability.[46]

However, it may be both possible and desirable in the future to move away from reliance on an American in-theater nuclear presence as the cornerstone of the U.S.-European nuclear partnership. Several of the traditional rationales for in-theater deterrence are of decreasing relevance to the emerging Europe. First, while further analysis of military and technological aspects of in-theater deterrence is left to Chapter 4, it is clear that, militarily, the new conventional balance in Europe reduces the need for nuclear weapons to counter the Soviet conventional threat. As the U.S. decision to withdraw battlefield nuclear weapons reflects, it thus eliminates the need for the kind of "use them or lose them" deployments believed necessary during the Cold War to make the U.S. deterrent threat more credible.

Political factors have changed as well. First, in the absence of a serious

---

[43]The July 1990 NATO London communiqué stated that nuclear weapons would "continue to fulfill an essential role in the overall strategy of the Alliance to prevent war by ensuring that there are no circumstances in which nuclear retaliation in response to military action might be discounted." Text of the Final Declaration, *New York Times*, July 7, 1990, p. 5.

[44]Alan Riding, "NATO Will Cut Atom Weapons for Aircraft Use," *New York Times,* October 18, 1991, p. A1.

[45]Germany's Defense Minister, Christian Democrat Gerhard Stoltenberg, stated in a speech May 1, 1990 in Washington, D.C., that, "In the future, nuclear forces will serve not so much to deter an expressly designated political opponent, but rather to assure and stabilize a system of reciprocal security in Europe cemented by treaty." Quoted in Ottfried Nassauer, *NATO Nuclear Planning After the Cold War*, Report 90.2 (Washington, D.C.: British-American Security Information Council, May 1990), p. 15.

[46]Examples of this perspective include Leon Sloss, *Reexamining Nuclear Policy in a Changing World*, Report No. 11 (Los Alamos: Center for National Security Studies, Los Alamos National Laboratory, December 1990); Walter B. Slocombe, "The Continued Need for Extended Deterrence," unpublished manuscript, February 1991; Timothy Stanley, "American Strategy After the Cold War: The Price of Disengagement," *Comparative Strategy*, Vol. 10, No. 1 (January–March 1991), pp. 73–92.

threat to Europe, the need to rely on nuclear weapons as a "coupling" device for alliance relations is greatly diminished. This practice, associated especially with in-theater forces and the integrated NATO command structure, aimed to convince the Soviet Union (and the Europeans) that the United States was "coupled" to Europe, to keep Europeans coupled to each other, and to reassure everyone that the security of Bonn rested on that of all the other European capitals. In the context of the new Europe, political coupling appears to be an increasingly inappropriate and unnecessary role for weapons of mass destruction. Psychologically, Europe has long sought a more independent role in world affairs. Politically, European institutions such as the European Community and others increasingly fulfill—at least among Europeans—many of the "coupling" functions formerly ascribed to U.S. nuclear weapons. Germany, for example, thoroughly embedded in the network of European institutions, recognizes that its interests and sovereignty can be realized only through its commitment to "Europe." As for the core transatlantic link, many have argued that the key element of the U.S. commitment has always been U.S. troops on the front lines in Europe, a connection NATO could preserve.[47]

Second, some emphasize that an American nuclear presence will help dampen potential violence among Europeans.[48] However, this "pacifying role," which some envision as the major post–Cold War role for U.S. nuclear weapons in Europe, is, upon close inspection, somewhat vague, and risks serving as a rationale for deployments that lack meaningful military missions. To be sure, the mere existence of a continued American nuclear presence would help to remind Europeans that any war in Europe would be dangerous. But this existential effect would be created, at least to some degree, by French and British nuclear weapons as well.

Beyond this existential effect, however, in the foreseeable future it is difficult to imagine scenarios that would require any direct role for U.S. nuclear weapons. Most of the issues facing Europe—namely continuing reform in the former Soviet Union and Eastern Europe, and the establishment of political and economic stability—have little to do with the kind of security concerns that call for nuclear deterrence. And the most likely future conflicts in Europe—namely ethnic—are probably not deterrable with nuclear weapons. Europe's historical memory of two world wars and fear of a conventional World War III may well do more to incline Europeans against war than a more remote fear of nuclear use.[49] Likewise,

---

[47]For example, Timothy Kinnan advocates denuclearizing NATO but leaving U.S. troops in Europe in "To Defend the Atlantic Home," *Comparative Strategy*, Vol. 10, No. 1 (January–March 1991), pp. 91–105.

[48]For this view see Karl Kaiser, "From Nuclear Deterrence to Graduated Conflict Control," *Survival*, Vol. XXXII, No. 6 (November/December 1990), pp. 4–7; John Mearsheimer, "Back to the Future: Instability in Europe After the Cold War," *International Security*, Vol. 15, No. 1 (Summer 1990), pp. 5–56.

[49]For elaboration, see Stephen Van Evera, "Primed for Peace: Europe After the Cold War," *International Security*, Vol. 15, No. 3 (Winter 1990–91), pp. 7–57; and Mueller, *op. cit.*

Central European states' interest in presenting themselves as responsible candidates for membership in the European community will likely be the strongest factor in constraining their behavior.[50] Thus nuclear weapons cannot be discounted, but they are likely to be much less relevant than other factors in moderating behavior in Europe.

Thus, few advocate extending an explicit U.S. nuclear guarantee to Central European states.[51] Largely irrelevant to the region's turmoil, a nuclear guarantee would be worth considering only in the event that Germany acquired nuclear weapons, or possibly in the face of a reconstituted threat from Soviet territory. Barring these eventualities, a nuclear guarantee to Central Europe would appear excessively provocative to the former Soviet Union and would suffer the same, if not greater, credibility problems as the NATO nuclear guarantee. While Central European states desperately need overarching regional security institutions, these will be provided most effectively through multilateral, nonnuclear arrangements.[52] However, such near-term arrangements need not rule out an implicit nuclear guarantee to Central European states by virtue of their future membership in a European security institution. Nor need they foreclose an explicit guarantee should conditions change in the long term—should Central European states become objects of aggression of Soviet successor governments.

Finally, the oft-cited argument that the American nuclear umbrella, upheld by the American nuclear presence, is needed to prevent Germany from acquiring nuclear weapons no longer appears relevant to the world of the 1990s. Profound societal changes in Germany over the past 45 years render German interest in a nuclear arsenal highly unlikely in the foreseeable future. Nonnuclear status has become part of the German domestic consensus on foreign policy.[53] The conditions required to reverse this situation would have to present a threat approaching Cold War magnitude, combined with an unresponsive United States. Such conditions appear highly remote.

In sum, these rationales for an American nuclear presence in

---

[50]Robert Jervis, "The Future of World Politics: Will the Future Resemble the Past?" *International Security*, Vol. 16, No. 3 (Winter 1991–92).

[51]One who does is Slocombe, *op. cit.*, pp. 19–21.

[52]For further discussion, see Daniel Nelson, "Europe's Unstable East," *Foreign Policy*, No. 82 (Spring 1991), pp. 137–158; Curt Gasteyger, "The Remaking of Eastern Europe's Security," *Survival*, Vol. 33, No. 2 (March/April 1991), pp. 111–124.

[53]In August 1990, prior to unification, East and West Germany issued a joint declaration that a united Germany would honor previous commitments undertaken by both countries to forgo nuclear, biological, and chemical weapons and would support extension of the NPT beyond 1995. See Harald Mueller, "NPT Review: Western Europe Needs the Treaty," *Bulletin of the Atomic Scientists*, Vol. 46, No. 6 (July/August 1990), p. 28; also Wolfgang Kotter and Harald Mueller, *Germany and the Bomb: Nuclear Policies of the Two German States and United Germany's Non-Proliferation Commitments*, PRIF Report No. 14 (Frankfurt: Hessische Stiftung Friedens-Und Konflikt-Forschung, September 1990).

Europe—deterring Soviet conventional aggression, "coupling," dampening conventional violence, and forestalling German nuclear ambitions—appear of steadily diminishing relevance to emerging realities in the new Europe. This suggests that the degree of reassurance required by the Europeans could likely be provided in the future by a restructured nuclear partnership in which the main role of U.S. nuclear weapons is as a hedge against a highly contingent, remote threat from Soviet successor governments.

Explicitly modifying the U.S. nuclear guarantee to Europe to include deterring use of nuclear weapons only but not deterring or responding to conventional attack, as well as phasing out the American nuclear presence, would have several benefits. Operationally, it would reduce reliance on nuclear weapons for NATO planning purposes and increase reliance on conventional capabilities. Such a modification would simply make explicit for planning purposes what has come to be *de facto* employment policy anyway. That is, it would have the desirable effect of bringing *deployment* and *employment* practices more into line (thereby reducing the credibility gap).[54]

The political advantages of eliminating the U.S. nuclear presence in Europe—which would mean removing U.S. nuclear weapons from the NATO command structure—include, first, a reduction in the threat NATO may be perceived as posing to levels commensurate with NATO's own stated intent to play a constructive role in building new, less militarized security structures for Europe. Second, eliminating U.S. nuclear weapons in Europe would remove the outdated focus on nuclear weapons as a coupling device and encourage more relevant efforts at institution building in Europe. Third, it would reduce endless political controversies in NATO over the deployment and employment of nuclear weapons.

Such a modified U.S. nuclear guarantee to Europe would approach an existential deterrent, where simply the existence of U.S. nuclear weapons and the fact that an adversary could not be certain that they would not be used—and not their deployment on the front lines—provide the deterrent effect. But such a guarantee would be made real and credible, as it has always been, by the political and publicly stated U.S. commitment to

[54]For a variety of views advocating a much reduced role for nuclear weapons in Europe, see, for example, Kaiser, *op. cit.*; Ian M. Cuthbertson and David Robertson, *Enhancing European Security: Living in a Less Nuclear World*, Institute for East-West Security Studies (New York: St. Martin's Press, 1990); Matthias Dembinski, *Europe Without Tactical Nuclear Forces? Reflections on the Concept of Minimized Extended Deterrence*, PRIF Reports No. 15 (Frankfurt: Hessische Stiftung Friedens-Und Konflikt-Forschung, September 1990); Thomas Risse-Kappen, "Towards a Nuclear-Free Central Europe: The Future of Nuclear Weapons in Post–Cold War Europe," unpublished manuscript, Yale, 1990; Richard Smoke, "For a NATO Defensive Deterrent," in P. Terrence Hopmann and Frank Barnaby, eds., *Rethinking the Nuclear Weapons Dilemma in Europe* (New York: St. Martin's Press, 1988), pp. 205–220.

the security of Europe, backed up by the continued presence of U.S. troops on European soil.

What are the prospects for moving in this direction? Clearly, the massive cuts in tactical nuclear weapons that have already taken place represent a significant first step. As Chapter 4 describes, advances in conventional capabilities enable this kind of shift away from the massive on-scene nuclear deployments that began in the 1950s toward nuclear forces that could be brought to bear from a distance. Certainly, large segments of the European public will be happy to see American nuclear weapons go. The great majority will likely be indifferent, while some European elites will undoubtedly voice the oft-heard concerns associated with fear of an American disengagement from Europe. It is necessary to consider existing habits of mind, like those of the Germans who value their participation in alliance nuclear policy,[55] but it is also important to remember that such attitudes are not fixed in stone. Physically hosting nuclear weapons need not be a criterion for consultation in alliance policy, and both Germans and Americans can learn to be comfortable with out-of-theater deterrence. The important burden-sharing aspect of the alliance can be shifted away from nuclear to conventional weapons. While support for relying on conventional capabilities was conspicuously absent among European allies during the Cold War, the withdrawal of Soviet forces from Eastern Europe and the reduction in conventional force levels on both sides may well bring the conventional defense of Europe within the realm of both political and economic feasibility for NATO members.[56]

Clearly, the future form of the U.S. nuclear guarantee depends greatly on as yet unknown developments in Europe. For reassurance purposes, European leaders may well seek a U.S. nuclear guarantee that includes a continuing small American nuclear presence, a situation to which the United States need not object in the short-term. On the other hand, the United States should not engage in divisive political debates with the allies over preserving unwanted roles for nuclear weapons. As time passes, and as nuclear weapons recede into the background of European politics, the perceived need for them may diminish. The United States should encourage such trends.

Finally, while the American nuclear guarantee remains an important component of European security, one can imagine developments in the long-term future that would reduce the need for it. A European deterrent could develop, in which French and British nuclear weapons would pro-

---

[55]Holger H. Mey and Michael Ruhle, "German Security Interests and NATO's Nuclear Strategy," *Aussenpolitik* (Eng. ed.), Vol. 42, No. 1 (1991), pp. 20–30.

[56]Early in 1990, Chairman of the House Armed Services Committee Les Aspin concluded (based on testimony of U.S. military officials) that the United States and its NATO allies could now—for the first time in the history of NATO—defeat invading Soviet forces without resorting to nuclear weapons. *San Francisco Chronicle*, March 14, 1990, p. A1.

vide the main nuclear guarantee. Additionally, strong evidence suggests that democracies do not fight each other.[57] If solid democracies emerge in Europe and on Soviet territory, the need for extended deterrence could diminish even further.[58]

Extended Deterrence in the Context of Potential Proliferation: East Asia   A reorientation toward the principle that U.S. nuclear weapons should be relied on only to deter the use of nuclear weapons would also promote U.S. security policy goals in the Asia-Pacific region. In addition to deterring aggression against allies, these include maintaining a regional balance of power, managing regional rivalries, and avoiding an arms race. The American military presence remains widely supported in East Asia, where it has traditionally balanced Soviet power, assisted South Korea in deterring attack by North Korea, reassured Japan and reassured others about Japan, and otherwise helped dampen regional tensions.[59] But as the United States adjusts its role in the Pacific to account for the changing regional dynamics described in Chapter 1, two factors stand out as most relevant for assessing the future role of U.S. nuclear weapons in the region: the residual Soviet threat and proliferation dynamics on the Korean peninsula.[60]

The diminution of the Soviet threat drastically reduces the perceived Cold War need to rely on U.S. nuclear weapons to contain Soviet expansion in Asia. Nevertheless, Soviet military retrenchment has proceeded more slowly in Asia than in Europe, and the Soviet Union retains a formidable nuclear presence near Japan, the primary U.S. ally in the region.[61] Thus the United States should continue to rely on its nuclear forces to deter Soviet nuclear attack, however unlikely, and to counter any Chinese nuclear threats against Japan or other regional allies. It should therefore continue to extend a nuclear guarantee, as part of its larger security commitment, to Japan. But in the future, given a reduced threat, the means upholding this guarantee may change.

---

[57] Michael Doyle, "Kant, Liberal Legacies and Foreign Affairs," *Philosophy and Public Affairs*, Vol. 12, No. 3 (Summer 1983), pp. 205–235.

[58] This point is made in Risse-Kappen, *op. cit.*, pp. 18–19.

[59] Recent discussions of East Asian security include William J. Crowe and Alan D. Romberg, "Rethinking Security in the Pacific," *Foreign Affairs*, Vol. 70, No. 2 (Spring 1991); and Peter Palomka, "Towards a 'Pacific House'" *Survival*, Vol. 33, No. 2 (March/April 1991), pp. 173–182.

[60] For a thorough discussion of U.S. security alternatives in the region see Jonathan D. Pollack and James A. Winnefeld, *U.S. Strategic Alternatives in a Changing Pacific*, Rand Report R-3933-USCINCPAC (Santa Monica, Calif.: The RAND Corporation, June 1990).

[61] For a comprehensive statement of Soviet naval capabilities see testimony of Director of Naval Intelligence Rear Admiral Thomas A. Brooks before the Seapower, Strategic, and Critical Materials Subcommittee of the House Armed Services Committee on Intelligence, March 7, 1991, pp. 11–33.

Potentially more serious and destabilizing than either the waning Soviet threat or the Chinese nuclear capability is the hostile situation on the Korean peninsula, which North Korea's apparent pursuit of nuclear weapons could dangerously exacerbate.[62] As the previous chapter described, the prospect of a nuclear arms race in the region, involving the two Koreas and possibly Japan, is a frightening one. Preventing this outcome is a foremost U.S. policy objective in the region. Although a reduced Soviet threat gives the United States greater flexibility in its nuclear policy in Asia, the uncertain and potentially complex proliferation dynamics make the costs and benefits of particular options much less clear-cut. Here, the dilemmas and challenges of balancing the reassuring and the provocative aspects of reliance on U.S. nuclear guarantees are well illustrated.

Developments in the region are shifting the main rationale for the U.S. nuclear guarantee away from deterring a North Korean conventional attack on the South toward dampening any South Korean aspirations for its own nuclear weapons in the face of a clandestine and threatening nuclear program in the North. North Korea's continued refusal to allow inspections of its nuclear installations, as required under the Non-Proliferation Treaty, to which it is a signatory, has dramatically increased the perceived urgency of reducing nuclear tensions on the peninsula.

Steps taken in 1991 by both the United States and South Korea to deemphasize the role of nuclear weapons in their security policies could facilitate this process and help stem proliferation in the North. The United States' October 1991 decision to remove all its nuclear weapons from South Korea, originally based there to bolster its policy of extended deterrence, reflects not only the declining military utility of such weapons, but also the pressing need to make nuclear weapons a less desirable acquisition to the North.[63] South Korea's public pledge in early November 1991 that it would not "manufacture, possess, store, deploy or use nuclear weapons" likewise represents a positive step toward establishing the peninsula as a nuclear weapons–free zone.[64]

Combined with economic and diplomatic measures designed to isolate North Korea, such moves could place increased pressure upon the North to open its facilities for inspection. North Korea has long demanded the

---

[62]For details see Leonard S. Spector and Jacqueline R. Smith, "North Korea: The Next Nuclear Nightmare?" *Arms Control Today*, Vol. 21, No. 2 (March 1991), pp. 8–13; Andrew Mack, "North Korea and the Bomb," *Foreign Policy*, No. 83 (Summer 1991), pp. 87–104.

[63]David E. Rosenbaum, "U.S. to Pull A-Bombs from South Korea," *New York Times*, October 20, 1991, p. A3.

[64]David E. Sanger, "New Data Raises Fears of Nuclear Moves by North Koreans," *New York Times*, November 10, 1991, p. 6. North Korea proposed in 1986 to turn the peninsula into a nuclear weapons–free zone, but it is only more recently that it has evidenced genuine interest in arms control and tension-reduction measures. John Wilson Lewis, "Reciprocal Unilateral Measures on the Korean Peninsula," unpublished manuscript, Stanford, Calif., November 20, 1990.

removal of American nuclear weapons from the peninsula and has sought legal assurances that the United States would not pose a nuclear threat to the North.[65] While the United States has consistently rejected these demands as illegitimate, it appears to have estimated that, given alternative means of reassuring South Korea, the previous advantages of a U.S. nuclear presence on the peninsula are now outweighed by the need for greater leverage over the North.

The United States had never ruled out the use of tactical nuclear weapons in response to a North Korean invasion, but many long viewed such a response as highly unlikely.[66] Both South Korea and the United States now possess sophisticated conventional capabilities, and neither the Soviet Union nor China would be likely to support North Korea in a war on the peninsula. With relations among all major parties (except North Korea) improving and the isolation of the North increasing, North Korea may come to recognize that problems on the peninsula must be solved by political means only, not force.[67]

U.S. officials have made clear that long-time ally South Korea will continue to be protected by the American nuclear umbrella. Arguments for retaining a U.S. nuclear guarantee to the South emphasize the continuing importance of a clear U.S. commitment to the South's security, not only to deter North Korean attack but more importantly to reassure the South and stem its latent nuclear ambitions.[68] In addition, some emphasize that such a nuclear guarantee would counter any political advantages the North might hope to derive from its proliferation threat, such as weakening the U.S.–South Korea security link, and would demonstrate to the North that its pursuit of nuclear weapons can bring it only disadvantages.[69]

As long as North Korea appears to be building nuclear weapons, such

---

[65]North Korea has been the sole nuclear aspirant in the developing world to face an overt nuclear threat from a superpower. Spector, *op. cit.*, p. 9. The annual U.S. "Team Spirit" exercises, for example, tended to worsen tension on the peninsula, if only temporarily, as they were perceived by North Korea as a rehearsal for nuclear war.

[66]According to Noel Gayler, former commander of U.S. forces in the Pacific, there was no area in the Pacific Command where "it would conceivably have made sense to explode nuclear weapons in order to carry out military objectives. . . . My evaluation, together with that of the senior generals, both Korean and American, responsible for the [Korean] Demilitarized Zone . . . was that it simply was not necessary to contemplate a nuclear strategy." Gayler, "A Commander-in-Chief's Perspective on Nuclear Weapons," in Prins, ed., *op. cit.*, p. 16.

[67]See the discussions in *The Transformation of the Asian-Pacific Region: Prospects for the 1990s*, Conference report (Stanford, Calif: Center for International Security and Arms Control, 1991). The entry of both Koreas into the United Nations represents the first step toward terminating the state of war between the two countries.

[68]I.M. Destler and Michael Nacht, "Beyond Mutual Recrimination: Building a Solid U.S.-Japan Relationship in the 1990s," *International Security*, Vol. 15, No. 3 (Winter 1990–91), p. 112.

[69]Burrus Carnahan, James Tomashoff, and Joseph Yager, *Nuclear Non-Proliferation Policy and the Korean Peninsula* (MacLean, Va.: Science Applications International Corporation, April 29, 1991), p. 5–7.

a rationale is sound. However, over the longer term, while a continuing need for a U.S. commitment to the South's security appears clear, the value of a *nuclear* guarantee should be weighed against a common U.S. and South Korean interest in delegitimizing the role of nuclear weapons in the region. Should North Korea demonstrate clearly that it is not a nuclear power and is not seeking to become one, the U.S. nuclear guarantee to South Korea could no longer be justified in terms of a need to deter an adversary's use of nuclear weapons. While the U.S. commitment to the South's security should remain ironclad, given modern conventional capabilities it need not be undergirded by a nuclear commitment should there be no direct nuclear threat. Were circumstances to change once again and North Korea to renew its pursuit of a nuclear capability, the United States could restore the nuclear guarantee to the South.

What impact would eliminating the nuclear guarantee have on South Korea's perceptions of its interests? Phasing out the U.S. nuclear guarantee should take place only in the context of establishing the peninsula as a nuclear weapons–free zone, a situation clearly in the South's interest. Such an arrangement could be monitored through a variety of diplomatic mechanisms, including inspections of facilities and other arms control and confidence-building measures.[70] For example, even if North Korea had its nuclear facilities inspected, it could still have reprocessed fuel stored (legally) on its territory, a situation that might provoke insecurity in South Korea. Thus, arrangements would need to include measures to curtail North Korea's stockpiling of plutonium. Additionally, American troops could remain on the ground in South Korea, as they do now, as a visible expression of the U.S. security commitment. Clearly, progress toward denuclearizing the region depends heavily on future political circumstances on the peninsula and the nature of the regime in the North.

In sum, U.S. interests, along with those of the Soviet Union and China, lie in maintaining a stable strategic and political environment on the Korean peninsula. The United States should continue to extend a nuclear guarantee to South Korea as long as North Korea fails to demonstrate convincingly that it does not seek nuclear weapons. But should the South no longer face a direct nuclear threat, the nature of the U.S. security guarantee should be altered to eliminate the nuclear component (for further discussion, see Chapter 4).

Extended Deterrence in the Context of Regional Conventional Aggression: The Middle East   The United States has extended its nuclear umbrella to the Persian Gulf since 1980 when the convergence of several events—the Iranian revolution, the fall of the shah, and the Soviet invasion of Afghanistan—raised the specter of a Soviet invasion of the Gulf. Concerned especially about protecting Iranian oil fields from Soviet control,

---

[70]James Goodby, "Confidence- and Security-Building on the Korean Peninsula: A Negotiating Agenda," in *The Transformation of the Asian-Pacific Region*, pp. 129–142.

President Jimmy Carter made a dramatic commitment to repel outside aggression "by any means necessary, including military force."[71] Although no mention was made of a specifically nuclear response, conventional defense against a Soviet invasion was almost universally regarded as infeasible. Since then, it has been presumed that the United States would rely on nuclear weapons to deter large-scale Soviet aggression in the Gulf region, and U.S. war planning in the region has provided for nuclear contingencies.[72]

With the easing of the Cold War, the dominant scenario is no longer a Soviet invasion of Iran, but rather aggression on the part of a regional power that threatens the balance of power in the Middle East, U.S. and allied access to oil, or Israel. In order to maintain secure access to oil supplies, the United States has sought to protect the security of Arab oil-producing states friendly to the West, such as Saudi Arabia and Kuwait. Iraq's invasion of Kuwait in August 1990 raised in a stark way the new kind of threat the United States faces in the post–Cold War era. Iraq's extensive conventional capabilities, past history of chemical use, known interest in acquiring nuclear weapons, and revisionist ambitions made it a textbook case of a post–Cold War Third World adversary.[73]

A desert scenario such as this actually presents very favorable conditions for the militarily effective use of nuclear weapons. A low-yield tactical nuclear weapon could have been used against massed Iraqi troops with minimal damage to civilians. Additionally, nuclear weapons could have destroyed the many underground Iraqi targets more easily than conventional weapons. Some reports during the Gulf crisis even suggested that under certain circumstances, using nuclear weapons would have resulted in fewer deaths in the coalition *and* on the Iraqi side than using the conventional weapons needed to assure victory.[74]

Because of the political costs associated with breaking the nuclear taboo, serious consideration of a nuclear option would most likely arise only in an extreme situation where U.S. troops were being overrun and the United States was faced either with great loss of American lives or humiliating withdrawal or defeat. Although some have advocated nuclear use in such situations, in the Gulf War U.S. officials wisely resisted entreaties to use nuclear weapons, estimating that nuclear use would be the best

---

[71]"The State of the Union," January 23, 1980, *Public Papers of the Presidents: Jimmy Carter, 1980–81*, p. 197.

[72]Joshua M. Epstein, *Strategy and Force Planning: The Case of the Persian Gulf* (Washington, D.C.: The Brookings Institution, 1987), p. 16.

[73]This section considers only conventional threats. Alternative U.S. responses to nuclear use by Nth countries are discussed in the following.

[74]John Barry, "The Nuclear Option: Thinking the Unthinkable," *Newsweek*, January 14, 1991, p. 17.

way to win the war and lose the peace.[75] Any immediate military benefits of nuclear use against Iraq would likely have been outweighed by the longer-term political and military costs of initiating nuclear use. Nuclear use, especially in a case where the U.S. homeland is not under attack, would likely ignite domestic protest, outrage allies, and jeopardize American relations with the Arab world. It could also increase the likelihood that the United States would face a nuclear-armed adversary on the battlefield in the future. It would thus not be in the United States' long-term security interest to suggest in any way that nuclear weapons are useful instruments for warfighting. If U.S. goals are to discourage other states from developing or expanding their own nuclear forces, the United States should avoid actions that suggest nuclear weapons have any value beyond deterring the use of nuclear weapons.

Thus, it would appear unwise for the United States to either use or threaten to use nuclear weapons in circumstances of regional conventional aggression. In fact, it has been U.S. policy since 1978 not to use nuclear weapons against nonnuclear parties to the NPT not allied or acting in concert with a nuclear state.[76] In a future conflict, however, the United States might not enjoy the conventional superiority it possessed in the Gulf War, and nuclear weapons might become relatively more attractive. In such cases it will be all the more important for the United States to remain committed to a policy of nuclear restraint.[77] As it did in the Gulf War, the United States should rely on conventional capabilities to protect allies in the region from conventional aggression and should reserve nuclear guarantees only for countering nuclear threats. Progress in arms control, both nuclear and conventional, particularly in regions like the Middle East, will be important in assuring a security environment that minimizes the need for nuclear deterrence.

To Deter the Use of Other Weapons of Mass Destruction   During the Cold War, the argument that the United States should rely on nuclear weapons to deter the use of chemical weapons was made primarily in discussions of possible Soviet use of chemical weapons in an attack on

---

[75]According to some accounts, U.S. officials effectively ruled out nuclear or chemical use in the Gulf crisis. According to one senior military official, the consequences of using nuclear weapons—some of which are unpredictable—"outweigh their military utility." R. Jeffrey Smith and Rick Atkinson, "U.S. Rules Out Gulf Use of Nuclear, Chemical Arms," *Washington Post*, January 7, 1991, pp. A1, A22.

[76]The United States, along with other nuclear weapons states, has regularly reaffirmed this qualified "negative security" guarantee, most recently at the 4th NPT Review Conference in September 1990. Van Doren and Bunn, *op. cit.*, p. 10.

[77]Joseph S. Nye, Jr., "Nuclear Restraint—Now and Later," *Boston Globe*, February 21, 1991, p. 13.

Western Europe. Up until the mid-1980s, even though the NATO alliance maintained a chemical weapons (CW) retaliatory capability, the main deterrent of chemical use by the Warsaw Pact was to be NATO conventional and nuclear forces, with CW forces in support.[78] Even after the Reagan administration renewed emphasis on the U.S. CW capability in 1986, NATO members recognized that "any use of CW by the Soviet Union might represent such a grave escalation of conflict as to compel NATO to consider the use of nuclear weapons in response."[79]

NATO has subsequently moved away from relying primarily on nuclear deterrence of Soviet chemical attacks, doubting the credibility of a nuclear response and questioning the wisdom of a policy that would seem to lower, rather than raise, the nuclear threshold.[80] And with the disappearance of the Soviet threat, the salience of the issue has receded and attention has shifted to regional scenarios such as the Gulf War, where Iraq threatened to use chemical weapons against U.S. troops and Israeli citizens. Here again, the question is whether the United States should rely on nuclear weapons to deter or respond to chemical use.

It has often been assumed that the United States would rely on nuclear weapons to *deter* chemical attack in circumstances where it did not fear nuclear retaliation. Although this has been cited as one role for the Israeli nuclear arsenal, in practice few, if any, seriously advocate such a deterrent role for U.S. nuclear weapons in developing country scenarios.[81] Given the current weakened taboo against chemical use, and the strong taboo against nuclear use, a U.S. threat to retaliate with the greater destructiveness of nuclear weapons might not be credible enough to deter chemical use by an adversary who felt backed into a corner. Moreover, such a threat would confer an undesirable legitimacy on nuclear threats in the eyes of

---

[78]Julian Perry Robinson, *NATO Chemical Weapons Policy and Posture*, ADIU Occasional Paper No. 4 (Sussex, UK: University of Sussex, Armament and Disarmament Information Unit, Science Policy Research Unit, September 1986), p. 9. See also Valerie Adams, *Chemical Warfare, Chemical Disarmament* (Bloomington, Ind.: Indiana University Press, 1990), pp. 22–24, 159. The Alliance as a whole does not possess a chemical capability; chemical weapons deployed by the United States are not declared to NATO and remain under U.S. national control. Adams, *ibid.*, p. 211.

[79]Aspen Strategy Group, *Chemical Weapons and Western Security Policy* (Lanham, Md.: University Press of America, 1987), p. 2. European states traditionally preferred to rely on nuclear weapons to deter a CW attack as a way of rejecting chemical weapons capabilities. They argued that expanding the intrawar chemical deterrent against CW would weaken overall deterrence against any Warsaw Pact aggression and degrade the nuclear deterrent (thus making protracted CW on German soil more, not less, likely). The nuclear retaliatory threat thus obviated the need for an in-kind deterrent. Robinson, *ibid.* p. 15.

[80]Aspen Strategy Group, *op. cit.*, p. 46.

[81]Personal communications with Elisa Harris, senior researcher, The Brookings Institution, and Professor Matthew Meselson, chemical weapons expert, Harvard University, November 1990.

potential proliferators and potentially harm U.S. interests in the longer term.[82]

It might be argued, however, that in the event of a massive chemical attack on U.S. troops, a nuclear *response* might be the best option for ending the war quickly and saving American lives. Although in a worst-case scenario nuclear use might appear a compelling option, it is difficult to imagine circumstances in which a nuclear response to a chemical attack would be justified. First, according to most experts, CW is vastly overrated as a military capability, especially against protected troops and when compared with high explosive (HE) conventional weapons.[83] The more serious concern is the ability of an adversary's chemical capability to degrade U.S. performance on the battlefield by forcing U.S. troops to "suit up" in unwieldy protective gear, thereby rendering them more vulnerable to conventional attack. More serious yet might be a chemical attack on a U.S. base or a U.S. ally's city. If protective gear were unavailable, the results could be tragic. But ultimately, in all these cases, a chemical attack, no matter how bad, would not threaten the survival of the United States[84] or its allies, nor cause the level of sheer destruction likely to result from a nuclear attack.

This leads to the second reason why a nuclear response to a chemical attack is difficult to justify: It would constitute a disproportionate use of force. It is difficult to see how the United States could justify the use of "population killing" weapons (i.e., nuclear) as long as it possessed adequate conventional capabilities with which to respond. While chemical weapons are undoubtedly terrifying weapons, they have a psychological effect out of proportion to what they really do; they still present a much lesser threat than nuclear weapons. As U.S. officials concluded in the Gulf War, ultimately it is more important that the Pandora's box of nuclear use remain closed.[85]

The related question of whether nuclear weapons should be relied on

---

[82]The Gulf War raised several interesting, if unanswerable, questions about what deters use of chemical weapons. Israeli nuclear weapons may well have deterred Iraqi chemical use. On the other hand, in the wake of the war, the threat of a massive conventional response to deter chemical use could well be more credible.

[83]Matthew Meselson and Julian Perry Robinson, "Chemical Warfare and Chemical Disarmament," *Scientific American*, Vol. 242, No. 4 (April 1980), pp. 8–11. Soldiers wearing antichemical protective gear are far more vulnerable to conventional attack than they are to attack with chemicals.

[84]This is, of course, true of any kind of attack on U.S. troops in the Third World.

[85]Options U.S. officials considered for responding to Iraqi chemical attack included a "visible" acceleration of conventional warfare, including a more concerted and overt attempt to kill Iraqi President Saddam Hussein and his top advisers, and pressing for war crimes trials for Iraqi commanders implicated in such an attack. R. Jeffrey Smith, "Iraq's Chemical Weapons Still a Threat to Ground Troops, U.S. Says," *Washington Post*, February 19, 1991, p. A7.

to deter or respond to the use of biological weapons has received little public attention, primarily because biological weapons are of such questionable military utility, at least so far. The United States does not possess an in-kind deterrent for biological capabilities, having rejected this option in the early 1970s, presumably for reasons of military unreliability and of redundancy given the U.S. nuclear capability.[86] Under optimum conditions, biological weapons are comparable to nuclear weapons in that they can kill populations over large areas. They therefore present a more dangerous threat than chemical weapons, but one that is much more remote because of the difficulties associated with using them effectively.[87] The unlikelihood of biological weapons use against the United States or its troops in all but the most extreme circumstances, and the existence of alternative U.S. responses, suggest that the same basic arguments for ruling out a nuclear response to chemical attacks would apply to biological warfare as well.[88]

Expanding Roles

To Deter or Respond to Nuclear Use by Nth Countries   Had Iraq, Kuwait, or Saudi Arabia possessed nuclear weapons in the Gulf War, the U.S. response to that crisis might have been very different. As described in Chapter 1, the spread of nuclear and ballistic missile capabilities to new, primarily Third World, states raises the possibility of a future crisis involving the United States and one or more nuclear-capable Third World actors. The potential use of nuclear weapons in the Third World poses a tremendous policy challenge to U.S. leaders, one to which they must devote much serious thought. As the following analysis suggests, the fading of the East-West confrontation, rather than giving new utility to U.S. nuclear weapons in regional conflicts, is likely to reinforce already severe constraints on their use.

As discussed in the previous chapter, although an Nth country (nuclear-armed, non-Soviet) threat to U.S. territory cannot be ruled out, more likely are either nuclear threats to U.S. troops or allies, or a nuclear exchange between two Nth countries where U.S vital interests are not

---

[86]For an extensive discussion of the attractions and liabilities of biological weapons see *The Problem of Chemical and Biological Warfare*, Vol. II (Stockholm: Stockholm International Peace Research Institute, 1971), pp. 116–159. A more recent discussion is Erhard Geisler, ed., *Biological and Toxin Weapons Today*, Stockholm International Peace Research Institute (New York: Oxford University Press, 1986).

[87]For example, biological weapons must be delivered in aerosol form and their effectiveness is therefore highly dependent upon weather and wind conditions. There is always the risk that they will infect the forces or population of the country that deployed them. *Ibid.*, pp. 136–137.

[88]Chemical protective gear also protects against biological weapons.

deemed to be directly at stake.[89] Examples of the former include an attack by a nuclear-armed Iraq against Saudi Arabia, Israel, or U.S. troops; by a nuclear-armed Middle Eastern or North African country against Europe[90]; or by North Korea against South Korea. Examples of the latter include a nuclear exchange between India and Pakistan or Iran and Iraq.[91]

Under what circumstances would the United States need to rely on nuclear weapons to meet a new nuclear threat? A full answer would require consideration of the range of possible scenarios and available alternatives, and is beyond the scope of this chapter. Here we will briefly sketch the major alternatives, including diplomacy, deterrence, conventional means, and nuclear use. In evaluating these options, the two primary considerations for the United States are the significance of the threat to U.S. interests and the capabilities of the adversary.

Clearly, diplomatic efforts to manage regional conflict, prevent hostilities, and control nuclear proliferation will be of utmost importance in minimizing new threats. Such efforts might address underlying sources of regional instability, check arms transfers, foster regional arms control and confidence-building measures, develop monitoring and arms control institutions, and strengthen the nonproliferation regime and the International Atomic Energy Agency.

Yet if such measures are not fully successful, the United States must consider how to operate in a proliferated world. Depending on the circumstances, the main options are nuclear deterrence, conventional measures of response, and actual use of nuclear weapons. These are considered in turn.

Some have argued that the U.S. nuclear arsenal would deter nuclear use by a small adversary, since such use would be both suicidal and irrational.[92] This may be logical, yet it ignores both new uncertainties about how

---

[89]Nuclear terrorism against the United States with one or more smuggled weapons is also a small, but real, possibility. However, it is not something that can be deterred with nuclear weapons (although perhaps with other means), and it is difficult to defend against.

[90]Central and Western Europe are currently beyond the range of Third World states' missile forces, but may not be for long. Turkey, a NATO member, can be hit by Syrian, Iraqi, Israeli, Iranian, and Saudi Arabian missiles. The former Soviet Union, concerned about Muslim fundamentalism to the south, can be targeted by missiles from Iraq, Iran, and Saudi Arabia, as well as Israel. See Martin S. Navias, "Is There an Emerging Third World Ballistic Missile Threat to Europe?" *The RUSI Journal* (Royal United Services Institute for Defence Studies), Vol. 135, No. 4 (Winter 1990), p. 12.

[91]Various scenarios are developed in Jerome H. Kahan, *Hedging Against the Unthinkable: U.S. Military Responses to Third World Nuclear Crises*, CNA Professional Paper No. 484 (Alexandria, Va.: Center for Naval Analyses, July 1990); and Robert Hunter, "Small Nuclear Forces in the Middle East: The Years 2000–2010," in Rodney Jones, ed., *Small Nuclear Forces and U.S. Security Policy* (Lexington, Mass.: Lexington Books, 1984), pp. 63–88.

[92]For this argument in the context of the Gulf War see Richard Rhodes, "Bush's Atomic Red Herring," *New York Times*, November 27, 1990, p. A23. More generally, see Kenneth N. Waltz, *The Spread of Nuclear Weapons: More May Be Better*, Adelphi Paper No. 171 (London: International Institute for Strategic Studies, 1981).

deterrence will operate in Nth country nuclear scenarios and old lessons about incentives to preempt in crises.

Unfortunately, lessons from the U.S.-Soviet experience of nuclear deterrence are unlikely to be easily transferred to new nuclear scenarios. For a variety of political, historical, and technological reasons, the calculus of deterrence in new nuclear scenarios may be very different. New nuclear states will have small nuclear arsenals designed primarily to deter regional adversaries and to either avoid or engage in nuclear intimidation. Third World states may therefore be more likely to challenge deterrent threats and less reluctant to use weapons of mass destruction (as Iraq's use of chemical weapons during the Iran-Iraq War suggests). They may be more willing to use nuclear weapons as instruments of terror than as means of achieving military objectives, although the two need not be mutually exclusive. For a variety of reasons, they may believe that the United States would be unlikely to retaliate in kind against nuclear use, thus leading them to use nuclear weapons.[93] Additionally, the superpower nuclear relationship benefited from the evolution over several decades of rules and norms of cooperation and survival (as well as by geographical distance), a situation not paralleled in the developing world. With fragile political regimes and with command and control capabilities comparable to or even less sophisticated than those of the United States in the 1950s, nuclear-armed Third World nations may be a long time in achieving relationships of stable nuclear deterrence.[94] Also, in contrast to the early U.S.-Soviet experience, a nuclear threat by a Third World country is likely to provoke the involvement of other equally or more powerful states, vastly complicating the situation.

Second, in a crisis an Nth country could have powerful incentives to use its nuclear weapons early, since it would know that, aside from defenses, the only way for the United States to avoid or limit damage from a nuclear attack on its troops or allies would be to attack first (with either conventional or nuclear weapons). Hence *it* would be tempted to launch first to escape preemption.[95] Additionally, because of the destabilizing effects of ongoing proliferation, and the volatility of regions such as the Middle East and South Asia, even deterrence and explicit retaliatory nuclear threats may be of limited, uncertain, or even counterproductive utility to the United States in dealing with new nuclear states.[96]

---

[93]Stephen M. Meyer, "Small Nuclear Forces and U.S. Military Operations in the Theater," in Jones, *op. cit.*, pp. 163–164.

[94]Military and political factors that contribute to stable nuclear deterrence and that may be absent in Third World regions are discussed in Karl Kaiser, "Non-Proliferation and Nuclear Deterrence," *Survival*, Vol. 31, No. 2 (March/April 1989), pp. 123–136; Meyer, *ibid.*, pp. 163–164; and Hunter, *op. cit.*, pp. 74–84.

[95]On the other hand, a nuclear threat could be worth more than its implementation, since a successful bluff would produce the desired deterrent effect.

[96]These dynamics are aptly discussed in Hunter, *ibid.*, passim. Some may suggest that the United States extend a nuclear guarantee to friendly states facing a new nuclear threat in

Thus until norms and institutions to stabilize deterrence and provide reassurance develop in regional contexts, and technical advances in command, control, and safety occur, relying on deterring new threats, especially if it depends upon the "rational" behavior of aggressive states, may appear unacceptably risky.[97] At that point decision-makers may face the choice, well depicted by the Gulf War, between "waiting" for deterrence to fail, with unknown consequences, and taking positive action such as using conventional weapons to destroy new nuclear capabilities.[98]

Conventional preemption itself is fraught with difficulties, yet for many will seem the lesser of two evils when compared with the dangers of nuclear use. Because of the existence of conventional alternatives, it would be difficult for the United States to justify a first use of nuclear weapons against a Third World nation, especially if U.S. territory were not at risk. An exception to this rule might be a nuclear strike to preempt an adversary's use of its small nuclear stockpile, where the risk of failure using conventional weapons would be judged too high. Nevertheless, such a course of action would be extremely controversial, with its attendant risks of failure and escalation, civilian casualties, transgression of the nuclear taboo, and political fallout from "going first."

If all other measures failed, and a nuclear weapon were used by an adversary, the United States would have to determine how to respond. Certainly nuclear retaliation in response to nuclear attack is widely considered the most justifiable use of nuclear weapons. Still, as long as a strike left the U.S. homeland unscathed, a nuclear response would not necessarily be in the U.S. interest.

For example, depending upon the scale and nature of the attack, options for response again include diplomacy, use of conventional force, or use of nuclear weapons. A diplomatic response alone would likely be perceived as insufficient and therefore unacceptable. A massive conventional response to eliminate remaining nuclear capabilities might be appropriate if the adversary possessed few nuclear weapons (and the United States knew where they were) and either the United States could successfully preempt any further attacks or U.S. troops and allies could ride out a small nuclear attack.[99] The final possibility would be a range of nuclear responses, from a nuclear demonstration shot to a full-scale nuclear attack.

---

order to stabilize a situation and dampen further proliferation. However, the credibility of such a guarantee would be questionable, especially to states that have not traditionally been defined as key U.S. allies.

[97]For a detailed discussion of how new nuclear forces could affect future U.S. capacities to project conventional military power in a region, see Meyer, *op. cit.*, passim.

[98]The fact that U.S. bombing during the Gulf War failed to destroy the Iraqi nuclear capability, as was originally claimed by President Bush, can be attributed more to weaknesses in U.S. intelligence than to shortcomings of military action itself. Elaine Sciolino, "Iraq's Nuclear Program Shows the Holes in U.S. Intelligence," *New York Times*, October 20, 1991, p. 5.

[99]Israel's restraint in responding to Scud attacks during the Persian Gulf War serves as a model, though on a much lower scale of lethality. See Chapter 8 for a discussion of defenses.

Clearly, all these scenarios involve the weighing of tremendous un-knowns and uncertainties. In general, it is difficult to imagine any case in which anything beyond a small nuclear response would be appropriate against a smaller nuclear-armed adversary. For example, a "massive" nu-clear response to demonstrate that first use does not pay could, because of unknown consequences, end up demonstrating that large-scale second use does not pay either. Furthermore, the long-term political and military advantages of not responding with nuclear weapons might well outweigh those of an in-kind retaliatory response, especially if the United States possessed alternative means of retaliation. U.S. restraint would strengthen a weakened taboo and would help avoid the dangerous consequences of a complete breakdown of normative and political constraints on nuclear use.[100]

Because of the tremendous dangers and uncertainties associated with any use of nuclear weapons, even in a remote corner of the globe, preven-tion of nuclear use by others should remain one of the highest priorities of the United States. Yet this must be tempered by a recognition that not all situations will be amenable to U.S. influence, nor will it necessarily be in the U.S. interest to intervene militarily to prevent nuclear use if diplo-macy fails. In a nuclear crisis between India and Pakistan, for example, U.S. conventional intervention could well set off a larger war than the one the action was intended to prevent. U.S. nuclear intervention would likely escalate the conflict, alarm Russia and China, and provoke controversy among the American public.[101]

It is clear that the best way to deal with an emerging nuclear threat is before it happens—through diplomatic and political measures. New nuclear threats will pose risks to the security of many states; strategies for managing them should reflect the shared interest of the international community. One possibility, for example, would be for the United States and Russia to jointly threaten to respond to a new nuclear threat, using a combination of diplomatic and conventional military measures. Addi-tionally, the experience gained by the United Nations Security Council and the IAEA in carrying out the inspection and destruction of Iraqi nuclear facilities after the Gulf War has increased the need to strengthen

---

[100]Though the taboo against the use of chemical weapons has been weakened in recent years, the perception that only "pariah" states would resort to such use was given a boost in the public mind by U.S. determination after the Gulf War to rule out chemical response to a chemical attack and to continue to push for a convention banning chemical weapons. Fred Kaplan, "U.S. Would Destroy All Its Poison Gas if Treaty Is Signed," *Boston Globe*, March 14, 1991, pp. 1, 4.

[101]It has been pointed out that such third party nuclear crises do open the door to nuclear "blackmail" of the United States, however. For example, in an Arab-Israeli war, either side might threaten to use nuclear weapons unless the United States became involved (either on the side of Israel if Israel were losing, or restraining Israel if Israel were winning). In the Persian Gulf War the United States successfully restrained Israeli intervention. See Kahan, *op. cit.*

the monitoring capabilities of the IAEA and has raised the possibility of a new role for the Security Council (under Chapter 7 of the UN Charter) in the oversight of a nuclear nonproliferation regime.[102]

Operationally, the United States should take every possible step to preclude having to use nuclear weapons itself. It should maintain or acquire the necessary conventional capabilities, devote resources to analyzing what objectives would be worth considering the use of nuclear weapons, and place greater emphasis on means of deescalating a conflict. Nevertheless, the magnitude of the U.S. military victory in the Gulf War should not obscure the fact that military intervention poses uncertain risks and dangers, the more so as Third World states acquire ever more lethal arsenals. Additionally, elevating military solutions for planning purposes may undercut the awareness of political dynamics of proliferation in peacetime.[103] It is crucial to take militarily relevant technology transfers to other countries in peacetime seriously, so that the United States is not left to face more lethal arsenals in time of crisis.

In sum, while deterring the use of nuclear weapons by new nuclear states constitutes a valid role for U.S. nuclear weapons, under many circumstances U.S. officials may lack confidence in its robustness. The United States must therefore think beyond deterrence to other measures. Specifically, it should ensure that it possesses adequate conventional capabilities and options so that, in a crisis with a new nuclear state, or if deterrence fails, it does not need to resort to nuclear weapons in response.

CONCLUSIONS AND RECOMMENDATIONS

- The threat to use nuclear weapons should be made only to deter use of nuclear weapons. While nuclear weapons may also have the effect of deterring conventional aggression between two nuclear-armed adversaries, this should not serve as the basis of policy. The fuse between conventional and nuclear war should be lengthened as much as possible. Nuclear weapons are no longer needed to deter conventional aggression in Europe. Beyond the protection of vital interests and key allies, nuclear threats possess doubtful credibility, the marginal efficacy of which may be offset by the fear they provoke in an adversary. Such fears may lead countries to seek their

---

[102]The UN Security Council authorized in Resolution 687, which brought the Gulf War to a ceasefire, a UN Special Commission to conduct inspections of Iraq's nuclear facilities and to destroy its nuclear weapons equipment and other weapons of mass destruction. Combined with UN-imposed economic sanctions on Iraq, such moves constitute important precedents for a more coercive nuclear monitoring regime. Paul Lewis, "Atomic Agency Maps Plans to Go After Nuclear Cheats," *New York Times*, October 11, 1991.

[103]Janne E. Nolan, *Trappings of Power: Ballistic Missiles in the Third World* (Washington, D.C.: The Brookings Institution, 1991).

own nuclear arsenals. Additionally, threatening nuclear use when it is not intended weakens the global norm against nuclear use. Operationally, this "deterrence-of-use-only" policy should lead to decreased emphasis on nuclear weapons and increased reliance on conventional capabilities for planning purposes.

- Basic deterrence (deterrence of nuclear attack on the U.S. homeland) should remain the primary role of U.S. nuclear weapons. With the disappearance of the Soviet threat, however, the requirements of deterrence will likely be lessened.

- In a policy of extended deterrence (protection of U.S. troops or allies), the United States should not rely on nuclear weapons to deter conventional attacks against its troops or allies. The United States should continue to make explicit security guarantees to important allies—Europe, Japan, South Korea—but should reserve nuclear guarantees for countering actual nuclear threats. In the absence of such, the United States should rely on conventional capabilities to deter or respond to aggression.

- The United States should not rely on nuclear forces to deter or respond to the use of chemical and biological weapons. It is doubtful whether a U.S. threat of nuclear retaliation in response to a chemical or biological attack would credibly deter such an attack. Additionally, the United States possesses sufficient conventional capabilities to respond to such an attack. It should therefore base its plans for dealing with such threats on nonnuclear means. While all weapons of mass destruction should ideally remain unused, it is most important that nuclear weapons remain unused.

- While deterrence of nuclear use by new nuclear states constitutes a valid role for U.S. nuclear weapons, the possible unreliability of deterrence in such circumstances may require the United States to consider other measures. U.S. nuclear use in response to an Nth country nuclear attack should be a highly contingent option. Even if another country breaks the nuclear taboo, it may be in the United States' long-term interest to refrain from nuclear use itself. The United States should ensure that it possesses adequate nonnuclear capabilities and options so that it does not need to resort to nuclear use in response, and should emphasize measures that promote regional deterrence and stability in new nuclear scenarios.

- The United States should reduce its reliance on nuclear deterrence and increase its reliance on alternatives. Policy-makers should design policies and postures that will enhance U.S. security without excessively threatening the security of others. Scholars have distinguished between conditions under which deterrence may be an effective policy and those under which it may provoke precisely the kind of behavior it is intended to prevent. The United States needs to reduce the incentives of potential adversaries to resort to force and to persuade them that they can achieve at least some of their goals by other means. This requires increased attention to the incentives states have to change the status quo and the use of reassurances and inducements as well as deterrence and threats as instruments of statecraft.

SUGGESTED READINGS

Betts, Richard. *Nuclear Blackmail and Nuclear Balance*. Washington, D.C.: The Brookings Institution, 1987.

Bundy, McGeorge. *Danger and Survival: Choices About the Bomb in the First Fifty Years*. New York: Random House, 1988.

Freedman, Lawrence. *The Evolution of Nuclear Strategy,* 2nd ed. New York: St. Martin's Press, 1989.

Gaddis, John Lewis. "The Origins of Self-Deterrence: The United States and the Non-Use of Nuclear Weapons, 1945–1953." In Gaddis, ed. *The Long Peace: Inquiries into the History of the Cold War*. New York: Oxford University Press, 1987, pp. 104–146.

————. "The Long Peace: Elements of Stability in the Postwar International System." In Gaddis, ed. *The Long Peace: Inquiries into the History of the Cold War*. New York: Oxford University Press, 1987, pp. 215–245.

George, Alexander L. and Richard Smoke. *Deterrence in American Foreign Policy: Theory and Practice*. New York: Columbia University Press, 1974.

Herken, Gregg. *The Winning Weapon; The Atomic Bomb in the Cold War*. New York: Alfred A. Knopf, 1980.

Jervis, Robert. *The Meaning of the Nuclear Revolution*. Ithaca: Cornell University Press, 1989.

Lynn-Jones, Sean M., Steven E. Miller, and Stephen Van Evera, eds. *Nuclear Diplomacy and Crisis Management*. Cambridge, Mass.: MIT Press, 1990.

Newhouse, John. *War and Peace in the Nuclear Age*. New York: Alfred A. Knopf, 1989.

Stern, Paul, et al., eds. *Perspectives on Deterrence*. New York: Oxford University Press, 1989.

Chapter
3

The Future of U.S. Nuclear Strategy

Michael C. Brower

One of the ironies of the nuclear age is that, even though the main purpose of having nuclear weapons is to avoid war, military planners spend much of their time thinking about how these weapons might be used in war. Deterrence is an abstract concept, but one that rests on concrete war plans. These plans, and the policies and principles that shape them, make up the anatomy of nuclear strategy.

Though rarely discussed in public, U.S. nuclear strategy has been the subject of continuing and often passionate debate among specialists both inside and outside government. The basic requirement of deterrence has never been in dispute: The United States must maintain a nuclear force that is capable of surviving attack and retaliating in kind. But although this minimum condition has long been met, other issues have been hotly debated. How many survivable weapons are needed to assure an adequate level of deterrence? At what kinds of targets—military or civilian, nuclear or nonnuclear—should the weapons be aimed? Should U.S. nuclear strategy seek to deter conventional as well as nuclear aggression? If so, what additional requirements are placed on U.S. nuclear capabilities?

It is fair to ask whether such details really matter where deterrence is concerned. The theory of "existential deterrence" holds that the mere existence of nuclear weapons exerts a powerful deterrent effect on potential nuclear adversaries independent of the adversaries' particular strategies and capabilities. The history of U.S.-Soviet relations, which has witnessed no direct conflict and a steady decrease in the incidence of serious crises, lends some credence to this view. The problem is that one can never be entirely sure that the details of strategy would *not* count heavily in some future crisis or conflict, and thus prudence demands that one pay close attention to them.

Throughout the Cold War, U.S. nuclear strategy was shaped by the twin objectives of deterring a Soviet nuclear attack on the U.S. homeland (basic deterrence) and deterring a Soviet conventional attack on Western Europe (extended deterrence). Of the two, however, the latter had by far the greater influence. It was the Soviet conventional threat to Western Europe that provided the original justification for the United States' growing reliance on nuclear weapons in the late 1940s and 1950s. And it was the need to maintain the credibility of extended deterrence in the face of ever-improving Soviet nuclear capabilities that led to the creation in the 1960s of the flexible response doctrine, which remains the basis of U.S. nuclear strategy today.

What, then, can be said about the future of U.S. nuclear strategy now that the threat of a Soviet-led invasion of Western Europe has disappeared and the Soviet Union itself is in the throes of disintegration? These recent events raise the possibility that relations between the United States and the former Soviet Union (or whatever state or states succeed it) could over time become as friendly as, say, relations between the United States and France. In that case, many basic assumptions about strategy and deterrence would have to be discarded or radically revised. Without a clear enemy, the United States would have no rational basis for maintaining a nuclear arsenal of any substantial size. Under these conditions, the United States and the former Soviet Union, as well as other nuclear powers, might well decide to reduce their arsenals to very low levels.

Yet even if this occurs, it will take perhaps a decade or longer to negotiate and implement radical reductions in nuclear forces and to solidify a truly peaceful, cooperative relationship between the former Cold War adversaries. In the meantime, questions of nuclear strategy vis-à-vis the former Soviet Union will continue to be of importance. In the years ahead, the United States must choose a strategy that reflects the greatly reduced military threats facing it and its allies today, yet at the same time hedges against new threats that could arise in the future. The most likely threats to which deterrence might be relevant involve: the emergence of a newly hostile Soviet (or successor) government, intent, perhaps, on regaining some of the influence it lost in Eastern Europe; and the spread of nuclear weapons to unstable or unfriendly nations, particularly in regions like the Middle East where the United States has vital interests or key allies. Of course, whatever strategy is chosen must also serve—or at least not undermine—other aims of U.S. security policy and must operate within the constraint of a declining defense budget.

This chapter seeks to design a new strategy for the near term (the next five to ten years) that conforms to these broad guidelines. Although strategies for responding to non-Soviet threats will be discussed, the focus of the chapter is on the U.S.-Soviet deterrent relationship, as this will most likely continue to drive U.S. nuclear policy for some years to come. Because sensible decisions about force posture will be difficult without a firm grounding in strategy, a central aim of the chapter is to guide later discussions in the book on nuclear weapons modernization and arms control policy. First, the chapter briefly reviews what is publicly known or inferred about current U.S. nuclear strategy and its development during the Cold War. Then it discusses why this strategy will be difficult to sustain in the future and proposes ways to revise it. A sample target list reflecting these guidelines is offered as a basis for determining weapons requirements.

U.S. NUCLEAR STRATEGY IN THE COLD WAR

When discussing U.S. nuclear strategy, it is important to distinguish between declaratory policies—what the government says in public—and employment policies, which actually determine how nuclear weapons would be used in war. Declaratory policies tend to be malleable, bending with the winds of politics and bureaucratic infighting. Employment policies, in contrast, tend to be far more resistant to change, reflecting both the physical constraints of military operations and the traditional dominance of career military officers over all matters involving nuclear weapons.

Throughout the history of U.S. nuclear strategy, there have been large swings in declaratory policy, but the war plans themselves have evolved in a fairly consistent manner.[1] The dominant trend has been a continuing effort by weapon designers and military planners to enhance the credibility of deterrence—particularly extended deterrence—by making nuclear weapons more effective and usable instruments of war. To this end, strong emphasis has been placed on threatening Soviet military assets, broadly defined to include nuclear facilities, command-and-control assets, the military and political leadership, conventional forces, and war-supporting industry.

This approach—sometimes, though perhaps confusingly, referred to as warfighting[2]—has long been the subject of controversy among strategic

[1] A great many articles and books have been written on the development of U.S. nuclear strategy. Except where otherwise noted, the historical material in this chapter was drawn from the following sources: Lawrence Freedman, *The Evolution of Nuclear Strategy* (New York: St. Martin's Press, 1989); David Alan Rosenberg, "U.S. Nuclear War Planning, 1945–1960," in Desmond Ball and Jeffrey Richelson, eds., *Strategic Nuclear Targeting* (Ithaca, N.Y.: Cornell University Press, 1986), pp. 35–56; Desmond Ball, "The Development of the SIOP: 1960–1983," *Ibid.*, pp. 57–83; Janne E. Nolan, *Guardians of the Arsenal: The Politics of Nuclear Strategy* (New York: Basic Books, 1989); and Desmond Ball, "Revising the SIOP: Taking War-Fighting to Dangerous Extremes," *International Security*, Vol. 14, No. 4 (Spring 1990), pp. 65–92.

[2] All nuclear strategies are warfighting strategies to the extent that they envision the use of nuclear weapons in war. In recent years, however, the term warfighting has been attached to any strategy that sees the ability to achieve some measure of military advantage over a nuclear adversary as not only a legitimate aim of nuclear war planning, but also a necessary ingredient of deterrence.

specialists. Some have defended it passionately, arguing that deterrence cannot rest solely on a threat to destroy an adversary's society if one's own society is equally vulnerable to nuclear destruction. Others have argued that the current approach does little to enhance deterrence—and may even undermine it in a crisis—but merely creates unnecessary demands for new and more sophisticated weapons, thus helping to fuel the arms race. To understand how the balance of these arguments has shifted over the years and where compromises might now be possible, it is useful to review the factors that have influenced the evolution of U.S. nuclear strategy since the start of the Cold War.

Early Strategy: 1945–1960

In the years immediately following World War II, U.S. nuclear strategy was shaped not by policy guidance but by capability. The supply of atomic bombs was limited—only 50 were in existence by mid-1948. In addition, the bombs were extremely heavy, took days to assemble, and could be delivered only by a relatively small number of specially equipped B-29 bombers. Under these conditions, there would have been little point in wasting the bombs against military targets. Instead, following the pattern of Hiroshima and Nagasaki, they were reserved for use against cities.

By the early 1950s, U.S. nuclear capabilities had improved to the point that military planners could afford to be more discriminating in their choice of targets. In 1950, the Joint Chiefs of Staff (JCS) formally organized Soviet targets into categories and assigned top priority to the "destruction of known targets affecting the Soviet capability to deliver atomic bombs."[3] The aim was to be able to destroy the Soviet Union's nuclear capability before it could be used against the United States, an objective later known as damage limitation; in effect, it was a strategy of preemption. Second and third priorities were given to the destruction of support facilities for Soviet ground forces in Eastern Europe and economic and industrial assets, respectively.

At the same time, and quite independently of this military planning, civilian officials began to think seriously about how nuclear weapons could be used in support of foreign policy objectives. A defining event was the Berlin crisis of 1948, during which President Truman ordered "atomic-capable" B-29 bombers to Britain as a warning to the Soviet government, thus effectively extending America's nuclear umbrella over its allies in Europe.[4] Throughout his time in office, however, Truman remained skep-

---

[3] David Alan Rosenberg, *op. cit.*, p. 40.

[4] Government press releases at the time described the B-29s as being "atomic capable," but in fact they were not. The B-29s equipped to carry atomic bombs were kept in the United States and placed on 24-hour alert during the crisis. Scott D. Sagan, *Moving Targets: Nuclear Strategy and National Security* (Princeton: Princeton University Press, 1989), p. 15.

tical of the morality and military utility of nuclear weapons,[5] so it was left to President Eisenhower to integrate them fully into U.S. military doctrine and planning. Eisenhower's doctrine of massive retaliation, formally adopted by the United States in 1954, was designed to deter Soviet and other Communist-inspired aggression by raising the specter of a possible nuclear response. Together with his "New Look" defense policy, which shifted much of defense spending from conventional forces to less-expensive nuclear forces, it had the effect of greatly increasing the U.S. military's reliance on nuclear weaponry. On the battlefield, in particular, finding ways to augment conventional forces with nuclear weapons became the order of the day.[6]

The principal rationale for the doctrine of massive retaliation was the protection of Europe from a massive Soviet conventionally armed invasion. By the time nonstrategic nuclear forces, including artillery rounds and gravity bombs, were first deployed to Europe in 1952, it was already apparent that the fledgling alliance could not financially and politically afford to field a credible conventional defense against a numerically superior Soviet military machine sitting just across the border in Eastern Europe.[7] Defense plans adopted by NATO in 1957 called for NSNF to be used at the start of a conflict to stop attacking Soviet forces. Their use would be followed by a full-scale attack on Soviet territory by U.S. strategic forces. In effect, the nonstrategic forces played the part of a trip wire that guaranteed the use of America's strategic forces in the event of a European conflict.

Despite its strong endorsement by the Eisenhower administration, the doctrine of massive retaliation drew criticism from various quarters. To many it seemed reckless, although this was not entirely fair, since the doctrine did in fact allow for some flexibility and restraint in responding to Communist-inspired aggression, at least outside Europe. Even so, toward the end of the 1950s—especially as Soviet nuclear capabilities improved—it was increasingly perceived as lacking credibility. A key devel-

---

[5]In a letter to David Lilienthal on the atomic bomb, Truman wrote: "You have got to understand that this isn't a military weapon. It is used to wipe out women, children, and unarmed people, and not for military use. So we have to treat this differently from rifles and cannon and ordinary things like that." Quoted in Freedman, op. cit., pp. 51–52.

[6]The push to develop nuclear equivalents of all manner of conventional weapons had some peculiar results. For example, the Redstone missile deployed with U.S. Army units in Europe "was supposed to function as corps artillery but . . . had to be moved about by a nine-vehicle caravan, one component of which was a 25-ton, 90-foot crane." See Ernest R. May, "History of the Development and Deployment of BNW," in Stephen D. Biddle and Peter D. Feaver, eds., Battlefield Nuclear Weapons: Issues and Options (Cambridge, Mass.: Center for Science and International Affairs, 1989), pp. 17–18.

[7]U.S. nonstrategic nuclear forces cover the entire range of missions short of strategic attack on the former Soviet Union. Over time, they have included a wide variety of weapons, from short-range missiles to artillery shells, from bombs for tactical aircraft to torpedoes, from air-defense missiles to land mines. See Chapter 4 for a more detailed discussion.

opment was the Soviet acquisition of long-range bombers in 1956–1957 and ICBMs in 1958, which for the first time put the United States clearly and directly at risk of nuclear attack. From then on, the threat to use nuclear weapons massively in response to any but the most dire threats to Western security could not be taken seriously.

Nonstrategic Nuclear Forces and the Rise of Flexible Response

President Kennedy came into office intent on renouncing massive retaliation. His determination was reinforced by the 1961 Berlin crisis, which demonstrated just how few military options the United States had, short of a full-scale nuclear attack, for responding to Soviet provocations in Europe. The strategic war plan (the Single Integrated Operational Plan, or SIOP) then in effect called for launching all available weapons within 24 hours; the only variable was the mix of targets that would be hit. Although the Joint Chiefs of Staff assured the president that, if U.S. forces struck first, American deaths in the ensuing Soviet retaliation could be kept to less than 10 million, this option was, to say the least, unappealing.

In the wake of the Berlin crisis, Secretary of Defense McNamara and his team of analysts set to work devising a new doctrine, which became known as flexible response.[8] Described in a series of speeches by McNamara in 1962, the doctrine had two key elements. First, it stressed the need for flexibility in U.S. nuclear war planning. A nuclear attack would be met by a proportionate nuclear response; a conventional attack would be met by a conventional or nuclear response, depending on the circumstances. Second, the doctrine stressed the importance of making Soviet military forces, not cities, the targets of U.S. nuclear weapons. For this reason, the strategy is sometimes referred to as flexible counterforce.[9]

NATO   The flexible response doctrine found its clearest application in Europe, where in 1967 it was adopted by NATO defense ministers as the basis of alliance defense strategy.[10] According to the new plan, the defense

---

[8]The author is grateful to Kurt M. Campbell for his invaluable contribution to this discussion of nonstrategic nuclear forces and strategies for their use.

[9]Nolan, *op. cit.*, uses this terminology. The term counterforce is often used in reference solely to targeting nuclear facilities, but in this chapter it refers to all military targets, nuclear and nonnuclear.

[10]Except where otherwise noted, the historical material on NATO strategy for nonstrategic weapons was drawn from the following sources: Jane E. Stromseth, *The Origins of Flexible Response: NATO's Debate over Strategy in the 1960s* (London: Macmillan, 1988), pp. 14–62; Daniel Charles, *Nuclear Planning in NATO: Pitfalls of First Use* (Cambridge: Ballinger, 1987); Richard Hart Sinnreich, "NATO's Doctrinal Dilemma," *Orbis*, No. 19 (Winter 1975), pp. 461–476; Leon V. Sigal, *Nuclear Forces in Europe: Enduring Dilemmas, Present Prospects* (Washington, D.C.: Brookings Institution, 1984), pp. 25–62; Gregory Treverton, "Managing

of Europe would follow a sequence of three steps: If the Warsaw Pact attacked with conventional forces, NATO would respond first with a conventional (or direct) defense; if that failed, NATO could escalate to the local use of tactical and theater nuclear weapons; as a last resort, the United States could escalate to strategic nuclear attacks. This shift in strategy forced NATO to place greater emphasis on its conventional forces. Nevertheless, nuclear weapons remained the backbone of the NATO defense plan, in large measure because of its continued commitment to the forward defense of Germany.[11]

Flexible response was adopted by NATO only after extended debate, and the final form of the new defense strategy reflected as much a political compromise between the United States and its European partners as a coherent military plan. The United States sought to reduce the risk of nuclear escalation in a European war by securing a commitment from the Europeans to increase the conventional component of NATO's defense. The Europeans, for their part, sought to ensure that the conventional defense would not become so dominant that the United States would be tempted to withdraw or weaken its nuclear commitment. Even so, many European officials and defense specialists expressed growing doubts that the United States would actually be willing to risk nuclear war on behalf of its allies in the event of a Soviet invasion.

The political squabbles among NATO allies hardly touched the surface of problems and issues surrounding NATO's nuclear strategy, however. While the *political* roles of nonstrategic nuclear forces (discussed in Chapter 2) were fairly clear and received strong support on both sides of the Atlantic, the *military* roles of these forces were far more dubious. Since the 1950s the U.S. military had argued that short-range tactical nuclear weapons could be highly effective against massed Soviet armor and thus would help correct the imbalance of NATO-Warsaw Pact conventional forces. Once the Soviet Union deployed similar weapons of its own, however, this argument lost a good deal of its persuasiveness. Analysis suggested that the first use of nuclear weapons would be unlikely to result in a significant military advantage for NATO; on the contrary, it would make conventional military operations vastly more difficult for both sides and would quite likely lead to a very messy stalemate.

There were other problems, as well, not least among them that the use of tactical weapons (such as artillery shells and short-range rockets) on a large scale would cause immense destruction to the very countries NATO was created to protect. For this reason, naturally, European members of NATO were much less inclined than the United States to support the

NATO's Nuclear Dilemma," *International Security*, Vol. 7, No. 4 (Spring 1983), pp. 93–155; and Gregory Treverton, *Nuclear Weapons in Europe*, Adelphi Paper No. 168 (London: International Institute of Strategic Studies, 1981).

[11]For a concise history of NATO defense strategy, see David N. Schwartz, "A Historical Perspective," in John D. Steinbruner and Leon V. Sigal, eds., *Alliance Security: NATO and the No-First-Use Question* (Washington, D.C.: The Brookings Institution, 1983), pp. 5–16.

deployment and use of these weapons and instead favored intermediate-range missiles and aircraft. In addition, the deployment of nuclear weapons in the European theater placed significant burdens on conventional military operations—troops had to be trained in their use, the weapons had to be stored in secure facilities, and personnel and equipment had to be held in reserve to transport the weapons to the front when needed. What is more, the deployment of some weapons near the front lines created the danger that they would be overrun by the enemy and that commanders would be placed in the position of having to decide whether to "use 'em or lose 'em." Because of this concern and flexible response's requirement that nonstrategic weapons be used discriminately, the United States put considerable effort in the 1960s and 1970s into improving tactical command-and-control procedures; it also unilaterally removed several classes of short-range weapons thought to pose especially serious risks because of their lack of modern safety controls and their proximity to the front lines. (See Chapter 4 for a more detailed overview of NSNF deployments.)

Yet if nonstrategic weapons—particularly of the tactical variety—offered no clear benefits and many disadvantages on the battlefield, they were still believed to provide a critical link in America's strategy for deterring conventional war in Europe. The problem, in a nutshell, was how to make the threat of an American nuclear response to a Soviet nuclear attack on Western Europe appear credible, when such a response carried the clear risk of inciting a massive Soviet attack on the American homeland. The solution, according to the prevailing view, was to create a broad spectrum of nuclear response options, ranging from the smallest tactical nuclear strikes to full-scale strategic attacks, which gave at least the appearance of permitting "controlled escalation" of a nuclear conflict.

Not everyone agreed that this strategy of escalation control—or, as it was sometimes more optimistically referred to, "escalation dominance"—was realistic or credible. Some NATO planners and strategic specialists argued that any use of nuclear weapons would almost certainly lead to uncontrolled escalation if for no other reason than because of the extreme technical difficulty of managing nuclear operations amid the confusion and destruction of a nuclear exchange. Moreover, it was the Soviet Union's position that *any* use of nuclear weapons by NATO would result in immediate and massive retaliation against the United States.[12]

Nevertheless, flexible response remained deeply entrenched in NATO strategy through the 1980s, although over time it evolved to place

---

[12]See, for example, David N. Schwartz, *NATO's Nuclear Dilemmas* (Washington, D.C.: Brookings Institution, 1983), pp. 176–177 and 221. In fact, as Schwartz notes, the notion that tactical nuclear warfare would inevitably lead to strategic war was an integral part of McNamara's original flexible response scheme, which called for a conventional defense so strong that pressure would mount on the *Soviet Union* to initiate nuclear conflict. This concept was dropped in the subsequent NATO debate, resulting in a strategy of early nuclear use.

much less emphasis on nuclear warfare near the front and more on selective and limited strikes, particularly against the Soviet homeland. Reduced emphasis on tactical nuclear weapons was the product both of concern about the command-and-control and security problems of tactical weapons mentioned earlier, and of advances in computers, sensors, and other technologies that permitted so-called "smart" conventional weapons, such as sophisticated antitank weapons, to assume some missions previously assigned to NSNF.[13] Increased emphasis on selective strikes against Soviet territory was evidenced by the 1979 decision to deploy modernized intermediate-range nuclear forces (the Pershing II and ground-launched cruise missile, or GLCM), which were intended to increase NATO's ability to destroy rear-echelon Warsaw Pact forces and military facilities supporting or moving to reinforce the front line.[14]

In 1987, the United States and the Soviet Union signed the INF Treaty eliminating all of their intermediate-range ground-based missiles. This agreement was unprecedented in many respects, most importantly in its asymmetrical cuts, its actual destruction of weapons, and its inclusion of highly intrusive, on-site inspections. Some observers faulted the treaty, however, for ignoring tactical weapons. Ironically, many of the latter were already being withdrawn unilaterally, and many more would follow as a result of announcements by Presidents Bush and Gorbachev in the fall of 1991. Estimates put the overall number of nonstrategic nuclear weapons remaining in Europe in 1991 at around 4,000 weapons.[15]

Despite the many questions surrounding NATO's nuclear strategy, there is some evidence that it indeed had an impact on Warsaw Pact force deployments and, by implication, on deterrence.[16] After NATO deployed Honest John nuclear-capable rockets and nuclear artillery rounds in the mid-1950s, the Soviet Army was observed to have redeployed its forward

---

[13]Some of the new conventional technologies and their strategic implications are discussed in Samuel P. Huntington, "Conventional Deterrence and Conventional Retaliation in Europe," *International Security*, Vol. 8, No. 3 (Winter 1983–1984), pp. 72–91, and Andrew J. Pierre, ed., *The Conventional Defense of Europe: New Technologies and New Strategies* (New York: Council on Foreign Relations, 1986). See also Charles A. Zraket, "Impact of the New Technologies on Industrial Economies and Military Systems," *Facing the Future: American Strategy in the 1990s* (Lanham, Md.: Aspen Institute for Humanistic Studies, 1991), pp. 79–118.

[14]On the issue of Soviet INF deployments and the U.S. response, see Richard Burt, "The SS-20 and the Eurostrategic Balance," *The World Today*, Vol. 33, No. 2 (February 1977), pp. 43–51; Stephen M. Meyer, *Soviet Theater Nuclear Forces*, Adelphi Papers No. 187 and 188 (Winter 1983/1984); Christoph Bertram, "The Implications of Theater Nuclear Weapons in Europe," *Foreign Affairs*, Vol. 61, No. 2 (Winter 1981), pp. 305–326; and Raymond L. Garthoff, "The Soviet SS-20 Decision," *Survival*, Vol. 25, No. 3 (May/June 1983), pp. 110–119.

[15]See "Nuclear Deterrence in Europe," *The Military Balance* (London: International Institute of Strategic Studies, 1991), pp. 214–215.

[16]See Michael A. Yaffe, *Origins of the Tactical Nuclear Weapons Modernization Program, 1969–1979* (University of Pennsylvania Ph.D. Dissertation, forthcoming).

divisions over a much larger area so as to reduce their vulnerability to nuclear attack. Similarly, following NATO's deployment of the Lance short-range missile in 1973, Warsaw Pact forces were observed in exercises to have split into two-echelon formations stretched to a depth of 60 kilometers. These changes in tactical deployment, if carried through in combat, would have significantly reduced the Warsaw Pact's ability to mount a massive assault using concentrated armor.

Korea   Of course, nonstrategic nuclear forces were not deployed only in Europe. Since the 1950s, beginning after the Korean War, the United States stationed land-based and air-delivered nuclear weapons in South Korea. The exact number of such weapons remains secret, but it is generally believed to have diminished over time and was in 1991 perhaps no more than 100.[17] These weapons have played much the same role—and raised many of the same issues—as they have in Europe. They were believed to couple the security of South Korea to that of the United States and to play an equalizing role (at least until recently) by offsetting the superior conventional forces of the North.[18]

Naval Non-Strategic Forces   Nonstrategic nuclear weapons have also been deployed at sea. Like the other armed services, the navy developed its own plans for the use of these weapons (although the distinction between nonstrategic and strategic uses was often blurred). From the first deployments of medium-range, carrier-based, atomic-capable aircraft in 1949 and 1950, the navy fielded a wide range of nuclear weapons designed for a variety of missions, from antisubmarine and antiship warfare to land attack.[19] As conventional weapons technology improved and Soviet naval capabilities expanded, the navy redirected its nuclear emphasis to land-attack missions using long-range cruise missiles and air-delivered bombs. Navy strategists—acutely aware that Soviet naval nuclear weapons could do great damage to American ships and submarines—believed that by holding the Soviet homeland at risk, the Soviet Union could be deterred from initiating nuclear war at sea.[20] Some criticized this strategy, however, on the basis that it would increase the likelihood that the use of

---

[17]Don Oberdorfer, "U.S. Decides to Withdraw A-Weapons from S. Korea," *Washington Post*, October 19, 1991, p. A1.

[18]For a description of the evolving military situation on the Korean peninsula, see *Strategic Survey 1990–1991* (London: International Institute for Strategic Studies, 1991), pp. 196–204; and *Military Balance 1990–1991* (London: IISS, 1991), pp. 166–168.

[19]Karl Lautenschlager, "Technology and the Evolution of Naval Warfare," in Steven E. Miller and Stephen Van Evera, eds., *Naval Strategy and National Security* (Princeton: Princeton University Press, 1988), pp. 205–209; Dominic A. Paolucci, "The Development of Navy Strategic Offense and Defensive Systems," *Naval Institute Proceedings*, Vol. 16, No. 3, May 1970, pp. 205–223.

[20]See, for example, Linton F. Brooks and Franklin C. Miller, "Nuclear Weapons at Sea," *Naval Institute Proceedings* (August 1988), pp. 41–45.

nuclear weapons at sea would escalate to the strategic level. The best response to the Soviet threat, according to this view, was to negotiate the elimination of tactical naval nuclear weapons by both sides.[21]

Recent Developments   The collapse of the Warsaw Pact and dissolution of the Soviet Union have sparked major changes in nonstrategic weapons deployments and, to a lesser degree, in strategy. By 1990, it had already become clear that nonstrategic nuclear weapons would have a far more limited role in deterring Soviet aggression in the future. In recognition of this, the NATO powers declared that nuclear weapons would henceforth be used only as a "last resort." On the surface this represented no substantive change in official strategy, since nuclear weapons had always been proclaimed to be weapons of last resort; but it had important symbolic value nonetheless. In the fall of 1991, after the failed August coup in the former Soviet Union, President Bush announced that all U.S. land-based nonstrategic weapons would be withdrawn from the theaters in which they were deployed and destroyed.[22] The NATO powers subsequently issued a joint statement confirming that the prospect of nuclear war had become "even more remote" and announcing, as a result, that NATO's nonstrategic arsenal would be cut by 80 percent, including half of the roughly 1,400 nuclear bombs for tactical aircraft in Europe.[23]

Yet NATO did not state a willingness to abandon NSNF entirely. Specifically, there was no move to eliminate all U.S. nonstrategic air-delivered bombs from Europe (and of course Great Britain and France retain considerable nonstrategic forces themselves). Nor was there any move to adopt an explicit strategy of "no first use," a seemingly logical step considering that there is now no credible conventional threat to NATO against which first use of nuclear weapons might be contemplated. Thus, in theory at least, the strategy of flexible response remains in place, though with fewer nuclear weapons and no clear enemy to define its role.

Much the same may be said of U.S. nuclear strategy in Korea. There the enemy remains intact, but the steady decrease of political support for North Korea by its principal benefactors, the former Soviet Union and China, coupled with the growth of South Korea's own military strength, has greatly diminished fears of an invasion. In response—and in part to

---

[21]See Ivo H. Daalder and Tim Zimmerman, "Banning Naval Nuclear Weapons," *Arms Control Today*, Vol. 18, No. 9 (November 1988), pp. 17–23.

[22]For the prepared text of President Bush's speech, see "Remarks by the President on Reducing U.S. and Soviet Nuclear Weapons," *New York Times*, September 28, 1991, p. A4. More details on the proposals were provided in a briefing by Secretary of Defense Cheney and Chairman of the JCS Powell. See "Excerpts from Briefing at Pentagon: 'It Will Make the World a Safer Place,'" *New York Times*, September 29, 1991, p. A10. This initiative is discussed in greater detail in Chapter 4.

[23]R. Jeffrey Smith, "NATO Approves 50% Cut in Tactical A-Bombs," *Washington Post*, October 18, 1991, p. A28.

discourage North Korea's efforts to acquire a nuclear bomb—the United States has declared its intention to withdraw all nuclear weapons from South Korean soil.[24] In theory, however, the nuclear umbrella will remain in place.

The decision not to abandon entirely the flexible response strategy in Europe and Korea is primarily political, rather than military, in nature. As Chapter 2 suggests, it reflects a strong U.S. interest in maintaining political stability in these regions and in discouraging its allies from seeking to develop nuclear weapons of their own. Only in the case of naval nonstrategic weapons has the Cold War strategy been unambiguously abandoned. The announcement by President Bush (echoed by President Gorbachev) of the intention to withdraw and either store or destroy all nonstrategic naval weapons, including Tomahawk sea-launched cruise missiles and gravity bombs, has virtually closed off the possibility of nuclear war at sea.[25]

Flexible Response and Strategic War Planning

At the strategic level, no less than at the tactical and theater level, the flexible response doctrine led to major changes in U.S. nuclear war planning. It resulted directly in the formulation of a new SIOP, approved in 1962, which contained the first so-called limited attack options. (The options were limited in name only, however, as even the smallest would have entailed the launch of thousands of weapons.) Of these, the most notable was the "no cities" option, which exempted Soviet cities from destruction in the initial stages of a nuclear exchange. Such a purely counterforce option was regarded as essential to the credibility of extended deterrence, as it created at least the possibility that a war in Europe might escalate to the strategic level without immediately causing the destruction of American cities.

Because flexible response put more emphasis on striking military targets, however, it had the unintended consequence of providing the U.S. military, especially the Strategic Air Command (SAC), with a basis for demanding large increases in nuclear weapons. By 1962, the JCS were requesting a force of 2,000–3,000 Minuteman ICBMs and 900 RS-70 bombers to be deployed by the end of the decade. General Power, the commander of SAC, went so far as to appeal personally to Kennedy to increase the planned Minuteman force to 10,000.[26]

---

[24]Don Oberdorfer, *op. cit.*; and David E. Rosenbaum, "U.S. to Pull A-Bombs from South Korea," *New York Times*, October 20, 1991, p. A3.

[25]"Remarks by President Bush on Reducing U.S. and Soviet Nuclear Weapons," *op. cit.*; and "Gorbachev's Remarks on Nuclear Arms Cuts," *New York Times*, October 6, 1991. p. A12.

[26]At the time, the United States had several hundred long-range B-52 bombers and was building up to a planned force of 1,000 Minuteman ICBMs.

Such demands led McNamara quickly to back away from "no cities" and propose the new strategic doctrine of assured destruction (later, mutual assured destruction, or MAD). Essentially a force sizing criterion, assured destruction required that U.S. forces be able to survive a Soviet attack and wreak "unacceptable damage" on Soviet cities and industry. The threshold for unacceptable damage was defined, through an analysis of diminishing returns, to be one-half to two-thirds of the Soviet Union's industrial capacity and one-fifth to one-fourth of its population. This degree of destruction could theoretically be accomplished with about 400 equivalent megatons of surviving nuclear firepower—far less than the United States already possessed.[27]

Although the concept of assured destruction had a powerful symbolic value—the Reagan administration continued to criticize it 20 years later, long after it had fallen from official grace—its impact on strategic war planning is debatable. (NATO war planning was not affected at all.) Assured destruction was an effective political device that enabled McNamara to head off the military's demands for additional weapons; but the SIOP never changed and damage limitation and counterforce targeting remained central elements of U.S. strategy.

By the early 1970s, assured destruction was all but dead as a matter of official doctrine, the victim of many of the same complaints that had doomed massive retaliation. Under the Nixon, Ford, and Carter administrations, flexible response experienced a rebirth—only now the motivation to develop truly limited counterforce options was even stronger, as the Soviet Union had achieved an assured destruction capability of its own and was finally approaching strategic parity with the United States. The result was SIOP-5, issued in 1976, which divided retaliatory options into four categories: Major Attack Options (MAOs), Selective Attack Options (SAOs), Limited Nuclear Options (LNOs), and Regional Nuclear Options (RNOs). These options were further divided into various suboptions and withholds, the latter intended to show restraint and exert bargaining leverage over the Soviet leadership.[28]

But this did not satisfy MAD's critics. Over the next several years, a number of strategists inside and outside government argued that the United States needed to be able to do more than simply respond in a flexible manner to Soviet attacks: It needed a demonstrable capacity to fight and win a nuclear war at all levels of conflict. One of the most outspoken proponents of this view was Colin Gray, who wrote in 1979 that

---

[27]Equivalent megatonnage is defined as the number of one-megaton explosions that would create a given amount of blast damage over a given land area.

[28]According to official statements cited by Ball, *op. cit.*, p. 81, LNOs are "designed to permit the selective destruction of fixed enemy military or industrial targets," whereas RNOs are "intended, for example, to destroy the leading elements of an attacking force."

U.S. strategy must be based on a "theory of victory": "First and foremost, the Soviet leadership fears *defeat*, not the suffering of damage—and *defeat* . . . has to entail the forcible demise of the Soviet state."[29]

In part, the arguments of Gray and others reflected growing concern about Soviet nuclear employment policy, which appeared to attach considerable importance to preemption as a means of limiting damage to the Soviet homeland in a nuclear war. To some observers, at least, it seemed that the Soviet general staff believed a nuclear war to be winnable. Why else, it was theorized, was the Soviet Union deploying highly accurate, MIRVed (multiple warhead) ICBMs presumed capable of destroying U.S. ICBMs in a first strike; or devoting immense resources to civil defense; or providing thousands of Soviet government personnel with hardened shelters for protection in a nuclear attack?[30] Skeptics countered that there was no evidence that Soviet political leaders shared the military's views and, moreover, that a dispassionate review of U.S. weapons deployments, taken in isolation, could lead one to conclude that the United States had also adopted a first-strike strategy.[31]

The culmination of this period of debate was President Carter's signing, in July 1980, of Presidential Directive (PD) 59.[32] Building on previous documents such as National Security Decision Memorandum (NSDM) 242, PD-59 made flexible counterforce the cornerstone of official strategic doctrine. Besides reaffirming the importance of targeting Soviet nuclear forces, PD-59 codified two important new elements of doctrine. First, deterrence should be based on a threat to destroy what the Soviet leadership "values most," namely, its personal survival and ability to control the state apparatus. Second, U.S. nuclear weapons and command-and-control systems should be able to survive and function in a *protracted* nuclear war lasting up to several months.

PD-59 was adopted with little modification by the Reagan administration in National Security Decision Directive (NSDD) 13. The contents of both documents remain secret, but it is apparent that the ability to "prevail" over the Soviet Union in a protracted nuclear war should deterrence fail was—and is—a goal of the strategy. A secret Pentagon policy document called the five-year defense guidance, leaked to the press in 1982,

---

[29]Colin S. Gray, "Nuclear Strategy: the Case for a Theory of Victory," *International Security*, Vol. 4, No. 1 (Summer 1979), p. 30. (Emphasis in the original.)

[30]See, for example, Richard Pipes, "Why the Soviet Union thinks it could fight and win a nuclear war," *Commentary*, Vol. 64, No. 1 (July 1977), pp. 21–34.

[31]See Michael E. Howard, "On Fighting a Nuclear War," *International Security*, Vol. 2, No. 4 (Spring 1978), pp. 6–7.

[32]A fascinating account of the development of PD-59 is found in Thomas Powers, "Choosing a Strategy for World War III," *The Atlantic Monthly*, Vol. 250, No. 5 (November 1982), pp. 82–110.

stated: "Should deterrence fail and strategic nuclear war with the USSR occur, the United States must prevail and be able to force the Soviet Union to seek earliest termination of hostilities on terms favorable to the United States."[33] The meaning of "prevail" has never been entirely clear. When the policy was announced, some critics of the Reagan administration interpreted it as an indication that the United States was intent on achieving the capability to launch a disarming first strike against the Soviet Union. According to officials involved in crafting the defense guidance, however, the term actually embodied the more limited objective of forcing the Soviet Union, subsequent to an invasion of Western Europe, to retreat to its prewar borders and restore the status quo ante.[34]

The principles embodied in PD-59 and NSDD-13 provided the rationale for several strategic programs that started in the 1970s and reached fruition in the 1980s.[35] The programs included a variety of highly accurate, "hard-target-kill" weapon systems, such as the MX ICBM, the air-launched cruise missile (ALCM), and the Trident II/D-5 submarine-launched ballistic missile (SLBM). They also included more enduring and flexible command-and-control systems like the Milstar communications satellite.

In addition, PD-59 and NSDD-13 led to the creation of a new war plan, SIOP-6, the latest version of which, SIOP-6G, went into effect in the fall of 1991. From what is publicly known about this plan, it appears to represent a continuation of earlier trends toward greater targeting flexibility and increased emphasis on counternuclear and counterleadership targeting.[36] In the latest version, some targeting adjustments have been made to reflect the withdrawal of Soviet forces from Eastern Europe and to make more efficient use of weapons in anticipation of strategic arms reductions.[37]

Perhaps most intriguingly, the targeting and war-planning process itself is being made much more adaptable to unexpected circumstances that might arise in a future crisis or conflict. New computers and electronics have been installed in missiles and bombers to permit more rapid retargeting of weapons during a conflict, and experiments in automation are being conducted to reduce the time needed to generate a new SIOP

---

[33]Michael Getler, "Administration's Nuclear War Policy Stance Still Murky," *Washington Post*, November 10, 1982, p. A24.

[34]Fred Ikle, Center for Strategic and International Studies, personal communication (1991).

[35]Jeffrey Richelson, "PD-59, NSDD-13, and the Reagan Strategic Modernization Program," *Journal of Strategic Studies*, Vol. 6, No. 3 (June 1983), pp. 125–146. For more details on developments in U.S. strategic forces and command-and-control, see Chapters 6 and 9.

[36]Ball and Toth, *op. cit.*, pp. 69–72.

[37]Fred Kaplan, "U.S. Eyes Cuts in Nuclear Warheads," *Boston Globe*, July 4, 1990, p. 1; and Robert C. Toth, "U.S. Scratches Nuclear Targets in Soviet Bloc," *Los Angeles Times*, April 19, 1991, p. A1.

"from months to weeks or even days."[38] In 1991, the then Strategic Air Command announced that it was revamping the war-planning process, reducing reliance on preplanned targeting (the heart of the SIOP) and shifting the responsibility for targeting from the Joint Strategic Target Planning Staff to the planning division of the newly formed Strategic Command. The aim of these changes—which include renaming the SIOP itself—is to give the National Command Authorities greater ability to pick and choose targets in response to new or changing circumstances, including regional conflicts not involving the former Soviet Union. (See Chapter 8.) However, the full scope and implications of these changes are not yet clear.

TOWARD A NEW STRATEGY

The disintegration of the Warsaw Pact and the resulting shift in the balance of power in Europe, coupled with revolutionary changes within the Soviet Union itself, have undermined much of the original justification for the flexible response strategy. Yet this does not mean that the concept of flexible response has no place in future U.S. strategy, though it is clear that existing strategy will have to be radically revised. Although NATO's position as the predominant power in Europe appears secure, the former Soviet Union, or the republics that succeed it, will retain most of its strategic weapons and possibly a good many nonstrategic weapons, and collectively they may still field an imposing conventional military force. Future confrontations with some of these republics over, say, Eastern Europe or the Middle East cannot be ruled out. In addition, other challenges to U.S. security may arise. The dangers posed by the spread of nuclear weapons to unstable regions of the world were made abundantly clear during the 1990–1991 Persian Gulf crisis, in which Iraq's reputed desire to obtain nuclear weapons boosted American public support for military action. The breakup of the former Soviet Union may add impetus to nuclear and ballistic-missile proliferation, as some republics will be tempted to export nuclear materials, components, and expertise to other countries, or even to develop weapons of their own.

The task in revising U.S. strategy is to balance the goal of deterring such potential threats with other, possibly competing, goals of U.S. security policy within reasonable political and economic constraints. In the past, deterring deliberate aggression by a patently hostile Soviet government was the paramount objective of U.S. strategy. In the future, the United States will almost certainly tolerate a more relaxed deterrent pos-

---

[38]Maj. Gen. Richard B. Goetze, "SIOP: A Plan for Peace," *Combat Crew*, January 1987, p. 15. See also Patrick Tyler, "Air Force Reviews 'Doomsday' Plan," *Washington Post*, July 11, 1990, p. A17.

ture in exchange for greater assurance of long-term stability and the opportunity to further reduce, through negotiated arms reductions, both the magnitude of the Soviet nuclear threat and U.S. defense spending. In the following sections, our proposed approach to striking such a balance is described.

Objectives

Over the years, a number of possible objectives for nuclear strategy have been expounded, some obvious and familiar, others less so. In the past, these objectives have been defined largely in terms of the Soviet threat; but in the future they may be extended, with modifications, to other circumstances as well. The principal objectives are (in rough order of increasing ambition):[39]

1. basic deterrence
2. extended deterrence
3. crisis stability
4. war termination
5. escalation control
6. damage limitation
7. victory

As Chapter 2 pointed out, basic deterrence—deterrence of nuclear attacks on the homeland—remains the most important role for nuclear weapons and hence the most important objective for nuclear strategy. Yet it is also by far the easiest objective to meet. Few doubt that a nuclear attack by the Soviet Union (or any other country) on the United States would lead to immediate retaliation, or that, under present circumstances, the United States would have more than enough surviving weapons after an attack to wreak "unacceptable damage" on the attacker. Hence the effectiveness and credibility of basic deterrence are rarely questioned. A problem for the future will be to decide how far strategic arms reductions can go without undermining basic deterrence. This will require a decision—subjective though it may be—on how many and what kinds of targets must be held at risk by survivable U.S. forces. Since the former USSR will remain for the foreseeable future the only entity capable of a massive nuclear attack on the U.S. homeland, debate over this question will inevitably revolve around the nature of the U.S.-Soviet deterrent relationship.

In contrast to basic deterrence, extended deterrence has always been a difficult objective to satisfy with any confidence. Many observers on both sides of the Atlantic have remained unconvinced that a defense strategy calling for nuclear weapons to be used in retaliation for conventional

---

[39]Adapted from the Harvard Nuclear Study Group, *Living with Nuclear Weapons* (New York: Bantam, 1983), p. 135.

attack could ever be credible, and some have urged the United States to declare a policy of "no first use," in effect reserving nuclear weapons only for cases involving *nuclear* attacks on U.S. allies.[40] With the virtual disappearance of the Soviet conventional threat to Europe, the logic of no first use has been considerably strengthened, and indeed the previous chapter concluded that, as a matter of policy, the United States should henceforth rely on nuclear weapons to deter only nuclear attacks on its allies and forces overseas. In the near term, at least, this objective can be met easily by a small number of nonstrategic or strategic weapons (presumably land-based air-delivered) of theater or global range. (See Chapter 4.)

Relying on nuclear weapons to deter only nuclear attacks does not necessarily imply a *public* commitment to no first use, however. The United States may, in fact, want to avoid making such a commitment in order not to undermine whatever residual capacity nuclear weapons may have to deter conventionally armed aggression. This was the strategy adopted during the Gulf War, when U.S. officials refused to rule out publicly and explicitly the possibility of a nuclear response to Iraqi chemical attacks, even though such an option was not seriously considered. In this manner, U.S. leaders hoped to encourage some measure of restraint on the part of Saddam Hussein. (Israel adopted a similar stance to discourage chemical attacks on its territory, although in this case, the possibility of a nuclear response seemed more plausible.)

However, the possible benefits of this somewhat schizophrenic approach to the no-first-use question must be balanced against its possible long-term cost, namely, the risk that other countries will perceive nuclear weapons as legitimate instruments of war precisely because the United States and other nuclear powers refuse to renounce their own right to use them first. Until now, the need to deter a Soviet conventionally armed attack against Western Europe has been perceived as far outweighing any possible benefit of a no-first-use declaration in the realm of nonproliferation policy. But the conventional military threats facing the United States and its allies are now greatly diminished—even Iraq's vaunted million-man army and modern air force proved no match for Western military forces—while the relative threat of nuclear proliferation has increased, so this assessment may have to be reexamined.

Crisis stability has long been recognized as a critical requirement of deterrence, and it will continue to be so in the future, for three reasons. First, even though the chance of a major confrontation between the United States and the former Soviet Union now seems remote, the possibility cannot be entirely discounted. Second, the danger of instability may rise as U.S. and Soviet strategic arsenals are reduced because each side

---

[40]McGeorge Bundy, George F. Kennan, Robert S. McNamara, and Gerard Smith, "Nuclear Weapons and the Atlantic Alliance," *Foreign Affairs*, Vol. 60, No. 4 (Spring 1982), pp. 753–768.

could be left with a smaller reserve of forces dedicated to assured retaliation. Third, the risk of inadvertent war, particularly acute during crises, will persist as long as each side's command-and-control system relies on quick response to minimize the consequences of being damaged or destroyed in a first strike.

To maximize stability in the future, the United States must adopt a strategy that places a premium on the survivability of U.S. nuclear forces and command-and-control systems and avoids putting Soviet strategic forces and command-and-control system unduly at risk of prompt destruction. (The former Soviet Union, of course, should adopt the same principles with regard to the United States.) It should be recognized, however, that changes in strategy alone may not significantly enhance stability in the near term, since the physical vulnerabilities and capabilities of each side's forces are the critical factors affecting stability, and these change only slowly over time.[41]

Interestingly, the calculus of crisis stability may be much different in situations involving adversaries other than the Soviet Union. Because of the extreme asymmetry in forces that would exist, a non-Soviet adversary could not expect its nuclear forces and command-and-control system to be immune from prompt destruction (even by U.S. conventional forces), nor could it have any hope of seriously damaging U.S. nuclear capabilities. Yet it might be tempted to use nuclear weapons against U.S. forces or allies in a crisis if its leadership feared preemption or calculated (however mistakenly) that the U.S. response would be restrained. In such a case, it is difficult to say what particular strategies and capabilities, if any, would serve to enhance stability.

The last four objectives concern what would happen if deterrence failed. In that event, the first and foremost objective should be "to terminate [the war] as quickly as possible and with the least amount of damage possible—on both sides."[42] If negotiated war termination fails, then the next objective should be to prevent the conflict from escalating out of control. As we will see in what follows, in the context of a U.S.-Soviet war, there is no guarantee that either of these objectives could be met if the initial nuclear exchange involved more than a small number of weapons.[43] Nevertheless, it would be prudent to take steps to enhance the prospects for war termination and escalation control wherever possible.

---

[41] This is not to say that a statement of intent to avoid targeting one another's nuclear forces would not improve the atmosphere of U.S.-Soviet relations, hence promoting greater confidence that a crisis would not lead to war. But counting on such statements alone to enhance stability would be foolish.

[42] Bernard Brodie, "Development of Nuclear Strategy," *International Security*, Vol. 2, No. 4 (Spring 1978), p. 79.

[43] For somewhat contrasting viewpoints, see Desmond Ball, *Can Nuclear War Be Controlled?* Adelphi Papers 169 (London: IISS, 1981), and Paul Bracken, "War Termination," in Ashton B. Carter, John D. Steinbruner, and Charles A. Zraket, eds., *Managing Nuclear Operations* (Washington, D.C.: The Brookings Institution, 1987), pp. 197–214.

A more ambitious objective would be to limit damage to the United States, either by means of strategic defenses (discussed in Chapter 7) or by destroying the enemy's nuclear forces before they are launched. A related objective would be to "prevail" over the enemy by forcing it to abandon its military objectives (occupying Europe, for example). Since the 1960s, the argument for a strategy designed to meet these two objectives has been based in large part on the need for credible escalatory options to support extended deterrence in Europe—a need that has been greatly reduced, if not eliminated, by the collapse of the Soviet threat to Western Europe. Moreover, we will make the case in the following that under foreseeable circumstances both objectives are technologically demanding, if not infeasible, and tend to undermine the more realistic objectives of crisis stability and war termination.

Against nuclear powers other than the former USSR, damage limitation and victory might well be realistic objectives for the United States. A question requiring further study (beyond the scope of this book) is whether these goals could be met just as easily with conventional forces alone. Experience in the Gulf War, at least, suggests that they might.

Targeting Policy

What strategy, then, will strike the best balance among these sometimes competing objectives? In the U.S.-Soviet context, much of the debate over this question will center on targeting policy. The four basic missions that U.S. nuclear forces could perform in a nuclear war would involve attacks on, respectively, enemy nuclear forces and their associated command-and-control facilities, the military and political leadership, conventional military forces and their command-and-control assets, and cities and industries. None of these missions is ideal, but for reasons discussed in the following, a combination of the last two (countermilitary and countervalue targeting) is much to be preferred over the first two (counternuclear and counterleadership targeting).

Counternuclear Targeting   Traditionally, counternuclear targeting has been accorded the highest priority in the U.S. strategic war plan. From a military perspective, this makes perfect sense: One of the aims of war is to destroy the enemy's ability to damage one's own military assets. But as many analysts have noted, serious problems arise where nuclear weapons are concerned. An obvious problem with counternuclear targeting is that it could be truly successful only if the United States were to go first, in a massive, disarming strike. Even then, U.S. military planners could not be sure that the Soviet Union would not launch its missiles on receipt of warning or while under attack. Furthermore, the Soviet nuclear arsenal is large enough that even a well-executed preemptive strike by the United States could not meaningfully reduce the number of American deaths that would result from the subsequent Soviet retaliation.[44] At the levels of destruction now attainable, damage limitation is an abstract concept at best.

In addition, Soviet nuclear forces are becoming increasingly difficult to target effectively. Since the mid-1980s, several hundred truck-mounted SS-25 ICBMs and scores of rail-mobile SS-24 ICBMs have been deployed, and the Defense Department projects that, by the end of the 1990s, two-thirds of Soviet ICBMs will be on mobile launchers.[45] The Soviet Union has also deployed numerous mobile command posts and backup communications facilities on trucks, trains, aircraft, and even ships.[46] The Defense Department is attempting to compensate for these measures by developing new weapon systems and sensors, but effectively targeting highly mobile systems such as these is likely to prove extremely difficult and costly, and in a period of declining defense budgets, "it looks like a losing battle."[47]

In addition to these practical considerations, a counternuclear targeting strategy—at least to the extent that it is reflected in U.S. nuclear capabilities—affects Soviet perceptions and, hence, crisis stability. A change in targeting policy that resulted in changes in weapons procurement and deployment policies could reduce Soviet fears of preemption and ease pressures to launch early in a crisis. Practically speaking, however, the ability of the United States to damage Soviet nuclear forces will remain largely unaffected by any change in targeting policy in the near term. The accuracy of U.S. missiles is already such that most fixed, hardened targets can be destroyed with high confidence by one or two warheads. Efforts to hold at risk relocatable targets, on the other hand, are unlikely ever to be so successful that they pose a "prompt" threat to highly mobile systems that have been properly dispersed and hidden.[48]

Problems posed by dispersal, hardening, and mobility may also affect

---

[44]The death toll on both sides would be largely independent of which side went first, because attacks on urban targets would account for most deaths, and both countries now have more than enough survivable weapons to cover urban targets. This would be true even if arms reductions reduced forces to a level of 3,000 weapons on each side. See Michael M. May, George F. Bing, and John D. Steinbruner, *Strategic Arms Reductions* (Washington, D.C.: The Brookings Institution, 1988), p. 67.

[45]However, President Gorbachev announced in the fall of 1991 that construction of new mobile ICBMs would stop, and existing mobile ICBMs would be deployed only in their garrisons. See "Gorbachev Remarks on Nuclear Arms Cuts," *op. cit.*

[46]U.S. Department of Defense, *Soviet Military Power 1990* (Washington, D.C.: Government Printing Office, 1990), pp. 51–52, and U.S. Department of Defense, *Soviet Military Power 1988* (Washington, D.C.: Government Printing Office, 1988), pp. 17, 45, 47.

[47]Leon Sloss, *Reexamining Nuclear Policy in a Changing World* (Los Alamos: Center for National Security Studies, 1990), p. 9. For more on the technical prospects of targeting Soviet mobile ICBMs, see Brower, *op. cit.*

[48]The deployment of satellites intended to locate and track relocatable targets could affect crisis stability, however, if it prompted the former USSR to develop new antisatellite weapons. See Brower, *op. cit.*, p. 442. Such weapons are discussed in an appendix to Chapter 7.

the ability of the United States to target the offensive nuclear forces of other countries. Despite overwhelming superiority in the air, the U.S.-allied Persian Gulf force was unable to stop Iraq from launching dozens of mobile Scud missiles against Saudi Arabia and Israel. This lesson is not likely to be lost on other countries contemplating the acquisition of a nuclear force.

Counterleadership Targeting The principal stated rationale for counterleadership targeting has been that it maximizes deterrence by threatening what Soviet leaders purportedly value most—their personal survival and ability to control the state apparatus. Needless to say, this argument is out of date. The Soviet leadership today is highly fragmented, divided deeply along both national and ideological lines. It is thus no longer possible to identify a coherent leadership body or ascribe to it clear motives that could be used as a basis for deterrence.

Yet even ignoring recent changes in the Soviet government—or supposing that such changes could be reversed—counterleadership targeting raises problems of both a practical and theoretical nature. Practically speaking, the set of Soviet leadership targets is potentially large and many of them are difficult to target effectively. Destroying key governmental buildings and military headquarters alone could require hundreds of weapons, while destroying the many hardened leadership shelters reported to have been built could require thousands more. Moreover, a few of the latter are buried so deeply underground that they might not be vulnerable to existing weapons, and even with the deployment of weapons specifically intended for such targets it is not certain that they could be destroyed.[49] Finally, top Soviet leaders would have the option of dispersing to mobile command facilities, which probably could not be targeted at all.

On theoretical grounds, counterleadership targeting is more dubious still. In a war, massive counterleadership attacks would virtually eliminate any chance for negotiated war termination. Thus, at the very least, prompt leadership destruction should be ruled out. But even if the Soviet leadership is retained as a withhold in the SIOP, the counterleadership strategy creates requirements for weapons that could be destabilizing in a crisis. Instability could arise because of the perceived threat both to the survival of the top leadership and to the leadership's ability to control the nuclear forces. Three types of weapons now under development by the United States might create significant new threats to the connectivity and control of Soviet nuclear forces: the microwave-enhanced weapon, which has the potential to disable or destroy mobile and fixed command-and-control facilities by overloading their electronic circuitry; the earth-penetrating

---

[49]One reason destroying deeply buried shelters could be difficult is that satellite photographs can determine the locations of only the shelter entrances, not the shelters themselves. A second reason—if bomber weapons were to be used—is that hardened shelters and command posts could be protected by dense air defenses.

weapon, which would burrow underground before exploding to enhance its effectiveness against deeply buried targets, including command posts; and the terminally guided maneuvering reentry vehicle (MaRV), which could achieve greater accuracy than ordinary ballistic reentry vehicles (hence making it more effective against hardened targets) and could ultimately be given the capability to seek out and destroy mobile command-and-control systems.[50]

In the case of an adversary other than the former Soviet Union, the most obvious problem with counterleadership targeting is that it would almost certainly require the destruction of enemy cities. This prospect was perhaps tolerable in the context of a massive U.S.-Soviet exchange in which both countries would be devastated, but not when the adversary is a relatively weak and, probably, poor Third World country. Even if U.S. forces overseas were the target of a deliberate nuclear attack, international opinion would scarcely tolerate a response that took tens or hundreds of thousands of civilian lives. In this situation, the destruction of enemy leadership targets would be far better left to conventional "smart" munitions like those used in the Gulf War.

Countermilitary Targeting   The third basic mission of U.S. nuclear forces—one that has received increasing support from strategists of various political persuasions as a possible future basis for U.S. deterrent strategy[51]—would be to destroy an adversary's conventional, rather than nuclear, capabilities. Likely conventional military targets include army units, divisional headquarters, military bases and airfields, communications facilities, ammunition dumps and supply depots, air-defense radars and missiles, and chemical and biological weapons facilities.

A strategy based on countermilitary targeting presents several advantages. It would be perceived by the adversary (whether it is the former Soviet Union or another country) as a credible deterrent because it would threaten assets essential to achieving war aims (such as occupying Europe or the Persian Gulf). It would be sensible from a military perspective, as well, because it would aim to destroy an adversary's war-making capabilities, not its society. At the same time, it would not be as challenging technologically as counterleadership or counternuclear targeting, since most conventional military targets are not substantially hardened and could be destroyed by existing weapons (with the possible exception of mobile army units). Finally, and perhaps most importantly, the strategy would not require capabilities that would threaten Soviet nuclear forces and command-and-control with prompt destruction.

---

[50]For discussion of weapons under development, see Brower, *op. cit.*, p. 441; Theodore Taylor, "Third-Generation Nuclear Weapons," *Scientific American*, Vol. 256, No. 4 (April 1987), pp. 30–39; Matthew Bunn, *Maneuvering Reentry Vehicles: Missions, Implications, and Prospects for Control* (Washington, D.C.: Arms Control Association, undated), pp. 13–15.

[51]See Sloss, *op. cit.*, pp. 9–11; and Michael J. Mazarr, "Beyond Counterforce," *Comparative Strategy*, Vol. 9, No. 2 (1990), pp. 147–162.

Two important issues need to be addressed, however. The first concerns the number and types of conventional military targets the United States would have to be able to destroy with survivable weapons to assure an adequate degree of deterrence. Since the Soviet military is by far the largest the United States would confront in the foreseeable future, the Soviet conventional military target set should define the upper limit of required capabilities. As McNamara discovered when he proposed his "no cities" approach, however, the Soviet conventional military target set is potentially extremely large and its boundaries difficult to define clearly. Three basic approaches to resolving this issue can be considered (in order of decreasing ambition).

In the first approach, the goal would be to be able to destroy the entire Soviet conventional military as an effective fighting force. Determining the number of facilities that would have to be targeted to meet this requirement would entail analyzing Soviet military structure and operations in great detail in order to define a threshold of destruction that would render the organization functionally useless. Needless to say, opinions on the appropriate threshold might vary widely depending on the analytical methods and assumptions used.

In the second approach, the goal would be to be able to destroy the former Soviet Union's capacity to project power beyond its borders. Determining what is required to achieve this more limited objective would entail identifying those military forces and facilities that would be called on to lead an invasion or provide direct support for invading forces. This would presumably be a fraction of the entire Soviet military machine.

In the third and last approach, countermilitary targeting would be viewed not as a means to disable the Soviet military, but merely as providing a set of credible response options in the event a conventional war escalated to a "limited" nuclear exchange. In that case, it would not be necessary to be able to destroy even a fraction of the Soviet military apparatus, but only a limited number of military assets; the ultimate deterrent would remain explicitly and unequivocally the threat to damage or destroy Soviet society. This approach, which might be called a flexible assured-destruction strategy, would lead to far lower weapon requirements than would the first two. For reasons discussed in the following, however, we recommend adopting the second approach in the near term.

Countervalue Targeting The last basic mission of strategic nuclear forces would be to attack the enemy's society, particularly its critical economic and industrial capacity. This mission—countervalue targeting—is widely regarded as the ultimate deterrent threat, the mission for which a portion of the U.S. strategic nuclear force should always be reserved as a last resort. Indeed, many strategic specialists would be uncomfortable with a deterrent posture that did not, directly or indirectly, threaten an adversary's society. The United States would be most unlikely to execute countervalue strikes, however, unless its own cities and industries were directly attacked.

Current U.S. policy on population targeting is somewhat ambiguous. The United States has ostensibly ruled out targeting the Soviet population *per se*, but even so, hundreds of Soviet cities would be severely damaged or destroyed if the SIOP were fully executed because of their proximity to industrial or military facilities or because they house government organs.[52] Destruction of Soviet industry, on the other hand, has always been an explicit goal of U.S. war planning. Industrial targets are usually divided into two broad categories: industry that supports the Soviet military machine, and industry that would contribute to the Soviet Union's long-term economic recovery after a nuclear war. Since the late 1970s the latter has been deemphasized, mainly because of uncertainty over how effective such a strategy would be.

Some observers believe that the countervalue threat alone could provide an adequate basis for deterrence at very low levels of forces (perhaps a few hundred strategic weapons).[53] Yet most others believe that such a minimum-deterrent posture would lack credibility in any realistic military context, and most certainly it would if the enemy posed no direct threat to the U.S. homeland. As we saw earlier, there is potentially a middle ground: a flexible assured-destruction strategy in which the countervalue threat would remain the ultimate deterrent, while a limited number of countermilitary options would be available to enhance credibility.

Proposed Targeting Approach   In sum, the United States should adopt a targeting approach for its strategic forces that includes some combination of countermilitary and countervalue targeting and eschews as much as possible counterleadership and counternuclear targeting. For the near term, we propose that the emphasis be placed on threatening the former Soviet Union's capacity (or the capacity of any of its republics) to project power in a sustained fashion beyond its borders. Because of its potentially large weapons requirements, the first countermilitary option discussed earlier—targeting the entire Soviet military apparatus—seems out of keeping with recent trends in U.S.-Soviet relations and internal Soviet politics. On the other hand, while the flexible assured destruction approach has points in its favor, it runs against the current trend (evident in the war against Iraq) away from targeting civilian populations and toward ever more discriminating use of military force. The approach we recommend strikes a middle ground. It would eliminate most nuclear and leadership targets from the SIOP while retaining a restricted number of conventional military and industrial (countervalue) targets. Our proposed

---

[52]Jeffrey Richelson, "Population Targeting and U.S. Strategic Doctrine," in Ball and Richelson, *op. cit.*, pp. 243–244.

[53]See McGeorge Bundy, "The Bishops and the Bomb," *New York Review of Books*, June 16, 1983, pp. 3–8; and Herbert F. York, *"Remarks" about Minimum Deterrence* (Livermore, Calif.: Lawrence Livermore National Laboratory Center for Technical Studies on Security, Energy, and Arms Control, January 25, 1991), p. 1.

Table 3.1. NOMINAL AND PROPOSED TARGET LISTS

Target Class	Nominal	Proposed
Strategic nuclear	2400	120
Leadership/C^{3}I	1100	150
Other military	930	300–600
Economic/Industrial	1500	500–1000
Total	5930	1070–1870

Sources: The nominal list is based on the one used by May, Bing, and Steinbruner. (Personal communication from George F. Bing to Warner Schilling, July 18, 1989.)

target list is compared for reference to a nominal list in Table 3.1. Several points should be made about these target lists. First, they are notional only. We do not pretend to have access to classified information concerning the exact number and types of targets in the current National Strategic Target Data Base; moreover, the actual number of targets attacked would depend on which attack option was executed. The nominal list is based on one used by May, Bing, and Steinbruner in their nuclear exchange calculations.[54] The numbers of strategic nuclear targets were adjusted somewhat to reflect recent changes in the Soviet ICBM force, namely, the increased deployment of mobile ICBMs and the retirement of SS-11, SS-13, and SS-17 silo-based ICBMs.

Second, the proposed list represents what we believe to be a plausible *upper bound* on the number of targets that must be held at risk. Above a range of 1,500-2,000 targets, the marginal contribution to deterrence would probably be small, and in a war, "a prudent military command would presumably choose to preserve any remaining weapons rather than expend them in redundant and unnecessary retaliation."[55] On the other hand, some might argue that a number below 1,000 would be adequate for deterrence if U.S.-Soviet relations continue to improve and there is no reversion to authoritarian rule within the Soviet republics, especially Russia.

Third, we have not eliminated all nuclear, command-and-control, and leadership targets. In particular, strategic air bases, naval ports, and mobile ICBM garrisons were retained on the grounds that they are part of the Soviet nuclear infrastructure that would be required for reconstitution after a nuclear war, and that having the capability to destroy them would have little impact on stability, because in time of crisis most weapons based at such facilities would be dispersed. Secondary command-and-control facilities were also retained, on the assumption—impossible to verify with-

---

[54]Personal communication from George F. Bing to Warner Schilling, July 18, 1989.

[55]May, Bing, and Steinbruner, *op. cit.*, p. 6.

out access to classified information—that they are dedicated to conventional military forces and hence are valid targets for attack. All antiballistic missile sites and some surface-to-air missile (SAM) sites were retained to ensure penetration of ballistic missiles and bombers; but early-warning radars, which are used for attack assessment and warning and hence whose survival would be crucial to war termination and escalation control, were eliminated from the list.

Finally, the nominal list of "other military targets" was reduced by one- to two-thirds to reflect the requirement to target only power-projection forces. The number of economic/industrial targets was reduced by the same fractions on the grounds that the breakup of the Soviet Union has already resulted in a large decrease in the size of this target base. Naturally, these estimates are quite crude and further study is needed.

Response Policy

Although targeting policy usually receives the most attention, response policy—which encompasses the scale and timing of retaliatory strikes—is an equally important component of strategy. In this area, too, significant changes in policy are needed, though the changes are less dramatic and their effects would be felt mainly in the longer term. The most important task is to strengthen stability by reducing the reliance of both U.S. and Soviet strategic forces on prompt, massive response to warning of strategic attack. In addition, the United States must ensure adequate flexibility and security of its command and control system to respond to regional nuclear contingencies.

Attack Options   As noted earlier, the SIOP currently contains a wide variety of attack options. The most important for the purposes of war termination and escalation control would be extremely limited options involving very few weapons, ranging from one or two up to perhaps a few dozen. Such options would be intended primarily to show U.S. resolve, though in certain situations they could also have a significant military objective. Limited attack options could also be useful for nuclear contingencies not involving the former Soviet Union. In both cases, it would be important that the weapons used be of relatively low yield so as to minimize civilian damage and reduce the risk of further escalation. If strategic weapons were used, the attack-planning process itself would have to be extraordinarily flexible to accommodate fast-changing conditions. Existing procedures are probably not up to this task, but with improvements in automation now under way, and if the proposed revamping of strategic war planning procedures is implemented, they may soon be.

In between extremely limited and full-scale options are intermediate options incorporating perhaps hundreds of weapons. Although their ostensible purpose is to support escalation control, their practical utility is doubtful. By the time such options might be contemplated, communications would probably be disrupted and many command posts destroyed, rendering fine control of nuclear attacks difficult, if not impossible. In addition, it is unlikely that the Soviet leadership would perceive an attack involving hundreds of weapons as "limited," no matter what the intent of the attack might be. As one observer wrote, nuclear weapons "are not suited to signaling any precise and unambiguous message but, on the contrary, are supremely capable of degrading the whole environment of communications."[56] This would be especially true, of course, if portions of the Soviet leadership and command-and-control network were themselves destroyed in the attack.

Besides the scale of retaliation, its possible timing is also an important factor to consider. Once the National Command Authorities (NCA) had concluded that an enemy attack was imminent (and hence deterrence had failed), three basic response options would be available: preemption, prompt launch (launch on warning or launch under attack), and retaliation after attack, or ride out.[57]

Preemption Preemption would involve launching U.S. strategic missiles and bombers on receipt of strategic warning, that is, on indications from one or more intelligence sources that enemy nuclear forces were preparing to attack. (Such indications might include the sudden departure of leaders from Moscow, the dispersal of bombers from bases or the surging of submarines from home ports, and an increase in communications traffic.) This response option is usually discounted by strategic experts because events unrelated to preparations for a nuclear attack could be misconstrued as strategic warning, although as we will see, tactical warning, on which U.S. response strategy currently depends, might also be based on error in some circumstances.

In any case, the NCA would be very unlikely to choose preemption for a number of reasons. First, if there were the remotest chance that the strategic warning was mistaken, preemption would close off any chance of avoiding nuclear war. Second, U.S. leaders would want to consider the scale and intent of the enemy attack before deciding on the appropriate response, and this could only be done after weapons had been launched. Third, there would be no guarantee that a preemptive strike on the Soviet Union would gain a significant military advantage for the United States or would prevent internal disintegration of the United States in the subsequent Soviet retaliation. As noted earlier, the Soviet Union might be able to launch many of its ICBMs promptly on warning of a U.S. attack; and dispersed bombers and submarines would survive in any event. Indeed,

[56]Ball, "Critique of Strategic Nuclear Targeting," in Ball and Richelson, *op. cit.*, p. 31.

[57]See Kurt Gottfried and Bruce G. Blair, eds., *Crisis Stability and Nuclear War* (New York: Oxford University Press, 1988), pp. 82–89; and Walter Slocombe, "Preplanned Operations," in Carter, Steinbruner, and Zraket, *op. cit.*, pp. 132–137.

far from limiting damage to the United States, a preemptive strike could precipitate a massive Soviet response, causing vast destruction on both sides.

Prompt Launch   Prompt launch is the response U.S. leaders would most likely choose under present circumstances if sufficient tactical warning were received that a major Soviet attack were under way.[58] The current reliance on prompt launch is dictated by vulnerabilities in the U.S. command-and-control system and nuclear forces (especially ICBMs), portions of which could be seriously damaged or destroyed if U.S. leaders chose to ride out an initial Soviet attack. Two prompt launch options would be available: launch on warning (LOW) and launch under attack (LUA). Under LUA, the NCA would wait until confirmation had been received of nuclear detonations on American soil before ordering retaliation. Under the less demanding requirements of LOW, confirmed detection of missile launches from at least two types of sensors—such as ground-based radars and satellites—would be enough.

The importance of being able to launch weapons promptly has been defended for two reasons. First and more important, the ability to launch ICBMs on warning or while under attack preserves the synergy of bomber and ICBM survivability—that is, if both bombers and ICBMs are on alert, it would be impossible for the former Soviet Union, with its present forces, to destroy U.S. ICBMs without giving bombers on alert enough warning to take off, and vice versa. Second, if damage limitation is the objective, then missiles must be launched promptly to have any hope of catching Soviet weapons on the ground or of disrupting Soviet communications before all weapons have been launched.

There are several clear—and quite frightening—difficulties associated with the prompt-launch response strategy, however. The most obvious is that it greatly compresses the time available to determine the best response to an attack—or even if an attack has really occurred. From launch it would take Soviet ICBMs 25–30 minutes to hit U.S. ICBMs; SLBMs launched from offshore could hit some critical targets, like Washington, D.C., in as little as 5–10 minutes. Considering the time that would be required initially to detect the attack and assess its scale and broad intent (to destroy U.S. nuclear forces, command-and-control assets, or other sets of targets), and, at the other end of the timeline, to issue and execute launch orders, no more than 5-10 minutes might be available for the NCA to review options and select an appropriate response.

---

[58]There is no well-defined threshold of attack above which the NCA would be likely to opt for prompt launch. Much would depend on the ability of military commanders to discern the intent and likely consequences of the attack and, in particular, whether it posed a serious threat to the U.S. command-and-control system or ICBM force. It seems likely, however, that a few hundred Soviet warheads would have to be detected heading toward the United States for a prompt launch to be considered.

In the short time available for prompt-launch decisions, several problems could arise. First, it could be very difficult to determine the true extent and nature of the Soviet attack, especially as some sensors might be destroyed early on. Second, possible single or multiple failures of sensors at critical junctures could send misleading information to the NCA that could not be corrected before a decision had to be made. In the worst case, sensors could indicate that an attack was underway when in fact it was not. To these potential problems must be added the tremendous psychological stress that would be placed on leaders in such a situation, leading possibly to tragic errors of judgment.[59]

Finally, reliance on prompt launch requires the ability to shift rapidly from a state of absolute negative control (designed to ensure that weapons cannot be launched accidentally or without authorization) to one of absolute positive control (to allow instantaneous weapons launch). As a result of this requirement, there is a disincentive to invest in devices or procedures that could reduce the risk of unauthorized launch yet would complicate or delay prompt launch. This may help explain, for example, why there are no feedback loops built into the current U.S. command system to ensure the accuracy of commands received by missile launch crews.[60]

Ride-out The last response option would be to wait until the brunt of an attack had been absorbed (30 minutes to an hour for Soviet ballistic missiles, up to 15 hours for Soviet bombers and cruise missiles) before ordering retaliation. This approach has the very attractive features of giving the NCA more time to consider retaliatory options, resulting perhaps in a more restrained response, and of virtually eliminating the chance that war might start because of an error of tactical warning. For these reasons, the NCA might elect to ride out a relatively small Soviet attack or an attack by a country other than the former Soviet Union.

However, there is considerable doubt that the existing U.S. command-and-control system could support the execution of deliberate and controlled responses after riding out a major Soviet attack *unless* the former Soviet Union intentionally avoided destroying key command-and-control facilities. This does not mean that no retaliation would occur. However, it would most likely be massive and uncoordinated, for two main reasons.

---

[59]In peacetime, the chance that false sensor readings could lead to mistaken retaliation is vanishingly small, because commanders would naturally seek to verify unusual sensor readings by all means available. Of significant concern, however, is the possibility that false warning might occur in the midst of a serious crisis. Then commanders would be more willing to accept that an attack was underway, and pressures to respond quickly could lead to inadequate confirmation of warning. (One is reminded of the shooting down of an Iranian airliner by the U.S. cruiser *Vincennes*, which was caused by misinterpretation of radar warning data by officers and crew under combat stress.)

[60]Bruce G. Blair, the Brookings Institution, personal communication (1991). See also Bruce G. Blair and Henry W. Kendall, "Accidental Nuclear War," *Scientific American*, Vol. 263, No. 6 (December 1990), p. 53.

First, if warning and assessment sensors were destroyed early, it would be difficult or impossible for the NCA to assess accurately the attack's intent and likely consequences; the natural inclination would be to assume the worst. Second, faced with the uncertain prospect of additional attacks, the NCA would be under strong pressure to order retaliation by all remaining forces since airborne command posts, bombers, and refueling tankers would not be able to stay in the air for more than several hours.

The difficulties of carrying out deliberate and controlled actions in a nuclear war of any substantial scale illustrate a key fallacy of recent U.S. strategic thinking: the notion that, through the development of more enduring weapons and command-and-control systems, one side could somehow influence the course of a protracted nuclear war so as to "prevail" over the other. On the contrary, the concept of protracted nuclear warfighting does not appear to offer a realistic basis for U.S. strategic war planning and acquisition policy, especially considering likely defense budget constraints.

We recommend that, in the future, emphasis should be placed on meeting two far less ambitious goals: enhancing the flexibility of limited nuclear response options involving up to a few dozen weapons, and improving the ability of U.S. nuclear forces and command-and-control systems to ride out, for a period of a few hours to days, a substantial nuclear attack and respond appropriately. Whether the latter goal, in particular, can be met within the constraints of a declining defense budget remains to be seen. (See Chapter 8.)

CONCLUSIONS AND RECOMMENDATIONS

In sum, U.S. nuclear strategy is at a crossroads. If the present strategy is maintained, the gap between what the strategy aims to accomplish and what is politically relevant or technologically feasible will inevitably grow. At the same time, it will provide no sound guidance for structuring U.S. strategic forces under arms reductions, leaving policy-makers to decide on an ad hoc basis which capabilities should be kept and which should be discarded. Amid such confusion, sensible decisions will be the exception, not the rule.

We propose a new approach that seeks to maintain deterrence and stability at greatly reduced levels of forces. It eliminates the more impractical and dangerous aspects of current strategy while retaining one of its central tenets—that deterrence should be based not solely on the threat to damage or destroy an enemy's society, but also on the ability to damage its military (but not nuclear) capabilities. To summarize our recommendations:

- The current policy of placing the highest priority on targeting Soviet strategic forces, command-and-control systems, and leadership should be abandoned.

- Instead, U.S. strategy should be based on targeting Soviet conventional forces and associated command-and-control systems needed for power projection, as well as war-supporting industry.
- The number of Soviet targets that should be held at risk in retaliation falls somewhere in the range of 1,100-1,900, with a consensus value (for determining weapons requirements in Chapter 5) of 1,500.
- The United States should continue to develop and refine flexible, limited strategic and nonstrategic attack options involving up to a few dozen weapons, preferably of relatively low yield, to support extended deterrence and as a hedge against the unlikely prospect of limited nuclear attacks by the former Soviet Union or other countries.
- Steps should be taken, where possible, to improve the ability of U.S. strategic forces and associated command-and-control systems to ride out a substantial Soviet nuclear attack and delay retaliation for up to hours or days. This would reduce reliance on prompt launch options and, as a result, the risk of inadvertent nuclear war.

SUGGESTED READINGS

Ball, Desmond and Jeffrey Richelson, eds. *Strategic Nuclear Targeting*. Ithaca, N.Y.: Cornell University Press, 1986.

Freedman, Lawrence. *The Evolution of Nuclear Strategy*. New York: St. Martin's Press, 1989.

Gottfried, Kurt and Bruce Blair, eds. *Crisis Stability and Nuclear War*. Ithaca, N.Y.: Cornell University Press, 1988.

Miller, Steven E., ed. *Strategy and Nuclear Deterrence: An International Security Reader*. Princeton: Princeton University Press, 1984.

Nolan, Janne E. *Guardians of the Arsenal: The Politics of Nuclear Strategy*. New York: Basic Books, 1989.

Rosenberg, David Alan. "The Origins of Overkill: Nuclear Weapons and American Strategy, 1945–1960." *International Security*, Vol. 7, No. 4 (Spring 1983), pp. 3–71.

Sagan, Scott D. *Moving Targets: Nuclear Strategy and National Security*. Princeton: Princeton University Press, 1984.

Schwartz, David N. *NATO's Nuclear Dilemmas*. Washington, D.C.: The Brookings Institution, 1983.

Sigal, Leon V. *Nuclear Forces in Europe: Enduring Dilemmas, Present Prospects*. Washington, D.C.: The Brookings Institution, 1984.

Steinbruner, John D. and Leon V. Sigal, eds. *Alliance Security: NATO and the No-First-Use Question*. Washington, D.C.: The Brookings Institution, 1983.

Chapter
4

The Future of U.S. Nonstrategic Nuclear Forces

George N. Lewis

*A*lthough strategic nuclear forces have received most of the attention in policy debates and the scholarly literature, the United States and the Soviet Union actually deployed more NSNF throughout much of their nuclear arms race. By the late 1980s and early 1990s, however, many types of NSNF had come to be seen as anachronisms, rendered obsolete by advances in technology and changes in the global political environment. Nevertheless, limiting or reducing these weapons posed a difficult challenge for arms control, particularly because verifying limits on NSNF appeared to be more difficult than monitoring constraints on strategic weapons. The unilateral initiatives announced by Presidents Bush and Gorbachev in September and October 1991 revolutionized nonstrategic arms control; they swept away most of the old problems in this field and even made the elimination of all NSNF a plausible goal.

This chapter begins with a brief review of the history of nonstrategic weapons and nonstrategic arms control up until the initiatives of September and October 1991. Particular emphasis is placed on the growing concern over the security of Soviet nuclear weapons, both strategic and nonstrategic, which played an important role in stimulating the Bush and Gorbachev unilateral initiatives. After summarizing the implications of these initiatives for NSNF, the chapter considers whether or not the United States needs to retain a nonstrategic force, and, if so, what form this force should take. Further arms control measures for NSNF and several issues that are relevant to both nonstrategic and strategic nuclear weapons are then discussed. The latter include: what the United States can do to minimize the nuclear dangers inherent in the breakup of the Soviet Union; the ultimate fate of the fissile plutonium and uranium in eliminated nuclear weapons and the prospects for a U.S.-Soviet agreement to end production of fissile material for weapons; and the possibilities for cooperatively verifying the destruction of nuclear warheads. The chapter concludes with a set of recommendations.

NONSTRATEGIC NUCLEAR WEAPONS

Nonstrategic nuclear weapons are a very diverse class of weapons intended for the entire range of nuclear missions short of strategic attack on the United States or the Soviet Union.[1] Many of these weapons had very short ranges (i.e., tens of kilometers) and were intended for tactical battlefield use, both on land and at sea. Other longer-range weapons (i.e., hundreds to a few thousand kilometers) were intended for use within one theater of military operations, such as Europe, and provided a link between battlefield nuclear weapons and strategic nuclear forces.

First deployed by the United States in the early 1950s, NSNF rapidly proliferated until a nuclear variant had been developed for virtually every feasible type of delivery system. On land, U.S. NSNF included short- and intermediate-range missiles, artillery shells, air defense missiles, ground-launched cruise missiles, and land mines (atomic demolition munitions). Air-based systems included bombs for tactical aircraft and air-to-air missiles. Naval variants of many of these weapons were also developed, as were nuclear torpedoes and depth bombs. U.S. deployments of NSNF peaked in 1967 at about 20,000 warheads.[2] Although Soviet deployment of NSNF began later, the Soviet Union ultimately fielded an equally large and diverse force. As late as 1988, it was estimated that the Soviet arsenal included roughly 18,000–19,000 nonstrategic warheads.[3]

As discussed in Chapter 3, the primary military rationale behind U.S. land- and air-based NSNF has always been to defeat or deter an attack on Western Europe by numerically superior Soviet and Warsaw Pact ground forces. This task was widely viewed as being difficult or impossible to accomplish at an acceptable financial cost with conventionally armed forces. At sea, where U.S. conventional forces were vastly superior to those of any possible opponent, NSNF were viewed primarily as more effective

---

[1]The dividing line between strategic and nonstrategic weapons is sometimes ambiguous. In particular, both long-range nuclear sea-launched cruise missiles and some types of nuclear air-defense weapons can be regarded as either tactical or strategic weapons. Because these weapons are very similar to certain types of NSNF, they will be treated as NSNF here.

[2]Thomas B. Cochran, William M. Arkin, and Milton M. Hoenig, *Nuclear Weapons Databook, Volume I: U.S. Nuclear Forces and Capabilities* (Cambridge, Mass.: Ballinger, 1984), p. 14.

[3]Thomas B. Cochran, William M. Arkin, Robert S. Norris, and Jeffrey I. Sands, *Nuclear Weapons Databook, Volume IV: Soviet Nuclear Weapons* (New York: Harper & Row, 1988), pp. 32–33. This figure includes air defense weapons.

versions of existing conventional weapons and as a means of deterring the use of Soviet nuclear weapons against the U.S. fleet.

Although NSNF provided U.S. conventional forces with greatly enhanced firepower, they also had serious drawbacks. Most importantly, once the Soviet Union deployed corresponding weapons, any use of U.S. NSNF could be expected to bring Soviet retaliation; in addition, first use of NSNF by the Soviets became a concern. Not only was it unclear how nonstrategic U.S. or NATO forces could benefit from engaging in nuclear combat with comparably armed Soviet forces, but the prospect of escalation to strategic nuclear strikes loomed large over any use of these weapons. Further, the use of NSNF in densely populated areas such as Europe could inflict great damage on the very people and territory they were intended to defend. Thus their deployment often aroused opposition among the publics of the nations in which they were deployed. In addition, given the natural reluctance of decision-makers to authorize the use of nuclear weapons, the availability of these weapons in even the most extreme military circumstances was highly uncertain. There were many other more mundane problems with NSNF as well: They imposed substantial security and training burdens on the units with which they were deployed, they often displaced more usable conventional weapons, and it was feared that their use would adversely impact increasingly sensitive and important sensors and communications equipment.

These factors, together with the growing sophistication and effectiveness of conventional weapons and the aging of the first generation of NSNF, led to a gradual decline in the number of U.S. nonstrategic nuclear weapons to less than 14,000 in 1980.[4] Although a few new nonstrategic weapons, such as the Tomahawk nuclear SLCM and, briefly, the Pershing II and the GLCM, were deployed, the pace of retirements accelerated in the mid- and late-1980s. All U.S. land- and air-based nuclear air defense weapons were withdrawn, as were all atomic demolition munitions. In 1989, the U.S. Navy announced plans to speed the retirement of most of its remaining weapons systems for nuclear combat at sea.[5] This left Tomahawk SLCMs and air-delivered depth and strike bombs as the U.S. Navy's only remaining nonstrategic nuclear weapons.

In the mid- to late-1980s, changes in the Soviet Union and improvements in U.S.-Soviet relations also began to affect NSNF deployments. The 1987 INF Treaty banned all U.S. and Soviet ground-based missiles with ranges between 500 and 5,500 km. By mid-1991, developments such as the INF Treaty, the Conventional Forces in Europe Treaty, the end of the Cold War, the withdrawal of Soviet forces from Eastern Europe, the collapse and dissolution of the Warsaw Pact, and the reunification of Ger-

---

[4]Cochran, Arkin, and Hoenig, *op. cit.*, p. 14.

[5]Michael Gordon, "Navy Phasing Out Nuclear Rockets for Close Combat," *New York Times*, April 30, 1989, p. A1.

many had undercut much of the rationale for those NSNF still in Europe. In particular, the new European map did not appear to leave a plausible or politically acceptable military role for ground-based U.S. nuclear weapons that lacked the range to reach the Soviet Union. Recognizing this, President Bush announced in May of 1990 the cancellation of both the Follow-On to Lance short-range missile and the modernization of U.S. nuclear artillery shells.[6] By the middle of 1991, the number of U.S. nonstrategic warheads had fallen to less than 7,000,[7] and the withdrawal—either by treaty, informal agreement, or unilateral action—of all U.S. nuclear short-range (i.e., range less than 500 km) missiles and nuclear artillery shells seemed likely within the next few years.

Further, only one new nonstrategic nuclear weapon was on the drawing board and its future was highly uncertain. The Short-Range Attack Missile—Tactical (SRAM—T) was a roughly 400-km range missile that was to be derived from the U.S. Air Force's new strategic Short-Range Attack Missile II (SRAM II). The SRAM—T was intended to fill NATO's requirement for a tactical air-to-surface missile (TASM) that could be launched from tactical aircraft and was slated to be deployed to Europe in the mid-1990s. However, its ultimate fate was uncertain due to technical problems, congressional opposition, and the potentially divisive NATO politics surrounding its deployment.

Although much less detailed information is available on Soviet NSNF trends, it appears that a similar but much less dramatic decline in the number of Soviet nonstrategic nuclear weapons also occurred in the 1980s and early 1990s. One estimate puts the Soviet nonstrategic arsenal at about 15,000 warheads in mid-1991, a decrease of 23 percent from a similar tabulation of three years earlier.[8] However, compared to U.S. forces, the Soviet armed forces remained highly nuclearized, particularly at sea.

NONSTRATEGIC ARMS CONTROL UP TO SEPTEMBER 1991

Nonstrategic nuclear weapons have historically received less attention in arms control negotiations than strategic nuclear weapons. Prior to the announcement of President Bush's unilateral initiative in September

---

[6]Ann Devroy, "Bush Calls for Major Review of NATO's Policies, Missions," *Washington Post*, May 4, 1990, p. A1.

[7]Robert S. Norris and William M. Arkin, "Nuclear Notebook: U.S. Nuclear Weapons Stockpile (June 1991)," *Bulletin of the Atomic Scientists*, Vol. 47, No. 5 (June 1991), p. 49.

[8]Robert S. Norris and William M. Arkin, "Nuclear Notebook: Estimated Soviet Nuclear Stockpile," *Bulletin of the Atomic Scientists*, Vol. 47, No. 6 (July/August 1991), p. 48, and Vol. 44, No. 5 (July/August 1988), p. 56. The figures cited here include air-defense weapons.

1991, only the negotiations leading to the 1987 INF Treaty had focused on NSNF.[9] The INF Treaty required the United States and Soviet Union to eliminate all conventional and nuclear land-based cruise and ballistic missiles with ranges between 500 and 5,500 km, and resulted in the elimination of over 2,600 missiles, two-thirds of which were Soviet. This treaty also established an unprecedented regime of cooperative verification measures, including perimeter-portal monitoring of missile production facilities and several types of on-site inspections.[10]

As the Soviet military threat to Western Europe receded, the interest in and prospects for further NSNF agreements increased. In announcing the cancellation of modernization plans for the Lance and nuclear artillery shells, President Bush also called for negotiations on short-range nuclear missiles in Europe to begin shortly after the CFE Treaty was signed.[11] The July 1990 NATO summit in London affirmed Bush's proposal to open talks on short-range missiles and further declared that "once negotiations begin on short-range nuclear forces, the Alliance will propose, in return for reciprocal action by the Soviet Union, the elimination of all its nuclear artillery shells from Europe."[12] Given repeated Soviet calls for reductions in or elimination of short-range nuclear forces in Europe, these developments suggested that an agreement limiting nonstrategic weapons in Europe could be successfully concluded in the near future.[13]

At the same time, pressure was growing on the United States to con-

---

[9]In addition, U.S. and Soviet deployments of quasi-strategic long-range nuclear sea-launched cruise missiles are nominally limited (to a maximum of 880 each) by a separate agreement reached in the START negotiations.

[10]See Office of Public Affairs, U.S. Arms Control and Disarmament Agency, *Understanding the INF Treaty* (Washington, D.C.: U.S. Government Printing Office, 1988); and Arms Control Association, "Special Supplement: Summary and Text of the INF Treaty and Protocols," *Arms Control Today*, Vol. 18, No. 1 (January/February, 1988).

[11]The previous NATO position was that such talks would only begin once CFE implementation was well underway. The CFE Treaty was signed on November 19, 1990.

[12]"Text of the Declaration After the NATO Talks," *New York Times*, July 7, 1990, p. A5.

[13]Some weapons, such as nuclear artillery shells, might have been dealt with outside the formal negotiations.

Analyses of European nonstrategic arms control issues, written prior to the 1991 unilateral initiatives, include: William D. Bajusz and Lisa D. Shaw, "The Forthcoming 'SNF Negotiations,'" *Survival*, Vol. 32, No. 4 (July/August, 1990), pp. 333–347; Martin Butcher, Dan Plesch, Otfried Nassauer, and David Shorr, *Short-Range Nuclear Force Negotiations*, BASIC Report 90.5/1 (Washington, D.C.: The British American Security Information Council, 1990); Catherine Guicherd, "Nuclear Weapons in Europe: Modernization and Arms Control" in Eric H. Arnett, ed., *Science and International Security: Responding to a Changing World* (Washington, D.C.: American Association for the Advancement of Science, 1990), pp. 329–360; Catherine M. Kelleher, "Short-Range Nuclear Weapons: What Future in Europe," *Arms Control Today*, Vol. 21, No. 1 (January/February 1991), pp. 17–21; and Sergei Kortunov, "Negotiating on Nuclear Weapons in Europe," *Survival*, Vol. 33, No. 1 (January/February 1991), pp. 45–52.

sider arms control limits on naval nonstrategic nuclear weapons.[14] The Soviets had long argued for limitations on both conventional and nuclear naval forces.[15] At the December 1989 Malta Summit, Soviet President Gorbachev proposed that all tactical nuclear weapons be eliminated from surface ships and submarines.[16] In his May 1990 appearance before the Senate Armed Services Committee, Marshall Akhromeyev, chief military advisor to Gorbachev, although speaking unofficially, renewed Soviet demands for limits on naval forces and naval tactical nuclear weapons, and threatened that future progress in other areas of arms control could be dependent on U.S. agreement to enter into naval arms control negotiations. He further added that the Soviets were willing to include Soviet land-based naval aviation in negotiations on naval nuclear forces.[17]

The U.S. government and the navy had historically resisted even discussing arms control limits on naval forces.[18] This hostility resulted from several causes, including: the traditional independence of the navy, the belief that any limit on U.S. maritime capabilities would be detrimental to U.S. security, fear that verification measures associated with arms control could interfere with naval operations or compromise security, con-

---

[14]The category of naval NSNF does not include intercontinental submarine-launched ballistic missiles, but it does include land-based weapons specifically intended for use against naval targets, such as naval aviation aircraft equipped with bombs or Soviet ship-attack air-launched cruise missiles.

[15]Preunilateral initiatives discussions of naval nuclear arms control include: Ivo H. Daalder and Tim Zimmermann, "Banning Nuclear Weapons at Sea: A Neglected Strategy," *Arms Control Today*, Vol. 18, No. 8 (November, 1988), pp. 17–23; Richard Fieldhouse, "Naval Nuclear Arms Control," in Richard Fieldhouse, ed., *Security at Sea: Naval Forces and Arms Control* (New York: Oxford University Press, 1990), pp. 158–186; Cathleen S. Fisher, "Limiting Nuclear Weapons at Sea," in Barry M. Blechman, William J. Durch, W. Phillip Ellis, Cathleen S. Fisher, and Mary C. Fitzgerald, eds., *The U.S. Stake in Naval Arms Control* (Washington, D.C.: Henry L. Stimson Center, 1990), pp. 353–393; J.R. Hill, "Tactical Nuclear Weapons at Sea," in *Arms Control at Sea* (London: Routledge, 1990), pp. 107–132; and Valerie Thomas, "Reducing Tactical Naval Nuclear Weapons," in Eric H. Arnett, ed., *Science and International Security: Responding to a Changing World* (Washington, D.C.: American Association for the Advancement of Science, 1990), pp. 391–409.

[16]Michael R. Gordon, "Gorbachev Said to Seek End to Naval Nuclear Weapons," *New York Times*, December 6, 1989, p. A16. Although it was initially unclear whether or not this proposal extended to submarines, Soviet Col. Gen. Chervov subsequently stated that the offer applied to both surface ships and submarines. R. Jeffrey Smith, "Soviets May Shift on Multiple Warheads," *Washington Post*, January 21, 1989, p. A11.

[17]Patrick E. Tyler, "Soviets Insist on Sea Talks," *Washington Post*, May 9, 1990, p. A16.

[18]This resistance applied to measures that attempted to go beyond avoiding or minimizing accidents or incidents at sea. See Steven E. Miller, "Naval Arms Control and Northern Europe: Constraints and Prospects," in Sverre Lodgaard, ed., *Naval Arms Control* (London: Sage Publications, 1990), pp. 84–117. The U.S. Government position opposing arms control for naval NSNF was laid out in U.S. Department of Defense, *Report on Naval Arms Control*, submitted to the Senate Committee on Armed Services and the House Committee on Armed Services (Washington, D.C.: U.S. Department of Defense, April, 1991).

cern that naval nuclear arms control would be only the first step down a "slippery slope" leading to limits on U.S. conventional naval forces, and the belief that naval arms control agreements could not be adequately verified.

However, in the late 1980s and early 1990s, there were increasing signs of cracks in the previously monolithic U.S. opposition to naval nuclear arms control. In 1988, Paul Nitze, special advisor to the president and secretary of state on arms control matters, suggested that the United States propose banning all nonstrategic nuclear weapons deployed at sea.[19] In 1990, shortly after retiring as the chairman of the Joint Chiefs of Staff, Adm. William J. Crowe, Jr. suggested that the United States should consider negotiating the elimination of tactical naval nuclear weapons.[20] Also in 1990, Chief of Naval Operations Adm. Carlisle Trost, responding to Akhromeyev's testimony before the Senate Armed Services Committee, told the Committee that if Soviet compliance could be assured, then it could be in the U.S. interest to enter into negotiations to ban nuclear weapons that threatened ships on either side.[21] Further, the Bush administration was coming under increasing pressure from Congress, allied countries, and other sources to consider entering into naval arms control discussions. Thus by mid-1991, while negotiations on naval NSNF did not seem imminent, the prospects for negotiated reductions in naval nuclear weapons appeared to be improving.

GROWING CONCERNS OVER THE SECURITY OF SOVIET NUCLEAR WEAPONS

By mid-1991, concern about the safety and security of Soviet nuclear weapons, both strategic and nonstrategic, was increasing with the growing turmoil in the former Soviet Union. This concern became a key factor in stimulating further nuclear arms reductions.

The Soviet Union, like the United States, has gone to great lengths to assure that its nuclear weapons are under firm central control.[22] All Soviet

---

[19]Michael R. Gordon, "U.S. Aide Offers Plan to Cut Arms at Sea," *New York Times*, April 6, 1988, p. A3.

[20]R. Jeffrey Smith, "Crowe Suggests a New Approach on Naval Nuclear Arms Cuts," *Washington Post*, January 8, 1990, p. A1.

[21]Patrick E. Tyler, "Top Admiral Sees Talks on Sea Arms Possible," *Washington Post*, May 12, 1990, p. A12.

[22]Bruce Blair, "Prepared Statement to Defense Policy Panel of the Committee on Armed Services, U.S. House of Representatives," July 31, 1991; Edward L. Warner III, "Prepared Statement to Defense Policy Panel of the Committee on Armed Services, U.S. House of Representatives," July 31, 1991; Bruce G. Blair and Henry W. Kendall, "Accidental Nuclear War," *Scientific American*, Vol. 263, No. 6 (December, 1990), pp. 53–58; David Holloway and Condoleeza Rice, "The Evolution of Soviet Forces, Strategy, and Command," in Kurt Gottfried and Bruce G. Blair, eds., *Crisis Stability and Nuclear War* (New York: Oxford Univer-

nuclear weapons are heavily guarded, and all strategic missiles, as well as many other Soviet nuclear weapons are equipped with devices that prevent their use unless special codes, held only by the highest Soviet authorities, are entered. Nevertheless, even before the failed coup of August 1991, the security of Soviet nuclear weapons was a growing worry to many in the United States given the uncertain future of the Soviet central government.[23]

Nonstrategic weapons raised particularly disturbing security problems for several reasons. In addition to being widely distributed geographically, their small size and mobility make them more vulnerable to seizure.[24] Furthermore, some of them, particularly naval weapons and older land- and air-based weapons, might not be equipped with devices to prevent their unauthorized use. Moreover, NSNF would be the most likely type of nuclear weapon to be used in a Soviet civil war. Strategic weapons raised different but no less serious concerns, because their large size and high visibility makes them more difficult than nonstrategic weapons to withdraw from troubled areas and because they have the range to reach the United States.

Prior to 1990–1991, nuclear weapons were believed to have been widely distributed throughout the Soviet republics.[25] Although the bulk of Soviet nuclear weapons were in Russia, large numbers (a thousand or more in each republic) were also deployed in the Ukraine, Kazakhstan, and Byelorussia, with smaller numbers in the other republics. Ethnic strife and the possibility of Soviet disintegration raised concerns that some Soviet nuclear weapons could find their way into the hands of extremists or terrorists. Reports of an attack in January 1990 on a Soviet military base near Baku, in Azerbaijan, at which nuclear weapons were stored seemed to confirm the validity of these fears.[26]

In 1990 and 1991, there were reports that the Soviets were pulling

---

sity Press, 1988), pp. 126–158; and Stephen M. Meyer, "Soviet Nuclear Operations," in Ashton B. Carter, John D. Steinbruner, and Charles A. Zraket, eds., *Managing Nuclear Operations* (Washington, D.C.: Brookings Institution, 1987).

[23]David C. Morrison, "Loose Soviet Nukes: A Mountain or a Molehill?" *Arms Control Today*, Vol. 21, No. 3 (April 1991), pp. 15–19. For a comprehensive discussion of the nuclear weapons-related dangers posed by the breakup of the Soviet Union, as well as suggestions for reducing these dangers, see Kurt M. Campbell, Ashton B. Carter, Steven E. Miller, and Charles A. Zraket, *Soviet Nuclear Fission: Control of the Nuclear Arsenal in a Disintegrating Soviet Union*, CSIA Studies in International Security No. 1 (Cambridge, Mass.: Center for Science and International Affairs, Harvard University, November 1991).

[24]See John J. Fialka, "The Risk Now Posed By the Soviet 'Nukes' Is One of Management," *Wall Street Journal*, November 20, p. 1, for a description of some of the problems that the Soviets may be facing in safely storing and transporting their NSNF.

[25]For an estimate of the number of nuclear weapons in each republic, see Robert S. Norris and William N. Arkin, "Nuclear Notebook: Where the Weapons Are," *Bulletin of the Atomic Scientists*, Vol. 47, No. 9 (November, 1991), pp. 48–49.

[26]See Warner, *op. cit.*, p. 3, and Morrison, *op. cit.*, p. 15.

back nonstrategic nuclear weapons from some republics to the Russian Republic and taking other steps to enhance their control over these weapons,[27] and, according to one assessment, most of the nonstrategic weapons had been withdrawn to the Russian Republic by early 1991.[28] However, the Soviet government initially denied most of these reports,[29] and the true extent of Soviet NSNF deployments remains unclear. At a minimum, strategic nuclear weapons are still deployed outside Russia in Belarus, Kazakhstan, and Ukraine, and nonstrategic weapons may remain in these republics as well as in a number of others.[30]

The failed coup converted growing concern over the security of Soviet nuclear weapons into a much more immediate problem. Not only was it reported that the coup leaders had seized the Soviet Union's nuclear authorization codes from President Gorbachev,[31] but the coup attempt greatly accelerated the breakup of the Soviet Union. Russian President Boris Yeltsin stated his intention to control nuclear weapons on Russian territory[32] and the president of Kazakhstan said that his republic would take control of nuclear weapons on its territory.[33] Ukraine, after issuing a declaration of independence, called for the removal of all nuclear weapons from its territory, but insisted that any weapons presently on Ukrainian territory be destroyed there.[34] Although in the months following the

---

[27]R. Jeffrey Smith, "Soviets Remove Some Nuclear Arms from Areas Marked by Ethnic Strife," *Washington Post*, June 23, 1990, p. A24; Michael Wines, "Soviets Are Said to Pull Nuclear Arms from Some Restive Regions," *New York Times*, June 23, 1990, p. A43; George Lardner, Jr., "Soviets Are Concerned About Security of Their Nuclear Arms, Webster Says," *Washington Post*, May 31, 1991, p. A23.

[28]Blair, "Prepared Testimony," p. 5.

[29]"Moscow Denies It Is Moving Nuclear Arms from Regions," *New York Times*, June 27, 1990, p. A7; "Soviets Deny Having Moved Nuclear Arms," *Washington Post*, October 4, 1990, p. A43.

[30]Shortly after the coup attempt, Petr Deynekin, the commander in chief of the Soviet Air Force, said that there were no nuclear weapons in troubled regions of the USSR. He said: "There are none in the Baltic republics, the Transcaucasus, or along the Western borders. They are only deep inside the country." "Air Force Chief on Military, Nuclear Weapons," *Moscow Rossiyskaya Gazeta*, September 2, 1991, p. 2 (in Russian, translation in U.S. Foreign Broadcast Information Service, *Daily Report–Soviet Union*, September 6, 1991, pp. 61–62).

[31]Douglas Waller, "Nuclear Codes and the Coup: Weapons in the Wrong Hands?" *Newsweek*, September 2, 1991, p. 57; "Where Was the Black Box," *Time*, September 2, 1991, p. 43. However, possession of these codes did not necessarily mean that the coup plotters would have been able to launch Soviet nuclear weapons. For a detailed discussion of the possible roles that the Soviet president's codes might play in preventing or ordering the use of Soviet nuclear weapons, see Campbell, Carter, Miller, and Zraket, *op. cit.*, pp. 5–11.

[32]"Yeltsin Seeks Control of Nuclear Arms," *Washington Times*, September 4, 1991, p. 1.

[33]Clinton O'Brien, "Nukes Ruled Out for Kazakhstan," *Washington Times*, September 17, 1991, p. B5. The title of this article refers to statements by Soviet officials that they would not allow Kazakhstan to gain control of these weapons.

[34]Peter Mass, "Ukrainian Leader Asks Removal of Soviets' Nuclear Weapons," *Washington Post*, August 30, 1991, p. A29; Peter Mass, "Ukraine, Russia Debate Nuclear, Border Issues,"

coup attempt the republics seemed to accept that central control of the nuclear weapons on their territory was necessary, the strength of both antinuclear sentiment and nationalism in the republics makes the future evolution of their policies toward these weapons impossible to predict with certainty. Even in cases where republics ultimately renounce nuclear weapons, they may be unwilling simply to give them to Russia.

The postcoup turbulence led President Gorbachev's science advisor, Yevgeny Velikov, to call for the international community to participate in controlling the Soviet nuclear arsenal.[35] More importantly, it prompted the U.S. government to intensify its search for ways to help assure continuing control of Soviet nuclear weapons and to seek talks with the Soviet government on this issue.[36] Indeed, one of the primary objectives of President Bush's announcement of unilateral nuclear arms reductions (discussed in the following) was to encourage the Soviets to improve the control and security of their nuclear weapons.[37] Besides arms reductions, President Bush also proposed discussions and technical cooperation with the Soviets on "safe and environmentally responsible storage, transportation, dismantling, and destruction of nuclear warheads," on "existing arrangements for the physical security and safety of nuclear weapons and how these might be enhanced," and on "nuclear command and control arrangements, and how these might be improved to provide more protection against the unauthorized or accidental use of nuclear weapons."[38]

THE BUSH AND GORBACHEV INITIATIVES OF SEPTEMBER–OCTOBER 1991

President Bush's surprise announcement of September 27, 1991, was a dramatic turning point for arms control and for nonstrategic arms control in particular.[39] In a few minutes, he pledged NSNF reductions that had

---

Washington Post, August 29, 1991, p. A39; Robert Seely, "Ukraine to Use Nuclear Stock as Bargaining Chip," *London Times*, September 16, 1991, p. 10; "Ukraine Asks Joint Control of Arsenal," *Boston Globe*, October 24, 1991, p. 4.

[35]Fred Hiatt, "Soviet Official Questions Nuclear Arsenal's Safety," *Washington Post*, August 28, 1991, p. A1.

[36]William Beecher, "U.S. to Seek Talks on Control of Soviet Nuclear Arms," *Minneapolis Star-Tribune*, September 9, 1991, p. 7; Barton Gellman, "General Withdrew Missiles to Shelters During Coup," *Washington Post*, August 28, 1991, p. A18.

[37]Michael R. Gordon, "The Nuclear Specter: Bush Took Steps After Soviet Coup Stirred Concern Over Control of Atomic Stockpile," *New York Times*, September 28, 1991, p. 1; Michael Kranish, "Bush Proposes Steep Arms Cuts," *Boston Globe*, September 28, 1991, p. 1.

[38]"Remarks by President Bush on Reducing U.S. and Soviet Nuclear Weapons," *New York Times*, September 28, 1991, p. A4.

[39]For the prepared text of President Bush's speech, see "Remarks by President Bush," *op. cit.* More details on the proposals were given at a briefing by Defense Secretary Dick Cheney

previously been expected to require years of complex negotiations. All U.S. nuclear artillery shells and short-range nuclear missile warheads would be withdrawn and destroyed. All U.S. naval nonstrategic weapons, including Tomahawk cruise missiles, would be withdrawn from the ships, submarines, and airplanes on which they were deployed and placed in storage, and all nuclear depth bombs would be destroyed. Once implemented, these reductions would leave the United States with only one type of deployed nonstrategic nuclear weapon: air-delivered bombs based in the United States, Western Europe, and South Korea. These reductions would be undertaken unilaterally, although Bush in return called on the Soviets "to destroy their entire inventory of ground-launched theater nuclear weapons: not only their nuclear artillery, and nuclear warheads for short-range ballistic missiles, but also the theater systems the U.S. no longer has—systems like nuclear warheads for air-defense missiles, and nuclear land mines."[40] However, it was also clear that the weapons in storage could be redeployed if the former Soviet Union failed to reciprocate.

The Soviet Union quickly responded to Bush's challenge with measures and proposals that matched and, in some cases, went beyond the U.S. initiative. On October 5, 1991, President Gorbachev announced that the Soviet Union would also destroy all of its nuclear artillery shells and nuclear warheads for short-range missiles, and that all Soviet naval nonstrategic weapons, including those belonging to naval aviation, would be withdrawn and either placed in storage or destroyed.[41] In addition, he pledged that all Soviet nuclear mines would be destroyed and that the nuclear warheads on Soviet antiaircraft missiles would be removed and placed in storage. Gorbachev also responded positively to Bush's proposals for discussions on storage, transportation, and safety of nuclear weapons and announced that, to achieve improved control, all strategic nuclear weapons, including those for strategic defense, would be placed under a single operational command. In a further move to increase the security of Soviet nuclear weapons, he also announced that all nuclear weapons for strategic bombers would be placed in storage and rail-mobile ICBMs would be confined to their garrisons.

Once implemented, these Soviet moves would enhance the security of Soviet nonstrategic nuclear weapons by collecting them into a relatively small number of presumably well-guarded central locations. In addition, the proposed changes could serve as a basis for bringing most or all of Soviet NSNF back to the Russian Republic, if this had not already occurred.

---

and Chairman of the Joint Chiefs of Staff Colin Powell, "Excerpts from Briefing at Pentagon: 'It Will Make the World a Safer Place'," *New York Times*, September 29, 1991, p. A10.

[40]"Remarks by President Bush," *op. cit.*

[41]For an excerpt of Gorbachev's statement, see "Gorbachev's Remarks on Nuclear Arms Cuts," *New York Times*, October 6, 1991, p. A12.

Subsequently, NATO announced that it would cut its NSNF arsenal in Europe by 80 percent, from 3,500 to about 700.[42] Most of the reduced weapons were the nuclear artillery shells and short-range missiles whose elimination had previously been announced by President Bush; however, half of the roughly 1,400 nuclear bombs, including 100–200 British ones, for tactical aircraft would now also be withdrawn. Shortly thereafter, the United States also announced that it would withdraw its remaining nuclear weapons from South Korea.[43]

The full implementation of the reductions and withdrawals announced in September and October 1991, together with previous unilateral withdrawals and the INF Treaty, will dramatically reduce U.S. and Soviet deployments and stockpiles of nonstrategic nuclear weapons. Table 4.1 on page 116 illustrates the scope of these reductions. They will leave the United States with only one type of nonstrategic nuclear weapon deployed: bombs for land-based tactical aircraft. Even these will be reduced in number and will be deployed only in the United States and Western Europe. Of the other nonstrategic weapons, long-range nuclear SLCMs and naval strike bombs will be in storage; all others will have been withdrawn for destruction. Thus U.S. NSNF will have fallen from over 10,000 weapons in 1987 to about 3,000 at the end of 1991, many of which are in storage.

Further, Bush's speech in effect terminated the only U.S. nonstrategic nuclear weapon then under development, the TASM. While weapons for tactical aircraft were not directly affected by Bush's announcement, and the TASM was not explicitly mentioned, the TASM program was effectively ended by the announced cancellation of Short-Range Attack Missile II on which the design of the TASM was to be based. However, the Pentagon emphasized that the SRAM-II cancellation was primarily due to technical difficulties in its development program and that the United States has not ruled out developing a TASM based on a new design.[44]

Soviet NSNF reductions will be similar in scope, although details of how many weapons will be stored rather than destroyed are unclear. Further, Gorbachev proposed that the United States and former Soviet Union agree to destroy all naval NSNF, including those in storage, and to place in storage all nuclear weapons for land-based tactical aircraft. If this proposal were adopted, no U.S. or Soviet nonstrategic nuclear weapons would be deployed, although several thousand would remain in storage.

---

[42]Jonathan Kauffman, "NATO to Cut Nuclear Arms 80%," *Boston Globe*, October 18, 1991, p. 1; R. Jeffrey Smith, "NATO Approves 50% Cut in Tactical A-Bombs," *Washington Post*, October 18, 1991, p. A28.

[43]Don Oberdorfer, "U.S. Decides to Withdraw A-Weapons from S. Korea," *Washington Post*, October 19, 1991, p. A1; David E. Rosenbaum, "U.S. to Pull A-Bombs from South Korea," *New York Times*, October 20, 1991, p. A3.

[44]"SRAM II Canceled for Cause; Doesn't End TASM Mission, Option Cited," *Aerospace Daily*, October 2, 1991, p. 13.

Table 4.1   NONSTRATEGIC NUCLEAR WEAPONS, 1987–1991

United States

Intermediate-range ballistic missiles	Eliminated by INF Treaty
Ground-launched cruise missiles	Eliminated by INF Treaty
Demolition munitions/land mines	Eliminated unilaterally
Naval surface-to-air missiles	Eliminated unilaterally
Antisubmarine missiles/rockets	Eliminated unilaterally
Artillery shells	To be destroyed
Short-range missiles	To be destroyed
Depth bombs	To be destroyed
Long-range SLCMs	Stored
Naval bombs	Stored
Land-based aircraft bombs	Withdrawn from Korea, some withdrawn from Europe

Soviet Union

Intermediate-range ballistic missiles	Eliminated by INF Treaty
Ground-launched cruise missiles	Eliminated by INF Treaty
Demolition munitions/land mines	To be destroyed
Artillery shells	To be destroyed
Short-range missiles	To be destroyed
Land-based surface-to-air missiles	Stored, ½ of warheads to be destroyed
Naval surface-to-air missiles	Stored[a]
Antisubmarine missiles/rockets	Stored[a]
Naval bombs/depth bombs	Stored[a]
Torpedoes	Stored[a]
Short-range SLCMs	Stored[a]
Ship-attack ALCMs	Stored[a]
Long-range SLCMs	Stored[a]
Sea mines	Stored (if still deployed)[a]
Land-based aircraft bombs	Unaffected, storage proposed

[a]1/3 of above Soviet naval weapons will be destroyed.

DOES THE UNITED STATES STILL NEED NSNF?

The changes in the political environment and in technology that led to the dramatic reductions just discussed raise the question of whether or not the United States still needs any NSNF at all, and if so, what type of force is required.

In announcing the unilateral U.S. reductions, President Bush stressed that U.S. air-delivered nuclear weapons would remain in Europe, calling them "essential to NATO's security."[45] However, with the disappearance

---

[45]"Remarks by President Bush," *op. cit.*

of the Soviet military threat to Europe, there is no remaining military need for the United States to deploy nuclear weapons in Europe. On the other hand, as described in Chapter 2, there are still some residual political rationales for continued deployment: to provide reassurance of a continued U.S. commitment to Europe's defense, and to remove any justification for nonnuclear NATO nations to develop their own nuclear weapons. For these reasons, it may not be desirable to remove immediately all U.S. nuclear weapons from Europe. Ultimately, however, their complete withdrawal from Europe is both feasible and desirable, with the pace of this withdrawal to be determined in consultation with the European allies.

As the Soviet threat has faded, however, regional nuclear contingencies have received increasing attention. The war against Iraq and postwar revelations about the extent of its nuclear program focused attention on the possibility that the United States might someday find its forces in some part of the world under attack by overwhelming conventional forces, chemical weapons, or even nuclear weapons. Although it is difficult to devise regional scenarios in which the use of NSNF is both militarily effective and likely to be in the long-term interests of the United States, concern about such scenarios is increasingly voiced and could become the primary rationale for retaining a force of nonstrategic nuclear weapons. More generally, although the traditional battlefield role of NSNF has been largely swept away, there may still be a need to be able to strike mobile military targets of the type that have been traditionally assigned to NSNF, for example, in support of the anti-power-projection targeting strategy outlined in Chapter 3.

Any assessment of future requirements for NSNF must take into account the fact that much of the distinction between strategic and nonstrategic forces has disappeared. The NSNF most distinct in character from strategic nuclear forces, the land-based and naval NSNF intended strictly for battlefield use, have been or soon will be withdrawn. The only nonstrategic nuclear weapons remaining deployed are bombs for tactical, land-based aircraft, and, at least in principle, U.S. strategic nuclear forces could perform any mission that these remaining NSNF might be assigned. Although this would require changes in the way the strategic bomber force is trained and operated,[46] such a change appears consistent with the direction the U.S. strategic bomber force is now taking. Under recently announced plans, greater emphasis will be placed on the use of U.S. strategic bombers for conventional missions.[47] Other U.S. strategic nuclear weapons, such as ballistic missiles or air-launched cruise missiles, could also be used against certain types of nonstrategic targets, primarily those at

---

[46]It might also require transferring lower yield weapons from the tactical to strategic forces.

[47]John D. Morrocco, "Shift in U.S. Military Strategy Calls for Increasing SAC's Conventional Role," *Aviation Week and Space Technology*, May 13, 1991, pp. 27–28; Melissa Healy, "Strategic Air Command Tries to Plot New Course," *Los Angeles Times*, June 24, 1991, p. 1. See Chapter 8 for more details on this issue.

fixed locations. In addition, U.S. strategic force and nuclear war planning are likely to place increasing emphasis on flexibility of forces and operations, which will enlarge the capability of the strategic forces to carry out heretofore nonstrategic missions.

Thus, practically speaking, whatever decisions may be made on the fate of the remaining U.S. nonstrategic nuclear weapons, the United States is certain to retain a formidable capability to launch nuclear attacks against any target, strategic or nonstrategic. The fundamental question is how these forces should be configured.

Currently deployed U.S. nonstrategic forces consist of dual-capable (conventional and nuclear) tactical aircraft. These forces could be retained in their present form, a separate "nuclear contingency force" of aircraft dedicated exclusively to nonstrategic nuclear missions could be formed, or the nonstrategic forces could be merged with the strategic forces (this option includes the possibility of eliminating all nonstrategic nuclear weapons). In evaluating these options in the following, it is assumed that naval weapons in storage have been eliminated.

Retaining the present force structure, where large numbers of tactical aircraft have a nuclear capability, seems excessive, particularly if U.S. air-delivered weapons are ultimately withdrawn from Europe, as we recommend. In essentially any conceivable scenario involving the use of NSNF, the number of weapons used and the number of aircraft likely to be required to deliver these weapons are quite small. In addition, retaining a large and diversified force of tactical nuclear-capable aircraft could complicate future arms control efforts involving these aircraft and/or strategic bombers. On the other hand, moving quickly toward a smaller force posture could be useful in encouraging the Soviets to take similar steps with their air-delivered nuclear forces, thereby enhancing the security of these forces.

A small "nuclear contingency force" of dedicated tactical aircraft for nonstrategic missions would be more appropriate in scale. Such a force would be uniquely capable of sending "signals" in a crisis and could employ specially trained personnel. Its structure and daily operations could be considerably different from those of the strategic bomber force, since it need not possess the same type of survivability against nuclear strikes directed at the United States. However, such a force would likely require the very same type of aircraft (stealthy penetrators, such as the F-117) that would be much in demand for the conventionally armed forces; this could be a serious drawback from a financial point of view. Further, establishing such a force could send the wrong message to potential proliferators about the military utility of nuclear weapons.

The third option would be to merge the nonstrategic and strategic forces. Such a result would practically be a *de facto* outcome of posture changes that seem sensible once the air-based NSNF are withdrawn from Europe; and such changes could begin even before such a withdrawal. In particular, it would be desirable to withdraw tactical nuclear bombs to a limited number of airbases and to restrict nuclear capability to a few types of highly capable attack aircraft, such as F-117s, F-15Es, or their successors. The resulting force would strongly resemble the strategic bomber force, with its new emphasis on conventional missions, differing, of course, in range and payload characteristics. Given this situation, the integration of these nuclear capabilities into a single organization would allow the most appropriate aircraft, whether formerly strategic or nonstrategic, to be selected for any given mission.[48]

The complete elimination of all NSNF is, in a sense, a subset of the case of merging the forces. However, even if all tactical aircraft were denuclearized, it would likely still be desirable to transfer some of their bombs to the strategic forces so as to maintain as wide a range of yields, particularly low ones, as possible. It might also be desirable to retain a nuclear capability in some of the more capable tactical aircraft to avoid straining the resources of the strategic bomber force or to retain any unique capabilities the tactical aircraft might provide.

An important and related issue is whether or not a new air-to-surface missile is needed. Although President Bush's initiative of September 27 effectively killed the TASM program, the possibility that a replacement could be developed was left open. In principle, the development of such a weapon, presumably in conjunction with a new and possibly identical missile for the strategic bomber force, could be desirable because it would enhance the capability of the bomber force to strike heavily defended targets. At present, however, there is no urgent need to restart the TASM program; U.S. bombers appear to have a more than adequate capability to penetrate defenses to deliver a nuclear weapon to any nonstrategic or strategic target. In the longer term, any decision on such a weapon should be based on an integrated assessment of the needs and capabilities of both strategic and nonstrategic nuclear forces to attack heavily defended targets and to penetrate deep into hostile airspace.

OBJECTIVES OF FUTURE NONSTRATEGIC ARMS CONTROL

The initiatives of September and October 1991 accomplished many of the goals that had been advanced by advocates of NSNF reductions. Nevertheless, as we shall argue, it would be in the best interests of both the

---

[48]In addition, relying on strategic forces for nonstrategic missions would have the advantage that such forces could carry out their missions while remaining securely based in the United States. While tactical aircraft could be forward deployed to theater airbases in a crisis (as could strategic bombers), such a step could potentially be destabilizing if only a relatively small number of airbases were available, since it might be viewed by a nuclear-armed adversary as providing an opportunity to eliminate the U.S. theater nuclear capability with an attack on these bases.

United States and former Soviet Union to seek further NSNF reductions. More specifically, both countries should seek to eliminate stored naval and air defense weapons and to significantly restructure their tactical nuclear air forces. Further, the opportunities that nonstrategic and strategic arms reductions provide to enhance the safety and security of the Soviet nuclear arsenal should be fully exploited. Finally, the United States and former Soviet Union should stop producing fissile material for nuclear weapons, eliminate from their weapons stockpile some or all of the fissile material from weapons being retired, and consider implementing a program of verified destruction of nuclear warheads. These recommendations are discussed in greater detail in the following.

Naval Weapons

The unilateral initiatives will leave the United States with about 1,300 stored naval nuclear weapons, and the former Soviet Union with an unknown, but probably similar or larger, number of weapons in storage. Prior to their withdrawal, these weapons provided the United States with little in the way of important military capabilities. At the same time, their deployment placed an operational burden on the navy, displaced more usable conventional weapons, raised problems with port visits, and increased the risk of accidents involving nuclear weapons (such as a collision or fire involving a nuclear-armed ship). Not only did pulling these weapons out of the fleet eliminate or greatly reduce these problems, but the reciprocal Soviet withdrawal removed the greatest military threat to the U.S. Navy. Assuming no crisis or other event leads to the redeployment of these weapons, they are likely to become increasingly irrelevant as they become obsolete and as both countries become acclimated to the idea of navies without nuclear weapons.

However, a number of reasons remain for going beyond storage to the destruction of these weapons, as called for by Gorbachev in his response to Bush's initiative, and to an agreement formalizing the prohibition of naval NSNF. Both sides may be concerned by the breakout potential these weapons provide the other side. This may be particularly true if reductions in strategic weapons proceed to levels well below those set by the START Treaty. The breakout threat posed by nuclear SLCMs is particularly important because, as mentioned in Chapter 5, redeployment of these weapons, particularly in a crisis situation, would raise serious concerns about nuclear surprise attack, since neither country has a warning system capable of detecting a small-scale SLCM attack.[49] In addition, the task of maintaining these weapons ready for redeployment in secure stor-

---

[49]George Lewis and Theodore Postol, "SLCMs—Ignored, the Stored," *Bulletin of the Atomic Scientists*, Vol. 47, No. 9 (November 1991), pp. 26–28; Theodore A. Postol, "Banning Nuclear SLCMs: It Would Be Nice If We Could," *International Security*, Vol. 13, No. 3 (Winter 1988/89), pp. 191–202.

age may be increasingly viewed as an unnecessary burden. Finally, both countries may be concerned that as nuclear proliferation proceeds, other countries may begin to deploy such weapons, possibly leading to their redeployment by the United States and former Soviet Union.

These considerations suggest that it would be in the best interests of both countries to move beyond withdrawal of naval nonstrategic weapons to their complete elimination. They should also encourage other countries with naval NSNF to eliminate theirs as well[50] and should seek to establish a general prohibition against all naval nonstrategic nuclear weapons.[51]

Air-Defense Weapons

Soviet nuclear air defense weapons are the other class of nuclear weapons that have been entirely withdrawn from deployment and placed in storage. The United States has no comparable weapons and should push the Soviets to eliminate these weapons as soon as possible. Such an action could be taken in return for U.S. agreement to Soviet proposals to eliminate stored naval weapons or to place in storage nuclear warheads for tactical aircraft. However, since these weapons could be used for strategic defense as well as for tactical purposes, it is possible that the Soviets would link their elimination to developments in the strategic offense or defense fields.

Air-Delivered Weapons

The unilateral initiatives will leave only one type of nonstrategic nuclear weapon deployed—bombs intended for delivery by tactical aircraft.[52] However, Gorbachev proposed that "on a reciprocal basis," these weapons also be removed from deployment and placed in storage.[53]

In the U.S. case, air-delivered weapons are now deployed only in the United States and Western Europe. At the time the initiatives were announced, U.S. nuclear weapons in Europe were kept in special bunkers at

---

[50]The only other nations known to deploy naval nuclear weapons (other than SLBMs) are Britain and France. Following the announcement that the United States would withdraw its naval NSNF, Britain announced that it would also do so.

[51]This raises potentially difficult issues involving submarine-launched ballistic missiles. For at least the near term, a ban on SLBMs is likely to be unacceptable to the United States and Soviet Union because these are the most survivable component of their strategic forces. Other countries may also wish to develop submarine-based nuclear forces because of their potential survivability, but may choose to do so with weapons that would be considered to be nonstrategic in the U.S. or Soviet navies, such as short-range missiles or even cruise missiles.

[52]In the Soviet case, some short-range missiles intended for delivery by tactical aircraft may also remain.

[53]"Gorbachev's Remarks on Nuclear Arms Cuts," *op. cit.*

airbases where the aircraft that would carry them were deployed.[54] As we have already discussed, it is desirable to withdraw these weapons from Europe, but at a pace set by alliance considerations. However, this would not necessarily preclude a quick acceptance of Gorbachev's offer, as these nuclear weapons could be withdrawn from operational airbases to a few central storage sites in Europe. Following Gorbachev's proposal, U.S. Secretary of Defense Dick Cheney said he saw some merit in such an approach.[55]

Such a withdrawal could contribute significantly to the security of both U.S. and Soviet nuclear weapons, would create a significant political barrier to their subsequent redeployment, and should be implemented as promptly as possible. However, it may also be desirable to adopt some additional measures, since simply storing the weapons does not affect the capabilities of the aircraft that are intended to deliver them. Both countries could, for example, agree to denuclearize a large portion of their tactical aircraft, leaving only a few types with nuclear-capabilities, and possibly to deploy the remaining nuclear-capable tactical aircraft at only a small number of known airbases. Aircraft to be denuclearized would have specialized nuclear circuitry and electronics removed, would not be used in nuclear-related training, and would not be operated out of bases where nuclear weapons were stored. Such a combined approach of nuclear bomb storage and aircraft denuclearization would be compatible with an eventual merger of the strategic and tactical forces.

Other Objectives

It is clear that one of the key objectives of U.S.-Soviet arms discussions, agreements, and cooperation should be to enhance the security and safety of all nuclear weapons, both deployed and stored. This is not a controversial objective. The question is how to go about achieving it, which is discussed in the next section, on implementation.

An additional, and somewhat related, question is the fate of eliminated nuclear warheads as well as the fissile plutonium and uranium they contain. The disposal of large numbers of nuclear weapons as a result of the unilateral initiatives, the START Treaty, previous agreements, and unilateral retirements not only raises safety and environmental concerns, but also the fundamental question of whether the fissile nuclear materials (plutonium and highly enriched uranium) they contain should be recycled for use in new nuclear weapons, permanently disposed of, or converted

---

[54]For many years, a number of NATO aircraft were designated as being on "quick-reaction alert." These aircraft were armed with nuclear weapons and kept ready to take off on short notice. This practice was reportedly discontinued in the late 1980s, and the nuclear weapons removed to the storage bunkers. R. Jeffrey Smith, "Cheney Open to Bomb Storage," *Washington Post*, October 16, 1991, p. 30.

[55]Smith, "Cheney Open to Bomb Storage."

to civilian use. At the same time, these unprecedented reductions, together with concerns about the ultimate fate of Soviet nuclear weapons and the troubled state of the U.S. nuclear weapons production complex, provide both an opportunity and an incentive to focus on the elimination of U.S. and Soviet nuclear warheads and on the destiny of their fissile materials.

The United States and the former Soviet Union should agree to halt production of fissile material for nuclear weapons and open all of their facilities, both military and civilian,[56] that could produce nuclear materials to inspection and safeguards.[57] Even before the unilateral initiatives, both countries had military stockpiles of plutonium and highly enriched uranium far in excess of the amounts required for their nuclear forces. The United States stopped producing highly enriched uranium for weapons in 1964, and plutonium production came to a halt in 1988 as a result of environmental and safety problems at the reactors where this production took place.[58] In early 1991, the U.S. Department of Energy (DOE) stated that no further production of plutonium or uranium for weapons was planned,[59] since more than enough fissile material could be obtained by recycling retired weapons. In 1990, the U.S. Congress directed the president to produce a study on verification issues associated with warhead

---

[56]The United States has already agreed to permit IAEA inspections and safeguards at its civilian nuclear facilities. However, at present the IAEA lacks the resources to monitor more than a small fraction of these facilities. The Soviets have also opened up some of their civilian nuclear facilities to IAEA safeguards.

[57]Frank von Hippel, "Warhead and Fissile-material Declarations," in Frank von Hippel and Roald Sagdeev, eds., *Reversing the Arms Race: How to Achieve and Verify Deep Reductions in the Nuclear Arsenals* (New York: Gordon and Breach, 1990), pp. 61–81. An excellent source on a fissile material cutoff, fissile material disposal, and warhead dismantlement is Federation of American Scientists, *Ending the Production of Fissile Materials for Weapons— Verifying the Dismantlement of Nuclear Warheads: The Technical Basis for Action* (Washington, D.C.: Federation of American Scientists, June 1991).

[58]For a brief description of the U.S. nuclear weapons production complex, see Thomas B. Cochran, William M. Arkin, and Robert S. Norris, "U.S. Nuclear Weapons Production: An Overview," *Bulletin of the Atomic Scientists*, Vol. 44, No. 1 (January/February 1988), pp. 12–16. For recent discussions of some of the problems facing the U.S. nuclear weapons production complex, see David Albright, Peter Gray, and Tom Zamora, "A Smaller, Safer Weapons Complex Through Arms Reductions," *Bulletin of the Atomic Scientists*, Vol. 47, No. 6 (July/August 1991), pp. 3–10; Allan Krass, *The Future of the U.S. Nuclear Weapons Complex* (Cambridge, Mass.: Union of Concerned Scientists, May 1991); Paul Leventhal, Milton Hoenig, and Deborah J. Holland, "Crisis in the U.S. Nuclear Weapons Infrastructure," in Eric H. Arnett, ed., *Science and International Security: Responding to a Changing World* (Washington, D.C.: American Association for the Advancement of Science, 1990), pp. 433–460; and U.S. Office of Technology Assessment, *Complex Cleanup: The Environmental Legacy of Nuclear Weapons Production* (Washington, D.C.: U.S. Office of Technology Assessment, February, 1991).

[59]This conclusion was stated in U.S. Department of Energy, *Nuclear Weapons Complex Reconfiguration Study*, DOE/DP-0083, January, 1991.

dismantlement, disposal of fissile material from dismantled weapons, and a ban on production of fissile material for weapons.[60]

The Soviet Union reportedly stopped producing highly enriched uranium for weapons in 1989, has shut down 7 of its 13 plutonium-producing reactors, and plans to shut down the rest by the year 2000.[61] It is likely facing environmental and safety problems with its nuclear weapons complex that are even more severe than those that led to the shutdown of many U.S. facilities.[62] Soviet officials, including President Gorbachev, called for a verifiable ban on fissile material production in recent years.[63] Gorbachev repeated this theme in his October 1991 initiative when he stated, "We also want to agree with the United States on a controllable cessation of the production of all fissionable materials which are used for the manufacture of weapons."[64]

Beyond stopping production of fissile material for weapons, the two countries should further agree that some or all of the fissile material from the weapons eliminated by the unilateral initiatives and other recent actions should either be converted to civilian use or otherwise permanently disposed of, or at a minimum, placed in secured, monitored storage. Further, they should consider destroying some or all of the warheads themselves through a bilateral, verifiable process.

These steps, taken together, would provide a number of significant benefits. They would formalize the closure of fissile material production sites that has occurred in the United States, and avoid the tremendous and unnecessary financial costs involved in reopening or replacing these facilities. They would also impose a significant barrier to U.S. and Soviet nuclear forces ever again being built up to their former levels. The verified elimination of nuclear warheads would ease concerns that large numbers of cores from eliminated weapons, the "pits" that contain the fissile materials, were being recycled into new weapons or stockpiled for possible future use in new weapons. In addition, implementing these measures

---

[60]An unclassified summary of this report was released in July 1991. The report discusses some the issues that would be involved in ending production of fissile material, verifying the dismantlement of nuclear warheads, and disposing of fissile materials, but does not offer an opinion on whether any of these would be in the U.S. interest. *Report to Congress: Verification of Nuclear Warhead Dismantlement and Special Nuclear Material Controls, Executive Summary*, July 1991.

For a discussion of previous congressional action on ending the production of fissile material, see Warren H. Donnelly, *Proposals for Ending U.S. and Soviet Production of Fissile Materials for Nuclear Weapons* (Washington, D.C.: U.S. Congressional Research Service, October 26, 1990).

[61]Federation of American Scientists, *op. cit.*, p. 13.

[62]See Thomas R. Cochran and Robert S. Norris, "A First Look at the Soviet Bomb Complex," *Bulletin of the Atomic Scientists*, Vol. 47, No. 4 (May 1991), pp. 25–31.

[63]Donnelly, *op. cit.*, p. 4.

[64]"Gorbachev's Remarks on Nuclear Arms Cuts," *op. cit.*

could provide important opportunities to enhance the security of Soviet nuclear weapons and to minimize the impact of the Soviet Union's disintegration on nuclear proliferation. Finally, these steps could significantly strengthen the international nonproliferation regime and, in particular, would be an important step toward placing all nuclear production facilities worldwide under safeguards.

IMPLEMENTATION ISSUES

Many of the most important questions about the measures discussed in this chapter are concerned primarily with how they should be implemented. Indeed, for some issues, such as the security of Soviet nuclear weapons, it is difficult to distinguish between the measures themselves and their implementation. In this section, we consider issues related to putting the objectives laid out earlier in this chapter into practice. We begin with a discussion of the possible role of different types of agreements and verification regimes in future agreements on NSNF. Next we discuss the implementation and monitoring of the Bush and Gorbachev initiatives. We then consider how the further NSNF reductions suggested in this chapter could be realized. Finally, we consider approaches to enhancing the safety and security of nuclear weapons, Soviet ones in particular, as well as approaches to warhead dismantlement and fissile material control.

Form of Agreement and Verification

As the Bush and Gorbachev initiatives and subsequent developments dramatically illustrate, further progress on NSNF and other arms issues need not proceed by means of formal, negotiated agreements or treaties. Yet it is important to realize that these initiatives, although taken unilaterally, were nevertheless tacit agreements. While some aspects of the reductions announced by Bush were probably irreversible, others were implicitly conditioned on corresponding Soviet reductions, and Bush aides reportedly indicated that the initiative would be rescinded if the Soviets did not match it.[65] Similarly, while some of Gorbachev's announced reductions were clearly unilateral, others, such as the elimination of stored naval NSNF and placing nuclear bombs for tactical aircraft in storage, were offered as proposals for U.S.-Soviet discussion and agreement.

Future U.S.-Soviet agreements could take many forms, ranging from treaties, to less formal negotiated agreements that would be politically rather than legally binding, to coordinated unilateral actions. The changes in the international political environment and the precedents set by the Bush and Gorbachev initiatives suggest that less formal approaches will

---

[65]Kranish, *op. cit.*

take on much greater importance in the future. In particular, less formal agreements appear to offer tremendous advantages in terms of flexibility and speed of negotiation and implementation over formal treaties. (For example, they might avoid the potentially arduous process of obtaining the U.S. Senate's advice and consent to ratification that is required for formal treaties.[66])

A key aspect of less formal approaches is that they are compatible with reduced standards of verification. Prior to Bush's September 27, 1991 announcement, verification appeared to be the most important technical problem standing in the way of NSNF arms control.[67] NSNF pose a very different and in many ways much more difficult verification problem than strategic weapons. As a class, they tend to be small, easily concealable, mobile or readily transportable, and dual-capable. Thus most types of NSNF cannot be monitored with high precision and confidence by national technical means (NTM).[68]

It is, however, possible to design verification regimes that could provide a high degree of confidence that NSNF were not being deployed on a routine, continuing basis. Such regimes would almost certainly require inspections of naval vessels and facilities on land, such as airbases and other deployment sites as well as potential storage areas. The INF, CFE, and START treaties have established a considerable precedent for inspection of facilities on land, but the United States has been unwilling to accept shipboard inspections.[69] While such inspections might not need to be as intrusive as the small size of many nonstrategic nuclear weapons would suggest,[70] the overall cost and complexity of an NSNF inspection regime

---

[66]A more detailed discussion of different approaches to arms control can be found in Chapter 9.

[67]Although the INF Treaty established extensive and effective verification provisions, the missiles eliminated by this treaty were, from a verification point of view, more like strategic than nonstrategic weapons, both because they were large and distinctive enough for national technical means to contribute significantly to their monitoring and because it was possible to eliminate their conventional variants and launchers. These conditions do not apply to most of the remaining NSNF.

[68]National technical means is the set of national intelligence gathering systems, such as reconnaissance satellites, used to observe other countries, and in particular to monitor their military activities and compliance with arms control agreements.

[69]This unwillingness is rooted in the belief that such inspections would be unacceptably intrusive and could interfere with naval operations and with the navy's policy of neither confirming nor denying the existence of nuclear weapons on its ships.

[70]Many NSNF, particularly naval ones, have significant operational limitations that could ease their verification. For example, on submarines, which are often said to present the most difficult verification problems, it is not possible to move weapons such as torpedoes or SLCMs out of the torpedo room into other parts of the submarine. Thus inspectors need only inspect the torpedo room. For discussions of such considerations in the context of naval and SLCM arms control, see George N. Lewis, Sally K. Ride, and John S. Townsend, "Dispelling Myths about Verification of Sea-launched Cruise Missiles," *Science*, Vol. 246 (November 10, 1990),

could still be very large because hundreds of ships and land facilities would be involved.[71]

Detecting or preventing rapid breakouts poses a much more difficult problem, and a small-scale covert breakout might go entirely undetected.[72] Such a breakout could be accomplished using hidden stockpiles of weapons that were either never reported, covertly produced, or covertly converted from conventional variants. Unless conventional variants of nonstrategic nuclear weapons are eliminated, it is unclear if any practicable verification regime could provide a high degree of confidence that a covert breakout would not go undetected and it may be impossible to prevent an overt breakout on a short time scale.

This discussion suggests that attempting to limit and verify NSNF in the same way as strategic weapons may not only be inappropriate but may also produce immense, expensive, and intrusive verification regimes of only partial effectiveness. However, the changed political environment and the perceived lack of utility of many types of NSNF now make it possible to consider arms reduction agreements with greatly relaxed verification standards, or even with no verification at all.

Even before the announcement of Bush's initiative, the apparent U.S.-Soviet agreement on an unverified coordinated unilateral withdrawal of nuclear artillery shells from Europe and, to a lesser degree, the START side agreement on SLCMs, demonstrated that a relaxation of verification standards could work, at least in certain cases. The initiatives of September and October 1991 made the leap to full acceptance of such standards. Although some of the U.S. NSNF reductions were ultimately dependent on reciprocation by the Soviets, no cooperative verification of this reciprocation was required.[73] Of course, the extensive NTM capabilities of each country could provide a considerable measure of assurance that the announced reductions were taking place.

Thus, although strict verification may still be necessary for deep reductions in strategic forces, these developments may mark the end of verification's central role in nonstrategic arms control. Even so, verifica-

---

pp. 765–770; John Parmentola, "Using Shipboard Inspections to Monitor Limits on SLCMs," *Science and Global Security*, Vol. 1, Nos. 3–4 (1990), pp. 335–338; and Valerie Thomas, "Verification of Limits on Long-range Nuclear SLCMs," *Science and Global Security*, Vol 1., Nos. 1–2 (1989), pp. 27–57.

[71]According to one estimate, U.S. verification of and compliance with the START Treaty will involve one-time costs of $410 to $1,830 million and continuing annual costs of $100 to $390 million. U.S. Congressional Budget Office, *U.S. Costs of Verification and Compliance under Pending Arms Treaties* (Washington, D.C.: U.S. Congressional Budget Office, September 1990).

[72]A breakout is a large-scale deployment, usually on a short time scale, of weapons or other systems in excess of agreed limits.

[73]Michael R. Gordon, "A New Era: Trust Without Verifying," *New York Times*, September 29, 1991, p. A12.

tion may still play a useful, if reduced, role in some of the measures discussed in this chapter, for example, in efforts to assure the safety and security of Soviet nuclear weapons. This role will be discussed as we consider the implementation of various measures.

Implementing and Monitoring the Initiatives

Some of the measures announced by Bush and Gorbachev, such as taking strategic bombers off alert, were implemented almost immediately, while others, such as the withdrawal of U.S. naval weapons, were expected to require about half a year,[74] while still others, such as the withdrawal of U.S. tactical ground-based weapons from Europe, are likely to require several years.[75] Thus it would be possible for the United States and the former Soviet Union to agree to monitor cooperatively some of these reductions, and discussions on this subject reportedly have been held.[76] Such cooperative monitoring is desirable if it can be accomplished without introducing delays into the reductions process. With one important exception, it is likely that any such monitoring will be relatively informal and provide less than airtight verification, and will therefore be useful primarily for confidence building. The exception, which will be discussed in more detail in the following, is verification measures to enhance the security of Soviet weapons and smooth the way for pulling them out of some of the republics.

It may be equally or more important to reach agreement on monitoring weapons once they have been withdrawn and placed in storage. This applies to both naval weapons and to Soviet land-based air-defense warheads. It could also apply to tactical air-delivered nuclear weapons if Gorbachev's proposal to place these in storage were accepted. Together these weapons and warheads could constitute a substantial breakout capability, at least in terms of numbers, and thus measures that provide assurance that the warheads remain stored may be useful. Such measures might include short-notice inspection of storage areas or weapons storage in secure areas that are then sealed and/or monitored electronically (which

---

[74]Naval weapons were removed almost immediately from ships at port in the United States. However, many ships were on extended overseas deployments, and would retain their nuclear weapons until they returned to the United States. R. Jeffrey Smith, "6th Fleet at Ease on A-Arms Loss," *Washington Post*, October 12, 1991, p. A40.

[75]A senior NATO official was cited as saying that the withdrawal of these weapons will probably be accomplished in less than two years, and that "the emphasis will be more on safety and security during that withdrawal process than on speed." Sally Jacobsen, "NATO Expects to Scrap Some Nuclear Arms in Two Years," *Washington Times*, October 9, 1991, p. 8.

[76]Michael Parks, "Leaders Approve Ways To Verify Arms Cutbacks," *Los Angeles Times*, October 30, 1991, p. 1.

could be done using procedures similar to those used by the International Atomic Energy Agency to monitor adherence to the Nuclear Non-Proliferation Treaty). However, as we have argued, rather than retain these weapons in such a stored state for an extended period, it would be better to seek their elimination.

One essential measure that should be implemented as quickly as possible is a mutual data exchange on the NSNF withdrawn, eliminated, or left deployed. This is particularly true from a U.S. point of view since the United States routinely releases much more information on its nuclear and other weapons programs than does the Soviet Union,[77] and it would generally be desirable to encourage an increasingly democratic Soviet Union to be more open with such information. Information exchanged should include the type, number, location, delivery platforms, and safety and security arrangements for all NSNF, whether stored or deployed. Such a data exchange would be extremely useful in assisting U.S. monitoring of the Soviet reductions, working toward cooperative verification measures, and providing a fuller understanding of the problems involved in assuring the safety and security of Soviet nuclear weapons.

Implementing Further NSNF Reductions

How should further NSNF reductions, such as the elimination of naval weapons and air-defense weapons recommended previously, be brought about? Since only the Soviets hold nuclear air defense weapons, the United States should press for their unilateral withdrawal and destruction. For the remaining naval NSNF, it would be simplest to remove and destroy these weapons on a mutual unilateral basis. While a rigorous and airtight verification regime would not likely be required in this case, it might nevertheless make sense to formalize their elimination in an agreement. Not only would such an agreement provide a stronger political barrier against the future reintroduction of U.S. and Soviet naval NSNF, but it could also serve as the basis for a multilateral agreement banning such weapons worldwide. For this last reason, a program of inspections or other verification measures aimed primarily at confidence-building could be useful in illuminating verification issues that might arise in such a global agreement.

If, as recommended here, air-deliverable NSNF were merged into the strategic forces, the most practicable approach would be to limit and verify these weapons in the next strategic arms agreement. Since future strategic agreements are likely to continue to require highly effective

---

[77]As an illustration, see Thomas Cochran and Christopher Paine, "Classes of Data About Nuclear Weapons and Nuclear-Weapon Materials Production that Have Been Declassified by the United States but Not by the Soviet Union," Appendix A of Federation of American Scientists, *op. cit.*

verification, these weapons could pose a difficult verification challenge. However, it would be no worse than that posed by existing bombs on strategic bombers, and at least the problem of distinguishing between strategic and nonstrategic bombs would be avoided.

In the interim, if Gorbachev's proposal to place air-deliverable tactical nuclear weapons in storage and/or if other measures, such as the denuclearization of some tactical aircraft, were agreed to, then an inspection regime at current and former deployment sites could be implemented. To provide very high assurance of compliance, a highly intrusive verification regime, perhaps involving "anywhere, anytime" inspections, would probably be required. However, given the financial costs involved and the marginal military utility of these weapons relative to remaining strategic weapons, neither country is likely to have much interest in such a complex and strict regime. Rather a program of inspections would be useful primarily as a confidence-building measure, as a tool for managing the security of Soviet nuclear weapons, or as an example for possible future global nuclear weapons limits. Whether such a regime of inspections would be necessary or desirable will depend on the future development of Soviet society and U.S.-Soviet relations.

Enhancing the Security and Safety of Soviet Nuclear Weapons

As discussed earlier in this chapter, it is in the interest of both the United States and the former Soviet Union to take steps to assure that Soviet nuclear weapons remain under firm central control and to limit the extent to which the Soviet Union's disintegration contributes to nuclear proliferation.

A central goal of U.S. policy should be that all Soviet nuclear weapons remain firmly under control of the central government and that any nuclear weapons outside the Russian republic should either be destroyed or withdrawn back to Russia. There are many ways in which the United States could contribute to this objective:

- The United States should work with the Soviet central government and the republics to bring about the rapid fulfillment of the Bush and Gorbachev initiatives.
- The United States and former Soviet Union should immediately commence and vigorously pursue the proposed discussions on cooperation on nuclear safety issues. Where appropriate, these discussions should include representatives of relevant republics. The United States should be prepared to extend immediate technical assistance to either the Soviet center or individual republics to help assure the security of nuclear weapons that are stored, deployed, or to be moved.

- As discussed earlier, the United States and former Soviet Union should agree to a comprehensive and immediate data exchange on weapons eliminated or withdrawn, as well as those remaining deployed. This exchange should involve not only information on numbers and locations of weapons, but also information on steps taken to ensure their security. Such an exchange would be extremely useful in providing a greater understanding of the Soviet weapons security problem and in formulating approaches to deal with it.

- The United States should strongly urge any republics that have achieved or are considering independence to renounce nuclear weapons and to commit themselves to either the prompt destruction or the removal, under U.S. or international observation, of all nuclear weapons on their territory. The United States, along with other nations, should also insist that any newly independent republic sign the Nuclear Non-Proliferation Treaty and accept full International Atomic Energy Agency safeguards over all its nuclear facilities. Agreement to these conditions should be a requirement for diplomatic recognition and economic or other forms of aid.[78]

- Individual republics may insist, as some already have, that any weapons on their territory must be destroyed on their territory rather than moved to Russia. This is of concern because it may unduly delay the removal or destruction of these weapons and because some of the individual republics may not have the technical or financial resources to eliminate the weapons on their soil safely. There are ways that the United States could help resolve this situation. It could negotiate an agreement with the republics and the Soviet central government (or with Russia) guaranteeing that the weapons would be removed to the Russian republic or some other site and destroyed under U.S. or international supervision.[79] Alternatively, the United States could provide technical and financial assistance in destroying the weapons within each republic, again under U.S. or international supervision.

- The United States could also consider negotiating an agreement with the Soviet government and with any relevant republics under which all nuclear weapon storage sites would be continuously moni-

---

[78]The United States in October 1991 had already warned Ukraine that it would not recognize its independence or provide aid if Ukraine attempted to assert control over Soviet weapons on its territory. Doyle McManus and Douglas Jehl, "Ukraine Has U.S. Nervous," *Philadelphia Inquirer*, October 27, 1991, p. 3; Doyle McManus and Michael Parks, "At Summit Discussions, It Will Be a Whole New Ballgame," *Los Angeles Times*, October 28, 1991, p. 4.

[79]It would not be necessary to return an entire weapon for destruction, only the warhead. For example, in the case of an ICBM, the missile itself could be destroyed at its deployment site, while the warhead would be removed to a different site for destruction.

tored or subject to joint or international inspections to assure continued compliance with the unilateral initiatives as well as the security of the weapons.[80] Such an agreement might require inspections on U.S. as well as Soviet territory.

- The United States should consider negotiating with the Soviets additional reductions beyond START aimed at eliminating those strategic weapons still outside of the Russian Republic. Gorbachev's unilateral announcement of a 1,000 warhead reduction below the START limit could be formalized into an agreement that would eliminate those weapons outside Russia in exchange for some further reduction in U.S. strategic forces. Such an agreement could contain provisions for the verified destruction of these weapons that might ease objections in the republics where they are now deployed.
- Finally, the United States needs to think through how it will respond if it ultimately proves impossible to avoid the emergence of several nuclear-armed republics. The United States could offer technical assistance in areas such as command and control and permissive action links to help ensure the security and safety of their nuclear weapons. However, this approach could be counterproductive if it were seen as encouraging or rewarding nuclear proliferation.[81]

The fate of existing Soviet nuclear weapons is, however, not the only concern raised by the breakup of the former Soviet Union. The collapse of central authority raises the prospect that some of the substantial nuclear expertise and infrastructure that resides in Russia and the other republics could end up contributing to nuclear proliferation in other countries or in newly independent republics. In light of this threat, U.S. pressure on newly independent republics to renounce nuclear weapons and accede to the Nuclear Non-Proliferation Treaty, and to other agreements such as the Missile Technology Control Regime, in exchange for recognition and aid is even more essential. The United States should also consider assisting the newly independent republics of the former USSR in developing and applying export controls on nuclear technologies.[82]

---

[80]This could be accomplished by electronically monitoring or sealing storage sites. Many of the techniques developed by the International Atomic Energy Agency could be applicable to this monitoring. Some of the IAEA monitoring techniques are described in G. Robert Keepin, "State-of-the-Art Technology for Measurement and Verification of Nuclear Materials," in Kosta Tsipis, David W. Hafemeister, and Penny Janeway, eds., *Arms Control Verification: The Technologies That Make It Possible* (Washington, D.C.: Pergamon-Brassey's, 1986), pp. 323–337.

[81]For a fuller discussion of possible U.S. responses to the emergence of nuclear-armed republics, see Campbell, Carter, Miller, and Zraket, *op. cit.*, pp. 107–116.

[82]Newly developing private enterprises that might export Soviet nuclear expertise and technology are a serious concern. William J. Broad, "A Soviet Company Offers Nuclear Blasts for Sale to Anyone with the Cash," *New York Times*, November 7, 1991, p. A18.

Warhead Elimination and Fissile Materials Control

The unilateral reductions announced by Bush and Gorbachev differ from previous nuclear arms reductions by calling for the destruction of not only weapons but also their warheads. Over 3,000 U.S. nonstrategic nuclear warheads are being eliminated as a result of these reductions; this number could grow substantially if those weapons put in storage were also eliminated. Further, many weapons have been or soon will be retired due to previous unilateral withdrawals and the INF and START treaties. If the reductions suggested in this book were implemented, the total number of U.S. nuclear warheads would fall from about 25,000 in mid-1987[83] to roughly 5,000, a decrease of about 20,000 warheads. This flood of retired nuclear weapons will severely stress existing warhead storage and dismantlement capabilities in both the United States and the former Soviet Union; at a minimum, the dismantlement of these weapons would take a number of years and new facilities might be required.

According to U.S. officials, U.S. warheads will be dismantled at the Pantex factory in Texas, which is the only U.S. facility for assembling or disassembling nuclear weapons.[84] The plutonium-containing "pits" or cores of these weapons will then be stored at Pantex and at military bases until a plan for their permanent disposal is developed, the selection of which is likely to take "a matter of years."[85] The long period that may be required for warhead dismantlement and disposal represents a particular point of vulnerability for Soviet nuclear weapons.[86] Thus it is important that the United States and the former Soviet Union promptly commence discussions and technical cooperation, as proposed by President Bush, on the "safe and environmentally responsible" dismantling and disposal of warheads.[87] These efforts should also be extended to include the disposal of the fissile materials contained in the warheads, as proposed by Gorbachev.

In the past, retired nuclear warheads were either put into storage or dismantled, and their fissile material was eventually recycled into new

---

[83]Robert S. Norris and William M. Arkin, "Nuclear Notebook—U.S. Nuclear Weapons Stockpile (June 1987)," *Bulletin of the Atomic Scientists*, Vol. 43, No. 5 (June 1987), p. 56.

[84]The U.S. nuclear weapons complex is able to produce, retire, or modify 3,500 to 4,000 warheads per year. Cochran, Arkin, and Norris, "U.S. Nuclear Weapons Production," p. 15. For a brief description of what occurs when a nuclear weapon is dismantled, see Joseph Albright, "U.S. Must Disarm 3,050 Bombs," *Atlanta Journal-Constitution*, October 6, 1991, p. 6.

[85]Thomas W. Lippman, "Disarmament's Fallout: 50 Tons of Plutonium May Require Disposal," *Washington Post*, October 18, 1991, p. A1; Earl Lane, "When Arms Go, Warheads Remain," *Long Island Newsday*, September 29, 1991, p. 19.

[86]According to a group of Soviet nuclear weapons experts, it may take up to ten years to collect and destroy the Soviet tactical nuclear weapons. Fialka, *op. cit.*

[87]"Remarks by President Bush," *op. cit.*

warheads. With rapidly shrinking U.S. and Soviet nuclear arsenals, only a small portion of the fissile material contained in retired weapons will be needed for new warheads. Thus these weapons reductions will free up a great deal of excess fissile material. As of the early 1980s, the U.S. nuclear arsenal was believed to contain about 100,000 kg of plutonium and 500,000 kg of highly enriched uranium.[88] According to one estimate, Bush's initiative and previous arms reductions will leave more than 42 tons of plutonium,[89] and likely several times this amount of highly enriched uranium, available for disposal. The amount of Soviet fissile material available for disposal is likely to be comparable.[90]

According to U.S. Defense Secretary Cheney, highly enriched uranium from eliminated U.S. weapons "would go into the stockpile and it would be available, for example, for navy use in their reactors," and that the plutonium would likely be processed into a safer, more stable form[91] that could be later retrieved and used in new warheads.[92] However, a variety of options also exist for disposing of fissile material in ways that would make it extremely difficult to reuse in new nuclear weapons.

Disposal of highly enriched uranium is relatively straightforward, since almost all U.S. and Soviet nuclear power reactors run on natural or low-enriched uranium. Thus the uranium from eliminated nuclear weapons could be diluted with natural or depleted uranium for use in commercial power reactors.[93]

Plutonium poses greater disposal problems. Not only is plutonium difficult to handle and extremely toxic, but neither the United States nor the former Soviet Union currently uses a significant amount of plutonium in civilian power reactors. Thus plutonium removed from weapons stockpiles would likely be difficult to dispose of permanently. However, weapons-grade plutonium can be mixed with highly radioactive waste to render it unusable for nuclear weapons.[94] This material can then be disposed of as if it were nuclear waste.

---

[88]Federation of American Scientists, *op. cit.*, p. 11.

[89]Estimate by James D. Werner, an environmental engineer with the Natural Resources Defense Council, cited in Lippman, *op. cit.*

[90]One estimate is that the current Soviet arsenal contains about 115–140 metric tons of plutonium, or roughly 15–40 percent more than the U.S. stockpile. Cochran and Norris, "A First Look," p. 31.

[91]In the metallic form used in nuclear warheads, plutonium can burn spontaneously if it comes into contact with air.

[92]Lane, *op. cit.*

[93]At current prices, the fuel value of the enriched uranium in the U.S. weapons stockpiles is about $12 billion. Federation of American Scientists, *op. cit.*, p. 35.

[94]The plutonium could, of course, be reextracted using essentially the same nuclear reprocessing technique used to produce it in the first place, but this would be a difficult and costly process, and would be vulnerable to detection if a fissile material production cutoff were imposed.

The problem of disposing of plutonium from nuclear weapons is closely related to that of disposing of plutonium produced in commercial power reactors and should be viewed in that context. U.S. civilian power reactors are currently accumulating 20,000 kg of plutonium, or about 20 percent of all the plutonium the United States has produced for weapons purposes, every year.[95] Neither the United States nor the former Soviet Union has yet determined how it will ultimately dispose of plutonium and other nuclear wastes. While no completely satisfactory scheme has been developed so far, the disposal of plutonium from civilian power reactors is a problem that will ultimately have to be solved, and any plutonium eliminated from weapons stockpiles could be disposed of in the same way. Until such methods are developed, the plutonium removed from weapons stockpiles should be placed in secured, safeguarded storage areas.

Given the large amounts of fissile materials in the present weapons stockpiles, it is unlikely that even a 50-percent cut in these stockpiles would significantly affect either country's ability to maintain its nuclear arsenal once START and the unilateral initiatives have been implemented.[96] If the reductions recommended in this book were implemented, much deeper cuts in fissile materials stocks would be possible. In the meantime, such a 50-percent reduction would be a large step toward more meaningful limits on fissile material and an unmistakable sign that the United States and the former Soviet Union were truly serious about permanently reducing their nuclear stockpiles. It is a reasonable first step that both countries should take. The reduced material could initially be securely and verifiably stored, but should ultimately be converted to civilian use or otherwise permanently disposed of.

Prior to such a reduction in fissile material stockpiles, it would be necessary to conduct a comprehensive data exchange on fissile material production facilities and stocks. This exchange should include not only data on present stocks and production facilities, but also production records. Such production data would be a valuable first step toward enabling each country to confirm the other's declarations.[97]

In order for reductions in fissile material stockpiles to be significant,

---

[95]Federation of American Scientists, *op. cit.*, p. 40.

[96]This is suggested by the fact that the U.S. nuclear arsenal at one time contained over 30,000 nuclear weapons, and START and the unilateral reductions will reduce it to slightly more than one third of that level. From another perspective, a 50-percent reduction would leave the United States with about 50,000 kg of plutonium. Assuming a force level of roughly 10,000 warheads after START and the unilateral reductions, this is roughly 50 kg of plutonium per weapon. However, even the first plutonium bomb, the one dropped on Nagasaki, contained only 6 kg of plutonium, and design improvements since then have greatly reduced the amount of plutonium required to produce a fission explosion. See von Hippel, "Warhead and Fissile Material Declarations," note 20 (p. 81).

[97]This process of using production records and other information to reconstruct fissile material stockpiles has been dubbed "nuclear archeology." Von Hippel, "Warhead and Fissile Material Declarations," p. 72.

they must be accompanied by an agreement to stop producing further fissile material for weapons. Thus the United States and the former Soviet Union should agree to shut down, and eventually dismantle, all of their facilities dedicated to the production of nuclear material for military purposes.[98] As previously discussed, the United States currently is neither producing any fissile material nor projecting any need to do so in the future. Since nuclear reactors produce a great deal of heat, the shutdown of production reactors would be easily verified using satellite-borne remote sensors.[99] However, on-site inspections of some types of facilities, such as those used to reprocess plutonium or to produce tritium or fuel for naval reactors, would likely be required. In addition, all civilian facilities capable of producing significant amounts of fissile material would be placed under safeguards. To avoid straining IAEA resources, these safeguards should initially be implemented on a bilateral basis, although with some IAEA participation.[100] Such an agreement would place the United

---

[98]There are two important possible exceptions that should be mentioned. Both U.S. and Soviet nuclear weapons contain small amounts of tritium, which is used to enhance the weapons' yields and is produced in nuclear reactors. Unlike fissile uranium or plutonium, which have half-lives of thousands or millions of years, the half-life of tritium is only 12.3 years, which means that it decays at a rate of 5.6 percent per year. Thus the supply of tritium in nuclear weapons must be periodically replenished if they are to produce their full yield. While the tritium removed from the many weapons being eliminated will be adequate to maintain the remaining weapons for a number of years, unless the number of nuclear weapons continues to decline steadily, at some point it will be necessary to produce more tritium. (According to one estimate, current tritium stockpiles could support an 8,000-warhead stockpile to the year 2008 and a 3,000-warhead stockpile to the year 2026. See Krass, *op. cit.*, p. 19). The amount of tritium needed, however, is small and could be produced at one or a few reactors. Inspections and other safeguards could be employed at tritium production sites to assure that they are not being used to produce fissile material for weapons. For a description of how tritium is produced and the role it plays in nuclear weapons, see David Albright and Theodore B. Taylor, "A Little Tritium Goes a Long Way," *Bulletin of the Atomic Scientists*, Vol. 46, No. 1 (January/February 1990), pp. 39–42.

The other exception that needs to be considered is the use of uranium in naval reactors. In the U.S. case, this uranium is even more highly enriched (97.3 percent) than the uranium used in nuclear weapons (roughly 94 percent). Thus some provision would have to be made, again under safeguards, to allow limited production of enriched uranium for naval reactors. The Non-Proliferation Treaty allows production of enriched fissile material for nonexplosive military uses.

[99]For a discussion of verification of a ban on fissile material production, see Federation of American Scientists, *op. cit.*, pp. 13–26; E.V. Weinstock and A. Fainberg, "Verifying a Fissile-Material Production Freeze in Declared Facilities, with Special Emphasis on Remote monitoring," in Tsipis, Hafemeister, and Janeway, *op. cit.*, pp. 309–322; Frank von Hippel and Barbara G. Levi, "Controlling Nuclear Weapons at the Source: Verification of a Cutoff in the Production of Plutonium and Highly-Enriched Uranium for Nuclear Weapons," in Tsipis, Hafemeister, and Janeway, *op. cit.*, pp. 338–388; and von Hippel, "Warhead and Fissile-Material Declarations," *op. cit.*

[100]It has been estimated that extending IAEA safeguards to all U.S. and Soviet reactors would approximately double the IAEA's workload. See von Hippel, "Warhead and Fissile Material Declarations," p. 64.

States and the former Soviet Union in a strong position to attempt to persuade those countries that have not signed the Nuclear Non-Proliferation Treaty to renounce production of fissile material for weapons and to accede to full IAEA safeguards on their nuclear facilities. This effort should be vigorously pursued.

The verified destruction of some or all of the reduced nuclear warheads would also be desirable, and could work synergistically with fissile material reductions. At a minimum, verified warhead elimination could ensure that intact plutonium-containing pits of reduced nuclear weapons would not be recycled into new weapons or stockpiled for future use. In the last few years, interest has grown in the United States in simply recycling intact pits into new nuclear weapons, and a successful underground nuclear test of such a recycled warhead has been conducted.[101] Unless the pits from eliminated weapons are destroyed, they may represent a potential capability to produce new nuclear weapons rapidly.

The process of warhead elimination not only raises environmental and safety issues, but also risks revealing possibly sensitive warhead design information. However, approaches for verifiably dismantling warheads without compromising weapon design details have been proposed,[102] and in the 1960s the United States conducted field tests on the verification of warhead dismantlement.[103]

For maximum effectiveness, consideration should be given to implementing a program of verified warhead destruction in conjunction with fissile material reductions to assure that warheads are destroyed and that their fissile material is not stockpiled. The most obvious approach would be to destroy the warheads verifiably, with the fissile material from each warhead being submitted for disposal. However, to be foolproof this approach would require moderately complex procedures.[104] A simpler approach would require that warheads be verifiably destroyed and that a fixed amount of stockpiled fissile material, corresponding roughly to the

---

[101]So far, all U.S. nuclear weapons have used pits individually designed for each different type of weapon. However, since the December 1989 shutdown of Rocky Flats, the only U.S. facility at which the plutonium-containing pits of nuclear weapons were assembled or disassembled, the United States has been unable to produce new nuclear weapons; this has already prevented the production of 450 planned W88 warheads for the Trident II missile. R. Jeffrey Smith, "U.S. Rushes to Reopen Nuclear Weapons Plant," *Washington Post*, May 11, 1991, p. A1; R. Jeffrey Smith, "Ultimate Recycling: Nuclear Warheads," *Science*, May 24, 1991, pp. 1656–1657; Robert S. Norris and William M. Arkin, "Beating Swords into Swords," *Bulletin of the Atomic Scientists*, November 1990, pp. 14–16.

[102]Theodore B. Taylor, "Verified Elimination of Nuclear Warheads," *Science and Global Security*, Vol. 1., Nos. 1–2 (1989), pp. 1–26.

[103]See Frank von Hippel, "The 1969 ACDA Study on Warhead Dismantlement," *Science and Global Security*, Vol. 2, No. 1 (1990), pp. 103–108.

[104]For example, it would probably be necessary to design procedures that could confirm that the objects being destroyed were real warheads without giving away warhead design information.

amount in the weapons eliminated, be submitted for disposal for each warhead eliminated.[105]

In the near term, fissile material reductions and verified warhead elimination could play a useful role in support of more traditional limits on nuclear delivery systems and efforts to limit nuclear proliferation. In the longer term, a combined approach of fissile material reductions and verified warhead eliminations might even prove to be useful in directly controlling numbers of nuclear weapons. It is currently unclear whether or not this approach could be applied with sufficient accuracy to be successful at the warhead levels proposed in this book, much less at lower levels. Such an approach would require much more detailed information about fissile material stocks (and possibly past production) and about the amounts of fissile material in deployed nuclear weapons than are likely to be immediately available and verifiable. However, implementing a program involving a fissile material production cutoff, fissile material stockpile reductions, and verified warhead destruction as we have outlined would provide much of the information needed for evaluating the long-term feasibility of such an approach.

CONCLUSIONS AND RECOMMENDATIONS

The end of the Cold War calls for sweeping changes in U.S. nonstrategic nuclear forces and policies. These changes should be based on the following recommendations.

- Nonstrategic nuclear weapons have been rendered largely obsolete by changes in technology and the global political situation. The United States and the former Soviet Union should now seek to eliminate most or all of these weapons.
- The Bush-Gorbachev initiatives of September–October 1991 were a breakthrough in efforts to limit NSNF. A particularly notable feature of these initiatives is that they did not require cooperative verification. These initiatives should be implemented as quickly as possible consistent with safety and security considerations.
- The United States should accept the Soviet proposal to destroy all naval NSNF. Further, the two countries should consider formalizing a ban on naval NSNF and urge other nations to subscribe to such an agreement.
- U.S. air-delivered weapons based in Western Europe should eventually be withdrawn to the United States. This withdrawal should occur on a time scale determined in consultation the United States' NATO allies.
- The United States and the former Soviet Union should agree, as

---

[105]Several approaches to destroying warheads and disposing of fissile material, including this one, are outlined in Federation of American Scientists, *op. cit.*, pp. 28–33.

proposed by former Soviet President Gorbachev, to withdraw all air-delivered NSNF to a small number of highly secure storage areas. At least on an interim basis, some of the U.S. storage sites could be in Western Europe. The two countries should also consider denuclearizing a large portion of their tactical air forces. The United States should ultimately consider merging its remaining air-delivered weapons and nuclear-capable aircraft with its strategic bomber force to form a single integrated force.

- Arms control efforts for any remaining tactical air-delivered nuclear weapons should eventually be combined with those for the strategic forces.
- Enhancing the safety and security of Soviet nuclear weapons and minimizing the impact of the breakup of the former Soviet Union on nuclear proliferation should be central objectives of U.S. national security policy. There are many steps the United States could take to help reduce the nuclear dangers inherent in Soviet disintegration.
- The United States and the former Soviet Union should agree to halt the production of fissile materials for weapons. Further, since both countries have far more fissile material than is needed to maintain the arsenals that will result from START and the unilateral initiatives, they should also agree to remove some of this fissile material from weapons stockpiles and either convert it to civilian use or place it in secure, monitored storage. An initial 50-percent cut in fissile material stockpiles is suggested here.
- The United States and the former Soviet Union also should consider destroying in a cooperative, verified manner some of the warheads they plan to eliminate. They should also investigate the potential role that a program of verified warhead elimination and fissile material limits could play in directly limiting nuclear warheads.

SUGGESTED READINGS

"A New Era of Reciprocal Arms Reductions." *Arms Control Today*, Vol. 21, No. 8 (October 1991), pp. 3–10.

Albright, David, Peter Gray, and Tom Zamora. "A Smaller, Safer Weapons Complex Through Arms Reductions." *Bulletin of the Atomic Scientists*, Vol. 47, No. 6 (July/August 1991), pp. 3–10.

Campbell, Kurt M., Ashton B. Carter, Steven E. Miller, and Charles A. Zraket. *Soviet Nuclear Fission: Control of the Nuclear Arsenal in a Disintegrating Soviet Union*. CSIA Studies in International Security, No. 1. Cambridge, Mass.: Center for Science and International Affairs, Harvard University, November 1991.

Daalder, Ivo H. and Tim Zimmermann. "Banning Nuclear Weapons at Sea: A Neglected Strategy." *Arms Control Today*, Vol. 18, No. 9 (November 1988), pp. 17–23.

Federation of American Scientists. *Ending the Production of Fissile Materials for Weapons—Verifying the Dismantlement of Nuclear Warheads: The Technical Basis for Action*. Washington, D.C.: Federation of American Scientists, June 1991.

Kelleher, Catherine M. "Short-Range Nuclear Weapons: What Future in Europe." *Arms Control Today*, Vol. 21, No. 1 (January/February 1991), pp. 17–21.

Krass, Allan. *The Future of the U.S. Nuclear Weapons Complex*. Cambridge, Mass.: Union of Concerned Scientists, May 1991.

Morrison, David C. "Loose Soviet Nukes: A Mountain or a Molehill?" *Arms Control Today*, Vol. 21, No. 3 (April 1991), pp. 15–19.

Taylor, Theodore B. "Verified Elimination of Nuclear Warheads." *Science and Global Security*, Vol. 1, Nos. 1–2 (1989), pp. 1–26.

von Hippel, Frank. "Warhead and Fissile-Material Declarations." In Frank von Hippel and Roald Sagdeev, eds. *Reversing the Arms Race: How to Achieve and Verify Deep Reductions in the Nuclear Arsenals*. New York: Gordon and Breach, 1990, pp. 61–81.

———. David H. Albright, and Barbara G. Levi. "Stopping the Production of Fissile Material for Weapons." *Scientific American*, Vol. 253, No. 3 (September 1985), pp. 40–47.

Chapter
5

The Future of U.S. Strategic Offensive Forces

Michèle A. Flournoy

*I*n contrast to the political map of Europe and the tenor of U.S.-Soviet relations, the strategic nuclear forces of the United States and the former Soviet Union remain largely as they were a few years ago. Each country continues to deploy more than 10,000 nuclear weapons on intercontinental missiles and bombers aimed at the other's homeland. And each continues to value its strategic arsenal highly. For Russia, strategic nuclear forces are now, perhaps more than ever, symbols of great power status; for the United States, they underwrite the ultimate insurance policy against a nuclear threat from the former Soviet Union or a new nuclear adversary. Nevertheless, these forces are not immune to the end of the Cold War. Although they have been slow to reflect the dramatic changes of recent years, they appear destined to be reshaped by the changing security environment. In short, the question is not whether U.S. strategic forces should change in the future, but how.

The primary objective of U.S. strategic offensive forces is basic deterrence: to deter a deliberate nuclear attack on the United States. But because nuclear war might also result from the accidental, inadvertent, or unauthorized use of nuclear weapons, the United States must also seek to minimize the risk of miscommunication, miscalculation, accidents, or a breakdown in political or physical control over these forces. Together, these two objectives—maximizing nuclear deterrence and minimizing the risk of unintended nuclear war—should guide the number and type of strategic forces the United States deploys as well as the manner in which it deploys them. These two goals can, however, compete, presenting difficult trade-offs between positive and negative control over nuclear weapons.[1] Thus the challenge for U.S. policy is first to identify measures that enhance both negative control and positive control (or at least increase the former without decreasing the latter), and then, in cases where trade-offs are unavoidable, to strike an appropriate balance between the two.

This chapter presents guidelines and recommendations for the size and shape of future U.S. strategic offensive forces. For the near term—the next ten years—it seeks to design *a notional strategic force that fulfills the roles and meets the requirements designated in earlier chapters at the lowest possible force levels consistent with stability and within anticipated constraints.* This notional force is not intended as an ultimate endpoint or a permanent answer to the question, "How much is enough?" Rather it is presented as a next step in the context of negotiated reductions beyond START I. For the longer term, this chapter seeks to identify directions in which this force might evolve over time.[2]

As outlined in Chapter 3, U.S. strategic forces must be able to retaliate against a Soviet nuclear attack with sufficient force to threaten the ability of the Soviet Union (or any of its republics) to project power in a sustained fashion beyond its borders. They need not be able to destroy Soviet nuclear forces, nuclear command-and-control facilities, or leadership posts. In the long term, they should be able to ride out a Soviet nuclear attack and retaliate hours, or even days, later. It is assumed that these capabilities are being sought in the absence of nationwide ballistic missile defenses in the former Soviet Union. (See Chapter 7 for an analysis of defenses against nuclear weapons.)

The United States should seek to achieve these capabilities at the lowest possible force levels, for several reasons. First, deploying forces in excess of what is required for deterrence, as is currently the case, is a waste of national resources. Deep cuts in the U.S. strategic arsenal would likely save money in the long term. Second, significant reductions in U.S. and

---

[1]Positive control refers to the ability to ensure that an order to use nuclear weapons can be executed, whereas negative control denotes the ability to prevent the accidental, inadvertent, or unauthorized use of nuclear weapons. For more on potential trade-offs between the two, see Paul J. Bracken, *The Command and Control of Nuclear Forces* (New Haven, Conn.: Yale University Press, 1983); Bruce G. Blair, *Strategic Command and Control: Redefining the Nuclear Threat* (Washington, D.C.: The Brookings Institution, 1985); and John D. Steinbruner, "Choices and Trade-Offs," in Ashton B. Carter, John D. Steinbruner, and Charles A. Zraket, eds., *Managing Nuclear Operations* (Washington, D.C.: The Brookings Institution, 1987). It is important to note, however, that some technological innovations could contribute to both responsiveness and control. For examples, see Ashton B. Carter, John S. Quilty, and Charles A. Zraket, "Nuclear Command and Control: The Next Thirty Years of Technological Change" (Paper presented to "The Future of Nuclear Weapons: The Next Three Decades" conference, Center for National Security Studies, Los Alamos National Laboratory, June 6–8, 1988).

[2]Whereas this chapter provides a vision for future U.S. strategic offensive forces, the next chapter provides an arms control and modernization blueprint for achieving this vision.

Soviet strategic forces would create both an incentive and an opportunity to restructure these forces in a manner that would increase their survivability. If this opportunity were seized, crisis stability could be enhanced. Deploying fewer nuclear weapons would also reduce the risk of accident or loss of control, other things being equal. Finally, such reductions would encourage the continued evolution of U.S.-Soviet relations in more cooperative directions and would signal the willingness of both countries to decrease their reliance on nuclear weapons, which could, in turn, advance nuclear nonproliferation efforts.

Nevertheless, to remain consistent with stability, a reduced U.S. force must be robust against changing strategic conditions, such as a Soviet breakout from treaty limits—that is, a rapid move to significantly higher force levels in excess of treaty limits. However implausible such a breakout might seem under current conditions, it cannot be ruled out categorically, particularly in light of the former Soviet Union's highly uncertain political future. If undertaken on a large scale, such a breakout would have the potential to upset the U.S.-Soviet strategic balance, especially as overall force levels decline. Even if militarily irrelevant, a breakout could be quite damaging politically, undermining confidence in a party's reliability as an arms control partner and in the predictability of its future strategic activities.

Minimizing this risk should, therefore, be a U.S. priority. Specifically, the United States should seek to limit weapon systems that would, if deployed by the Soviets, give them significant breakout potential. For example, building out excess missile capacity as forces are reduced would make reversing warhead reductions far more difficult. Minimizing the risk of breakout should, however, be balanced against other, perhaps competing, objectives, and fears of breakout should be tempered by evidence of changing Soviet intentions, realistic assessments of its likely consequences, and verification measures that increase its costs and decrease its likelihood.

U.S. strategic forces must also be robust against any increases in the level of nuclear danger due to political reversals in the former Soviet Union, technological breakthroughs, the emergence of new nuclear weapons states, or other unpredictable events. Given the uncertain future of the former USSR, the often unpredictable nature of advances in technology, the potential for further nuclear proliferation, and the longevity of U.S. strategic weapons systems, these forces must be adaptable to the changing security environment. They must, in particular, be sufficient to deter Soviet nuclear aggression no matter what course U.S.-Soviet relations take in the next decade.

This chapter begins by considering the constraints within which future decisions about U.S. strategic offensive forces must be made. It then proposes the levels and types of strategic forces the United States should deploy and how these forces should be structured, offering specific suggestions for each leg of the triad. Finally, after exploring how the proposed force might be adapted to changing threats and conditions, the chapter concludes with a set of recommendations.

CONSTRAINTS

As the United States considers how to posture its strategic forces, the most immediate constraint is economic. In 1990, powerful and persistent pressures to reduce U.S. military spending resulted in the deepest cut in the U.S. defense budget since the end of the Vietnam War.[3] According to Defense Department plans for the next several years, defense budget authority can be expected to decline 22 percent after inflation between FY1990 and FY1996, continuing a trend that began in 1985.[4] Over the next four years, defense spending is expected to be more than $130 billion less than what the Bush administration requested in January 1990.[5] And Congress is likely to mandate still deeper cuts. In this context, defense planners and members of Congress are hunting for programs to defer, curtail, or kill.

In this budgetary environment, and in the context of post–Cold War reassessments of U.S. defense priorities, strategic nuclear weapons are prime candidates for the chopping block: They are expensive, they seem ill-suited to the security challenges the United States now faces, and they are in direct competition with conventional force programs, which are perceived, particularly in the wake of the Gulf War, to have far greater utility. Thus, future funds available for strategic programs will be restricted not only by the shrinking size of the defense spending pie but also by the potentially shrinking size of the slice devoted to nuclear weapons. This will place severe constraints on strategic modernization. As a result, cost can be expected to play an increasingly important role in U.S. force structuring decisions, as the debate over the B-2 bomber demonstrated.

Political constraints will also shape the future of U.S. strategic forces. There are, for example, domestic and international pressures for the United States to reduce its reliance on nuclear weapons now that the Cold War has ended. Domestically, large nuclear arsenals are likely to be viewed as increasingly anachronistic in the changing security environ-

---

[3]Defense Budget Project, "Final Congressional Action on the FY1991 Defense Budget: Authorization and Appropriations," November 7, 1990, p. 1.

[4]Budget authority dropped 22 percent between FY1985 and FY1991 in real terms, after having risen 55 percent between FY1980 and FY1985. Task Force on the FY1992–FY1997 Defense Plan, *Responding to Changing Threats* (Washington, D.C.: Defense Budget Project, June 1991), p. 6.

[5]Statement of Secretary of Defense Dick Cheney before the Senate Armed Services Committee in Connection with the FY1992–93 Budget for the Department of Defense, February 21, 1991.

ment. Internationally, reductions in strategic forces remain a priority in U.S.-Soviet relations and a vehicle for their further improvement. In June 1990, the United States and the Soviet Union agreed to consider further stabilizing reductions after START, which reduces U.S. and Soviet strategic forces by about one third. This commitment has since been echoed by leaders of various republics, and Gorbachev proposed that both sides begin "intensive negotiations on a radical reduction in strategic weapons, by about half."[6] In addition, for the foreseeable future, the fate of U.S. strategic forces will remain tied to that of the nuclear forces of other countries. Domestic politics are likely to render untenable anything less than rough parity with the former Soviet Union and a margin of superiority over Britain, France, China, and other nuclear powers.

Another possible restriction on the future of strategic forces is the sorry state of the Department of Energy's nuclear weapons complex, which includes 15 major sites in 13 states.[7] For the first time since World War II, U.S. nuclear weapons materials production has ceased entirely as environmental, safety, and health problems have closed key facilities. Most notable is the shutdown of Rocky Flats, the only plant that produces plutonium "pits" for nuclear warheads. This shutdown most immediately affects warheads currently in production, such as the W88 warhead for the Trident II missile, but could, if it continues, ultimately limit the U.S. ability to recycle existing warheads or manufacture new ones.[8]

Furthermore, the U.S. ability to produce tritium, which decays at the rate of 5.6 percent per year and must be replaced periodically in existing warheads, is also in question due to the closing of the Savannah River reactors. Although some tritium from retired warheads can be recovered and recycled, the lack of a new production capability would at some point constrain the U.S. ability to deploy new high-yield warheads and perhaps the size of the existing stockpile. Obviously, the smaller the stockpile and the more careful the management, the longer existing supplies of tritium could be stretched. In the longer term, however, the United States must either redesign its warheads to limit their reliance on tritium or find new

---

[6]"Gorbachev's Remarks on Nuclear Arms Cuts," *New York Times*, October 6, 1991, p. A12.

[7]For an overview of the problem, see *Complex Cleanup: The Environmental Legacy of Nuclear Weapons Production* (Washington, D.C.: Office of Technology Assessment, February 1991); Alan Krass, *The Future of the U.S. Nuclear Weapons Complex* (Cambridge, Mass.: Union of Concerned Scientists, May 1991); and Paul Levanthal, Milton Hoenig, and Deborah J. Holland, "Crisis in the U.S. Nuclear Weapons Infrastructure," in Eric H. Arnett, ed., *Science and International Security: Responding to a Changing World* (Washington, D.C.: American Association for the Advancement of Science, 1990).

[8]For an excellent discussion of options that could reduce or eliminate the need for plutonium operations at Rocky Flats, see Jonathan Medalia, William Boesman, Warren H. Donnely, Mark Holt, and Amy F. Woolf, *Rocky Flats and U.S. Nuclear Weapons Programs: Alternatives for the Future* (Washington, D.C.: Congressional Research Service, February 1991). For a discussion of warhead recycling, see R. Jeffrey Smith, "Ultimate Recycling: Nuclear Warheads," *Science*, Vol. 252 (May 24, 1991), pp. 1056–1057.

sources of the material (i.e., build a new reactor, as the Department of Energy has proposed).[9]

In sum, the uncertain fate of U.S. nuclear warhead production may well constrain or at least modify some strategic modernization programs. Whether the complex will be fully refurbished, as its supporters urge, or dramatically downsized, as its critics recommend, has yet to be decided. The outcome of this decision will determine whether new warheads will be produced as planned, modified to incorporate recycled components of systems already in the stockpile, or canceled altogether. This, in turn, will influence the number and type of nuclear warheads the United States will deploy in the future.

Finally, there is a possibility that further limitations on nuclear testing will be negotiated. Although the United States has long stated its commitment to a Comprehensive Test Ban (CTB) as "a long-term objective," the Bush administration has declined to participate in any new testing negotiations in the near term, as it "has not identified any further limitations on nuclear testing . . . that would be in the U.S. national security interest."[10] Indeed, the administration remains committed to continued nuclear testing until "we do not need to depend on nuclear deterrence to ensure international security and stability."[11] Nevertheless, the former Soviet Union and many other countries continue to call for near-term negotiations toward a CTB.[12] With the approach of the 1995 review of the Nuclear Non-Proliferation Treaty, which will determine whether the treaty expires or is extended, this issue is likely to receive greater atten-

---

[9]See *Nuclear Materials: Decreasing Tritium Requirements and Their Effect on DOE Programs*, GAO/RCED-91-100 (Washington, D.C.: Government Accounting Office, February 8, 1991); and *The Tritium Factor: Tritium's Impact on Nuclear Arms Reductions* (Washington, D.C.: Nuclear Control Institute and The American Academy of Arts and Sciences, December 1988). Some, including Soviet President Gorbachev, advocate halting the production of all fissionable materials for weapons as a method of forcing arms reductions. For contrasting views, see J. Carson Mark, Thomas D. Davies, Milton M. Hoenig, and Paul L. Levanthal, "The Tritium Factor as a Forcing Function in Nuclear Arms Talks," and W.G. Sutcliffe, "Limits on Nuclear Materials for Arms Reduction: Complexities and Uncertainties," in *Science*, Vol. 241, September 2, 1988, pp. 1166–1169. Such proposals are discussed further in Chapter 4.

[10]"U.S. Policy Statement on Nuclear Testing," memorandum from the executive secretary of the National Security Council, January 9, 1990. In September 1987, the United States and the Soviet Union agreed to initiate "stage-by-stage" nuclear testing negotiations to draft verification protocols to the then-unratified Threshold Test Ban Treaty and Peaceful Nuclear Explosions Treaty, pursue intermediate nuclear testing limitations, and eventually proceed to the ultimate goal of a CTB. Now that the two protocols have been negotiated, signed, and ratified, the Bush administration has sought a pause in the negotiations for a "period of implementation."

[11]*Ibid.*

[12]In his October 1991 initiative on nuclear arms, Gorbachev announced the beginning of a one-year unilateral Soviet moratorium on nuclear testing, urged other nuclear powers to follow suit, and called for the complete cessation of nuclear testing. See "Gorbachev's Remarks on Nuclear Arms Cuts," *op. cit.*

tion, as a number of developing countries view the CTB as a litmus test of the nuclear powers' commitment to reining in their own nuclear ambitions.[13] On the home front, there is substantial support in Congress for a reduction in the size and number of nuclear tests the United States and the Soviet Union conduct each year.[14] Given the serious possibility that additional constraints on nuclear testing will be imposed in the next decade, the United States would be wise to begin preparing to live with them, emphasizing warhead safety and "generic" warhead designs—designs with parts that can be recycled, interchanged, or easily modified—over exotica as it plans for the future.[15]

STRATEGIC FORCE REQUIREMENTS

Given these constraints, how many and what type of strategic offensive forces should the United States field in the context of negotiated reductions beyond START I?

Force Levels

It is impossible to determine exactly how many—or how few—nuclear weapons are needed to deter the former Soviet Union, as the targeting exercise in Chapter 3 emphasized. One must rely, therefore, on methods rooted in intuited comfort levels and educated guesses. Given this caveat, there are two prototypical approaches to ascertaining the desired level of strategic forces. In the first approach, the desired level of forces is reached by starting with existing or anticipated force levels and reducing from this

---

[13]In September 1990, the fourth NPT Review Conference failed to reach consensus on a final document due to a deadlock between pro-CTB signatories to the NPT, led by Mexico, and the United States and Britain, which object to near-term negotiations on a CTB. Article VI of the NPT requires each party to "pursue negotiations in good faith" on "cessation of the nuclear arms race at an early date," and the preamble of the treaty refers specifically to the commitment to work toward a CTB contained in the 1963 Limited Test Ban Treaty. For more details, see Charles N. Van Doren and George Bunn, "Progress and Peril at the Fourth NPT Review Conference," *Arms Control Today*, Vol. 20, No. 8 (October 1990), pp. 8–12.

[14]In April 1988, for the third year in a row, the U.S. House of Representatives passed an amendment to the defense authorization bill to halt all tests above one kiloton if the Soviet Union adheres to the same limit and permits in-country seismic monitoring acceptable to the Reagan administration. However, the amendment was again dropped in conference. In May 1989, 23 senators and 142 members of the House urged President Bush to adopt a step-by-step program for phasing out all nuclear tests by 1995. See "Chronology of the Comprehensive Test Ban," *Arms Control Today*, Vol. 20, No. 9 (November 1990), p. 35.

[15]The viability of this approach has already been demonstrated. The United States has used warheads from the Pershing II and ground-launched cruise missiles withdrawn under the INF Treaty to make B61 gravity bombs. Similarly, to compensate for the shutdown of Rocky Flats, the Navy plans to use W76 warheads from retired Trident I missiles on a large fraction of new Trident II missiles.

baseline by some percentage. This is an essentially intuitive approach, one that dictates force levels based on a broad and arbitrary concept or organizing principle.

In the second approach, the level of forces is calculated from a specific set of targets, taking into account estimated measures of weapons performance. This is a more analytical approach, one that logically deduces force levels from targets, capabilities, and missions. Although less arbitrary, this approach is also quite subjective, as any target set embodies a subjective set of beliefs about what deters, and as weapons performance estimates are unavoidably inexact.

In practice, a combination of both approaches has influenced U.S. strategic force planning and arms control policy. For example, at the 1985 Geneva summit, Presidents Reagan and Gorbachev emphasized the intuitive approach in defining the extent of START reductions. Both sides, they agreed, would reduce their strategic arsenals by 50 percent. However, subsequent application of the analytical approach within the U.S. government led the United States to introduce START counting rules that would result in overall reductions of 35 percent or less.

In contemplating START II reductions, most analysts have, to date, relied on the more general, intuitive approach. Many have concluded that a 50-percent cut from START I levels,[16] to a force of 3,000 accountable or roughly 4,000 actual warheads, would be acceptable.[17] Others have

---

[16]START I requires the United States and the Soviet Union to reduce their respective strategic arsenals to no more than 6,000 *accountable* warheads on 1,600 deployed delivery vehicles. Ballistic missile warheads each count as one warhead under the treaty, but bomber weapons are discounted. For example, the entire payload of a bomber that does not carry ALCMs, no matter how many gravity bombs and short-range attack missiles it includes, counts as only one warhead under the treaty. ALCMs are also undercounted, though to a lesser degree. As a result, the United States' 6,000 *accountable* warheads are expected to correspond to approximately 8,500 *actual* warheads. For a more detailed description of the START Treaty and its impact, see Michèle A. Flournoy, *Briefing Book on the Strategic Arms Reduction Treaty* (Boston: Council for a Livable World Education Fund, October 1990).

[17]Several experts in and outside government appear to be comfortable with such force levels. For example, former Secretary of Defense Harold Brown has endorsed between 1,000 and 3,000 strategic warheads on each side. See Harold Brown, "Navigating the Security Sea Change," *Arms Control Today*, Vol. 20, No. 4 (May 1990), p. 3. Gen. David C. Jones, retired Chairman of the Joint Chiefs of Staff, believes that roughly 2,000–3,000 strategic weapons would be sufficient. As quoted in "General David Jones: Redefining Security, Expanding Arms Control," *Arms Control Today*, Vol. 20, No. 8 (October 1990), p. 5. The National Academy of Sciences advocates reductions down to 3,000–4,000 warheads in the context of START II. See Committee on International Security and Arms Control, *The Future of the U.S.-Soviet Nuclear Relationship* (Washington, D.C.: National Academy Press, 1991). Former Special Advisor to the President and the Secretary of State on Arms Control Matters Paul Nitze argues that the United States "could afford to go as low as 3,000–5,000 [weapons] and still not have a material increase in risk." Interview with the author, July 19, 1990. And former National Security Advisor McGeorge Bundy has said that START II should aim for 3,000–5,000 strategic weapons on each side. See Sybil Francis, *The Role of Nuclear Weapons*

called for far more radical cuts, down to hundreds of weapons on each side.[18] Still others decline to recommend specific force levels and advocate instead a process of reducing U.S. and Soviet strategic forces as quickly and as deeply as possible within the bounds of strategic stability.[19]

Our analysis, however, takes the more uncommon analytical approach in an effort to ascertain a ballpark figure for the level of strategic forces appropriate to the targeting doctrine proposed in Chapter 3.[20] We begin by assuming that the United States retaliates only after absorbing a large-scale Soviet nuclear attack. However implausible this scenario may seem under current conditions, it remains the best basis for assessing the requirements of deterrence and sizing U.S. strategic forces for the next decade, as the former Soviet Union continues its transformation.

In setting the goals for a retaliatory strike, we assume that the United States would use only one warhead per target. Although a departure from current practice, this assumption is appropriate for the target set postulated in Chapter 3. U.S. targeteers have in the past sought to achieve 0.9 damage expectancy for strategic nuclear targets and between 0.5 and 0.7 for all other targets.[21] The higher damage expectancy requirement for strategic nuclear targets translates into assigning two or more warheads to each target, especially those that are hardened against nuclear effects. However, all of the targets in Chapter 3's notional set—including the 120 strategic nuclear targets—are soft. And one-on-one targeting on soft targets is generally assumed to result in a damage ex-

---

in the Year 2000: Summary of the Workshop Proceedings (Livermore, Calif.: Lawrence Livermore National Laboratory Center for Technical Studies on Security, Energy, and Arms Control, January 25, 1991), p. 5.

[18]For example, former Secretary of Defense Robert S. McNamara argues that if the risk of war between East and West were negligible, 500 warheads on each side would be enough to deter a nation from building nuclear weapons in secret and using them unilaterally. McNamara assumes that the Soviet Union would be allocated the same number of warheads as the United States, Britain, and France combined. Interview with the author, July 19, 1990. In addition, Professor Herbert York argues that the United States and the Soviet Union would need no more than 100 nuclear weapons for minimum deterrence. See Herbert F. York, "Remarks About Minimum Deterrence," (Livermore, Calif.: Lawrence Livermore National Laboratory Center for Technical Studies on Security, Energy, and Arms Control, January 25, 1991), p. 1.

[19]Conversation with MIT Professor Jack Ruina, October 22, 1990, Livermore, Calif.

[20]For another example of the analytical approach, see Michael M. May, George F. Bing, and John D. Steinbruner, *Strategic Arms Reductions* (Washington, D.C.: The Brookings Institution, 1988).

[21]Damage expectancy is the product of weapons reliability, probability of penetration to the target, and probability of destruction upon arrival. (Technically speaking, damage expectancy also includes prelaunch survivability, but that is treated separately here.) These figures are treated as rules of thumb, not as exact probabilities of accomplishing specific military objectives.

pectancy of about 0.7.[22] This is judged to be sufficient for the very few strategic targets in the postulated target set.[23]

As for the number of targets identified in Chapter 3 to be attacked, all 120 strategic targets and approximately 1,380 nonstrategic targets are included.[24] For the nonstrategic targets, we assume, based on the traditional damage expectancy goal of 0.5 for conventional force and economic targets, that destruction of half would be sufficient. Given that one-on-one targeting would result in a damage expectancy of about 0.7, one must target 70 percent (or 966) of these aimpoints in order to destroy half of them. Thus, a U.S. retaliatory force must be capable of striking a total of nearly 1,100 Soviet targets.

Finally, it is assumed that the United States would maintain a survivable strategic reserve of nearly 350 additional warheads (roughly 25 percent of the total that would survive a surprise attack).[25] Failing to do so could leave the country relatively disarmed after a nuclear exchange and vulnerable to blackmail or coercion by other nuclear powers.

How many strategic warheads would the United States need to cover roughly 1,100 targets and maintain a strategic reserve of approximately 350 survivable warheads? Three cases are considered in an effort to answer this question. Each case is based on a different set of assumptions about the alert rates—and thus the survivability—of U.S. forces when a Soviet attack arrives.

Case 1 assumes that the United States receives strategic warning of a Soviet nuclear attack and acts on it. In such a case, U.S. strategic forces are placed on fully generated alert (i.e., 95 percent of U.S. bombers are placed on runway alert and 75 percent of U.S. ballistic-missile submarines (SSBNs)

---

[22]This analysis estimates damage expectancy against soft targets to be .79 for ballistic missile warheads (i.e, .8 reliability × 1.0 probability of penetration × .99 probability of destruction upon arrival) and .61 for bomber weapons (.72 reliability × .85 probability of penetration × .99 probability of destruction upon arrival). The weighted average of these is .72.

[23]For lack of detailed information, we assume that none of the identified targets is collocated. This assumption would tend to inflate the number of warheads deemed necessary to destroy the target set. On the other hand, we also assume that each target encompasses only one aimpoint, even though in reality some targets might require multiple warheads to reach the desired damage expectancy.

[24]Although Chapter 3's notional target list identified a range of 1,070—1,870 targets, we use 1,500 targets—the approximate midpoint in this range—as a basis for force sizing.

[25]There is little consensus on the criteria by which a secure strategic reserve should be sized. For example, Roger Speed argues that a secure reserve of 100–150 medium-sized warheads would be sufficient to deter a nuclear attack on American cities, as they could probably destroy over 50 percent of the Soviet industrial capacity. See Roger Speed, *Strategic Forces: Future Requirements and Options* (Livermore, Calif.: Lawrence Livermore National Laboratory, Center for Technical Studies on Security, Energy, and Arms Control, November 1990), p. 14. By contrast, others call for a strategic reserve that is approximately 10 percent of the total arsenal. See May, Bing, and Steinbruner, *op. cit.*, p. 36.

are flushed from their ports),[26] and all alerted forces survive. However, no U.S. ICBMs are launched on warning or from under attack[27]; since all are silo-based, only 10 percent survive.[28]

Case 2 assumes that, based on negative changes in U.S.-Soviet relations, the United States returns its strategic forces to Cold War peacetime alert rates but stops short of believing that a nuclear attack is imminent. As a result, 30 percent of U.S. bombers and 66 percent of U.S. SSBNs survive the Soviet attack. Once again, no ICBMs are launched promptly and only 10 percent survive.

Finally, Case 3 assumes that the United States maintains its strategic forces at current levels of readiness (i.e., 66 percent of SSBNs and no bombers on alert), that it either does not receive strategic warning of a Soviet nuclear attack or fails to act on such warning, and that it does not launch its ICBMs promptly.

In Case 1, approximately 70 percent of U.S. strategic warheads survive.[29] In this case, the United States would need to deploy about 2,070 warheads to meet the targeting and reserve requirements described. It would, however, be imprudent for the United States to size its strategic forces based on Case 1, as strategic warning of a Soviet nuclear attack might not be clear or unambiguous enough to elicit a fully generated U.S. alert. Even if such warning were unambiguous, a U.S. president might not be willing to increase U.S. nuclear readiness so dramatically for fear that such action would be perceived as provocative by the adversary and might panic the American people.

In Case 2, an estimated 40 percent of U.S. strategic forces survive, and

---

[26]In all three cases, the SSBN force is assumed to be comprised entirely of Tridents. Generated alert assumptions are drawn from May, Bing, and Steinbruner, *op. cit.*, p. 35.

[27]The reasons why the United States should eschew prompt launch options for its land-based missile force are discussed below.

[28]Long-range nuclear sea-launched cruise missiles are not included in these calculations because they are no longer deployed and because we believe they should be eliminated entirely, as discussed in Chapter 4. Nuclear SLCMs add relatively little and nothing unique to U.S. nuclear capabilities overall. Therefore, keeping them in storage as a hedge against Soviet policy reversals is an unnecessary precaution in our view. Furthermore, the costs of failing to take up the Soviet offer to eliminate these weapons could be high, as the redeployment of Soviet sub-launched SLCMs would raise the possibility that the United States could not distinguish between a nuclear and a conventional SLCM attack and that it might not be able to determine whether an attack was even underway, given the very real possibility that SLCMs could escape detection. The former problem could pose the risk of inadvertent escalation (but only if U.S. ICBMs were launched on warning) and the latter the risk of decapitation, particularly given the paucity of U.S. cruise missile warning capabilities. See Theodore A. Postol, "Banning Nuclear SLCMs: It Would Be Nice If We Could," *International Security*, Vol. 13, No. 3 (Winter 1988/89), pp. 191–202; and Rose E. Gottemoeller, "Finding Solutions to SLCM Arms Control Problems," *International Security*, Vol. 13, No. 3 (Winter 1988/89), pp. 175–183.

[29]This assumes that 20 percent of U.S. strategic forces are deployed on ICBMs, 40 percent on SLBMs, and 40 percent on bombers.

approximately 3,600 warheads would be needed to cover the proposed target set and yield the desired reserve. This case assumes that the United States reacts to a dramatic downturn in U.S.-Soviet relations by putting some of its strategic bombers back on alert; however, it stops short of assuming that the United States would necessarily have strategic warning of a Soviet nuclear attack and respond to it by putting its strategic forces on fully generated alert. Consequently, it seems a more prudent basis of analysis than Case 1.

At the same time, Case 2 is more plausible than Case 3, in which only 28 percent of U.S. strategic forces would survive. Case 3 implies that a U.S. president would not adjust alert rates in response to a dramatic resurgence of U.S.-Soviet hostility. This assumption is, however, difficult to believe. We believe that a responsible, prudent leader would likely return to the peacetime alert rates of the Cold War period, as envisioned in Case 2, if worsening political conditions warranted such a change. In contrast to the steps postulated in Case 1, such an incremental step would be unlikely to be seen as provocative or to cause panic. Thus, the most rational set of assumptions on which to base our analysis of "how much is enough" for the next decade is Case 2. It is worth noting, however, that the force of 3,600 warheads prescribed by Case 2 would be able to cover more than the minimum Soviet targets cited and yield a reserve of over 200 warheads even if the unlikely conditions postulated by Case 3 obtained.

Force Characteristics

As the United States reduces its forces to the proposed level, certain force characteristics should be emphasized and others deemphasized, if not eliminated. The most important traits to accentuate are survivability, control and safety, and flexibility.[30] To the extent possible, these characteristics should be maximized as a set rather than each in isolation or one at the expense of the other.

As U.S. strategic forces become smaller, survivability will remain the cornerstone of crisis stability. As long as both sides' forces can endure attack, there is little incentive for either to strike first. Ideally, U.S. strategic forces as a whole should be survivable enough to ride out a nuclear attack and still meet the targeting requirements described in a retaliatory strike. Every system need not survive, only enough to meet this standard.

---

[30]The United States should also make every effort to reduce the yield of its strategic nuclear weapons over time—and to encourage the Soviets to do the same. If both sides moved toward strategic forces with only low-yield warheads, they would eventually lose the capability to destroy each other's nuclear forces and hardened targets. This could enhance crisis stability substantially. However, there are very real limits to how far this process can proceed in light of the incapacitation of the nuclear weapons production complex and the probability of future limits on nuclear testing. Thus, we do not address this issue further here.

There are essentially three paths to increased survivability: protecting a weapon from nuclear effects, making it more difficult to target, or making it not worth the cost to attack. The first is accomplished through hardening.[31] The second results from mobility (as in the case of mobile ICBMs) or deceptive basing (as in the case of the Multiple Protective Shelter basing scheme for ICBMs). The third is achieved by spreading one's warheads among so many launchers that an attacker would be forced to expend more warheads than it could hope to destroy. In the last case, individual weapons systems, though still vulnerable, become unattractive targets, as attacking them would reduce the attacker's forces more than those of the victim.[32]

In addition to survivability, a high premium should be placed on the control and safety of future U.S. strategic forces given that the most plausible path to nuclear war with the former Soviet Union may be the accidental, inadvertent, or unauthorized use of nuclear weapons. All nuclear weapons should be subject to physical and procedural safeguards against such use. Specifically, steps should be taken to reduce the chances that SLBMs could be launched without the authorization of the national command authorities. Additionally, the United States should explore means of destroying unintentionally launched missiles before they reach their targets. These measures will be discussed in greater detail in the following.

As forces shrink, they should also become more flexible. Given that the United States will have fewer surviving warheads with which to accomplish a broad range of missions, weapons should be procured (or retained) with a variety of missions in mind. To be adequately flexible, they should also be easy to reassign to new targets, if necessary, after riding out a nuclear attack.

At the same time, a number of force characteristics should be deemphasized, including: extensive MIRVing of ballistic missiles, particularly those that are vulnerable; hair-trigger postures; excess throwweight; and weapon systems that pose new threats to survivability.

Although cost-effective, MIRVing raises three concerns. On vulnerable systems, such as silo-based ICBMs, it creates incentives for the attacker to strike these highly lucrative targets and for the potential victim to launch a preemptive strike—to use its valuable weapons before it loses them. On less vulnerable systems, such as mobile ICBMs, MIRVing can heighten the risk of breakout. Because mobile missiles are difficult to track, there is a greater risk that they could be deployed in excess of treaty limits,

---

[31]Although both the United States and the Soviet Union have gone to considerable lengths to harden key nuclear assets, gains in hardening are often outstripped by gains in weapon accuracy and destructiveness over time.

[32]An adversary might nevertheless contemplate such an attack if it had a larger force than its opponent to begin with or the ability to attack other retaliatory forces with great efficiency.

a risk that would be further magnified if each missile carried more than one warhead.[33] Finally, MIRVing increases the damage and destruction that would occur if missiles were launched accidentally, inadvertently, or without authorization.

Concern about hair-trigger postures is raised by the U.S. capability to launch its land-based missiles on warning or under attack.[34] Both launch on warning, which enables ICBMs to be fired after confirmed warning of an attack[35] but before any warheads have exploded on American soil, and launch under attack, which enables them to be fired after the first incoming warheads have exploded but before the full attack has been absorbed, evolved as operational answers to ICBM vulnerability. Both are means of creating doubt in the minds of Soviet leaders as to whether U.S. missiles would still be in their silos by the time a Soviet attack arrived. However, actually using these capabilities would compress decision-making time into just a few minutes and increase the risk that nuclear weapons could be used as a result of false warning or miscalculation.[36] These prompt launch options should, therefore, be ruled out. As Chapter 3 recommends, the United States should focus its energies not on being able to launch its ICBMs quickly, but rather on being able to ride out a nuclear attack—that is, wait until the brunt of an attack has been absorbed in order to determine the origin, scope, and nature of the attack before retaliating. Admittedly, fulfilling this aspiration will require time and substantial investment in command and control systems. Nevertheless, it is a step worth taking to reduce the risk of inadvertent war or escalation, particularly in the context of Soviet instability in the near term and the spread of nuclear weapons to other potential adversaries in the longer term.

The strongest argument against this policy shift is that if the U.S. forces

---

[33]This risk is, however, likely to decline as the United States gains experience monitoring Soviet mobile missile deployments and as mobile missile verification schemes are refined over time.

[34]In September 1985, then Commander of the North American Aerospace Defense Command General Robert T. Herres told Congress that, "We in the military would like to provide the National Command Authority with the flexibility to be able to ride out at least some portion of a nuclear attack if that should be necessary. . . . We have been able to keep up with the capability to launch on warning, but to go beyond that takes quite a lot of invest- ment." See "Our Nation's Nuclear Warning System: Will It Work If We Need It?" Hearings before a Subcommittee of the U.S. House Committee on Governmental Operations, Septem- ber 26, 1985, p. 72. The Soviet Union is believed to have the same capability. Bruce G. Blair and Henry W. Kendall, "Accidental Nuclear War," *Scientific American*, Vol. 263, No. 6 (December 1990), p. 55.

[35]Confirmed warning denotes warning received from two independent sensors, such as a satellite and a ground-based radar.

[36]For more on launch on warning and the risks of accidental nuclear war, see Blair and Kendall, *op. cit.*; Kurt Gottfried and Bruce G. Blair, eds., *Crisis Stability and Nuclear War* (New York: Oxford University Press, 1988); and Bruce G. Blair, *The Effects of Warning on Strategic Stability* (Washington, D.C.: The Brookings Institution, 1991).

were at current alert levels and the former Soviet Union simultaneously launched its ICBMs and SLBMs (from subs off U.S. coasts) in a surprise attack, then most U.S. bombers and ICBMs would be destroyed in the attack. This outcome is essentially that predicted by Case 3, described earlier, in which only 28 percent of U.S. strategic forces—or about 1,000 of 3,600 warheads—survive. This scenario is, however, highly implausible under current political conditions. And if conditions changed enough to make it plausible, alert rates could and would likely be changed as well.

The United States should also consider eliminating excess throwweight on its strategic missiles if the former Soviet Union agrees to do the same. Excess throwweight is created when missiles are deployed with fewer warheads than the maximum number they can carry, as in the case of downloading where some of the reentry vehicles originally deployed on a missile are removed. This, in turn, creates a potential for breakout. That is, each side is in a position to deploy additional warheads rapidly, easily, and possibly without detection. As stated earlier, building out excess capacity as forces are reduced would build into the strategic balance a greater degree of stability.

Finally, the United States should seek to constrain technologies that, if deployed by the former Soviet Union, would pose new threats to the survivability of U.S. forces and the U.S. strategic command and control system. These include, among others: MaRVs, which can alter their trajectories during flight to strike their targets with pinpoint accuracy; earth-penetrating warheads, which burrow deep into the earth before exploding in order to destroy hardened, underground facilities such as leadership bunkers; and short-time-of-flight SLBMs, which threaten targets that depend on warning for their survivability, such as bombers.[37] Although the United States currently has a technological edge over the Soviet Union in all of these areas, past experience suggests that, in time, U.S. forces could be rendered equally vulnerable by Soviet versions of these weapons if they are permitted to be deployed. Furthermore, the hardened targets for which MaRVs and earth-penetrating warheads were designed are no longer included in the proposed target set.

FORCE STRUCTURE

In considering what forces would best meet these guidelines and how they should be structured, the obvious starting point is today's triad of ICBMs, SLBMs, and long-range bombers. Should the U.S. triad be maintained?

Although some argue that the United States should move to a dyad or

---

[37] Depressed trajectory SLBMs would have flight times of only 5–10 minutes as opposed to 10–15 minutes for SLBMs launched in the conventional manner from the same location. See Walter Slocombe, "Danger: Low-Flying Missiles," *Washington Post*, May 13, 1988, p. 23.

even a monad,[38] there are good reasons for maintaining a triad, at least in the next round of reductions. Deploying a diversity of forces complicates an adversary's attack planning, multiplying the factors that must be taken into account in the design and execution of an attack against U.S. forces. Diversifying strategic systems also hedges against the wholesale failure of one or more U.S. weapons systems, reduces the risk of a technological breakthrough in countermeasures against any one leg, and complicates the task of defending against a U.S. retaliatory strike. It also encourages adversaries to divide their resources among a broad range of countermeasures and defenses, lessening their ability to concentrate their efforts on defeating any one system.

In a world in which the existence of a determined and sophisticated adversary armed with a large number of nuclear weapons cannot be ruled out, these arguments make a fairly compelling case for continued diversification. However, one can at least imagine a post–Cold War world, sometime in the future, in which such an adversary would not exist. In that case, relying on only one or two types of strategic systems might be far less risky and far more appealing, particularly if forces were reduced to very low levels.

The current division of labor among the legs of the U.S. triad is the product of years of compromise among many strategic, technological, political, and economic factors.[39] As such, it represents a web of shared understandings, vested interests, and accepted practices born of technological developments, interservice rivalries, and congressional politics. Although there is nothing sacred about this division of labor, the triad has after 30 years become an institution resistant to dramatic change.

Nevertheless, this division of labor is constantly being adjusted at the margins as annual defense budgets pass through Congress and arms con-

---

[38]For example, some advocate getting rid of all ICBMs. See, for example, Thomas C. Schelling, "Abolition of Ballistic Missiles," *International Security*, Vol. 12, No. 1 (Summer 1987), pp. 179–183; and James R. Lynch, "Triad or Dyad?" *Proceedings*, Vol. 116, No. 1 (January 1990), pp. 61–65. Others argue, in the context of much lower levels of forces than those considered here, that U.S. and Soviet strategic forces should consist entirely of single-warhead ICBMs, both mobile and silo-based. See Committee of Soviet Scientists for Peace and Against the Nuclear Threat, *Strategic Stability Under the Conditions of Radical Nuclear Arms Reductions*, 2nd edition (Moscow: Committee of Soviet Scientists for Peace and Against the Nuclear Threat, November 1987), as cited in Harold A. Feiveson and Frank von Hippel, "Beyond START: How to Make Much Deeper Cuts," *International Security*, Vol. 15, No. 1 (Summer 1990), p. 166. Others have suggested relying exclusively on ballistic missile-carrying submarines. See, for example, Sam Cohen, "Needed: Perestroika for U.S. National Security Policy," *Journal of Social, Political and Economic Studies*, Vol. 15, No. 2 (Summer 1990), pp. 131–140. Finally, some, like former President Reagan, have proposed eliminating all ballistic missiles and relying exclusively on bombers for nuclear deterrence. See "Text of U.S. Document on Reagan at Summit," *New York Times*, October 24, 1986, p. A12.

[39]Currently, the United States deploys 20 percent of its strategic warheads on ICBMs, 42 percent on SLBMs, and 38 percent on bombers. The Soviet Union, by contrast, fields 58 percent of its strategic warheads on ICBMs, 33 percent on SLBMs, and only 9 percent on bombers.

trol agreements are negotiated. As these adjustments are made, several guidelines should be kept in mind. First, as already argued, the United States should seek to deploy forces that optimize desired characteristics and minimize undesired characteristics. Second, if it is to reap the triad's benefits, the United States must not allow any one leg to atrophy to the point where it ceases to be of serious concern to an adversary. Each leg should continue to pose a substantial threat to the adversary's assets and a substantial challenge to its defenses and countermeasures. Finally, in the current budgetary environment, the relative costs of different systems—both overall program costs and the cost per deliverable warhead—should play a pivotal role in determining the appropriate division of labor among the legs of the triad and the overall direction of force modernization and restructuring. (See Chapter 6.)

Based on these guidelines and on the assumption that there are no compelling reasons for a substantial redistribution of warheads, we will make the case for the following U.S. force structure:

Delivery systems	Deployed warheads
ICBMs	700
SLBMs	1,440
Bombers	1,440
Total	3,580

The ICBM Leg

In the context of a force of approximately 3,600 warheads, the United States should deploy roughly 700 single-warhead missiles in silos.[40] This would eliminate the most destabilizing element of the U.S. triad: MIRVed silo-based missiles. Although the economy of deploying multiple warheads on individual missiles would be lost, a valuable measure of crisis stability would be gained. Even though these missiles would remain vulnerable to destruction if attacked, the former Soviet Union would have little incentive to attack them as it would have to expend at least twice the number of warheads as it could hope to destroy. In the context of strictly limited strategic forces, this should be an extremely unappealing outcome for any attacker.[41]

---

[40]What type of missiles these should be—refurbished Minuteman IIs, downloaded Minuteman IIIs, or new Midgetman missiles—will be discussed in the next chapter.

[41]There are essentially two conditions under which single-warhead missiles in silos might be considered more attractive targets: (1) in the event that the vast majority of U.S. bombers and SSBNs were rendered vulnerable to Soviet attack, and (2) in the event that the former

Shifting to mobile or deceptive basing schemes would, of course, do even more to enhance ICBM survivability, but the added expense seems neither necessary, given the survivability of the triad as a whole, nor affordable, given budgetary constraints on procurement decisions, at the present time.[42]

Because single-warhead ICBMs would be unattractive targets, the United States would also be less subject to the use-'em-or-lose-'em pressures and therefore more able to eschew launch on warning and launch under attack. Rejecting these options would significantly reduce the risk of miscalculation and enhance stability in crisis, as previously discussed.

In addition to deploying single-warhead missiles in silos and abandoning prompt launch postures, the United States should explore technical safeguards that would moderate the disastrous consequences of an accidental, inadvertent, or unauthorized missile launch, such as "command destruct systems."[43] The 1971 U.S.-Soviet "Accidents Measures" Agreement required each party, in the event of an accidental or unauthorized launch of one of its nuclear weapons, to "make every effort to take necessary measures to render harmless or destroy such weapons without causing damage."[44] However, the United States is currently incapable of fulfilling this pledge.[45] Command destruct mechanisms would provide the United States with the capability to disarm or destroy a missile and its warheads after launch, or to help the potential victim to do so through the transmission of a code to the system. In order to be viable, these systems

---

Soviet Union were confident that it could destroy U.S. ICBM silos with only one warhead per silo. Neither of these conditions is likely in the foreseeable future.

[42]Cost comparisons of various options for the U.S. ICBM force are made in the next chapter.

[43]Congress has recommended that both the United States and the Soviet Union place these mechanisms, also known as postlaunch destruct systems, on all intercontinental ballistic missiles. See Conference Report on the National Defense Authorization Act for FY 1992–93 as cited in *The Congressional Record*, Vol. 137, No. 168 (November 14, 1991), p. 9879. For more on command destruct systems, see Raymond L. Garthoff, "Changing Realities, Changing Perceptions: Deterrence and U.S. Security after the Cold War," *The Brookings Review*, Vol. 8, No. 4 (Fall 1990), p. 20; Sherman Frankel, "Stopping Accidents after They've Happened," *The Bulletin of the Atomic Scientists*, Vol. 46, No. 9 (November 1990), pp. 39–40, and "Aborting Unauthorized Launches of Nuclear-armed Ballistic Missiles through Postlaunch Destruction," *Science and Global Security*, Vol. 2, No. 1 (1990), pp. 1–20; and Blair and Kendall, *op. cit.*, p. 58.

[44]See "Agreement on Measures to Reduce the Risk of Outbreak of Nuclear War Between the United States of America and the Union of Soviet Socialist Republics," in *Arms Control and Disarmament Agreements* (Washington, D.C.: U.S. Arms Control and Disarmament Agency, 1990), p. 120.

[45]Former Soviet Deputy Foreign Minister Viktor Karpov claims that the Soviet Union has the capability to destroy both its ICBMs and SLBMs after launch. Conversation with the author, May 10, 1991, Barnett Hill, England. But this claim is widely disputed. In addition, it should be noted that the United States does employ command destruct mechanisms on unarmed missiles during flight tests. The technical requirements of destroying a nuclear-armed missile safely and effectively would, however, be more demanding.

would have to preclude the possibility that an adversary could use them to foil an intentional attack. They should also be designed to minimize the environmental damage that would result from destroying the missile and warhead. The feasibility of such systems merits further study.

In sum, in the context of a reduced force, the United States should deploy 700 single-warhead missiles in silos. As a hedge against future threats to the survivability of the triad as a whole, it should also research and develop more survivable basing options, such as mobile and/or deceptive schemes. In an effort to reduce the risk of accidental or inadvertent missile launches, launch on warning and launch under attack should be formally abandoned. And in order to mitigate the consequences of unintended launches, should they occur, command destruct systems should be researched and, if viable, developed and deployed.

The SLBM Leg

Ballistic missiles deployed on submarines are generally believed to constitute the most survivable leg of the U.S. triad because they are difficult to detect and attack while on patrol. As the United States reduces its strategic forces to a fraction of their current size, safeguarding this survivability will be of utmost importance.

In the context of planned force retirements, budgetary constraints, and anticipated arms control limitations, the navy is expected to reduce its SSBN fleet from the 30 or so boats currently deployed to some 18 Trident submarines.[46] However, the decision to significantly reduce the size of the U.S. SSBN fleet is decades old.[47] The navy has long anticipated, without much apparent discomfort, living with fewer submarines but with roughly the same number of warheads on station.

The prospect of deeper cuts in U.S. strategic forces raises a fundamental question to which there appears to be no definitive answer: How many (or how few) subs constitute a survivable fleet? Underlying this question is the widely held view that the survivability of the fleet is directly proportional to the number of SSBNs. But this assumed relationship is not as clear as it may seem, for the relevance of numbers depends on the nature of the antisubmarine warfare (ASW) threat. If an adversary were able to use remote sensing to detect U.S. SSBNs at sea on a global scale, then the entire fleet would be vulnerable no matter how large its size. In that event, assessing SSBN vulnerability would depend more on qualitative judgments about an adversary's ASW and on the probability of future technological breakthroughs than on any quantitative calculations. If, however,

---

[46]Congress authorized funds for the Eighteenth Trident in FY1991.

[47]In 1972, the Navy decided to proceed with a plan to replace 41 smaller Polaris and Poseidon submarines with a smaller fleet of larger and quieter Trident boats. Polaris and Poseidon subs have 16 missile tubes each whereas Tridents have 24 tubes each.

the primary ASW threat were from attack submarines trailing or tracking U.S. SSBNs as they leave port, then the size of the U.S. SSBN fleet, relative to the size of the adversary's force of attack submarines, would be a central measure of survivability.

Because the United States is confident that the former Soviet Union and others remain far from being able to find its stealthy Tridents in open waters and because widespread trailing would be considered a provocative practice (and one that the navy thinks it could evade), few regard the shrinking size of the fleet as a source of concern based on assessments of the current and anticipated ASW threat.[48]

Nevertheless, little thought has been given to deploying fewer than 18 boats. Indeed, this prospect makes many analysts nervous, not because they have discovered some logical threshold of fleet survivability but because 18 subs have come to define a widely shared, if intuited, comfort level below which considerable uncertainty and anxiety arise. Because an in-depth analysis of SSBN fleet survivability is beyond the scope of this chapter, we accept the supposition that the U.S. SSBN fleet should continue to be made up of 18 boats, even as the number of U.S. SLBM warheads declines from the 3,456 anticipated under START to the 1,440 proposed for the future. Nevertheless, the issue of fleet survivability merits further study, particularly in light of the potentially declining resources the former Soviet Union may devote to antisubmarine warfare in the future and the relatively undeveloped ASW capabilities of other potential adversaries.

In order for the number of submarines to remain constant as SLBM warhead levels are reduced by almost 60 percent, fewer warheads must be deployed on each Trident submarine.[49] Although the proposed fleet

---

[48]Former Secretary of Defense Frank Carlucci stated that "When at sea, our SSBNs are considered to be 100% survivable by all recent assessments and are projected to remain so against foreseeable threats." See Secretary of Defense Frank Carlucci, *Annual Report to Congress FY1990* (Washington, D.C.: U.S. Government Printing Office, January 17, 1989), p. 188.

[49]Specific approaches to reducing the number of warheads on each Trident submarine—such as downloading SLBMs, disabling missile tubes, deploying a new type of SLBM that carries fewer warheads, or deploying a smaller sub with fewer missile tubes—will be explored in the next chapter. Whether Trident D-5 SLBMs should be equipped with new W88 warheads as planned or redesigned to optimize safety features is now open to question. For a review of the safety problems associated with the Trident D-5 missile and W88 warheads, see *Nuclear Weapons Safety*, Report of the Panel on Nuclear Weapons Safety of the Committee on Armed Services, U.S. House of Representatives, December 1990. In addition, tightening budget constraints have caused the navy to delay its plan to begin backfitting the first eight Trident submarines, which currently carry C-4 missiles, with D-5 missiles in 1993. See Statement of Vice Admiral Roger F. Bacon, assistant chief of naval operations, before the Subcommittee on Seapower and Strategic and Critical Materials of the House Armed Services Committee on Submarine Programs, March 20, 1991. Funding for this program does not appear in the Six Year Defense Plan for FY1992 to FY1997, and it is widely believed that the backfit will not occur. We believe that the added expense of backfitting would be

would be less cost-effective than a smaller fleet with more warheads per boat, the higher cost is judged to be worth paying if it provides a margin of safety and higher confidence in overall fleet survivability.

In addition to survivability, the potential risk of unauthorized SLBM launches should be highlighted. Although highly unlikely, this risk cannot be dismissed out of hand given the sheer magnitude of its consequences. Currently, SLBMs are the only U.S. strategic nuclear weapons that do not carry PALs—electromechanical locks that prevent warheads from exploding unless an unbreakable code, communicated when a launch has been properly authorized by the National Command Authorities, is inserted.[50] As a consequence, there is no *physical* barrier stopping an SSBN crew from launching its missiles without permission.[51]

For many reasons, the U.S. Navy has long resisted the use of PALs.[52] First, it does not perceive any need for such safeguards. It argues that SLBMs are relatively invulnerable to hostile takeover or terrorist attack, established procedures to minimize the risk of unauthorized use are adequate, and the personnel in charge of the weapons are well screened for reliability. Besides, it is argued, there has never been a problem stemming from inadequate control of the navy's nuclear arsenal. Thus the danger is judged insufficient to justify the cost of placing PALs on all SLBM warheads, particularly in the current budgetary environment.

In addition, the navy exhibits a strong psychological and cultural resistance to PALs because they are perceived to undermine the autonomy

---

particularly unnecessary in light of our proposed target set, which includes only "soft" targets.

[50]This discussion of the pros and cons of PALs is drawn from Peter Stein and Peter Feaver, *Assuring Control of Nuclear Weapons: The Evolution of Permissive Action Links*, Center for Science and International Affairs Occasional Paper Series, No. 2 (Lanham, Md.: University Press of America, 1987), pp. 70–77, 99–103, and 108–109; G. E. Miller, "Who Needs PALs?" *Naval Institute Proceedings*, Vol. 114, No. 7 (July 1988), pp. 50–56; John M. Weinstein, "Command and Control of Strategic Submarines," *National Defense*, Vol. 74, No. 445 (March 1989), pp. 19–21; Peter D. Zimmerman, "Navy Says No PALs for Us," *Bulletin of the Atomic Scientists*, Vol. 45, No. 9 (November 1989), pp. 37–41; and Dan Caldwell and Peter D. Zimmerman, "Reducing the Risk of Nuclear War with Permissive Action Links," in Barry M. Blechman, ed., *Technology and the Limitation of International Conflict* (Washington, D.C.: Foreign Policy Institute, School of Advanced International Studies, Johns Hopkins University, 1989).

[51]There are, however, *procedural* safeguards designed to prevent the unauthorized use of SLBMs. The launch of an SLBM requires several officers, other than the commanding officer, to verify the authenticity of the launch order and to execute the launch sequence itself. The best description of these procedural safeguards may be found in two unclassified memos from the Chief of Naval Operations (CNO): CNO, "SSBN Nuclear Weapons Control," message 272050Z (Washington, D.C.: September 27, 1984) and CNO, "Discussion Guide for Missile Release Procedures on Fleet Ballistic Missile Submarines," memo Ser 02/6U383394 (Washington, D.C.: July 11, 1986). Portions of each are reprinted in John M. Weinstein, *op. cit.*

[52]The best articulation of the navy's position on the risk of an accidental or unauthorized SLBM launch is CNO, "SSBN Nuclear Weapons Control," *op. cit.*

and authority traditionally given to navy commanders in the operation of their vessels. In short, in the navy's eyes, PALs are akin to "rudder orders from the beach."[53]

Furthermore, PALs are believed to present operational problems that could either degrade nuclear deterrence or lessen reliability. Because communications links with SSBNs are less survivable than the subs themselves, an adversary might think that an attack on these communications links would leave a PAL-equipped SLBM force paralyzed, since the submarines would be unable to launch their missiles without the codes to unlock PALs. Alternatively, even if these links were survivable, PALs would add a measure of complexity to an already complex system, and could therefore lessen the reliability of SSBN communications.

Those who advocate the placement of PALs on SLBMs see things somewhat differently. First, they argue, while the risk of the unauthorized use of SLBMs may indeed be low, the size of the nuclear firepower aboard a single submarine—as many as 192 warheads of 475 kilotons each[54] —makes this risk worth reducing still further. Second, although PALs may run counter to certain navy traditions, they ensure that the ability to use nuclear weapons remains contingent on the authority of the highest civilian decision-makers.

Third, the concern that PALs, in combination with vulnerable communications links, could render the entire SLBM force unusable bears further examination. Navy officials are the first to argue that "communication links to our strategic submarines are robust, reliable, redundant and readily reconstitutable."[55] Indeed, submarine communications have improved in recent years, narrowing the reliability differential between links to sea-based forces and links to land-based forces. Furthermore, given the variety of channels available for communicating with SSBNs,[56] it is almost certain that some links could be reconstituted, even after a massive nu-

---

[53]Miller, *op. cit.*, p. 53.

[54]This assumes a Trident submarine carrying 24 Trident D-5 missiles with high-yield W88 warheads. Under the proposed force levels, one Trident submarine would carry approximately 80 warheads.

[55]See for, example, the Testimony of Vice Admiral Bruce DeMars, assistant chief of naval operations for undersea warfare, before the Subcommittee on Seapower and Strategic and Critical Materials of the House Armed Services Committee on Undersea Warfare, March 9, 1988.

[56]SSBN communications span the radio spectrum—including extremely low frequency (ELF), very low frequency (VLF), low frequency (LF), high frequency (HF), and ultra high frequency (UHF) systems—and their transmitters are deployed in space, on aircraft, on land (both fixed and mobile platforms) and at sea. While electromagnetic pulses (EMP) from nuclear explosions would undoubtedly disrupt some SSBN communications, this would not occur across the entire radio spectrum. Furthermore, many transmitters are hardened against EMP.

clear strike, to transmit PAL codes to submarines before they would have to return to port.[57]

However, the crux of the matter is that this concern is arguably independent of the absence or presence of PALs. If in fact submarine commanders would only launch their missiles if they received proper authorization and if in fact this authority is not predelegated to individual commanders, then any breakdown in communications, with or without PALs, would mean that such authorization could not be received and the missiles would not be launched. To argue otherwise—that is, that the missiles might nevertheless be fired—only confirms that the risk of unauthorized launch is indeed real. Finally, the addition of PALs would not necessarily overburden the existing system with unworkable complexity; if the PAL code were included in the message to launch, unlocking the PAL and giving a missile its instructions would be one and the same action.[58]

On balance, we believe that the absence of PALs on SLBM warheads is a situation that needs to be rectified. The means of enabling the actual use of nuclear weapons must remain in the hands of the highest civilian and military authorities—and in their hands alone.[59] We therefore recommend installing PALs on all U.S. SLBM warheads[60] while taking steps to further improve the redundancy and reliability of submarine communications.[61]

In sum, in the context of the proposed reductions, the United States should reduce its SLBM force to 1,440 warheads on a fleet of 18 SSBNs, unless and until the ASW threat changes significantly. All SLBM warheads should be equipped with PALs to reduce the risk of unauthorized SLBM use, and the reconstitutability of submarine communications should be

---

[57]Indeed, Vice Admiral DeMars states that "the invulnerability of our submarines, combined with these and other enduring or restorable communication links, provides crisis stability through the assurance that National Command Authority orders can be delivered before, during or after an attack on the United States." DeMars, *op. cit.*

[58]See Zimmerman, *op. cit.*, p. 40 for more details.

[59]Ashton B. Carter, "Emerging Themes in Nuclear Arms Control," *Daedalus*, Vol. 120, No. 1 (Winter 1991), p. 239.

[60]Congress recently recommended the placement of PALs on all U.S. intercontinental ballistic missiles. See Conference Report on the National Defense Authorization Act for FY 1992–93, *op. cit.*

[61]For example, the United States might consider building a network of relay stations that could store authorization codes, once transmitted by the national command authorities, until individual submarines could surface, query the stations, and receive the forwarded information. See Stein and Feaver, *op. cit.*, pp. 100–101. This network would have to be survivable if the eventual transmission of enabling codes was to be assured. Such a network would also contribute to the United States' ability to ride out a nuclear attack. Although improving submarine communications via this alternative or others would probably be expensive, these costs might well be outweighed by the risks of not guarding against unauthorized SLBM use.

improved. As in the case of ICBMs, the viability of equipping SLBMs with command destruct mechanisms should be explored. Lastly, research and development should begin on future means of deploying fewer warheads per submarine.

The Bomber Leg

Like ICBMs and SLBMs, bombers have their own virtues. For example, they are the only strategic systems for which launch is not necessarily synonymous with use, since they can be recalled before striking their targets.[62] In addition, they are highly versatile, able to be used for both nuclear and conventional missions, and able to strike both fixed and, under some conditions, mobile targets.[63]

In the absence of compelling reasons to alter the strategic division of labor, the bomber force should continue to carry approximately 40 percent of U.S. strategic warheads—that is, 1,440 of the proposed force of 3,600. Assuming an average of 12 weapons per aircraft, this would allow the United States to deploy 120 strategic bombers.[64]

The central issue is, of course, what kinds of bombers these should be.[65] What is the appropriate mix of penetrators and cruise-missile carriers? Almost two-thirds of the current U.S. bomber force carry ALCMs and one-third serve as penetrators. Under START, the bomber force envisioned by the Reagan and Bush administrations would have tilted more toward the latter.[66] However, the following analysis suggests that the United States should decrease its emphasis on penetrating bombers and rely on cruise-missile-carrying bombers as the backbone of its future force.

Of the numerous missions that have been claimed for penetrating bombers, none is concurrently feasible, necessary, and able to be performed only by penetrators.[67] For example, hunting down "strategic

---

[62]The recallability of bombers is, however, far from assured in a nuclear environment where communications between national command authorities and pilots might be lost. Furthermore, once recalled, bomber forces would be extremely vulnerable to attack as squadrons regrouped.

[63]The capability to hunt and destroy mobile targets is, however, far from assured, as will be discussed in the following.

[64]This estimate of average bomber loading is based on aircraft carriage capability, weapons availability, and operational requirements. Actual loadings would vary according to mission.

[65]This chapter addresses what kinds of bomber *missions*, and thus what kind of bomber force, the United States should emphasize in the future. It is left to the next chapter to address the specific types of bombers—B-52s, B-1Bs, or B-2s—needed to fulfill these missions.

[66]Both administrations originally advocated full bomber force modernization, which would have resulted in a force of 132 B-2 bombers, 97 B-1B bombers, and 87 B-52 ALCM-carrying bombers under START.

[67]For a more in-depth discussion of these missions, see Michael Brower, "B-2: New Numbers, Old Arguments," *The Bulletin of the Atomic Scientists*, Vol. 46, No. 5 (June 1990), pp. 25–29,

relocatable targets," such as Soviet mobile missiles, is currently infeasible because the reconnaissance satellites necessary to track their movements do not exist and would cost billions of scarce defense dollars to acquire and deploy. This mission is, moreover, not necessary given the postulated target set. However, even if this mission were both feasible and desirable, it could be foiled by relatively inexpensive countermeasures, such as deceptive missile basing, camouflaging, electronic jamming, and the use of decoys. Witness Iraq's effective use of quite simple countermeasures, such as hiding mobile launchers and fielding decoys, to confuse U.S. sensors and pilots during the Gulf War. The difficulties associated with this mission would be compounded in a nuclear environment, with radioactivity, smoke, and dust in abundance.

The air force has also asserted that it needs penetrating bombers for postattack assessment and reconnaissance-strike missions. In such a mission, U.S. bombers would fly over Soviet territory in the wake of ballistic missile attacks in order to assess whether or not sufficient damage had been done to specific targets and to launch additional strikes as necessary. In a nuclear environment, however, this mission would likely be infeasible. And, even if it were feasible, it would add only marginal value at substantial cost. As then Army Chief of Staff Maxwell Taylor questioned in the early 1960s: "Is it worth several billion dollars . . . to be able to overfly Soviet targets with a few score of manned bombers looking for residual [targets] after each country . . . has already exchanged several thousand megatons of nuclear firepower on their respective target systems?"[68] We believe not.

Penetrating bombers have also been lauded as providing the most survivable hard-target-kill capability in the U.S. strategic arsenal. However, since hardened targets like Soviet nuclear forces and leadership posts are not part of our proposed target set, this capability is of little significance in our view.

Finally, some air force officials have advocated using strategic penetrating bombers, such as the B-2, in conventional missions.[69] Indeed, the

---

and Michael E. Brown, "The U.S. Manned Bomber and Strategic Deterrence in the 1990s," *International Security*, Vol. 14, No. 2 (Fall 1989), pp. 5–46.

[68]Maxwell Taylor as quoted in Alain C. Enthoven and K. Wayne Smith, *How Much Is Enough? Shaping the Defense Program, 1961–1969* (New York: Harper & Row, 1971), p. 246.

[69]General Lee Butler, then commander-in-chief of the Strategic Air Command, told Congress that "our new military strategy and the changing international security environment signal that it is clearly time to reinstitute the full conventional capacity inherent in the nation's bomber fleet, especially as its numbers shrink in the years ahead." Specifically, he argued that the B-2 Stealth bomber could "revolutionize the Conventional Warfighting Triad" (i.e., the triad of bombers, tankers, and strategic reconnaissance forces). See Statement of General Lee Butler before the Subcommittee on Defense of the Committee on Appropriations of the U.S. House of Representatives, April 30, 1991.

use of long-range bombers in conventional roles is a pillar of the 1991 air force reorganization. (See Chapter 8 for details.) Given the changing security environment and the declining defense budget, this is hardly surprising. The strategic bomber force will undoubtedly be more relevant and more cost-effective if it exercises its latent conventional capacity. However, the United States already has hundreds of land-based tactical and carrier-based aircraft dedicated primarily (if not exclusively) to conventional missions; the circumstances in which these would need to be supplemented by a significant force of strategic bombers are few.[70] Furthermore, in the event that strategic bombers were needed in a conventional conflict, past experience (in Vietnam and the Persian Gulf) suggests that existing bombers, such as the B-52, would more than likely be sufficient. It is doubtful whether the United States would need the stealthy capabilities of the newer B-2 bomber to penetrate the air defenses of non-Soviet adversaries. Therefore, conventional missions should continue to be considered a secondary rather than a primary role for penetrating bombers, particularly with regard to procurement decisions.

Aside from these missions, the air force also maintains that penetrating bombers, when deployed in combination with cruise missile carriers, complicate Soviet air defense efforts and splinter the application of Soviet resources to this task, thereby increasing the effectiveness of cruise missile carriers. But existing Soviet air defenses are no match for U.S. cruise missiles as it is; indeed, the air force claims that cruise missiles can penetrate existing Soviet air defenses with a high degree of confidence, placing an enormous amount of stress on the system.[71] And this is likely to remain the case for the foreseeable future, as the expenditure of billions of rubles to rectify the situation appears highly unlikely given current and anticipated economic conditions in the former Soviet Union. Furthermore, the deployment of the stealthy Advanced Cruise Missile (ACM) will only make an effective Soviet defense against cruise missiles less attainable.[72]

In sum, there is no foreseeable mission for penetrating bombers that is feasible, necessary, and able to be performed only by such bombers. Thus, the United States need not maintain a substantial force of them. Given the high cost of penetrating bombers, it should emphasize bombers

---

[70]If, for example, the number of U.S. overseas bases dwindled, the political costs of using them became prohibitive, and/or there were no carriers within striking distance of a given theater, the United States might want the ability to launch from its own soil a conventional air attack against a distant adversary.

[71]The air force estimates that currently deployed ALCMs (i.e., ALCM-Bs) will be able to penetrate Soviet air defenses throughout the decade. Roger Speed, *op. cit.*, p. 27.

[72]This is true not only because of the ACM's stealthy qualities but because it will have a range significantly greater than the ALCM-B, "allowing U.S. bombers to cover the entire Soviet Union from launchpoints beyond the range of far forward defense." Department of Defense, *Program Acquisition Costs by Weapon System for FY1991*, January 29, 1990, p. 76.

that carry ALCMs instead. The United States should, however, retain a residual penetration capability for unforeseen missions that may arise in the future.

Finally, as in the case of ballistic missiles, the United States should explore command destruct mechanisms for air-launched cruise missiles. Although the risk of accidental or unauthorized use associated with ALCMs is less than that associated with ICBMs and SLBMs, it does exist and should, therefore, be addressed.[73]

FORCE ADAPTABILITY

When contemplating the future of U.S. strategic offensive forces, it is important to remember that the strategic environment is neither static nor insulated from the winds of political change. Therefore, U.S. strategic forces must be designed to withstand and adapt to significant shifts in U.S.-Soviet relations and the level of nuclear danger. Such adaptability stems from how forces would be operated under different conditions. This section describes how the proposed forces could be adapted to two different scenarios: on one hand, a dramatic increase in the threat to U.S. forces and C³I and in the risk of deliberate nuclear war; and on the other, the continued positive transformation of U.S.-Soviet relations.

The first scenario envisions a world in which U.S.-Soviet relations take a sharp turn for the worse and the risk of deliberate nuclear war reemerges as a source of considerable concern. This world is not simply a return to the Cold War as we knew it,[74] but a world in which threats to the survivability of U.S. forces and command and control facilities markedly increase above Cold War levels. Such threats could take the form of potentially hostile operating practices, such as large numbers of Soviet ballistic- and cruise-missile-carrying submarines patrolling off U.S. coasts, or technological breakthroughs, such as a Soviet ability to detect and track U.S. SSBNs in the open sea. However unlikely, this scenario provides a worst-case basis for thinking through available options.

If such threats were to emerge, the United States would have a number of options for improving the survivability of its strategic forces. If, for example, the survivability of its strategic bombers were threatened, the

---

[73]Because bombers would arm and launch their cruise missiles only after hours of decision time had elapsed, the risk of accidental or unauthorized use is low. Nevertheless, one can imagine a situation in which human or technical error might lead to an unwanted or errant launch.

[74]In fact, a return to the status quo ante is not a real possibility, as many of the changes that have taken place—the liberation of Eastern Europe from Soviet domination, the reunification of Germany, and the dissolution of the Warsaw Pact—would be virtually impossible to reverse.

United States could take a number of steps to lessen their vulnerability. Day-to-day bomber alert rates could be increased,[75] bomber escape time improved, bombers and tankers redeployed from coastal to inland bases, and bombers more widely dispersed.[76] If the United States sought to improve the survivability of its ICBMs, it could deploy them on mobile launchers or in deceptive basing schemes, as discussed earlier. Finally, if a more survivable SSBN fleet were sought, the United States could consider increasing the number of boats on patrol, upgrading its ASW efforts, enhancing its efforts to foil Soviet ASW, and patrolling larger areas or patrolling only in protected sanctuaries, depending on the nature of the Soviet ASW threat. These options are, however, not equal, and their relative advantages and disadvantages would have to be assessed in light of the specific threat faced. The object of such an assessment would be to determine which option(s) would result in the greatest increase in survivable warheads at the least cost.

The second scenario envisions a world in which U.S.-Soviet relations continue to improve and the United States faces no new nuclear adversaries capable of posing a serious threat to the overall survivability of its nuclear forces or C³I.

In such a world, as in today's world, the most plausible path to nuclear war with the former Soviet Union would be the accidental, inadvertent, or unauthorized use of nuclear weapons. Therefore, the United States would be wise to make additional changes in its nuclear operations to reduce this risk. For example, as a follow-on to reducing alert rates and rejecting prompt launch options, the United States could consider removing nuclear warheads from units no longer on ready alert and placing them in the custody of civilian authorities.[77] By lengthening the time it would take to prepare nuclear weapons for use, separating warheads and delivery vehicles would lessen the risk of unintended nuclear weapons use still further. If, in the very long term, this approach were taken to its logical extreme and applied universally, it would be akin to putting the U.S. bomb back in the basement.

The primary risk of this approach is that, in the unlikely event of a crisis, reversing it could endanger stability. If, in a time of substantial tension or fear of war, the United States began remating warheads and delivery vehicles, this purely defensive action could reasonably be interpreted by the former Soviet Union to be a sign of preparation for offensive action. In short, reducing readiness in peacetime could actually increase the risk of miscalculation in crisis.

---

[75]In some cases, this might require the construction of additional runways in order to avoid stacking up bombers as they await takeoff.

[76]The latter two options might require the construction of additional bases. See Michael E. Brown, *op. cit.*, pp. 27–32, for a more detailed discussion of options related to increasing bomber survivability.

[77]See Blair and Kendall, *op. cit.*, pp. 53–58.

If, however, the United States and the former Soviet Union could conceive of and agree to "rules of the road" for nuclear alerting procedures and deployment practices, this risk could be lessened or at least managed. Whether or not such rules would be both workable and acceptable to the U.S. and Soviet militaries is not clear.[78] Should superpower relations continue to improve and the threat of deliberate nuclear war continue to decline, they should be the subject of U.S.-Soviet discussion.

Finally, the United States and the former Soviet Union could, in the second scenario, negotiate further stabilizing reductions in strategic weapons down to the minimum levels required for deterrence in such a less confrontational world.

In sum, if new threats to the survivability of U.S. nuclear forces and command and control were to emerge and the risk of deliberate nuclear war were to increase markedly, the United States would have a variety of means at its disposal for improving the survivability of the forces proposed in this chapter. If, on the other hand, U.S.-Soviet relations continue to improve, the United States could consider decreasing further the readiness and size of its strategic offensive forces.

CONCLUSIONS AND RECOMMENDATIONS

With the end of the Cold War, U.S. strategic offensive forces, operations, and policies seem destined to change. The only question is how. The following recommendations outline a set of changes that would bring U.S. strategic nuclear weapons more into line with the realities of the post–Cold War world.

- As the United States enters the first decade of the post–Cold War era, its strategic offensive forces should be designed to maximize the deterrence of deliberate nuclear war and minimize the risk of the accidental, inadvertent, or unauthorized use of nuclear weapons. These objectives should be met at the lowest possible force levels consistent with stability and within anticipated constraints.
- As a next step in the context of a U.S.-Soviet agreement beyond START I, the United States should seek to reduce its strategic nuclear forces to approximately 3,600 warheads. In the longer term, deeper reductions may well be warranted.
- As U.S. strategic offensive forces are reduced and restructured, the following force characteristics should be emphasized: survivability (to enhance crisis stability), control (to reduce the risk of unintended

---

[78]On one hand, precedents such as the Incidents at Sea Agreement and the more recent Dangerous Military Activities Agreement suggest that such rules of the road might be possible. On the other hand, one can expect some resistance from both the air force and the navy to any regulation of operations that could compromise the readiness and survivability of their nuclear forces in a crisis.

nuclear weapons use), and flexibility (to ensure that a smaller force can perform a range of missions).
- At the same time, a number of other force characteristics should be deemphasized, if not eliminated: extensive MIRVing, especially of silo-based missiles; hair-trigger postures; excess throwweight on ballistic missiles; and weapon systems that pose new threats to survivability, such as MaRvs, earth-penetrating warheads, and short-time-of-flight SLBMs.
- The United States should, at least in the near term, maintain a strategic triad as its forces are reduced, deploying roughly 700 warheads on single-warhead ICBMs in silos, 1,440 warheads on 18 ballistic missile submarines, and 1,440 warheads on 120 heavy bombers, primarily cruise-missile carriers.
- As a hedge against future threats to the survivability of the triad as a whole, more survivable ICBM basing options, such as mobile and/or deceptive schemes, should be kept open.
- Prompt launch options, such as launch on warning and launch under attack, should be abandoned in order to reduce the risk of miscalculation and inadvertent nuclear war. The United States should also seek the strategic forces and command and control capabilities necessary to ride out a large-scale nuclear attack, for a period of a few hours to days, and respond appropriately.
- PALs should be installed on all SLBM warheads to reduce the risk of unauthorized SLBM use, and research and development should begin on future means of distributing SLBM warheads over a larger number of submarines.
- As for heavy bombers, the United States should emphasize bombers that carry ALCMs and ACMs while retaining a residual penetration capability for unforeseen missions that may arise in the future.
- Finally, the United States should research command destruct systems and, if viable, develop and deploy them on all strategic offensive missiles in an effort to mitigate the consequences of accidental, inadvertent, or unauthorized missile launches.

SUGGESTED READINGS

Blair, Bruce G. and Henry W. Kendall. "Accidental Nuclear War." *Scientific American*. Vol. 263, No. 6 (December 1990), pp. 53–58.

Carter, Ashton B., John D. Steinbruner, and Charles A. Zraket, eds. *Managing Nuclear Operations*. Washington, D.C.: The Brookings Institution, 1987.

Cochran, Thomas B., William M. Arkin, and Milton M. Hoenig. *Nuclear Weapons Databook, Volume I: U.S. Nuclear Forces and Capabilities*. Cambridge, Mass.: Ballinger, 1984.

Flournoy, Michèle A. *Briefing Book on the Strategic Arms Reduction Treaty*. Boston: Council for a Livable World Education Fund, October 1990.

May, Michael M., George F. Bing, and John D. Steinbruner. *Strategic Arms Reductions*. Washington, D.C.: The Brookings Institution, 1988.

National Academy of Sciences. *The Future of the U.S.-Soviet Relationship*. Washington, D.C.: National Academy Press, 1991.

Speed, Roger. *Strategic Forces: Future Requirements and Options*. Livermore, Calif.: Lawrence Livermore National Laboratory, Center for Technical Studies on Security, Energy, and Arms Control, November 1990.

The START Treaty and Beyond. Washington, D.C.: Congressional Budget Office, October 1991.

von Hippel, Frank and Harold A. Feiveson. "Beyond START: How to Make Much Deeper Cuts." *International Security*. Vol. 15, No. 1 (Summer 1990), pp. 154–180.

Chapter
6

A Modernization and Arms Control Agenda for Strategic Offensive Forces

Michael F. Stafford

*S*ince the dawn of the nuclear age, the United States has modernized its strategic offensive forces to maximize their effectiveness as the ultimate deterrent to war. New systems have been deployed to maintain force capability as systems have aged and to enhance that capability in the face of increasingly capable Soviet strategic forces. Simultaneously, the United States has sought arms control agreements to constrain the Soviet threat.

Ideally, modernization and arms control efforts should reflect careful assessments of needs, available resources, applicable constraints, and their net effect on stability in light of likely Soviet reactions. They should also be synergistic, viewed not as independent endeavors but rather as mutually reinforcing means of achieving a common goal. In modernizing its forces, the United States should emphasize those force characteristics that will create the greatest potential for stabilizing arms control; in devising arms control proposals, it should emphasize those provisions that maximize the stabilizing effects of prospective forces.

Unfortunately, past modernization programs and arms control proposals have too frequently fallen short of these standards. At times, programs to modernize U.S. strategic forces have arisen for relatively narrow military reasons—a technological advance, a potential for greater efficiency, a new capability to handle a new mission—and have been advocated without due regard for their overall effect on the strategic balance. Most frequently cited in this regard is the U.S. program, beginning in 1970, to place multiple warheads on its ballistic missiles, which led to highly fractionated U.S. and Soviet ICBM forces that are widely considered to be destabilizing. Other programs have owed much of their success to political factors—industry alliances with key members of Congress, bureaucratic imperatives within the defense establishment—rather than to their contribution to deterrence. Still other modernization programs have run afoul of political or economic constraints. Several of the proposals for mobile basing of the MX ICBM, for example, could not obtain public acceptance. And the B-2 bomber and road-mobile Midgetman have been hampered by their high costs in a time of tight budgets.

Arms control efforts, likewise, have on occasion been based on overly narrow considerations. For example, the United States has at times resisted limits on certain capabilities in order to preserve its modernization options, despite the negative net consequences if the Soviet Union were to exercise the same options. The multiple warhead example cited earlier is a case in point. Chapter 5 noted two other cases: U.S. resistance to limits on maneuvering reentry vehicles and earth-penetrating warheads.

Finally, modernization and arms control efforts have too often proceeded on divergent paths. Certain modernization programs—such as nuclear sea-launched cruise missiles, which are very difficult to monitor—have created tough arms control problems, and certain arms control provisions—such as START I bomber weapon counting rules—have created incentives to which modernization efforts have had difficulty responding.

The aim of this chapter is to devise an agenda for strategic force modernization and arms control that meets the standards already cited—an agenda that is based on a comprehensive assessment of requirements for and effects of possible programs and provisions, that accounts for applicable political and economic constraints, and that is coherent. Beginning with the recommendations in Chapter 5 regarding the levels and characteristics of strategic offensive forces the United States should seek as it moves beyond the force structure mandated by the START I Treaty, we assess options for reaching those goals and for maximizing stability both during the transition and thereafter. Based on that assessment, we recommend a comprehensive program of strategic offensive force modernization and arms control for the immediate post–START I era.

A few basic axioms underlie this analysis:

First, as explained in earlier chapters, the fundamental objective of the U.S. nuclear force posture is to minimize the risk of war, particularly nuclear war, both deliberate and inadvertent. To forestall deliberate war, the United States should seek a posture that maximizes deterrence. To avoid inadvertent war, it should seek to minimize the chances of miscommunication, miscalculation, accidents, or a breakdown in political or physical control. Both force modernization and arms control can contribute to each of these efforts.

Second, the continuing uncertainty about the future political course of the former Soviet Union makes it important to insure U.S. security against shifts in the orientation of those who control the Soviet nuclear arsenal. For this reason, the modernization and arms control agenda should aim to create a strategic balance that is resilient to such shifts. In particular, we emphasize minimizing the risk of a rapid Soviet breakout from arms limits, especially because such a breakout could become increasingly significant as force levels are reduced. However implausible such a breakout may seem under current circumstances, it is in U.S. interests, as nuclear arsenals are reduced, to seek to eliminate excess missile capacity that could be exploited easily by future Soviet leaders who might have a different agenda than those presently in power. Minimizing this risk not only has implications for arms control proposals, it also means avoiding modernization options that would create breakout concerns if matched by the Soviets.

Third, as noted in Chapter 5, it is likely that strategic force modernization, like the rest of the defense budget, will continue to be relatively constrained for the foreseeable future, as a result of both deficit-cutting efforts and the widespread perception of a diminishing threat. This will place a premium on modernization options designed either to enhance force capabilities at low cost or to preserve more costly programs as options for future contingencies.

Finally, the key venue for the next phase of strategic arms control will be the START II negotiations, to which the United States and the former Soviet Union are already committed.[1] A commitment to significant reductions in strategic arms has been reaffirmed by both Soviet President Gorbachev and Russian President Yeltsin since the failed coup of August 1991.[2] It is further assumed that these talks will continue to be bilateral, with a single entity representing the Soviet center and those republics with strategic nuclear weapons on their soil. This assumption is based on what appears to be, as of this writing, an emerging consensus within the former Soviet Union (and in the West) that a single central authority should retain control over the Soviet nuclear arsenal. Yeltsin, for example, envisions a committee, representing both the center and individual republics, to control nuclear weapons.[3] This view has been echoed by others, including Ukrainian President Leonid Kravchuk.[4] Should this consensus collapse or take a different direction, the United States would have to adjust both the process and substance of its arms control efforts accordingly.

Furthermore, we do not expect other nuclear powers to participate in

---

[1]"The Joint Statement on Future Negotiations on Nuclear and Space Arms and Further Enhancing Strategic Stability," dated June 1, 1990, commits the sides to "new talks on strategic offensive arms" to begin "at the earliest practical date" following the signing of the START I Treaty. See *Arms Control Today*, Vol. 20, No. 5 (June 1990), p. 23.

[2]See "Gorbachev's Remarks on Nuclear Arms Cuts," *New York Times*, October 6, 1991, p. A12; and Boris Yeltsin, Interview on Cable News Network, September 3, 1991.

[3]Yeltsin, *op. cit.*

[4]Leonid Kravchuk, Remarks at National Press Club Luncheon, September 26, 1991.

such discussions, as they are opposed to joining the negotiations until U.S. and Soviet forces are reduced to lower levels and other conditions are met, and as their inclusion could greatly complicate what are already bound to be very complex talks. Nevertheless, as U.S. and Soviet forces *are* reduced further, it will become important that third-country forces be taken into account. The United States and the former Soviet Union can do this by seeking a political commitment from the British, French, and Chinese not to exceed their then-existing force levels in the aftermath of a START II Treaty or, failing that, by making START II limits contingent upon restraint by others.

It must be emphasized, however, that this focus on START II does not preclude pursuing some aspects of strategic offensive arms control through other independent channels. If, for example, outcomes other than binding limits were being sought, different countries were involved, or progress in negotiations could be accelerated, the talks could be held outside the START framework. Alternatively, the United States and the former Soviet Union could take steps unilaterally, without any negotiation at all, as Presidents Bush and Gorbachev did in withdrawing nuclear-tipped sea-launched cruise missiles from ships and submarines in the fall of 1991. Therefore, the arms control recommendations contained in this chapter, particularly those involving cooperative measures, are made without any judgment as to whether they should be implemented in START II or separately.

FORCE POSTURE OBJECTIVES

The objectives the United States should set for strategic offensive forces include the levels and characteristics specified in Chapter 5, as well as other goals that can produce a more stable strategic environment. As recommended in Chapter 5, the United States should seek to reduce its (and Soviet) strategic offensive forces to a level of about 3,600 warheads, while retaining a triad of land-based, sea-based, and air-based forces. The recommended distribution of U.S. warheads is 700 on ICBMs, 1,440 on SLBMs, and 1,440 on heavy bombers.

In structuring its forces and seeking to influence how the Soviets structure theirs, the United States should emphasize survivability, control, and safety, and deemphasize highly fractionated missiles (particularly those that are vulnerable), excess throwweight, new threats to survivability, and measures that create pressures to use weapons early.

Restructuring of the U.S. land-based leg should aim to maximize reliance on single-warhead ICBMs in silos in the near term, while retaining the option for mobile and/or deceptive basing in the longer term. The key objective for the sea-based leg should be to retain a sufficiently robust fleet of SSBNs to hedge against unforeseeable antisubmarine warfare advances; we judge 18 SSBNs to be sufficient. The air-based leg should deemphasize penetrating bombers in favor of cruise missile carriers. And nuclear sea-launched cruise missiles should be eliminated.

Other goals derive from additional, identifiable elements of the current strategic environment that tend to undermine stability or produce misunderstanding and thereby heighten the risk of war. For example, both the United States and, to a lesser extent, the Soviet Union have been plagued in the past by considerable uncertainty as to the nature of the other's strategic force operations and planning. The United States has dealt with this uncertainty through worst case estimates of the threat and its evolution that, in retrospect, have often been exaggerated and have produced unnecessary arms buildups and dangerous measures to improve survivability. Although this problem has decreased in recent years and is likely to decrease further if current trends in U.S.-Soviet relations continue, additional efforts to enhance transparency and predictability could accelerate this process. Similarly, each side has an inadequate understanding of the other's views of nuclear weapons and their appropriate roles, as well as an inadequate appreciation of aspects of its own behavior that the other side has found particularly threatening. Efforts to address these shortcomings and other sources of misunderstanding could reduce tensions.

MAINTAINING SYNERGY

As noted, it is important, in seeking to attain the desired force posture, that the United States design its force modernization and arms control efforts to be mutually reinforcing. Some of the force posture objectives we have specified translate straightforwardly into force modernization or arms control options. For others, however, synergy between modernization and arms control is a key to attaining the desired outcome.

For example, in the near term we would enhance the likelihood that ICBMs would survive a first strike by relying on single-warhead missiles that are unattractive to target because they would require at least two warheads each to destroy. In two ways, arms control can increase the probability that an adversary would be unwilling to attempt an attack in which it would expend more warheads than it could hope to destroy. First, by producing equal levels of warheads on each side, arms control could ensure that such an attack would leave the aggressor with fewer residual warheads than the victim. Second, by reducing the level of warheads to the point where differences of a few hundred become important, arms control would make this disadvantage for the aggressor more significant.

In the longer term, we would retain the option for further enhancing ICBM survivability through mobile or deceptive basing. Arms control can ensure that some of these missiles would survive even an all-out attack by reducing warheads below the number the potential attacker would need to barrage the full dispersal area for mobile ICBMs or to destroy all possible locations for deceptively based ICBMs.

One of the reasons cited in Chapter 5 for retaining both ICBMs and bombers in the U.S. force is the synergy between them that would prevent a hostile Soviet Union from being able to attack both legs simultaneously with short warning. Continuation of this effect would be endangered, however, if such a Soviet Union were able to deploy a sufficient number of highly accurate warheads on its SLBMs to conduct an SLBM-only attack against all ICBMs and bomber bases. Arms control reductions can substantially decrease that threat.

Finally, we recommend measures such as abandoning prompt launch postures to increase control over strategic forces and reduce the likelihood of their inadvertent use. Such measures become possible largely to the extent that modernization and arms control efforts reduce the prompt threat to those forces and thus relieve pressures for their early use.

MODERNIZATION OPTIONS

This section identifies and assesses options for modernizing U.S. strategic offensive forces as part of the effort to reach the recommended force posture. It strives to examine all options that are feasible candidates during the next decade for producing a force with the desired characteristics; options suggested by others that we judge to be either infeasible or inconsistent with the recommended force characteristics are not included.

The ICBM Leg

To get to the recommended near-term force of 700 single-warhead, silo-based ICBMs, it is assumed that the United States would eliminate the 50 MX ICBMs it currently deploys, and modernization would focus on smaller missiles. The following programs provide potential means of achieving this near-term goal and preserving the option for more survivable basing in the longer term:

1. *Refurbish Minuteman II.* The 450 Minuteman II ICBMs deployed since 1966 constitute the only single-warhead missiles in the land-based force. These missiles, which are reaching the end of their projected lives, have been taken off alert, and the air force plans to retire them over about six years beginning in 1992. Another option, however, is to extend their lives by replacing key missile components. A program to replace the stage one motors, motor liners, and propellant and to upgrade missile guidance systems would extend the operation of these missiles by about 17 years at a cost of approximately $2.9 billion.[5] This would thus be a relatively low-cost approach to deploying a modernized, single-warhead force.

---

[5]General Accounting Office, *Strategic Forces: Minuteman Weapon System Status and Current Issues*, GAO/NSIAD-90-242 (Washington, D.C.: General Accounting Office, September 1990), pp. 15–17.

2. *Download Minuteman III.* Another low-cost means of producing single-warhead ICBMs is to remove two of the three warheads from each of the 500 currently deployed Minuteman III missiles. The air force plans to begin doing that in 1995 in a program estimated to involve negligible cost.[6] To enable such a step, the START I Treaty allows the United States to download this missile in return for a Soviet right to download one or more missiles.[7]

3. *Deploy Midgetman in Silos.* The development of a new, single-warhead Small ICBM, or Midgetman, is projected to be completed near the end of the century. Although originally developed with road-mobile basing in mind, this missile could also be deployed in silos, with the option of shifting to mobile basing in the future. Silo deployment of 250 missiles would cost about $15 billion for acquisition, with annual operations and support (O&S) costs of $500 million.

4. *Develop and Deploy a New, Improved Small ICBM.* Having been in development for some seven years, the Midgetman is not based on the most advanced U.S. technology. A new missile incorporating state-of-the-art guidance systems, rocket motors, and propellants should prove more reliable and maintainable. The cost for 250 such missiles deployed in silos would likely be $30 billion or more, however.

5. *Resume Research and Development on Road-Mobile Midgetman.* The road-mobile basing concept for Midgetman promises a force that could disperse rapidly upon receipt of warning of attack, even if that warning came only after the attack was launched. Assuming the attacker would be unable to locate and attack the missiles discretely (certainly the case given current capabilities), it could eliminate the Midgetman force only by barraging the entire dispersal area with far more warheads than it would be trying to destroy.[8] This should make such an attack quite unattractive, if not impossible. Thus, road-mobile Midgetman promises high survivability, but at high cost, about $25 billion for acquisition of missiles and launchers and $750 million in annual O&S. In the current

---

[6]Except where noted otherwise, all cost estimates were provided by congressional analysts, based on projections from Department of Defense budget figures for comparable historical and current-generation programs and using then-year dollars.

[7]The treaty allows each side to download a total of 1,250 warheads from as many as three types of missiles—for the United States, the Minuteman III, and two other, unspecified, existing types; for the Soviet Union, the SS-N-18 and two other, unspecified, existing types.

[8]For example, the concept favored by the air force would place Midgetman missiles on hard mobile launchers in garages at current Minuteman silos, with two launchers per garage. The launchers would be able to dash on warning at average speeds of 30 miles per hour. If 250 missiles were deployed in this manner, they could, with as little as ten minutes of dash time, disperse into an area of almost 10,000 square miles. With a launcher hardness of 30 pounds per square inch when battened down, the attacker would need over 3,300 warheads of 500-kiloton yield or up to 10,000 100-kiloton warheads to barrage this area. These calculations are based on data provided in Roger D. Speed, *Strategic Forces: Future Requirements and Options* (Livermore, Calif.: Lawrence Livermore National Laboratory, Center for Technical Studies on Security, Energy, and Arms Control, November 1990), pp. 31–32.

economic and strategic environment, such a cost is quite difficult to justify, but it might seem reasonable under different circumstances in the future (such as those described in Chapter 5). Although President Bush decided to halt research and development (R&D) on this basing concept in September 1991, it could be resumed and completed for about $3 billion, preserving the option to implement it in the future should circumstances so warrant.

6. *Research and Develop a Multiple Protective Shelter (MPS) Basing Concept for a Small ICBM.* This approach, also known as the "shell game" concept, involves concealing each ICBM among a large number of potential silos or launch points. The object is to create a prohibitive price for destroying the ICBM by forcing the attacker to destroy all launch points in order to be assured of getting the missile. The major advantage of MPS basing is that, because it requires no extraordinary U.S. action, such as dispersal, to enhance survivability, it is just as effective against a surprise attack as against a forewarned one. This would allow a U.S. president to avoid actions in a crisis that could be perceived as provocative. The disadvantage is that, should the potential attacker develop a means of detecting the actual location of each missile, it becomes no more survivable than a single-warhead, silo-based missile. In addition, although verification of deployment numbers could be accomplished through random sampling techniques, the extra shelters could create a breakout concern if covert production of missiles seemed feasible.

A basing scheme of this type for the MX ICBM was rejected in the 1980s, but recent technological advances have produced a more attractive approach, called "carry hard."[9] Research and development on this concept could be completed for about $5 billion over five years.

Comparison of Options: Downloading the Minuteman III is the least expensive way of sustaining a substantial, single-warhead ICBM force into the future. The necessary allowance of similar Soviet downloading creates a greater capability for breakout, however. In this case, the Soviets would have the potential to rapidly restore 1,250 warheads on one or more types of ballistic missiles. For this reason, we would prefer that the START I Treaty not allow downloading and that the United States instead refurbish the 450 Minuteman II missiles and deploy 250 Midgetman missiles in silos to produce the 700-missile force. Nevertheless, the right to download is provided by the treaty, and there would be no additional harm in Washington's exercising that right.

---

[9]The carry-hard approach uses hardened, encapsulated missiles that are shuttled among austere, unhardened shelters. The hardness of the capsules, about 10,000 pounds per square inch when in the shelters, allows the shelters to be spaced more closely than under previous schemes, thus reducing the land requirements. The hardening of missile capsules rather than each individual shelter reduces the costs (about $35 billion to deploy 250 Midgetman missiles in a field of 5,000 launch points). For a fuller description of this concept, see Speed, *op. cit.*, pp. 36–39. The cost estimate for this option is derived from data provided by Speed.

This leaves the question of what missiles should complement the 500 Minuteman IIIs to fill out the force. The less expensive option would be to retain and refurbish 200 Minuteman IIs. With their high-yield warheads, these missiles would be particularly effective for area targets but inappropriate for targets where collateral damage was a concern. Alternatively, the United States could deploy 200 Midgetman missiles in silos. This would provide more modern missiles as well as the option to move more rapidly to mobile basing in the future, but at the cost of about an additional $10 billion. Under current funding constraints, we believe the additional capability does not justify the cost.

For the longer term, we believe it important to maintain the option to shift to more survivable basing of ICBMs, in case a threat arises that makes such a shift advisable. Therefore, we favor completing research and development of both the road-mobile and carry-hard basing concepts for a small ICBM.

Recommendations: The United States should exercise the right provided by the START I Treaty to download its 500 Minuteman IIIs to one warhead each and should refurbish 200 Minuteman IIs. To preserve more survivable basing options for the future, the United States should also complete R&D on both road-mobile and carry-hard basing for a small ICBM.

The SLBM Leg

To retain the desired number of 18 SSBNs in the fleet, the recommended 1,440 SLBM warheads would have to be distributed at about 80 warheads per sub. This represents an approximate 60-percent reduction of current loads, since a 24-missile Trident SSBN with the eight-warhead C-4 or D-5 SLBM carries 192 warheads. The following options provide means of reducing submarine loads by that amount:

1. *Remove or Disable SSBN Tubes.* Removing or disabling 14 of the 24 launch tubes on each Trident SSBN would cut its load to 80 warheads. Removal of tubes would be quite expensive and time-consuming. Several approaches to disabling tubes have been suggested, including: (1) inserting a concrete plug, (2) welding the hatch shut, and (3) severing the part of the tube that protrudes beyond the hull and pressure welding a steel cap over the remainder of the tube. These approaches would likely involve a relatively small, but not trivial, cost (on the order of $1–2 billion), since disablement would probably have to be accomplished outside the normal overhaul schedule. In choosing among them, the key would be to ensure that the disablement could not be easily or quickly reversed while also allowing for necessary safety inspections of the tubes.

2. *Download SLBMs.* Another way to reduce the number of warheads per sub would be to download all SLBMs from the current eight warheads per missile to, say, four. This could be done at minimal cost.

3. *Develop a New, Less Fractionated SLBM.* Instead of downloading existing SLBMs, the United States could, of course, develop a new SLBM that carries fewer warheads. A program to research and develop such a missile and procure 300–400 could be expected to cost about $20–25 billion.

4. *Develop a New, Smaller Submarine.* The United States could also develop a smaller submarine that carries fewer missiles than the Trident. One possibility is an advanced diesel sub, whose proponents argue that it would be cheaper (at about $500 million each) than a nuclear sub and that a mixed diesel/nuclear force would complicate Soviet antisubmarine warfare efforts by producing differing sonar signatures.

Comparison of Options: As with ICBMs, downloading SLBMs is the cheapest and easiest way to produce less fractionated missiles. Downloaded SLBMs would have greater range, allowing their submarines to patrol in wider ocean areas, and they would create greater targeting flexibility by reducing footprint constraints. But, as with ICBMs, securing the right to download SLBMs would create a greater breakout capability if the Soviets were accorded the same right. Downloading 360 SLBMs from 8 warheads per missile to 4, when combined with the 1,000 warheads downloaded from Minuteman IIIs, would require the United States to seek an allowance of 2,440 downloaded warheads per side. Given our desire to constrain excess missile capacity as arsenals are reduced, we would prefer to hold the line on downloading at the 1,250 warheads allowed by START I.

Disabling missile tubes, if duplicated by the Soviets, also creates some capability for breakout, but it should be possible to find a disablement technique whose reversal would require a visible and fairly slow process that would give the United States time to respond and make a breakout attempt less likely in the first place.

Deploying either a less fractionated missile or a smaller sub is prohibitively expensive in the short term, but we favor preserving these options in the longer term by conducting appropriate R&D.

Recommendations: The United States should disable 14 missile tubes on each of 18 Trident SSBNs. To preserve longer-term options, it should conduct research and development on both a low-MIRV SLBM and a small submarine.

The Bomber Leg

Chapter 5 recommends reducing the air-based leg to a 1,440-warhead force that relies increasingly on cruise missile carriers. Assuming the average bomber carries 12 warheads, this would translate into a force of 120 heavy bombers, compared to the more than 250 bombers now deployed. Options for constituting such a force would include the following:

1. *Retain 120 B-52Hs and B-1Bs as Cruise Missile Carriers.* All B-52Gs and most B-52Hs would either be retired or converted to conventional use.[10] The B-2 program would be canceled and the existing handful of B-2s would be retired, due to the economic inefficiency of maintaining such a small force. All B-1Bs would be converted to cruise missile carriers, at a cost of about $100 million. No penetrating bombers would be maintained in the heavy bomber force.

2. *Retain 90 B-52Hs and B-1Bs as Cruise Missile Carriers and 30 B-1Bs as Penetrators.* This option differs from the first in that a wing of the B-1Bs would not be converted to cruise missile carriers in order to retain some capability to perform penetrating missions.

3. *Use 15 B-2s as Penetrators and Retain 105 B-52Hs and B-1Bs as Cruise Missile Carriers.* This force would rely on a small number of B-2s to sustain a limited U.S. capability to penetrate air defenses with confidence farther into the future. Procurement of the 15 B-2s already in the pipeline would be completed at a cost of $9 billion. This amount would cover completion of R&D, conversion of R&D bombers to operational capability, and completion of procurement. The remainder of the 120-bomber force would consist of B-1Bs and B-52Hs carrying cruise missiles.[11]

Comparison of Options: As explained in Chapter 5, we favor retaining a modest capability to perform penetrating missions into the future. B-1Bs are highly likely to penetrate current air defenses, but their ability to do so can be expected to deteriorate if air defenses, particularly Soviet systems, are improved in the future. Whether the B-2s are worth the substantial additional cost is difficult to judge. We believe the advantage for future R&D of gaining experience with operational stealth bombers tips the scale in favor of finishing the current buy.

Recommendation: The United States should complete procurement of the 15 B-2s already in the pipeline and should retain 105 B-52H and B-1B bombers as cruise missile carriers.

Other Modernization

Finally, as recommended in Chapter 5, the United States should pursue at least two additional strategic modernization programs. First, it should equip all SLBMs with PALs. Second, it should conduct research and development on command destruct systems for all strategic offensive missiles. These steps would reduce both the risk of inadvertent and unauthorized missile launches and the consequences of such launches were they to occur.

---

[10]The START I Treaty allows the sides to convert up to 75 heavy bombers to conventional use. This creates a breakout problem in that they could be rapidly reconverted to a nuclear role. Therefore, the United States should seek to ban such conversion in START II.

[11]A variant of this option would be to fill out one wing of 30 B-2s to create a more economically sustainable force, but the additional 15 bombers would cost an extra $35–40 billion.

ARMS CONTROL OPTIONS

This section identifies and assesses arms control options for producing, in tandem with modernization efforts, the recommended force posture. It also addresses other options for using arms control to reduce the risk of war.[12]

As already noted, it is assumed that the primary venue for these arms control efforts will be the START II negotiations. We believe the START I Treaty provides, in general, a suitable baseline from which START II can proceed.[13] Accordingly, we propose that START II build on the START I regime to the extent possible rather than starting from scratch. To this end, we are inclined to retain the basic structure of limits contained in START I except in cases where we believe the value of individual limits is insufficient to justify the estimated negotiating difficulty of seeking to retain or tighten them.

Aggregate Limits

The START I Treaty contains aggregate limits on deployed strategic nuclear delivery vehicles (ICBMs, SLBMs, and heavy bombers) and warheads carried by those vehicles. Should START II include similar limits?

1. *Warheads.* Because it is the warhead, not the missile or launcher, that destroys a target, the warhead is the most appropriate unit for counting gross strategic capabilities. It also gained widespread acceptance as the basic accounting unit during the START negotiations. Thus, START II should likewise use a warhead ceiling as the central aggregate limit.

A second question is whether warheads should be counted on the basis of actual numbers or alternative counting rules. In START I, ballistic missile warheads are counted according to actual numbers deployed. Aircraft-delivered weapons, on the other hand, are "discounted": a full bomber load of gravity bombs and short-range attack missiles counts as one warhead, and a bomber carrying cruise missiles counts as 8–10 warheads (although it can carry 16–20). The discount is intended to serve two purposes. First, it adjusts for the fact that aircraft must face defenses unconstrained by an arms control agreement while ballistic missiles face, at most, tightly constrained defenses; thus an aircraft-delivered warhead has a lower probability of being effective than a ballistic missile warhead. Second, it provides an incentive for the sides to place greater reliance on aircraft, particularly penetrators.

---

[12]In addition to the recommendations included in this chapter, the recommendations made in Chapters 4 and 5 to ban nuclear SLCMs and in Chapter 7 to retain ABM Treaty limits on strategic ballistic missile defense programs would have important implications for the strategic environment.

[13]For a description of the START Treaty, see Michèle A. Flournoy, *Briefing Book on the Strategic Arms Reduction Treaty* (Boston: Council for a Livable World Education Fund, Inc., 1990), pp. 13–18.

For reasons discussed in the following, we do not favor counting rules that create incentives to favor one type of weapon system over another. We do believe it appropriate, however, to continue to adjust for the differing levels of defenses bombers and ballistic missiles face. Thus, we would count each heavy bomber, regardless of armament, as carrying six warheads, or about half its normal load.[14] This approach has the additional virtue of simplifying significantly the verification of accountable bomber warhead numbers; one need merely count bombers and multiply by 6.[15] We would continue to count ballistic missile warheads according to the number actually deployed.

With this counting approach, the force structure recommended in Chapter 5 can be accommodated within an aggregate limit of 3,000 accountable warheads, or 50 percent below the START I limit.

2. *Strategic Nuclear Delivery Vehicles (SNDVs).* One reason for an SNDV limit in the START I Treaty was to constrain the number of Soviet nuclear targets in order to ease U.S. targeting requirements. But, as Chapter 3 argues, targeting of most Soviet nuclear forces is not advisable in the future, and thus this rationale disappears. However, there are other reasons for retaining an SNDV limit. Each delivery vehicle provides added potential for a rapid breakout from treaty limits through the loading up of additional warheads on the missile or bomber. However, binding throw-weight limits would reduce this problem for ballistic missiles by constraining the ability of those missiles to carry additional warheads. Also, the exclusion, or even the easing, of SNDV limits in a START II Treaty could be misperceived by the public as a step away from the force cuts mandated by START I. On the other hand, SNDV limits, if too tight, would constrain each side's ability to shift to less highly MIRVed missiles in order to enhance survivability. A limit of 1,200 (25 percent below the START I limit) would allow room for 700 single-warhead ICBMs, 360 four-warhead SLBMs, and 120 heavy bombers.

Recommendations: START II should include central limits of 3,000 warheads and 1,200 strategic nuclear delivery vehicles.

Structuring of Triad Legs

The START I Treaty affects each side's decisions regarding the distribution of forces among triad legs through both direct limits—warhead subli-

---

[14]This 50-percent discount is the same as used for ALCM bombers in START I. Because bombers on each side would actually be allowed to carry their full load, this accounting approach would not create a risk of a breakout beyond treaty limits.

[15]To secure Soviet agreement to this approach, it might be necessary to add a limit of 12 warheads per ALCM bomber, similar to the START I limits of 16 for Soviet bombers and 20 for U.S. bombers, so that the discount for ALCM bombers remained strictly limited to 50 percent. Because such a limit creates difficult verification tasks, however, it should be avoided if possible.

mits on ballistic missiles, heavy ICBMs, and mobile ICBMs—and, as mentioned earlier, incentives—favorable counting rules for bomber weapons. U.S. support for such an approach was based on judgments that certain systems are more or less destabilizing than others. For example, it was asserted that slow-flying bombers are less destabilizing than fast-flying ballistic missiles because they are less capable of a surprise attack.[16] Similarly, U.S. officials argued that SLBMs are less destabilizing than ICBMs, particularly heavy ICBMs, because they are less capable (at least for now) of preemptive strikes against hard targets such as missile silos and are also less vulnerable to preemptive strikes.[17]

We are not convinced that distinctions of this nature will continue to exist. Stealth technology could enable bombers to present a growing threat of a short-warning attack (as demonstrated in the initial air strikes against Baghdad in the Persian Gulf War), greater accuracy should make SLBMs increasingly capable against hard targets, and other technological advances could blur previous differences among triad legs.

In addition, incentives have been known to backfire. For example, the START I counting rule substantially favoring penetrating bombers over cruise missile carriers was originally developed to reflect U.S. plans to build a large force of B-2 bombers. When the B-2 program ran into considerable trouble in Congress, one of the primary arguments used by its proponents to buttress their case was that the United States needed a full complement of B-2s to take advantage of the counting rule.[18] There is no indication that START policy-makers ever intended to create a rationale for a bomber that could not be justified on its own.

Therefore, we see no reason to incorporate into START II any provision designed to influence how the sides allocate weapons among legs of the triad.

Recommendation: Within the START II aggregate warhead and SNDV limits, there should be complete freedom to mix among ICBMs, SLBMs, and heavy bombers.

Low Fractionation

We recommend maximizing reliance on single-warhead ICBMs and placing fewer SLBM warheads on each submarine, possibly by relying on SLBMs that carry fewer warheads. The following options would move the sides in the direction of less fractionated missiles:

1. *Ban on Fixed, MIRVed ICBMs.* This provision would require the United States to eliminate or download its 500 Minuteman III missiles and

---

[16]"The Case for START Sublimits," *ACDA Issues Brief*, May 13, 1988, p. 1.

[17]*Ibid.*

[18]For example, see General John Chain, "Testing and Operational Requirements for the B-2 Bomber," Hearing before the Senate Armed Services Committee, July 21, 1989, p. 18.

either eliminate or shift to rail-mobile basing its 50 MX missiles. It is consistent with our recommended force of 200 refurbished Minuteman IIs and 500 downloaded Minuteman IIIs. The Soviets would have to eliminate their SS-17, SS-18, and SS-19 ICBMs, and either eliminate or shift to rail-mobile basing their silo-based SS-24 missiles. The resulting Soviet ICBM force could be expected to consist of both fixed and road-mobile SS-25s and rail-mobile SS-24s.

2. *Ban on All MIRVed ICBMs.* This provision, proposed by President Bush in September 1991, would ban mobile, as well as fixed, MIRVed ICBMs. It would require the United States to eliminate the MX and download Minuteman III, as we recommend. The Soviets would have to eliminate all modern ICBMs except the SS-25 and begin a massive procurement program to retain a substantial land-based force. The rationale for banning MIRVed mobiles is not that they are necessarily vulnerable to attack like their silo-based counterparts but rather that the difficulty of monitoring them, combined with the large number of warheads per missile, makes them a potentially significant means of rapid breakout from treaty limits. This could occur through covert production of illegal missiles to be used as reloads on legal launchers or covert production of illegal launchers and missiles. On the other hand, the United States has concluded that START I verification provisions are sufficient for it to monitor rail-mobile SS-24s with an acceptable level of confidence. Moreover, the experience gained through such monitoring should enhance confidence and lead to development of even more effective techniques for START II.

3. *Sublimit on Fixed, MIRVed, or All MIRVed, ICBM Warheads.* Rather than banning MIRVed ICBMs, the United States could propose placing a sublimit on them to allow the sides to move more gradually toward less fractionated forces, an effect that, given our recommendation to eliminate U.S. MIRVed ICBMs in any case, would primarily benefit the Soviets. The Soviets would likely favor a ceiling on the order of 1,000 warheads or more to accommodate a significant number of SS-18s and/or silo-based SS-24s, and would want to apply it only to fixed ICBMs, to protect the mobile SS-24. A possible tradeoff would be for the United States to offer to exempt mobile MIRVed ICBMs from the sublimit in return for a lower ceiling than the Soviets might otherwise like.

4. *Sublimit on MIRVed Ballistic Missile Warheads.* The Soviets have traditionally resisted U.S. efforts to single out ICBMs—the leg they most emphasize—for special limits, arguing that equity requires that such limits apply as well to SLBMs—the leg the United States most emphasizes. They could therefore be expected to parry a U.S. proposal for a sublimit on MIRVed ICBM warheads with one covering all MIRVed ballistic missiles. This would capture U.S. C-4 and D-5 SLBMs, as well as most Soviet SLBMs.

5. *Ban on Production of MIRVed ICBMs or MIRVed Ballistic Missiles.* This provision, in isolation or in conjunction with one of the sublimits outlined, would force a further evolution of the sides' force postures toward lower fractionation by ensuring that any ICBM, and possibly any

SLBM, produced after an agreed date would have but one warhead. The provision could apply to all missiles, whether new or modified versions of existing types. Banning production of MIRVed ICBMs would not constrain the modernization programs we recommend, since they focus solely on single-warhead ICBMs. However, it would probably not be most cost-effective for a future SLBM to have only a single warhead. On the other hand, as with the sublimit discussed earlier, the Soviets would likely oppose a provision that constrained ICBMs and not SLBMs. A possible compromise would be for the United States to agree to include SLBMs with more than, say, four warheads in this provision in return for Soviet agreement that (1) the agreed cutoff date would be such as to allow completion of necessary D-5 production, and (2) a MIRVed warhead sublimit would not include SLBMs.

Comparison of Options: Although a ban on fixed, MIRVed ICBMs is a desirable long-term outcome and would not affect the force posture we recommend for the United States, it would substantially alter Soviet forces. It would force elimination of all Soviet heavy missiles and, if accompanied by significant constraints on mobile ICBMs, require extensive Soviet procurement of fixed, single-warhead ICBMs at great cost to retain their current emphasis on the land-based leg. Therefore, the Soviets could be expected to oppose it strongly. A ban on all MIRVed ICBMs would affect the Soviets even more extensively, and thus would also likely engender strong opposition.

The sublimit options therefore seem to be more feasible for START II. We oppose extending such a sublimit to SLBMs, because all U.S. and almost all Soviet SLBMs are MIRVed, and thus the sublimit would have to be so high as to be practically meaningless. Instead we prefer to exempt SLBMs and mobile ICBMs as well, the latter in return for Soviet acceptance of a low ceiling.

The production ban suggested in the final option effectively complements the sublimit to push the sides toward even lower fractionation over the longer term, without interfering with recommended U.S. modernization programs.

Recommendations: START II should include a sublimit of 500 warheads on fixed, MIRVed ICBMs within the 3,000-warhead limit. There should also be a ban on future production of MIRVed ICBMs and, if necessary to win Soviet acquiescence, on production of SLBMs with more than four warheads.

Mobility Versus Breakout Potential

As noted earlier, although mobile basing for ICBMs promises enhanced survivability, it also creates heightened potential for a rapid breakout from treaty limits. To dampen this problem, START I includes a sublimit of 1,100 warheads on mobile ICBMs. Recognizing that the difficulty of breakout might increase as the United States gains experience monitoring mobiles under the START I regime, should it seek a similar sublimit in START II? Or should another type of constraint on mobiles be proposed? Options include:

1. *Ban on MIRVed Mobile ICBMs.* This would eliminate the greatest breakout potential among mobile ICBMs, since each additional missile of this type would add multiple warheads to the force. The Soviets would have to eliminate mobile SS-24s and the United States would forgo the rail-mobile MX, for which funding was halted in September 1991 in any event.

2. *Sublimit on Mobile ICBM Warheads.* The START I sublimit could be tightened further to discourage reliance on MIRVed mobiles. The United States would want the limit to protect deployment of up to 500 road-mobile Midgetman ICBMs, while the Soviets would prefer a limit that, combined with feasible options for fixed ICBMs, allowed them about 1,500 warheads on ICBMs. A limit of 750 warheads should fit this requirement.

Comparison of Options: As outlined earlier, a MIRVed mobile ban when combined with the recommended sublimit on fixed, MIRVed ICBM warheads, would force the Soviets into a massive and costly procurement program to maintain their current emphasis on the land-based leg. Therefore, they could be expected to oppose it strongly.

A warhead sublimit should also affect Moscow more than Washington, because the Soviets are almost certain to deploy more mobiles than the United States. Nevertheless, its inclusion in START I should make it easier to gain Soviet acceptance of a similar provision in START II. Therefore, even though the risk of breakout might be diminishing, the cost of securing this sublimit as insurance against negative changes in the security environment may be even smaller.

Recommendation: Within the warhead aggregate, there should be a sublimit of 750 warheads on mobile ICBMs.

Stricter Limits on Heavy ICBMs

START I cuts Soviet heavy ICBMs in half, to 1,540 warheads on 154 missiles, and bans new types of such missiles (effectively banning any U.S. heavy ICBM). Although increased accuracy can make other ICBMs effective hard-target killers, heavies remain the most threatening of Soviet strategic systems. The following options would tighten the constraints on these missiles:

1. *Ban on Heavy ICBMs.* The Soviets would be required to eliminate their remaining 154 SS-18s and deploy no more.

2. *Reduced Sublimit on Heavy ICBM Warheads.* Should a ban appear

to be too difficult to obtain, the United States could seek a further reduction below 154 missiles.

3. *Ban on Testing.* No further flight testing of heavy missiles would be allowed.

Comparison of Options: The ban is obviously the best option from the U.S. perspective. It is unclear how strongly the Soviets would oppose it. In the absence of SS-18s, they could easily deploy the same number of warheads on SS-24s and SS-25s. On the other hand, they recognize the negotiating leverage their heavy ICBM force affords them and might attempt to exact a steep price for banning it.

The Soviets would likely find it difficult to counter the argument that a reduction in the START I heavy ICBM sublimit was mandated by a reduction in the START I aggregate limit. This would argue for a further 50-percent cut to 770 warheads on 77 missiles. Allowing a sublimit this high would, however, require raising the sublimit on fixed, MIRVed ICBM warheads above 500.

In conjunction with a reduced sublimit, a ban on flight testing could heighten the momentum toward the elimination of heavies by leading to the eventual obsolescence of the existing force. The ban on future production of MIRVed ballistic missiles recommended previously would produce a similar effect, however, and should be easier to negotiate.

Recommendation: The United States should seek to ban heavy ICBMs but be prepared to accept a reduced sublimit, as long as the Soviets agree to ban future production of MIRVed ICBMs.

Reduced Throwweight

START I reduces Soviet ballistic missile throwweight by about half, to a ceiling of approximately 6 million pounds that is applicable to each side. Options for further throwweight reductions include:

1. *Reduced Limit.* The START I limit could be reduced by an additional 50 percent to 3 million pounds.

2. *Allowing Other Limits to Reduce Throwweight Indirectly.* Throwweight will automatically be reduced as the sides reduce the number and size of their ballistic missiles. The treaty could rely solely on this effect rather than codifying further throwweight cuts.

Comparison of Options: Current U.S. ballistic missiles total about 4.4 million pounds of throwweight.[19] Anticipated force reductions under

---

[19]Throwweight figures are derived primarily from data provided in International Institute for Strategic Studies (IISS), *The Military Balance, 1990–1991* (London: IISS, 1990), pp. 216–222.

START II should enable the United States to accommodate a 50-percent cut in the throwweight limit. Soviet reductions could leave them at a higher level than the United States but also below 3 million pounds. This, plus the START I precedent, should make it relatively easy to incorporate such a 50-percent cut into START II. It also helps that the difficult work of defining throwweight and determining how it is to be measured was completed in START I: The Treaty includes a Throwweight Protocol that defines throwweight and denotes means of measuring it in great detail.

Although the indirect effect of other cuts would reduce the need for a lower throwweight limit, it would not hurt to codify a throwweight reduction and a direct limit would help guard against large, single-war-head missiles on which extra warheads could be rapidly deployed in a breakout.

Recommendation: START II should require an additional 50-percent reduction in ballistic missile throwweight.

Missile/Warhead Destruction

One of the criticisms of START I is that, although its basic unit of account is warheads, its reductions require no actual destruction of warheads or even of most types of missiles.[20] The sides are allowed to salvage warheads from reduced missiles for other uses. And they are allowed to maintain, except in the case of mobile ICBMs, unlimited numbers of "nonde-ployed," or spare, missiles; any missiles above treaty limits can be con-verted to spares. Verification problems—the difficulty of monitoring war-head stockpiles and nondeployed missiles—underlie these approaches, as does the desire to use the missiles and warhead materials for other pur-poses. But critics argue that strategic forces have not really been reduced if the missiles and warheads remain intact. Options for requiring missile or warhead destruction are:

1. *Destruction Provisions for Missiles and Warheads.* The treaty could require that, for every missile launcher eliminated to comply with treaty limits, one missile of that type, and perhaps its warheads, be de-stroyed. Similarly, if a launcher were converted to handle a new type of missile, one missile of the older type and its warheads would be destroyed. An additional provision could require that, for each bomber eliminated or converted to nonnuclear use, a bomber load of weapons be destroyed.

2. *Limit on Nondeployed Missiles.* Combined with the SNDV limit, this would place a ceiling on all missiles possessed by each side, forcing destruction of any missiles above the ceiling.

3. *Direct Limit on Stockpiled Warheads.* The sides would be re-quired to eliminate all warheads above an agreed ceiling.

---

[20]The INF Treaty did not require destruction of warheads, either, a fact that was highlighted by its critics during the ratification debate.

Comparison of Options: The destruction requirements of the first approach would not, of course, prevent either side from building new missiles and warheads to replace those destroyed. But the side would have to bear the cost of doing so. In the case of warheads, it would also have to expend the necessary nuclear materials (unless salvage from destroyed warheads were allowed), which could, in the case of tritium, be difficult for the United States given current supply problems.

An advantage of this approach is that, with sufficient on-site inspection, the sides should be able to verify compliance with the requirement with high confidence. On the other hand, allowing inspectors of the other side to observe and verify the destruction of warheads could give them access to sensitive information regarding warhead design.[21]

A variant of this option would be to require that each side destroy 3,000 warheads (the difference between the START I and START II aggregate warhead limits) and a number of missiles equal to the number of launchers it reduces, without designating which ones must be destroyed. This would simplify the requirement while also according each side greater flexibility to destroy the missiles and warheads it values the least. On the other hand, allowing the sides to destroy their most obsolete weapons would make this provision even more cosmetic.

As noted, the second option, a limit on nondeployed missiles, could be difficult to verify with much confidence, since missiles are easier to hide than their larger, more cumbersome launchers. On the other hand, the experience of verifying the limit on nondeployed mobile ICBMs under the START I regime could improve verification techniques and raise U.S. confidence.

There is also a potential problem created by differing U.S. and Soviet procurement practices. To create economies of scale, the United States tends to buy a full complement of missiles rapidly, and then draws down the stocks slowly over time as missiles are used for test flights. The Soviet Union stretches out procurement over longer periods; combined with drawdowns for test flights, this produces more constant stockpile levels at relatively lower numbers. Thus, the United States tends to have a substantially higher percentage of nondeployed missiles than the Soviets. Absent expensive changes in U.S. procurement practices, nondeployed missile limits would have to be set so high—to accommodate U.S. practices—as to have no effect on the Soviets, or so low—to constrain the Soviets—as to force extensive U.S. reductions.

One way to work around this problem would be to set a limit on the number of nondeployed missiles of a given type that a side could possess over time, without limiting the number possessed at any one time. This

---

[21]Procedures for verifying warhead dismantlement without compromising security are discussed in Theodore B. Taylor, "Verified Elimination of Nuclear Warheads," *Science & Global Security*, Vol. 1, Nos. 1–2 (1989), pp. 1–26.

could complicate an already-difficult verification requirement, however, while also penalizing missile types that are retained over long periods.

The warhead limit would be even more difficult to verify than a limit on nondeployed missiles—despite the unique signatures associated with nuclear weapons storage, such as specialized security measures—due to the small size of warheads and uncertainty about the size of the current Soviet stockpile.

Recommendation: We believe some effort should be made to require destruction of missiles and warheads, but without creating a daunting verification task. Thus, the treaty should require that, for every missile launcher eliminated to comply with treaty limits or converted to a new type, one missile of the original type and its warheads be destroyed. START I–type limits on nondeployed mobile ICBMs would be retained. For the longer term, the United States should begin a determined effort to develop means of confidently verifying limits on warheads and nondeployed missiles.

Constraints on Future Threats

Chapter 5 recommended guarding against several types of future weapons that would pose new threats to survivability. Possible constraints are:

1. *Ban on Testing of Maneuvering Reentry Vehicles.* These weapons are capable of altering their trajectories during flight to evade antiballistic missiles or to strike targets with pinpoint accuracy. The United States is currently conducting low-level research and development on MaRV technology for strategic missiles, but has no plans for its deployment. The Pershing II intermediate-range missile, banned by the INF Treaty, was the only U.S. ballistic missile that had maneuvering reentry vehicles.

The United States chose not to address MaRV limits in START I because it wanted to protect the option to evade ABMs and did not know how verification efforts could differentiate between evading MaRVs and accuracy MaRVs. Because we would leave tight constraints on ABM systems, the need to evade ABMs seems insignificant (although MaRVs could provide a hedge against ABM breakout). As for accuracy, a maneuvering reentry vehicle, especially if it were combined with an earth-penetrating warhead, would have considerable capability against leadership and other hardened targets that we prefer not to attack or have attacked by the Soviets. Thus, it seems more important to foreclose Soviet options for such systems than to preserve U.S. options. A ban on all MaRV testing would seem fairly straightforward to verify.

2. *Ban on Testing of Earth-Penetrating Warheads.* These weapons burrow deep underground before exploding to destroy leadership shelters and other hardened targets. As with MaRVs, the United States has a low-level R&D program for this technology and chose not to address it in START I in order to protect the option for future deployment. Again,

because we choose not to attack hardened targets, it makes more sense to foreclose the Soviet option. The key verification difficulty in banning earth-penetration tests would be differentiating between such tests and normal tests of surface burst weapons that also impact the ground at the end of the missile's trajectory.

3. *Ban on Short-Time-of-Flight (STOF) SLBM Tests.* The trajectory of an SLBM could potentially be depressed or otherwise shaped to reduce significantly the time it takes to reach its target. This would substantially heighten the threat to systems, such as bombers, that rely on warning time for survivability. Neither the United States nor the former Soviet Union is currently developing a STOF capability for its SLBMs, and each realizes the threat such a capability would present. Accordingly, both sides have supported the concept of a STOF test ban, and they discussed it in START I.

But attempts to conclude a ban have encountered definitional problems. There is no clear threshold between STOF tests and normal ballistic missile tests, and, even if a threshold were established, it could be difficult to distinguish between a STOF test and a failure of a normal test. In START I, the United States finally proposed a ban based on the elapsed time of the test flight, but it foundered on Soviet attempts to expand this effort to incorporate such additional provisions as SSBN standoff zones and constraints on weapons using stealth technology.[22]

Recommendations: The treaty should ban testing of both MaRVs and earth-penetrating warheads if effective verification measures can be developed. Efforts should continue to define and negotiate a meaningful constraint on the short-time-of-flight threat.

COOPERATIVE MEASURES

Beyond the menu of more traditional strategic arms control provisions already outlined is a panoply of steps the United States and the former Soviet Union, and other nuclear powers, could take cooperatively to enhance mutual confidence and security and further reduce the risk of war. Many of these measures would hold particular promise for relieving potential causes of inadvertent war. The United States should draw as extensively as possible from the set of measures described in the following.

Verification Enhancements

The START I Treaty contains a robust verification regime including extensive data exchanges, a wide range of inspections, and a series of measures

---

[22]Interview with Soviet Foreign Ministry spokesman Gennadi Gerasimov, *FBIS Daily Report—Soviet Union*, February 1, 1990, p. 4; R. Jeffrey Smith, "U.S., Soviets Disagree on Trial Arms Inspections," *Washington Post*, October 24, 1989, p. A20.

designed to ease the monitoring task. Additional measures could both enhance the confidence with which the sides verify START II compliance and produce greater understanding of the nature of each other's strategic programs and posture. Such measures might include more movement restrictions and notifications for mobile ICBMs (without compromising survivability), more intrusive inspections of weapons to protect against conversion of conventional warheads to nuclear ones, and improved tags and seals for tracking treaty-limited items. Another possibility would be for the sides to exchange data on their warhead stockpiles and nuclear materials, and to begin monitoring each other's declared stocks, as a way of starting to get a handle on warhead inventories. Although this initial approach would leave unresolved the problem of ensuring that undeclared stockpiles were not being covertly maintained, it would nevertheless be a step in the right direction.

Transparency/Predictability Enhancements

As already explained, measures to enhance each side's understanding of the other's current forces and operational procedures, as well as its plans for future changes, can reduce the likelihood of misunderstanding or miscalculation exacerbating relations or leading toward conflict. Some such measures are:

1. *Expanded Notification of Strategic Activities.* The United States and former Soviet Union currently have in place agreements calling for advance notification of all strategic ballistic missile launches[23] and of one major strategic exercise per year.[24] Such notifications, of course, reduce the risk that such activities could be misperceived as threatening. Extension of the requirement to all strategic exercises involving activities that exceeded an agreed threshold could further reduce that risk.

2. *Increased Visits to Installations.* The transparency of each side's strategic programs and capabilities has been significantly enhanced by the series of visits over the past few years by policy-makers, military officers, and technical experts to installations of the other side. This trend could be furthered by a program of regular visits to operational bases, command and communications centers, production facilities, test sites, and research facilities.

---

[23]"Agreement between the U.S. and the USSR on Notifications of Launches of Intercontinental Ballistic Missiles and Submarine-Launched Ballistic Missiles," signed at the May/June 1988 Reagan-Gorbachev Summit in Moscow. See *Arms Control Today*, Vol. 18, No. 6 (July/August 1988), pp. 20–21.

[24]"Agreement between the U.S. and the USSR on Reciprocal Advance Notification of Major Strategic Exercises," concluded in September 1989. See *Arms Control Today*, Vol. 19, No. 8 (October 1989), p. 25.

3. *Launch Detection Systems.* Cooperative emplacement and maintenance of launch warning sensors in each other's ICBM fields and on SLBMs could enhance the ability of existing warning systems to provide indication of unintended launches as well as confirmation that no launch had occurred. The disablement of such a system could also warn that a deliberate strike might be in the offing. This option would be desirable, however, only if the sides could minimize reliability problems that could produce false alarms and heighten the risk of inadvertent war.

Safety/Control Enhancements

U.S.-Soviet discussions have devoted little attention to date to the risk of nuclear accidents and the possibility that a side could lose physical control of one or more of its nuclear weapons. A key reason for the dearth of discussion is that any detailed exchange could get into the particulars of warhead design. But an accidental detonation of a nuclear weapon, or its intentional detonation by a third party, could under some circumstances be misunderstood by the United States or the former Soviet Union as the initiation of nuclear conflict by the other and could lead to war.

The risk of loss of control over Soviet nuclear weapons was highlighted during the abortive Soviet coup of August 1991, and unrest in the republics has continued to raise concerns about this possibility. As discussed in Chapter 4, such concern appears to have been a primary motivation behind President Bush's September 1991 unilateral initiatives, particularly his proposal to explore cooperation in improving the safety and security of nuclear weapons, strengthening command and control, and reducing the risk of accidental or unauthorized use.

Efforts to improve nuclear weapons safety and control could include, among others[25]:

1. *Information Exchange on Warhead Safety.* Experts from the two sides could exchange information on techniques, such as insensitive high explosive, that can be used to reduce the risk of a nuclear accident. Although such a discussion might be more of a U.S. tutorial than an exchange, the United States would nevertheless benefit if the result were safer Soviet warheads.

2. *Information Exchange on Command Destruct and Warhead Enabling Devices.* The value of these devices was described in Chapter 5, which recommended researching command destruct devices for all strategic missiles and extending PALs to SLBMs. As with warhead safety measures, the United States benefits to the extent these devices are used with

---

[25]Other such efforts are discussed in Chapter 4.

Soviet weapons as well. As noted in Chapter 5, there is some indication that Soviet ballistic missiles already carry command destruct systems. A U.S.-Soviet exchange on these systems would be a logical follow-up to the 1971 U.S.-Soviet "Accidents Measures" Agreement.

As for PALs, it is believed that, like the United States, the Soviets use enabling devices on their ICBMs and bombers, but do not so equip their SLBMs.[26] An exchange on the technologies involved could help produce greater use of these safeguards.

Nuclear Risk Reduction Center (NRRC) Upgrades

When Senators Sam Nunn and John Warner first espoused the concept of NRRCs, they had in mind centers that would help prevent or defuse situations that could pose a heightened risk of nuclear war. For this purpose, the centers would provide a special communications channel between Washington and Moscow, and they would also be the sites of ongoing efforts by specialists to devise and implement measures to reduce the war risk.[27] In practice, however, the NRRCs have been little more than conduits for the routine exchange of notifications required by U.S.-Soviet arms control agreements. Part of this disparity is understandable; for example, crisis communications are already handled by the recently upgraded "hotline." But there are additional contributions the NRRCs could make. The original NRRC agreement calls for periodic reviews to consider additional tasks for the centers. Some candidates include yearly consultations on crisis management issues, discussion of means of war termination, joint conduct of some crisis management exercises, and conduct of some of the discussions outlined in the following.

"Hotline" Upgrades

As noted, the "hotline" was upgraded during the Reagan administration. Nevertheless, it continues to rely on communications satellites and cable and radio links that are vulnerable to accident and nuclear effects. Thus, it might go dead just when it was most needed. Dedicated, radiation-resistant satellites could improve the reliability of this system significantly.[28]

---

[26]Bruce G. Blair and Henry W. Kendall, "Accidental Nuclear War," *Scientific American*, Vol. 263, No. 6 (December 1990), p. 56.

[27]For details of proposals for NRRCs, see John Borawski, "U.S.-Soviet Move Toward Risk Reduction," *Bulletin of the Atomic Scientists*, July/August 1987, pp. 16–18.

[28]*Ibid.*, p. 58.

Other Exchanges

Finally, discussions of an even more general character could serve to relieve sources of tension and misunderstanding.[29] As noted earlier, each side has an inadequate understanding of the other's views toward nuclear weapons and their appropriate roles, and an inadequate appreciation of aspects of its own behavior that the other side finds particularly threatening. Efforts to ameliorate this situation could also be expanded to include other nuclear powers.

1. *Doctrinal Discussions.* The United States and Soviet Union engaged in limited discussions of nuclear doctrine during the START I negotiations, and more expansive discussions have occurred informally between officials and experts contemplating a radically reduced strategic balance. The latter have focused primarily on Soviet thinking. A thorough exchange in official channels on the roles of nuclear weapons in the post–START I world could stimulate further thought and understanding and be otherwise beneficial to both sides.

2. *Discussions of Particular Sources of Concern.* Both U.S. and Soviet participants in the START I negotiations and other recent exchanges reported that they had gained a new appreciation of how some of their country's practices were perceived to be provocative by the other side. Exchanges devoted explicitly to such problems could lead to a less wary attitude toward existing force postures or to changes in those postures, either of which would reduce tensions.

3. *Discussion of Third-Country Nuclear Capabilities.* As U.S. and Soviet force levels diminish, British, French, and Chinese nuclear capabilities and means of addressing them will become increasingly important. This discussion could facilitate a common understanding of the dimensions of the problem and a more cooperative approach to resolving it. (The dangers of proliferation of nuclear capabilities to other nations will also grow in importance, but regular U.S.-Soviet discussions of this problem are already established.)

CONCLUSIONS AND RECOMMENDATIONS

This chapter has sought to produce an agenda for strategic force modernization and arms control in the post–START I period that would move the United States safely to the stabilizing force posture recommended in

---

[29]Secretary of State Baker, for example, proposed a U.S.-Soviet dialogue on "the 'software' side of the arms competition: strategy and doctrine" in an October 19, 1990, speech to the American Committee on U.S.-Soviet Relations, as reprinted in *Foreign Policy Bulletin*, Vol. 1, No. 3 (November/December 1990).

Chapter 5. This agenda is intended to be a single, coherent plan for reaching the specified objectives with maximal efficiency. It takes into account both the need to economize in a time of funding constraints and the need to protect against uncertainty in a time of political instability in the former Soviet Union. As a result, emphasis is placed on modifying existing forces, rather than on procuring new ones, and on continuing research and development in key areas as a means of insuring the resilience of U.S. strategic forces in a changing and unpredictable security environment.

Table 6.1 summarizes the key elements of this agenda. Notional U.S. and Soviet forces that might result from these recommendations are depicted in Appendix A.

Table 6.1   A MODERNIZATION AND ARMS CONTROL AGENDA FOR STRATEGIC FORCES

Force Modernization

ICBMs	Download the 500 Minuteman IIIs to one warhead each, refurbish 200 Minuteman IIs, complete R&D on road-mobile and carry-hard basing for a small ICBM
SLBMs	Disable 14 tubes on each of 18 Trident SSBNs, do R&D on a low-MIRV SLBM and a small sub
Bombers	Complete procurement of 15 B-2s, retain 105 B-52Hs and B-1Bs as cruise missile carriers
Other	Equip all SLBMs with PALs, research and develop command destruct systems for strategic offensive missiles

Arms Control Provisions

Central limits	3000 warheads, 1200 SNDVs
Triad legs	Freedom to mix
MIRVed missiles	500 warheads on fixed, MIRVed ICBMs; ban on future production of MIRVed ICBMs and, if necessary, future production of SLBMs with more than 4 warheads
Mobile ICBMs	750 warheads on mobile ICBMs
Heavy ICBMs	Ban or reduced sublimit
Throwweight	50-percent cut below START I ceiling
Missile/warhead destruction	For every missile launcher eliminated to comply with limits or converted to a new type, one missile of the original type and its warheads must be destroyed
Future threats	Ban on testing of both MaRVs and earth-penetrating warheads if verification possible, continued effort to define and negotiate a meaningful constraint on the short-time-of-flight threat
Coop measures	Comprehensive menu

APPENDIX A

NOTIONAL U.S. AND SOVIET FORCES UNDER THE RECOMMENDED REGIME

United States	SNDVs	Accountable warheads	Actual warheads
ICBMs			
Minuteman II	200	200	200
Minuteman III	500	500	500
SLBMs			
Trident C-4/D-5	180	1440	1440
Bombers			
B-52H/B-1B	105	630	1260
B-2	15	90	180

Comparison to START II limits	Limit	U.S. total
SNDVs	1200	1000
Accountable warheads	3000	2860
Fixed, MIRVed ICBM warheads	500	0
Mobile ICBM warheads	750	0
Ballistic msl throwwt (million lbs)	3	2.0

Soviet Union	SNDVs	Accountable warheads	Actual warheads
ICBMs			
SS-19	83	498	498
SS-24 mobile	50	500	500
SS-25 mobile	225	225	225
SS-25 fixed	150	150	150
SLBMs			
SS-N-23	216	864	864
Bombers			
Blackjack	50	300	600
Bear H	75	450	600

Comparison to START II limits	Limit	Soviet total
SNDVs	1200	849
Accountable warheads	3000	2987
Fixed, MIRVed ICBM warheads	500	498
Mobile ICBM warheads	750	725
Ballistic msl throwwt (million lbs)	3	2.3

SUGGESTED READINGS

Arbatov, Alexei G. "START: Good, Bad or Neutral?" *Survival*. Vol. XXXI, No. 4 (July/August 1989), pp. 291–300.

———, ed. *The Security Watershed: Soviets Debating Defense and Foreign Policy After the Cold War*. Arms Control and Security Yearbook of the Institute of World Economy and International Relations of the Soviet Academy of Sciences, 4th ed. New York: Gordon and Breach, 1992.

Davis, Richard. *Potential START II Outcomes and Their Implications*. Unpublished Background Paper presented to a Workshop on START II sponsored by Lawrence Livermore National Laboratories, September 14, 1990.

Gottemoeller, Rose, ed. *Strategic Arms Control in the Post-START Era*. London: Pergamon-Brassey's, 1991.

National Academy of Sciences. *The Future of the U.S.-Soviet Nuclear Relationship*. Washington, D.C.: National Academy Press, 1991.

Warner, Edward L. and David A. Ochmanek. *Next Moves: An Arms Control Agenda for the 1990s*. New York: Council on Foreign Relations, 1989.

Chapter
7

Defenses Against Nuclear Weapons

Mark W. Goodman

*T*he preceding chapters tacitly assume that the United States and the former Soviet Union will not deploy significant new defenses against nuclear weapons. This chapter considers how defenses, and Soviet reactions to U.S. defenses, might affect the goals described in those chapters and how changes in the world and in nuclear weapons policy may shift the balance of arguments for and against defense. While previous chapters propose substantial changes in U.S. nuclear weapons policy, this one argues for continued restraint in the U.S. approach to defenses.

Nuclear weapons challenge common notions of offense and defense in a number of ways. First, nuclear weapons appear to make defenses especially attractive, but their tremendous destructive capacity poses requirements so severe as to cast doubt as to whether defenses can serve any useful purpose at all, especially given today's large and diverse nuclear arsenals. Second, nations that rely on nuclear deterrence as their ultimate instrument of security may not consider defenses benign but instead see them as a profound threat. Third, defenses can provoke reactions that at best reinforce deterrence at greater cost—and undermine the nuclear arms control process—and at worst create dangerous incentives for preemption.

Recognizing the drawbacks of attempting to defend against nuclear weapons, the United States and Soviet Union signed the Anti-Ballistic Missile (ABM) Treaty in 1972. This treaty severely constrains defenses against long-range ballistic missiles and forms the central legacy of arms control from the Cold War era. The end of the Cold War raises new questions for U.S. policy on defenses against nuclear weapons. Will improved relations with the Soviet Union allow a more cooperative approach to these defenses? Does the disintegration of the Soviet Union or the proliferation of ballistic missiles and nuclear weapons warrant a substantial effort at defense?

To address these and other questions, this chapter begins with a brief history of defenses against nuclear weapons and goes on to explain how changes in the world may affect the balance of arguments for or against such defenses. It then develops a framework for classifying and evaluating various types of proposed defenses and applies this framework to the cases of long-range missile defense, short-range missile defense, and air defense. A summary of recommendations appears at the end, and Appendix A discusses the related issue of antisatellite weapons (ASATs).

HISTORICAL SURVEY

The early Cold War years saw relatively little debate over defenses against nuclear weapons. The limited scale of the Soviet nuclear bomber threat made air defenses a natural and potentially effective response. Investments in air defense were discussed on the basis of technical feasibility and spending priorities—with strategic offensive forces being the top priority under President Eisenhower's austere New Look military budgets.[1]

Most of the issues in today's debates first arose in internal bureaucratic disputes over ABM defenses in the Department of Defense under Robert McNamara. These include technical problems of feasibility and countermeasures, strategic issues of vulnerability and arms race stability, and basic questions of the purpose and scope of the defense. These disputes led to a polarization of the debate between a "damage limitation" school, which supported unilateral U.S. actions—including active defenses—to limit damage from a Soviet nuclear attack, and an "arms control" school, which saw damage limitation as a hopeless task in the face of possible Soviet responses and sought instead to reduce the risk of nuclear war through cooperation and arms control.

McNamara became a pivotal figure in establishing the arms control school of thought and fought to restrain the army's increasingly ambitious ABM schemes. As an alternative, he proposed in 1967 to deploy a limited ABM system (Sentinel) intended to defend against the potential nuclear threat from China. Later transformed by the Nixon administration into a defense of ICBMs and strategic bomber bases (Safeguard), only a single site was ultimately deployed, and that only briefly.[2]

---

[1]James M. Eglin, *Air Defense in the Nuclear Age: The Post-War Development of American and Soviet Strategic Defense Systems* (New York: Garland, 1988) covers the early history in some detail. B. Bruce-Briggs, *The Shield of Faith: A Chronicle of Strategic Defense from Zeppelins to Star Wars* (New York: Simon & Schuster, 1988) offers an idiosyncratic but more comprehensive historical survey.

[2]Edward Randolph Jayne II, "The ABM Debate: Strategic Defense and National Security" (Ph.D. dissertation, Massachusetts Institute of Technology, 1969), provides a thorough and

McNamara also sought to open an arms control dialogue with the Soviets, hoping that limits on ABM defenses would facilitate limits on offensive nuclear forces as well. Without such limits, ABM systems would create too great an incentive to increase and improve offensive forces—to be sure of penetrating the defense and maintaining an effective deterrent capability. By 1972, the Strategic Arms Limitation Talks had produced the ABM Treaty, a treaty of indefinite duration that strictly limits ABM deployments and restricts activities that could facilitate breakout from these limits, but only an interim agreement to limit the expansion of strategic offensive forces.[3] Although McNamara's hope that defensive arms control would allow strict limits on offensive forces was not realized, the ABM Treaty may have prevented an even more costly arms competition between offensive and defensive forces.[4]

The arms control school held sway until 1983 when President Reagan revived debate with his "Star Wars" speech, in which he put forward the goal of "rendering . . . nuclear weapons impotent and obsolete."[5] The resulting debate over the Strategic Defense Initiative (SDI) produced a stalemate between the arms control school, which dominated in Congress, and the damage limitation school, which held sway in the executive branch. This stalemate lasted through the 1980s.

DEFENSES AFTER THE COLD WAR

The end of the Cold War has produced changes that require us to rethink the arguments over defenses against nuclear weapons. For example, as the risk of deliberate conflict between the United States and the former Soviet Union has declined, concerns about accidental or unauthorized nuclear attack and the proliferation of nuclear weapons have grown.

---

readable history of this period. Morton H. Halperin, "The Decision to Deploy the ABM: Bureaucratic and Domestic Politics in the Johnson Administration," *World Politics*, Vol. 25, No. 1 (October, 1972), pp. 62–95, and Ernest J. Yanarella, *The Missile Defense Controversy: Strategy, Technology, and Politics, 1955–72* (Lexington, Kentucky: University of Kentucky Press, 1977) are also very useful.

[3]For an insider's view of the ABM Treaty negotiations, see Gerard Smith, *Doubletalk: The Story of SALT I* (Garden City, N.Y.: Doubleday, 1980). John Newhouse, *Cold Dawn: The Story of SALT* (Elmsford, N.Y.: Pergamon-Brassey's, 1989) provides a broader overview of the SALT process. David N. Schwartz, "Past and Present: The Historical Legacy," in Ashton B. Carter and David N. Schwartz, eds., *Ballistic Missile Defense* (Washington, D.C.: The Brookings Institution, 1984), pp. 330–349, and Alexander Flax, "Ballistic Missile Defense: Concepts and History," in Jeffrey Boutwell and Franklin A. Long, eds., *Weapons in Space* (New York: Norton, 1986), pp. 33–52, provide more contemporary reviews of the history.

[4]"The Success of the ABM Treaty" in Matthew Bunn, *Foundation for the Future: The ABM Treaty and National Security* (Washington, D.C.: The Arms Control Association, 1990), pp. 16–17.

[5]President Reagan's March 23, 1983, speech is reprinted as Appendix B in Jeffrey Boutwell and Franklin A. Long, eds., *op. cit.*, pp. 369–371.

As discussed in Chapters 1 and 4, political instability in the former Soviet Union and the collapse of the central government have raised concerns over the control of Soviet nuclear forces. The elaborate physical and procedural safeguards on Soviet strategic forces[6] could prove difficult to maintain under conditions of political and social disintegration, and safeguards are generally less rigorous for nonstrategic forces.[7] It remains difficult to imagine a motivation for possible attack against the United States, but the weakening of the safeguards against such an attack is troubling, and has led to renewed calls for defenses.[8]

The collapse of the Soviet Union also provides new avenues for nuclear proliferation. First, newly independent republics may inherit nuclear weapons or significant elements of a possible nuclear weapons production complex from the former Soviet Union. Second, political, economic, and social collapse could facilitate the transfer of nuclear weapons, related technologies, and technical expertise to other countries with nuclear ambitions.

The proliferation of nuclear weapons may pose new threats to U.S. allies and forces overseas, to which active defense is one possible response. Now relatively limited, these threats could grow much larger in the next ten years, and a direct threat to U.S. territory could arise in the more distant future.[9]

The end of the Cold War has also raised the possibility that the Soviets would be less likely to respond aggressively to U.S. defenses now than before, both because they are less concerned about external threats and because they are less capable of mounting an effective response. Given the uncertain future of the former Soviet Union and the possible reestablishment of a strong central government, however, it would be unwise to assume that these conditions will continue. Worsening bilateral relations and the grim logic of deterrence could lead such a regime to pursue responses to U.S. defenses that could be quite effective.

Defenses could also have the more dangerous effect of undermining

---

[6]Bruce G. Blair and Henry W. Kendall, "Accidental Nuclear War," *Scientific American*, Vol. 263, No. 6 (December, 1990), pp. 53–58, Bruce G. Blair, Testimony to the Committee on Armed Services, United States House of Representatives, July 31, 1991, and Stephen M. Meyer, "Soviet Nuclear Operations," in Ashton B. Carter, John D. Steinbruner, and Charles A. Zraket, eds., *Managing Nuclear Operations* (Washington, D.C.: The Brookings Institution, 1987), pp. 470–531, provide accounts of the control system for Soviet strategic forces.

[7]Kurt M. Campbell, Ashton B. Carter, Steven E. Miller, and Charles A. Zraket, *Soviet Nuclear Fission: Control of the Nuclear Arsenal in a Disintegrating Soviet Union*, CSIA Studies in International Security, No. 1 (Cambridge: Mass.: Center for Science and International Affairs, Harvard University, 1991), describes how Soviet safeguards might break down.

[8]Sam Nunn, "Needed, an ABM Defense," *New York Times*, July 11, 1991, p. A19.

[9]Nuclear weapons could also be delivered by unconventional means, like sending a ship into a U.S. harbor. This chapter does not analyze the daunting task of defending against such unconventional means of delivery.

current U.S. efforts to promote the reduction of Soviet nuclear forces. The Soviets have long argued that the continued maintenance of the ABM Treaty is essential for progress in strategic arms reductions,[10] although recent statements indicate some interest in missile defense.[11] Soviet officials seem particularly interested in cooperating with the United States to improve their capabilities for early warning of ballistic missile attack, but there are indications that they might accept broader deployment of missile defenses than the ABM Treaty now allows.[12]

These changes have different implications depending on the type of defense and on the circumstances. The next two sections provide a classification scheme for defenses and a framework for analyzing their merits.

TYPES OF DEFENSES

This chapter deals with *active defenses*, which intercept incoming warheads before they reach their targets, but these must be considered in the context of other approaches to limiting damage from nuclear weapons. *Passive defenses* seek to limit damage by making the potential targets of nuclear attack harder to destroy, and include such measures as hardening, mobility, deceptive basing, and civil defense. *Counterforce* seeks to destroy nuclear weapons before they can be launched. *Operational measures* can improve the readiness of military forces and facilitate prompt response strategies to avoid the destruction of strategic forces prior to use. Finally, *arms control* can reduce the likelihood of nuclear war and the scope of damage in case of war. Throughout the Cold War, the United States devoted far more effort to these alternatives than to active defense.

Later sections on defenses against long-range ballistic missiles, against short-range ballistic missiles, and against aircraft and cruise missiles (air defenses) will follow the functional classification of active defenses according to the weapons or delivery systems they intercept. This section explores less tangible distinctions of purpose: What does a defense seek to protect, and what type of attack—and by whom—does it seek to thwart?

The aims of defenses fall broadly into two categories, the defense of military assets, especially strategic ones, and the protection of civil society.

---

[10]"Statements on the Relationship of START and ABM read at a meeting between U.S. Ambassador Brooks and Deputy Foreign Minister Obukhov on June 13, 1991," *START: Treaty between the United States of America and the Union of Soviet Socialist Republics on the Reduction and Limitation of Strategic Offensive Arms Signed in Moscow on July 31, 1991* (Washington, D.C.: U.S. Arms Control and Disarmament Agency, 1991), p. 277.

[11]See Matthew Bunn, "Yeltsin Suggests Joint Missile Defense," *Arms Control Today,* Vol. 22, No. 1 (January/February, 1992), p. 38; and Dunbar Lockwood, "Baker, Kozyrev Discuss Deep Cuts," *Arms Control Today,* Vol. 22, No. 2 (March, 1992), p. 21.

[12]John D. Morrocco, "Soviets Endorse U.S. Effort to Cooperate on ABM Systems," *Aviation Week and Space Technology*, October 14, 1991, pp. 20–21.

Because military facilities and equipment are normally designed to be robust against attack, and because the United States has put some effort into making its strategic forces survivable, defending these assets tends to be easier than protecting people and cities.

There are many types of military installations the United States might want to defend, ranging from hardened missile silos to softer C^3I facilities and bomber and submarine bases. Two factors make missile silos the easiest assets to defend. First, missile silos are hardened to withstand nuclear explosions more than a few hundred meters away, so the defense need only prevent nuclear explosions within this small radius. Second, the goal need not be to defend every silo but only to ensure that a sufficient fraction survive to provide an adequate deterrent.[13]

Lacking these advantages, the protection of small numbers of relatively soft assets, like strategic bomber and submarine bases, is much more challenging; even a single warhead penetrating the defense could destroy one of these bases. The defense of mobile or camouflaged assets provides an interesting intermediate case. In this case the tactic of selective defense can offer significant advantages; the defense may choose to intercept only those warheads that appear likely to destroy the assets in question. This tactic should work better for assets that are relatively hard and numerous, like mobile or deceptively based ICBMs, than for those that are relatively soft and few in number, like C^3I facilities.[14]

The protection of populations also embodies a range of possibilities, all of which involve broad area defense rather than point defense of localized military facilities. President Reagan's "Star Wars" speech envisioned the "ultimate goal" of providing complete protection against nuclear attack. A slightly less ambitious version of this goal would be to prevent the former Soviet Union from being able to inflict "unacceptable damage" on the United States (although this depends on what level of damage is deemed "acceptable"). It is widely recognized that such defenses are not feasible in the foreseeable future.[15] Even if it is impossible to reduce damage to acceptable levels, damage limitation remains a legitimate goal, second only to preventing nuclear war from occurring. The question is whether defenses can effectively accomplish this goal without increasing the risk of war.

Recent debate on SDI has focused on more limited visions of defense,

---

[13]For purely deterrent purposes, an even looser standard can be accepted. The defense need only be credible enough to deny the Soviets adequate confidence of destroying enough silos to prevent a U.S. response from causing unacceptable damage.

[14]See Theodore Jarvis, "Nuclear Operation and Strategic Defense," in Ashton B. Carter, John D. Steinbruner, and Charles A. Zraket, eds., *op. cit.*, pp. 661–678 for a description of how selective defense might be used for C^3I facilities.

[15]See Sanford Lakoff and Herbert F. York, *A Shield in Space?: Technology, Politics, and the Strategic Defense Initiative: How the Reagan Administration Set Out to Make Nuclear Weapons "Impotent and Obsolete" and Succumbed to the Fallacy of the Last Move* (Berkeley: University of California Press, 1989) for an analysis of the technical debate.

designed to limit or prevent damage from small-scale attacks.[16] These would include accidental or unauthorized launches of Soviet missiles or deliberate attacks from other countries that have or might develop ballistic missiles.

Specific defense systems may embody ambiguous or multiple roles that depend on the circumstance of their use and do not necessarily correspond to any single role previously described. For example, a "thin" area defense against limited attacks might also provide some protection for missile silos; with deep reductions in offensive forces, it might provide significant damage limitation. Because it would probably be more effective against a retaliatory second strike than a preemptive first strike, a defense system could also support counterforce strategies for damage limitation and create dangerous incentives for preemption. In addition, long-range ABM interceptors generally make effective ASATs and could be used against an opponent's space-based ABM components.

Combined with the inevitable uncertainties about the capabilities of a given system, these ambiguities could lead an opponent to see a threat even where none exists or is intended. A cooperative approach to the deployment of defenses, perhaps through agreed modifications to the ABM Treaty, could alleviate these problems of misperception.

DECISION CRITERIA

Decisions on the U.S. approach to defenses against nuclear weapons must take into account both technical and strategic policy issues. Without a specific deployment scheme, it is difficult to assess technical feasibility except in general terms; because a defense aims to defeat other manufactured systems, the most challenging problems it faces involve the possible responses of others, especially the former Soviet Union. These responses could take the form of offensive countermeasures, defensive deployments, or a retreat from the arms control process.

Some responses, like the deployment of decoys, would have the principal effect of negating the defense; their main effect would be the relatively benign one of reinforcing the status quo ante. Others, like the development of antisatellite weapons and the proliferation of offensive forces, have potentially dangerous side effects. A revived strong central govern-

---

[16]Senator Sam Nunn introduced the idea of an Accidental Launch Protection System (ALPS) in a speech to the Arms Control Association on January 19, 1988. The speech is reprinted as Sam Nunn, "Arms Control in the Last Year of the Reagan Administration," *Arms Control Today*, Vol. 18, No. 2 (March, 1988), pp. 3–7. The Bush administration adopted a more ambitious version with its 1991 GPALS proposal, described in Henry Cooper and Stephen J. Hadley, "Briefing on the Refocused Strategic Defense Initiative" (edited transcript), February 12, 1991. Spurgeon M. Keeny, Jr., "Limited ABM Defense: Dangerous and Unnecessary" and Michael Krepon, "Limited ABM Defense: A Prudent Step," *Arms Control Today*, Vol. 21, No. 8 (October, 1991), pp. 14–20, present a debate on the merits of limited ABM defenses.

ment in the former Soviet Union could also deploy extensive ABM defenses, which the United States might see as a threat to basic deterrence. Offensive or defensive, benign or threatening, these responses could alter the perceived requirements of deterrence and force the United States to reevaluate its nuclear force posture.

The cost-benefit calculations behind strategic policy decisions depend on many levels of analysis. Paul Nitze, an arms control adviser in the Reagan administration, first elaborated the technical criteria of survivability and favorable cost-exchange as U.S. government policy in 1985.[17] A defense system that could not survive a direct attack without severe degradation could provide an attractive target for preemptive attack and undermine crisis stability. This would be especially true if both sides deployed vulnerable defenses.

The cost-exchange criterion asserts that it should also cost less to maintain the defense in the face of offensive countermeasures than it costs to implement the countermeasures themselves. Otherwise, defenses could provoke an action-reaction cycle in which the offense would have the economic advantage; attempts to maintain the defense in the face of such a cost disadvantage would undermine arms race stability.[18] Direct cost comparisons ignore the differences in countries' abilities to bear those costs and the value they place on defense and deterrence; a proper comparison of social costs and values is necessarily a subjective and uncertain affair, one compounded by uncertainties about the future intentions and capabilities of the former Soviet Union.

The stability of the political relationship between the United States and the former Soviet Union is at least as important as these technical criteria. The ABM Treaty codifies each side's recognition of the importance of deterrence to the other and, as the first strategic arms control agreement between the nuclear superpowers, provides an important symbol of cooperation. Unilateral actions that threaten the treaty could undermine U.S.-Soviet relations and complicate the delicate process by which the United States hopes to encourage reductions in Soviet nuclear forces. A more stable cooperative relationship, on the other hand, could allow the nuclear superpowers to consider a mutual shift to a security posture in which defense plays a greater role.

Most of those who argue for perfect or near-perfect defenses generally recognize that these would require a highly cooperative arrangement between the superpowers to bring about a managed transition where extensive defenses would accompany complete or nearly complete nu-

[17]Paul H. Nitze, "On the Road to a More Stable Peace," speech to the Philadelphia World Affairs Council, February 20, 1985.

[18]Barry M. Blechman and Victor A. Utgoff, "The Macroeconomics of Strategic Defenses," *International Security*, Vol. 11, No. 3 (Winter, 1986–87), pp. 33–70, provides a framework for calculating the costs of various types of defense deployments, though the details do not correspond to current technologies or proposals.

clear disarmament.[19] Such a transition would face a number of potential obstacles. First, even the agreed deployment of strictly limited defenses could impede progress on strategic arms reductions by increasing the force levels required to maintain a given level of deterrence. However, simultaneously making strategic forces more survivable would protect deterrence and mitigate this effect. Second, the disarmament process would have to include all the major nuclear powers, any of which could see superpower defenses as a threat to its deterrent capabilities and could implement countermeasures to challenge the defense. While defense dominance, the goal of such a transition, might be less robust than the Cold War balance of terror,[20] it might be preferable in a less antagonistic world, and the added insurance against nuclear rearmament would surely provide greater stability than disarmament unaccompanied by defenses.

Finally, we must consider active defense in relation to the full range of alternatives to meeting U.S. security needs. Modernization efforts that emphasize passive defense or arms control agreements that promote stability and reduce the risk of accidents can provide many of the same benefits, often at lower cost and without many of the drawbacks of active defense.

With these criteria in hand, we now proceed to analyze various options for long- and short-range missile defense and air defense.

ABM DEFENSES

Since the development of long-range ballistic missiles, ABM defenses against these missiles have dominated the debate over defenses against nuclear weapons.[21] This section begins by reviewing the ABM Treaty and the current ABM programs of the United States and the former Soviet Union. An analysis of the prospects for general types of ABM deployments is followed by specific recommendations for the SDI program and for ABM arms control.

---

[19]Freeman Dyson, *Weapons and Hope* (New York: Harper & Row, 1984), makes the case for a cooperative defense-dominated future. According to A. Fenner Milton, M. Scott Davis, and John A. Parmentola, *Making Space Defense Work: Must the Superpowers Cooperate?* (Elmsford, N.Y.: Pergamon-Brassey's, 1988), p. 165, "the goal of a low-leakage population defense . . . would require more extensive mutual cooperation than the superpowers have ever experienced, even during their short-lived alliance in World War II." Daniel O. Graham, *High Frontier: A New National Strategy* (Washington, D.C.: The Heritage Foundation, 1982), provides a notable exception to this view, arguing that the United States can protect itself by dominating the "High Frontier" of outer space.

[20]Charles L. Glaser, "Defense Dominance" in Joseph S. Nye, Jr., Graham T. Allison, and Albert Carnesale, eds., *Fateful Visions: Avoiding Nuclear Catastrophe* (Cambridge, Mass.: Ballinger, 1988), pp. 47–68.

[21]We adopt the ABM Treaty's convention of using the term ABM to refer only to defenses against strategic ballistic missiles.

The ABM Treaty

The 1972 ABM Treaty restricted and reshaped both U.S. and Soviet ABM programs. Although both countries have pushed its limits, neither has yet been willing to risk killing the treaty altogether, either by formal withdrawal or by systematic efforts to circumvent or evade its central aims.[22] Given its importance in the arms control legacy, the ABM Treaty provides a crucial framework for evaluating current and prospective ABM activities.[23]

Article I states the central purpose of the ABM Treaty: to prevent either side from deploying a territorial ABM defense or even providing a base that would allow the rapid deployment of such a defense. The treaty therefore includes not only specific limits on allowed ABM deployments, but also general restrictions on the development and testing of ABM technologies and on the ABM capabilities of related systems.

The ABM Treaty allows each side to deploy a single ABM site around its national capital or at an ICBM field, with up to 100 launchers and interceptors.[24] At the time, the Soviet Union was deploying an ABM system around Moscow and the United States was deploying one at an ICBM field in North Dakota, which it later deactivated.

The treaty also restricts a variety of predeployment activities that might facilitate rapid ABM breakout. Large early-warning radars may be deployed only "along the periphery of the national territory and oriented outward." Weapons other than ABM systems and components may not be tested "in an ABM mode" or given "capabilities to counter strategic ballistic missiles or their elements in flight trajectory."

Another important provision restricts the development and testing of certain ABM systems and their components, although the precise scope of this restriction has been the subject of some controversy. Article V(1)

[22]Each country has charged the other with violating the ABM Treaty, but the only clear-cut violation has been the Soviet deployment of the Krasnoyarsk early-warning radar in an illegal location. As of this writing, this radar is in the process of being dismantled.

[23]For a more complete review of the ABM Treaty see George Schneiter, "The ABM Treaty Today," in Carter and Schwartz, eds., op. cit., pp. 221–250, or John B. Rhinelander and Sherri Wasserman Goodman, "The Legal Environment," in Antonia H. Chayes and Paul Doty, eds., Defending Deterrence: Managing the ABM Treaty into the 21st Century (Elmsford, N.Y.: Pergamon-Brassey's, 1989), pp. 43–69, and Gerard C. Smith, "The Treaty's Basic Provisions: View of the U.S. Negotiator," in Walther Stutzle, Regina Cowen, and Bhupendra Jasani, eds., The ABM Treaty: To Defend or Not to Defend (New York: Oxford University Press, 1987). The ABM Treaty and related statements, including unclassified summaries of subsequent agreed interpretations, are reprinted as Appendices A and B in Matthew Bunn, op. cit., pp. 162–169.

[24]The original 1972 treaty allowed each side to deploy two sites, one of each type, but the 1974 Protocol reduced this to one of either type. The restrictions on radars differ in the two cases, and a small number of additional launchers and radars may be deployed at agreed ABM test sites.

enjoins both countries "not to develop, test, or deploy ABM systems or components which are sea-based, air-based, space-based, or mobile land-based." According to the traditional interpretation, this restriction applies regardless of the technology involved. But in 1985 the Reagan administration introduced a new interpretation claiming that this restriction applies only to technologies embodied in the ABM systems of 1972.[25] We believe that the bulk of the evidence supports the traditional interpretation and argue in the following that the United States should continue to uphold this interpretation.[26]

As a treaty of unlimited duration, the ABM Treaty must be able to adapt to changes in technology and the world. It therefore provides for regular review conferences and a Standing Consultative Commission to address disputes over treaty compliance and interpretation and allow for amendments. These or other forums[27] could be helpful in resolving important ambiguities in the meaning of key terms in the treaty text, particularly "ABM capability," "tested in an ABM mode," and "development," and in the application of the term "component" to new types of systems and new technologies.

U.S. ABM Programs

The ABM debate in the United States has always balanced the promise of new technologies against the prospect of Soviet countermeasures. The earliest proposed ABM system, Nike-Zeus, would have used long-range missiles with nuclear warheads to intercept incoming warheads above the atmosphere. But the possibility that the Soviets might equip their missiles with light decoys, which are practically indistinguishable from warheads until they reenter the atmosphere, posed a severe problem then and remains a serious challenge today. Nike-X, which replaced Nike-Zeus in 1963, offered better performance with high-acceleration rockets and electronically steered phased-array radars, but it faced the objections that it would cost too much to reinforce the system in re-

---

[25]This new interpretation was based on Agreed Statement D, which contemplates the future development of ABM systems and components "based on other physical principles" and requires only that their deployment be subject to negotiation. Raymond L. Garthoff, *Policy Versus the Law: The Reinterpretation of the ABM Treaty* (Washington, D.C.: The Brookings Institution, 1987), provides a summary of the debate over this interpretation.

[26]The main argument comes from the treaty text. We believe that Article II, which defines ABM systems functionally and describes them as "currently consisting of" ABM launchers, interceptors, and radars, implies that the basic treaty restrictions apply to other types of systems as well. Furthermore, Agreed Statement D does not contradict Article V(1) if we interpret it to apply only to fixed land-based ABM systems. Publicly available records, including declassified portions of the negotiating record described in *ibid*. and references therein, generally support this analysis.

[27]The Reagan and Bush administrations have preferred to use the arms control forum of the Defense and Space Talks to address questions of ABM Treaty interpretation and clarification.

sponse to an expansion of the Soviet strategic arsenal and that the radars were vulnerable to blinding and destruction by nuclear explosions in the atmosphere.[28]

The Safeguard ABM system, deployed briefly at Grand Forks, North Dakota, used technologies from Nike-Zeus and Nike-X. The United States deactivated this system within a year of its completion in 1975, judging that its limited effectiveness did not justify its operational expense. The United States continued to support research and development on technologies for ABM systems at relatively low levels until President Reagan inaugurated the Strategic Defense Initiative in 1985.[29]

The initial promise of SDI was to develop new technologies for intercepting missiles in their boost phase, the period of flight when the exhaust plumes from their burning rocket motors make them easy to track and target and before they dispense their warheads and decoys. Directed-energy weapons, lasers and particle beams, were envisioned as destroying missiles instantaneously at long ranges; precision-guided kinetic-energy weapons would destroy them by collision at high speeds; high-resolution infrared sensors and expert computer software would guide the interceptors to their targets.[30]

But interception during the boost phase faces its own set of problems. It can only be done from space, leading to increased costs from putting interceptors into orbit and to large absentee ratios from orbiting defense satellites spending most of their time over other portions of the globe. Boost-phase defense is also susceptible to a number of new countermeasures; antisatellite weapons could threaten key defense satellites and fast-burning boosters would impose severe time constraints, especially for kinetic-energy interceptors.[31] Many of the proposed defense technologies, particularly directed-energy weapons, face severe technical challenges

---

[28]Richard L. Garwin and Hans A. Bethe, "Anti-Ballistic Missile Systems," *Scientific American*, Vol. 218, No. 3 (March 1968), pp. 164–174; "McNamara Explains 'Limited' Missile Defense for U.S.," *U.S. News & World Report*, October 2, 1967, p. 106.

[29]David N. Schwartz, "The Historical Legacy," in Carter and Schwartz, eds., *op. cit.*, pp. 330–349.

[30]An advisory panel led by James C. Fletcher designed the SDI program. Its report, an unclassified summary of which has been released as Department of Defense, *The Strategic Defense Initiative: Defensive Technologies Study* (Washington, D.C.: U.S. Government Printing Office, 1984), is known as the Fletcher Report.

[31]These challenges are well described in two reports by the Office of Technology Assessment: *Ballistic Missile Defense Technologies* (Princeton, N.J.: Princeton University Press, 1986) and *SDI: Technology, Survivability, and Software* (Washington, D.C.: U.S. Government Printing Office, 1988). The sections on countermeasures in the latter report were never declassified but public discussions of this issue can be found in Ashton B. Carter, *Directed Energy Missile Defense in Space*, background paper prepared for the Office of Technology Assessment (Washington, D.C.: U.S. Government Printing Office, 1984) and "Report to The American Physical Society of the study group on science and technology of directed energy weapons," *Reviews of Modern Physics*, Vol. 59, No. 3, Part II (July, 1987).

before they can be converted into workable weapons systems,[32] and therefore require extensive laboratory research and development to determine whether they can be candidates for ABM interception.

As illustrated in Figure 7.1, today's main candidates for space-based ABM interception are Brilliant Pebbles, so-named because of their improved design compared to earlier "smart rock" concepts. Each "pebble" would be an autonomous space-based interceptor with its own sensors and computer for warning, tracking, and guidance.[33] Still in the design phase, Brilliant Pebbles would reduce the problems of cost and vulnerability for space-based interceptors, but would still have problems in the face of relatively simple countermeasures.[34] Furthermore, their decentralized control would sacrifice some efficiency and predictability, and would create the dangerous precedent of a high-altitude ASAT.[35]

Ground-based interceptors form the remainder of the near-term SDI deployment options. The Exo-atmospheric Reentry-vehicle Intercept System (ERIS), which uses an infrared sensor to guide itself into collision with warheads before they reenter the atmosphere, is the most mature of these. A prototype for the future, smaller Ground-Based Interceptor (GBI), ERIS has been successfully tested against simulated warheads in space,[36] but both would have serious problems dealing with decoys.

The shorter-range Exo-atmospheric/Endo-atmospheric Interceptor (E²I), which would provide a second layer of ground-based defense, is still in the design phase. Although it avoids many problems of decoy discrimination, it faces the added technical problem of preventing atmospheric friction and heating from blinding its infrared sensors. Furthermore, launch of this interceptor might have to wait until warheads could be clearly distinguished from decoys, which would be stripped away by reentry into the atmosphere. This could greatly reduce the interceptor's effective range.[37]

---

[32]The challenges associated with directed-energy weapons include scaling up laser power as well as problems of atmospheric propagation and mirror design. See *ibid.* for details.

[33]Lowell L. Wood, " 'Brilliant Pebbles' Missile Defense Concept Advocated by Livermore Scientist," *Aviation Week and Space Technology*, June 13, 1988, pp. 151–155; Gregory Canavan and Edward Teller, "Strategic Defence for the 1990s," *Nature*, Vol. 344 (April 19, 1990), pp. 699–704.

[34]Richard L. Garwin, "Brilliant Pebbles Won't Do," *Nature*, Vol. 346 (July 5, 1990), p. 21; Roger Speed, "ASATs versus Brilliant Pebbles," informal report, Lawrence Livermore National Laboratory, UCRL-ID-103669 (March, 1990).

[35]See Appendix A for a discussion of ASATs. David C. Wright, "Brilliant Pebbles as ASATs: The Threat to Satellites in High Earth Orbits," *Inside the Air Force*, May 17, 1991, p. 16, describes the capabilities of Brilliant Pebbles as high-altitude ASATs.

[36]James R. Asker, "Army Eris Interceptor Destroys Dummy Warhead in SDI Test," *Aviation Week and Space Technology*, February 4, 1991, pp. 21–22.

[37]Philip Finnegan, "Critics Question Wisdom of New Interceptor," *Defense Week*, November 26, 1990, p. 3.

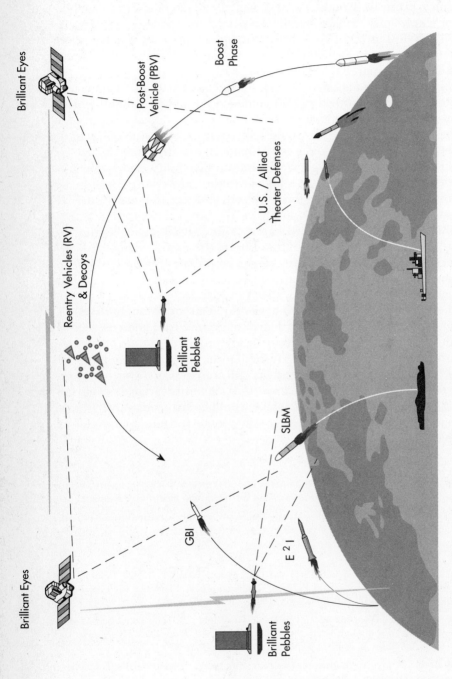

Figure 7.1 *Possible ballistic missile defense components.* Brilliant Pebbles in space would intercept long- and intermediate-range missiles above the atmosphere. Ground-based GBI and E²I interceptors would intercept reentry vehicles above or high in the atmosphere. Theater missile defenses would intercept shorter-range missiles. The space-based Brilliant Eyes sensors and ground-based radars would detect and track these missiles, as a ground-based command center coordinates the defense. (*Source:* Courtesy of the U.S. Department of Defense, Strategic Defenses

Though they are often overlooked, sensors are at least as important as interceptors to the functioning of an ABM system. Their functions include early warning, tracking, and interceptor guidance, as well as the more difficult task of discriminating decoys from warheads. Traditional ABM systems rely on ground-based radars for most of these functions, but future systems may need more capable sensors. The accuracy needed for kinetic-kill requires that interceptors have built-in sensors for terminal guidance, either infrared or active radar. Heat-sensing infrared sensors of various wavelengths can track boosting missiles, colder objects in space, or warheads heated by reentry. Laser rangefinders or laser radars could further improve tracking and discrimination capabilities in the future.[38]

SDI has pursued a variety of sensor concepts that integrate these technologies in various combinations and on various platforms. In addition to improvements in traditional early-warning satellites and ground-based radars, these concepts include constellations of infrared satellites for tracking objects in space,[39] optical sensors on aircraft, and sensor platforms, such as the Ground-based Surveillance and Tracking system, designed to be lofted into space temporarily upon warning of possible missile attack. As they have changed in the past, specific design concepts are likely to evolve in the future.

The greatest challenge for sensor systems is to discriminate between warheads and potential decoys. For this and other purposes, like the management and control of defense components during battle, an ABM system needs complicated and reliable computer software. The problems of developing this software become more severe as defense requirements become more demanding or unpredictable, and as the opportunities for realistic testing diminish.[40] This problem can be reduced but not eliminated by integrating software design and simulations into system concepts at an early stage.[41]

The most likely near-term deployment options embody the more ma-

---

[38]More exotic proposals include nuclear bomb-pumped X-ray lasers and neutral particle beams for "interactive" discrimination of decoys. See "Status and Prospects of Ballistic Missile Defense Sensor Technology" in Office of Technology Assessment, *SDI: Technology, Survivability, and Software*, pp. 73–102.

[39]Brilliant Eyes, the sensor offshoot of Brilliant Pebbles, are the current version of this concept. See Gregory Canavan and Edward Teller, "Brilliant Eyes Technology Provides Dual-Mode Viewing," *Signal*, Vol. 45, No. 4. (December, 1990), p. 29.

[40]The main failure of the Patriot system in the war against Iraq was reportedly caused by a software failure. See Eric Schmitt, "Army Is Blaming Patriot's Computer for Failure to Stop the Dhahran Scud," *New York Times*, May 20, 1991, p. A6. For a general discussion of the issue see David L. Parnas, "Software Aspects of Strategic Defense Systems," *American Scientist*, Vol. 73, No. 5 (September-October, 1985), pp. 432–440; and Herbert Lin, "The Development of Software for Ballistic-Missile Defense," *Scientific American*, Vol. 253, No. 6 (December, 1985), pp. 46–53.

[41]Jeffrey Rowe, "NTB—Simulating the Future of SDI," *Defense Electronics*, Vol. 23, No.4 (April, 1991), pp. 37–44.

ture ABM technology programs in SDI, including ground-based radars and interceptors. Some space-based sensors may also be included, but the more speculative Brilliant Eyes and especially Brilliant Pebbles have been controversial and may be modified in or disappear from future proposals.

Soviet ABM Programs

It is difficult to obtain detailed information on Soviet strategic activities, but the general outlines of the Soviet ABM effort are known.[42] The Soviets began deploying their first true ABM system, based on the Galosh missile, around Moscow in the mid-1960s. After an upgrade in the 1980s gave it a new high-acceleration ABM interceptor (the Gazelle) and the more capable Pushkino radar, the Moscow ABM system appears to be roughly comparable to the Safeguard ABM system the United States deployed in the mid-1970s.

The Soviets have also developed and deployed a number of long-range air defense systems whose Surface-to-Air Missiles (SAMs) have been tested against short-range missiles, notably the SA-5, SA-10, and SA-12B SAMs. The Reagan administration cited these as a potential breakout threat from the ABM Treaty, but their capability is probably limited to short-range missile defense.

Although most of their ABM efforts have been devoted to maintaining the Moscow ABM system, the Soviets have also put significant resources into R&D on directed-energy weapons.[43] They may also have developed and tested a laser ASAT with limited capabilities and have been constructing a larger laser facility.[44] Given the relative backwardness of their sensor and computer technologies,[45] which would be needed to turn these into usable ABM systems, the Soviets appear to be even further than the United States from directed-energy weapons with ABM capability.

ABM Deployment Options

Any initial U.S. ABM deployment would be limited in one of two ways: It might be capable of blocking only limited attacks or it might be capable

---

[42]See Sayre Stevens, "The Soviet BMD Program," in Carter and Schwartz, eds., *op. cit.*, pp. 182–220, and David Holloway, "The Strategic Defense Initiative and the Soviet Union," in Boutwell and Long, eds., *op. cit.*, pp. 257–278, and "The Soviet ABM Program," pp. 48–55, in Bunn, *op. cit.*, for descriptions of Soviet ABM programs.

[43]*Soviet Strategic Defense Programs* (Washington, D.C.: Department of Defense and Department of State, 1985).

[44]A visit by U.S. scientists to the laser research facility at Sary Shagan showed that it was many orders of magnitude short of ABM requirements. See "A Visit to Sary Shagan and Kyshtym," *Science and Global Security*, Vol. 1, Nos. 1–2 (1989), pp. 165–174. The newer laser research facility at Dushanbe has remained closed to foreigners.

[45]*Soviet Strategic Defense Programs*, p. 16.

of defending only a limited set of assets. We will consider these two cases in succession.

Defense Against Limited Attacks   Most of the current attention on ABM defenses focuses on relatively "thin" area defense concepts. Ranging from the deployment of a single ABM site to broader ground- and space-based deployments, these proposals aim to defend against relatively small nuclear attacks, accidental or unauthorized launches of Soviet missiles, or potential threats from other countries.

Three other countries now have the capability to attack the United States with long-range missiles: Britain, France, and China. Japan and Israel have space-launch capabilities that could be converted to ICBMs, and India also has a fairly advanced space-launch and missile program. These countries are unlikely to threaten the United States, however; their concerns lie elsewhere. Other countries have missile programs, including some, like North Korea and Libya, that are decidedly unfriendly to the United States, but these countries are much further from being able to pose a long-range missile threat.[46] Continued research and development of ABM technologies could provide useful insurance against the eventual emergence of this type of threat,[47] perhaps 10–20 years from now. The value of this insurance is undermined, however, by the prospect that these emerging missile capabilities could well be equipped with simple countermeasures—especially decoys—that would greatly complicate the task of defense.

For at least the next ten years the main threat of limited missile attack against the United States will come from the former Soviet Union. Although it is possible to imagine scenarios in which war among fragments of the former Soviet Union, for example, leads to nuclear threats or a deliberate nuclear attack against the United States, these do not seem particularly plausible. We will therefore concentrate on the more realistic possibility of accidental or unauthorized attacks.

There are many ways in which accidents could lead to nuclear attacks against the United States. The most prosaic form of accident, and probably the least likely, would be a hardware failure that causes a single missile to "launch itself." Yet events surprisingly similar to this have occurred in the United States and, reportedly, in the Soviet Union.[48] More likely causes of

---

[46]Two recent books dealing with the spread of ballistic missile capabilities around the world are Janne E. Nolan, *Trappings of Power: Ballistic Missiles in the Third World* (Washington, D.C.: The Brookings Institution, 1991), and W. Seth Carus, *Ballistic Missiles in the Third World: Threat and Response* (Westport, Conn.: Praeger, 1990).

[47]Les Aspin, "Patriots, Scuds and the Future of Ballistic Missile Defense," speech to the Washington Chapter of the National Security Industrial Association, April 24, 1991.

[48]David C. Morrison, "Loose Soviet Nukes: A Mountain or a Molehill?" *Arms Control Today*, Vol. 21, No. 3 (April 1991), p. 17.

accidents stem from the complexity of U.S. and Soviet nuclear forces and command structures and the unpredictable interactions between these two systems, especially in times of crisis. For example, false signals from warning sensors or cautionary alerts could start an action-reaction cycle that leads to nuclear attack.[49] Although the reduction in alert levels on both sides[50] makes such a cycle less likely, the continuing weaknesses of Soviet early warning capabilities could lead to dangerous miscalculation.[51]

Unauthorized launches provide another potential source of nuclear attack against the United States.[52] The Soviet Union implemented numerous safeguards, both physical and procedural, against unauthorized use of its strategic forces, reportedly including separate command systems for the release and arming of nuclear warheads.[53] But these rigorous safeguards may not survive the continuing fragmentation of the Soviet Union, especially if republics other than Russia choose to retain custody of and assert control over the forces now deployed on their territory. Even so, these republics would need to establish formal nuclear command systems, probably on the Soviet model.[54] A greater danger of loss of control could come from attempts to seize nonstrategic weapons,[55] which have less rigorous safeguards, although these weapons are scheduled to be removed to Russia.

Any of these scenarios could increase the chance of a nuclear attack against the United States. Given the rapid internal changes in the former Soviet Union, it is difficult to judge which scenario is most likely. It is perhaps a bit easier to estimate the possible scale of the resulting attack. A system-level failure of command and control would lead to a system-level response, perhaps a massive attack involving thousands of warheads or perhaps something much smaller. A missile accident or the seizure of nuclear weapons—or any initial missile capability of another country—would most likely lead to a very small attack. Unauthorized launches, whether from Russia or another republic, could lead to an intermediate scale of attack involving a few tens of missiles or a few hundred warheads.

[49]Paul Bracken, *The Command and Control of Nuclear Forces* (New Haven: Yale University Press, 1983); Bruce G. Blair, *Strategic Command and Control: Redefining the Nuclear Threat* (Washington, D.C.: The Brookings Institution, 1985); and Ashton B. Carter, "Sources of Error and Uncertainty," in Carter, Steinbruner, and Zraket, eds., *op. cit.*, pp. 611–639.

[50]"A New Era of Reciprocal Arms Reductions: Texts of President Bush's Nuclear Initiative and Soviet President Mikhail Gorbachev's Response," *Arms Control Today*, Vol 21, No. 8 (October, 1991), pp. 3–6.

[51]Stephen M. Meyer, pp. 479–481, *op. cit.* A lack of early warning capabilities could also help avoid crises that might otherwise have been caused by false warning information.

[52]Blair and Kendall, *op. cit.*, and David C. Morrison, *op. cit.*

[53]Kurt M. Campbell et al., *op. cit.* pp. 5–20.

[54]*Ibid.*, pp. 107–109.

[55]*Ibid.*, pp. 36–40.

The Bush administration's original GPALS proposal called for 1,000 space-based and 750 ground-based interceptors, with the aim of providing complete protection against small- to intermediate-scale attacks of up to 200 warheads.[56] The Congress has blocked plans to deploy Brilliant Pebbles in space while expressing support for significant ground-based deployments.[57]

Large ABM deployments like these would provide the base for a more comprehensive defense and undermine the central purpose of the ABM Treaty. By aggressively pursuing plans that clearly conflict with its arms control commitments, the United States would send an unfortunate signal to its negotiating partners in the former Soviet Union. This could greatly complicate the delicate processes of implementing current Soviet arms control commitments and negotiating further nuclear arms reductions. Furthermore, a revived strong government in the former Soviet Union could still implement effective countermeasures to these defenses.

A more modest defense along the lines of the Accidental Launch Protection System proposal by Senator Nunn[58] would aim only to block the smallest-scale attacks. A smaller system with only ground-based components could satisfy this objective and provide less cause for Soviet opposition. However, even such a system would require more than the one ABM site allowed by the ABM Treaty. Some have proposed redeploying the single ABM site permitted under the treaty, but this system probably could not protect either coast.[59]

As discussed in Chapter 5, there are a number of ways to address the threat of accidental or unauthorized attack that do not involve active defense. One approach would be to develop a more survivable force structure and reduce alert levels, moving away from prompt launch postures and reducing the risk of command and control accidents.[60] The most urgent task for the United States should be to help the former Soviet Union to maintain control over its nuclear forces. This could include continued arms control efforts to remove nonstrategic forces as well as technical assistance to implement current and possible future arms control agreements, as described in Chapter 4. Like defenses, any of these measures would take many years to implement. Finally, a concerted interna-

---

[56]Cooper and Hadley, *op. cit.*

[57]William J. Broad, "Quietly, Lawmakers Prepare to Approve an Antimissile Plan," *New York Times*, November 18, 1991, p. A1.

[58]Sam Nunn, "Arms Control in the Last Years of the Reagan Administration," *op. cit.*

[59]Even the deployment of a single ABM site involving GBI or E²I would require some discussion, because these interceptors rely on a different physical principle from older ABM systems, namely infrared rather than radar guidance.

[60]See "Reducing the Dangers of Accidental and Unauthorized Nuclear Launch and Terrorist Attack: Alternatives to a Ballistic Missile Defense System," Report of the International Foundation for the Survival and Development of Humanity, January 1990.

tional effort to discourage the proliferation of ballistic missile technologies could prevent or delay the emergence of long-range missile threats from other countries.[61]

Defense Against Counterforce Attacks   Limited defense of strategic forces to reinforce deterrence has been a persistent theme in the old ABM and more recent SDI debates, and may well resurface in the future. The ability to prevent a successful first strike against U.S. missile silos is often presented as a benefit of proposed defense systems, but rarely are such defenses designed specifically for this purpose; defending missile silos does not require long-range interceptors or multilayer defenses. A point defense that intercepts most warheads before they get close enough to damage missiles in their silos would suffice.[62]

Such a defense would be highly specialized, however, and would not provide a significant defense of anything other than missile silos. As such, it would offer neither the benefits nor the drawbacks of potential area defenses. The Soviets should not see it as a threat, but deployment beyond a single site would nonetheless require renegotiation of or withdrawal from the ABM Treaty.

Again, we must weigh such defenses against other means of achieving the same end. The three most obvious alternatives are arms control to reduce the scale of the threat, deMIRVing to reduce the attractiveness of ICBMs as targets, and mobile or deceptive basing to raise the costs of attacking them. Finally, we should consider whether the threat to deterrence is great enough to warrant any major response. The arguments of Chapters 5 and 6 suggest that we should consider research on defenses both as a hedge against possible future counterforce threats and as a possible step toward a more survivable ICBM force in the future.

Even though they are not optimized for the defense of missile silos, area defenses can provide some capability for this task. Even the relatively extensive GPALS proposal could be readily saturated or defeated by countermeasures, and would then provide little protection for missile silos. Still "thicker" area defenses could provide significant protection for ICBMs, but only at deployment levels that would probably provoke a proportionately greater Soviet response.

Defense could be considered for other strategic assets as well, such as bomber bases, submarine bases, and C[3]I facilities. But because these tar-

---

[61]Seven Western supplier countries formed the Missile Technology Control Regime (MTCR) in 1989, which a number of other suppliers have since joined and to which the Soviet Union also adheres. Janne Nolan, *op. cit.*, describes this and other possible approaches to controlling the spread of ballistic missiles in "Toward an International Technology Security Regime," pp. 131–167.

[62]Short-range ATBMs like ERINT could probably be adapted for this role. The low-altitude "swarmjet" proposal is described in Office of Technology Assessment, *Ballistic Missile Defense Technologies*, p. 157.

gets are relatively soft and few in number, such a point defense would face much more stringent requirements for range, leakage, and survivability. We should therefore not expect any more from such a defense than to raise the cost of attack by a modest factor. Given the overall survivability of U.S. strategic forces, it would be difficult to justify the cost of such defenses.

SDI Program Recommendations

Continued research and development of ABM systems provides a knowledge base for future U.S. decisions on defense and a hedge against threats and opportunities that could make limited defenses more attractive in the future.[63] Pushing the full-scale development of an ABM system without a well-thought-out system design concept or before the technology matures would be a waste of resources.[64] By raising costs, premature development could drain resources from essential research and encourage greater political opposition. For mobile, space-based, or sea-based ABM components, whose development and testing are forbidden under the traditional interpretation of the ABM Treaty, the United States must also consider the costs of violating or withdrawing from the treaty.

For deployment decisions, much stricter criteria apply: The United States should deploy an ABM system only if the benefits outweigh the costs, and only if equally effective alternatives are more costly. These costs would include those of violating or withdrawing from the ABM Treaty if deployment were undertaken without Soviet cooperation. A candidate defense must also show reasonable promise of meeting Nitze's survivability and cost-exchange criteria, suitably applied.

Ground-based Interceptors We recommend continued moderate rates of testing for the ERIS/GBI interceptor and, if a workable sensor design emerges, E²I. This will maintain the option of deployment in case future circumstances—increased risk of accidental or unauthorized Soviet attack or the proliferation of long-range missiles—warrant it. However, we cannot identify a deployment plan whose value currently outweighs its costs. Deployment at a single site would provide some operational experience with an ABM system but would offer little protection at significant operational expense. Deployment at multiple sites would exceed the bounds of the ABM Treaty.

---

[63]We distinguish between "research," which includes research and technology development with general applications in mind and "development," which encompasses the development and testing of prototype military systems. This definition would allow for research in space, particularly on sensor technologies.

[64]John C. Toomay and Robert T. Marsh, "The Nature and Purpose of ABM Research," in Chayes and Doty, eds., *op. cit.*, pp. 70–80.

Space-based Interceptors The development and testing of Brilliant Pebbles would violate the traditional interpretation of the ABM Treaty and signal a lack of commitment by the United States to its arms control obligations.[65] Given their cost and susceptibility to countermeasures, and the likelihood that they would add little to a ground-based limited ABM system, we recommend against further development of Brilliant Pebbles.

Directed-Energy Weapons These technologies hold some promise for more effective ABM defenses in the future, but continued research is required to resolve the many technical problems involved in converting them into weapons. Large-scale projects are justified only if their scale is essential to understanding the scientific issues, not as technology demonstrations. Every effort should be made to avoid expensive space-based experiments if cheaper ground-based ones can provide the same information.

Sensors It is more difficult to spell out limits on the testing and deployment of sensors. Sensors provide important collateral benefits, such as improved early warning, and limits may be difficult to verify. However, the deployment of ABM sensors would eliminate one of the main obstacles to ABM breakout and arguably provide a base for a territorial defense.

The ABM Treaty allows the testing of fixed ground-based radars at agreed test sites, but prohibits the development of mobile ABM radars, which would facilitate rapid ABM breakout. The United States should therefore refrain from developing modular transportable ABM radars.[66]

The ground-based GSTS platform provides a vehicle for testing most other types of sensors in a manner consistent with the ABM Treaty while leaving a significant buffer against breakout. We therefore recommend against testing Brilliant Eyes or other sensor platforms in orbit, which would violate the treaty.

Control Systems Software problems often cause serious delays and limitations in modern weapon systems. SDI should continue to place a high priority on software design, especially for ground-based ABM systems.

---

[65]Brilliant Pebbles have also been touted as a defense against short-range missiles, but the short time of flight and low altitude of these missiles presents challenges much like fast-burning boosters for ABM defense; they make the defense too thin or too expensive. David C. Wright and Lisbeth Gronlund, "Underflying Brilliant Pebbles," *Arms Control Today*, Vol. 21, No. 4 (May 1991), p. 16, and Richard Garwin, "Defense is Easier from the Ground," *Space News*, March 11–17, 1991, p. 15, present other arguments against Brilliant Pebbles as ATBMs.

[66]This recommendation could be modified if the United States can define a suitable threshold of mobility, preferably one arrived at through negotiation with the Soviets.

Program Organization We recommend separating U.S. ABM efforts into two sections, one for technology research and the other for developing possible ABM components and systems,[67] with strict criteria for progression from one level to the next. Immature technologies like directed-energy weapons and certain sensor concepts would be placed in the first section, as would space-based and mobile ABM concepts, whose testing would violate the traditional interpretation of the ABM Treaty. The development of ground-based interceptors and sensors would take place in the second section of SDI.

Countermeasures There are two reasons for the United States to pursue R&D on countermeasures to ABM defenses. First, a strong effort to understand countermeasures provides an essential foil against which to test ABM systems and concepts. Second, such R&D provides another means, beyond maintaining the ABM Treaty, to discourage and limit the danger of Soviet ABM deployments.[68] We recommend that the United States continue to give significant priority to R&D on ABM countermeasures, especially decoys, but because of its contrasting purpose this effort should remain administratively separate from SDI.[69]

ABM Arms Control Recommendations

Because of concern over possible Soviet reactions, we have argued that the SDI program should be pursued in a manner that does not undermine the ABM Treaty. In many cases the restrictions of the ABM Treaty are clear, and unilateral U.S. restraint will suffice. But because current technologies are far removed from those that existed when the ABM Treaty was negotiated, it is not always obvious how to apply general treaty constraints to specific systems.

Threshold Limits The United States should seek discussions with the former Soviet Union to clarify ambiguous ABM Treaty constraints. Rational definitions of the terms "ABM capability," "testing in an ABM mode," and "component," among others, in the form of verifiable threshold limits on specific technologies offer the most promising approach to resolving these ambiguities.[70]

---

[67]For reasons described in the following, we would place short-range missile defense programs in a third section of SDI.

[68]See "Hedging Against Soviet Breakout," in Matthew Bunn, *op. cit.*, pp. 86–87.

[69]Chapter 5 argues against the development of maneuvering reentry vehicles for other reasons.

[70]John Pike, "New Thresholds to clarify the ABM Treaty," *F.A.S. Public Interest Report*, Vol. 40, No. 7 (September, 1987), pp. 8–12. Threshold limits are the most explicit and readily verifiable means of implementing these definitions.

Interpretation   The United States may be able to finesse the dispute over the new interpretation of the ABM Treaty by agreeing to threshold testing limits for space-based ABM components. Some would use the interpretation issue for bargaining leverage, perhaps to achieve more favorable threshold limits or allow broader ground-based deployments, but the United States should resist this temptation; most likely, it would only complicate the more urgent tasks of strengthening control over Soviet nuclear weapons and reducing the size of the Soviet nuclear arsenal. In any case, our proposed restructuring of SDI would leave the United States with little to gain from the new interpretation.

Future ABM Roles   In the future, the United States and the former Soviet Union may wish to reconsider the specific deployment restrictions in the ABM Treaty. The proliferation of long-range missiles could make "thin" area defenses attractive to both countries. On the other hand, a desire for deep reductions in strategic forces could create incentives to ban all ABM deployment and testing. The president and Congress have agreed, for now, to call for amending the ABM Treaty to allow broader ground-based deployments, but we cannot now make a recommendation either way. Open-ended discussions of the strategic role of ABM defenses could pave the way for agreement in the future.

SHORT-RANGE MISSILE DEFENSES

The end of the Cold War has cast the problem of defending against shorter-range Tactical or Theater Ballistic Missiles (TBMs) in a new light. The INF Treaty and the collapse of the Warsaw Pact eliminated most of the missiles of concern—those that could strike Western Europe—from the Soviet arsenal, while the war against Iraq has increased concerns over the proliferation of ballistic missiles in other regions.

A number of countries beyond the avowed nuclear powers are developing ballistic missiles, and others have acquired them on the international market. Most of these missiles are very inaccurate and carry only conventional warheads, and therefore have little direct military significance.[71] Their use as terror weapons can have substantial political effects, however, as demonstrated by Iraq's Scud missile attacks against Israel.[72]

Most of the countries with emerging ballistic missile capabilities also

---

[71]W. Seth Carus, *op. cit.*, pp. 27–39, and Janne Nolan, *op. cit.*, pp. 63–97.

[72]The diversion of resources to deal with such a terror threat can have important indirect military effects, as evidenced by the redirection of air power to locate and destroy Iraq's Scud missile launchers.

possess chemical weapons and many also have programs to develop nuclear and biological weapons.[73] All of these pose great challenges to defenses. Chemical warheads must be intercepted at a high enough altitude or with the release of enough energy to disperse or destroy the chemical agent and prevent it from doing significant harm on the ground.[74] As an alternative, gas masks and other civil defense precautions can reduce the lethality of chemical weapons,[75] and protective suits provide essentially complete protection. Nuclear warheads must also be intercepted at high altitudes to prevent damage on the ground, and also pose a significant threat to crucial defense components like radars, making it particularly difficult to defend effectively against all but the smallest nuclear attacks.

Because of its geographic isolation, the United States does not face a direct threat from any of these TBMs, which may account for the relatively recent vintage of U.S. ATBM (Anti-TBM) efforts. But as long as it continues to define its interests globally, the United States must deal with emerging threats to its allies or to troops stationed abroad.

The upgrade of the Patriot air defense missile to an ATBM role was originally proposed in the early 1980s as a response to the improving capabilities of Soviet TBMs.[76] The U.S. Theater Missile Defense Initiative (TMDI), now directed mostly against Third World missile threats, includes

---

[73]Leonard Spector produces nearly annual volumes on the status of nuclear proliferation, including the most recent one with Jacqueline R. Smith, *Nuclear Ambitions: The Spread of Nuclear Weapons, 1989–90* (Boulder, Co.: Westview Press, 1990). The Aspen Strategy Group Report, *New Threats: Responding to the Proliferation of Nuclear, Chemical, and Delivery Capabilities in the Third World* (Lanham, Md.: University Press of America, 1990) surveys chemical weapons and ballistic missile proliferation as well. Rear Admiral Thomas A. Brooks, statement before the Seapower, Strategic, and Critical Materials Subcommittee of the House Armed Services Committee, March 7, 1991, describes the proliferation of biological weapons. Steve Fetter, "Ballistic Missiles and Weapons of Mass Destruction: What Is the Threat? What Should Be Done?" *International Security*, Vol. 16, No. 1 (Summer, 1991), pp. 5–42, assesses the threat from missiles with conventional and unconventional warheads.

[74]Theodore A. Postol, "The Prospects for Successful Air-Defense Against Chemically Armed Tactical Ballistic Missile Attacks on Urban Areas," Discussion Paper, Program in Defense and Arms Control Studies, Massachusetts Institute of Technology, discusses the technical challenges in intercepting chemical warheads.

[75]Matthew Meselson, "The Myth of Chemical Superweapons," *Bulletin of the Atomic Scientist*, Vol. 47, No. 3 (April, 1991), pp. 12–15, argues that such precautions can render even nerve agents no more lethal than conventional weapons, but others dispute this view. Such precautions would reduce the lethality of many types of biological weapons as well, but the effects on unprotected populations would be much greater.

[76]See Donald L. Hafner and John Roper, eds., *ATBMs and Western Security: Missile Defenses for Europe* (New York: Ballinger, 1988), and Jurgen Altmann, *SDI for Europe?: Technical Aspects of Anti-Tactical Ballistic Missile Defenses*, PRIF Research Report 3/1988 (Peace Research Institute Frankfurt, 1988), for discussions of this issue.

further upgrades of the Patriot as well as three other ATBM programs: ERINT, Arrow, and THAAD.[77] The apparent success of the Patriot in intercepting Iraqi Scuds had an important effect in keeping Israel out of the war against Iraq, but it remains unclear whether the Patriot actually reduced damage on the ground.[78] Indeed, the Patriot ATBM was not designed for the protection of broad urban areas but for low-altitude point defense of military assets.

With real or potential enemies in neighboring China, South Asia, the Middle East, and Europe, the former Soviet Union has special reason to be concerned about and to pursue defenses against shorter-range missiles. Indeed, it has tested SAMs against short-range missiles and may have deployed them with a dual ATBM role in mind. Many of these long-range SAMs appear to carry nuclear warheads,[79] which would enhance their ATBM capability but could also cause substantial damage to defended areas.

Approaches to ATBM Development

ATBM defenses against non-Soviet missiles, most of which are nonnuclear, raise a different set of questions from ABM defenses. The limited military threat posed by today's inaccurate, conventionally armed missiles may not warrant a costly deployment effort, but the prospect of more capable missiles in the future justifies a significant program of research and development. Similarly, the terror threat these missiles pose to urban areas may not warrant the deployment of area defenses, but the prospect of unconventional warheads makes the development of such systems a high priority. ATBMs are easily made mobile or transportable, so a small, relatively cheap contingency force could be kept in the United States and deployed in the event of a regional crisis. Ship-basing provides another approach to contingency deployment.[80]

---

[77]Originally designed for air defense, the Patriot was subsequently upgraded to give it some ATBM capability. Future upgrades, including an active radar seeker, should extend its range. Both Patriot and the Extended-Range Interceptor (ERINT), SDI's original ATBM, are short-range ATBMs. Israel is developing the longer-range Arrow and with mostly U.S. funding. Still in the design stage, the Theater High-Altitude Area Defense (THAAD) aims for the longest range and highest altitude of any of these ATBMs. The Corps SAM replacement for the Hawk air-defense system is being designed to have ATBM capabilities as well, and there has been some discussion of giving ATBM capabilities to the Standard ship-based SAM or making other ATBM interceptors deployable on ships.

[78]Theodore A. Postol, "Lessons of the Gulf War Experience with Patriot," *International Security*, Vol. 16, No. 3 (Winter, 1991/92), pp. 119–171, points out that damage levels increased after the Patriot was deployed to Israel, and offers several explanations for this observation.

[79]Thomas B. Cochran, et al., *Nuclear Weapons Databook Volume IV: Soviet Nuclear Forces* (New York: Ballinger, 1989), p. 117.

[80]Robert Holzer and Neil Munro, "Navy Extends New Mission With Aegis: Effort Aims to Guard Marines from Ballistic Missile Strikes," *Defense News*, November 4, 1991, p. 1.

In designing its ATBM program, the United States must also consider possible responses to its efforts at ATBM defense. Will U.S. programs prompt the development of countermeasures, perhaps available on the international market? Will countries be encouraged to develop cruise missiles as an alternative? Will defenses simply stimulate international commerce in high-technology weapons? The United States should be prepared in case its efforts to limit the diffusion of these technologies fail.

Finally, ATBMs can have considerable overlap with ABM systems, and the widespread deployment of highly capable ATBMs could help circumvent the deployment limits in the ABM Treaty. Although there is no sharp distinction between ABM and ATBM capabilities, most ATBMs would provide at best a point defense against nuclear ICBMs and SLBMs. The United States should take care not to undermine the ABM Treaty with its ATBM efforts.

ATBM Recommendations

ABM Treaty   The United States should seek in its discussions with the former USSR to establish thresholds to distinguish ATBMs from ABMs. The increasing range of some Third World missiles makes a careful definition of thresholds especially important.[81]

Program Organization   The United States has already taken the first step in rationalizing its approach to short-range missile defense by unifying its efforts into a single program, the Theater Missile Defense Initiative. This allows greater coordination and perhaps consolidation of overlapping ATBM programs. The different threat environment and the importance of maintaining the ABM Treaty provide strong reasons for keeping this program administratively separate from the rest of SDI, even in areas of technology overlap, like radar.

Short-range ATBMs   The limited capabilities of current Third World TBMs suggest a measured, evolutionary approach to ATBMs, using the existing Patriot system as a base. Given its dual air-defense role, the Patriot system offers an economical approach for near-term ATBM capabilities. ERINT is designed for integration into the Patriot architecture, also at relatively low cost. The mix of interceptors in an integrated air and missile defense system depends on costs and on technical and threat information, none of which are yet known. A mobile ATBM system for rapid deploy-

---

[81]These could include limits on the speed of the interceptor and the speed and altitude of the target warhead at interception. See Herbert Lin, "Rationalized Range/altitude Thresholds for ABM Testing," *Science and Global Security*, Vol. 2, No. 1 (1990), pp. 87–101. These threshold limits would apply equally to SAMs as well.

ment in regional contingencies should be cheap enough to satisfy cost-exchange and cost-benefit criteria.[82]

Long-range ATBMs   Systems like Arrow and THAAD require more powerful surveillance radars, resulting in much greater infrastructure costs. Because of the potential growth of the short-range missile threat, the United States (and Israel) should continue to develop and test these systems, but should defer any decision on deployment. The development of area ATBMs requires careful attention to the ABM Treaty, as THAAD in particular could have significant ABM capabilities. If given ABM capabilities are tested in an ABM mode, area ATBM components could be considered ABM components, with their deployment restricted by the ABM Treaty. Article IX of the ABM Treaty, which prohibits the transfer of ABM systems to other countries, could further complicate the deployment of such systems in regional contingencies.

Non-proliferation   The United States should continue its efforts, in coordination with other suppliers, to limit the spread of ballistic and cruise missile technologies. The widespread sale of ATBMs could, however, complicate this task. Although many of these technologies are already widely proliferated, there are still opportunities to limit improvements in missile range and accuracy, and perhaps even more promisingly, the spread of chemical and nuclear weapons. Though they face difficult challenges, attempts at regional arms control in the Middle East and elsewhere could also bear valuable fruit.

STRATEGIC AIR DEFENSE

Like fallen nobility, strategic air defense in the United States boasts a venerable history but has been reduced to poverty by years of neglect. After the legendary bomber gap of the 1950s, the advent of strategic missiles, followed by the ABM Treaty, left little motivation to defend against the least robust element of the Soviet strategic triad. The development of cruise missiles and stealth technology could, however, change this situation and pose a challenge for early warning, as mentioned in the next chapter.

History and Current Status

The development of nuclear weapons and strategic bombers by the Soviet Union prompted an immediate and massive U.S. effort at strategic air

---

[82]The cost-exchange ratio is probably not a very good criterion when the United States faces countries with relatively limited resources.

defense. This led to a significant technology push in radar and computing, as well as the development of improved fighter aircraft and the nuclear-tipped Bomarc and Nike air-defense missiles. In 1958, the United States and Canada established the North American Air (now Aerospace) Defense Command (NORAD) to defend the continent against Soviet bombers, and deployed a three-layered system of radars, with the crucial Distant Early Warning line of 78 radars spread across arctic Canada, Greenland, and Alaska.[83]

As costs rose, ambitious plans were scaled back somewhat, and U.S. and Canadian air defense deployments peaked in the early 1960s with over 3,000 interceptor aircraft and 90 long-range SAM batteries. Since then their numbers have fallen steadily. In the early 1980s the United States retired its last Nike-Hercules missiles and maintained just over 300 interceptor aircraft in the Air National Guard. In parallel with SDI, the Reagan administration launched the Air Defense Initiative to coordinate air defense activities, but funding has remained low and has concentrated on surveillance and warning systems.[84]

The Soviet Union has taken a different approach to air defense, maintaining and modernizing a robust network of radars, SAMs, and interceptor aircraft. This is due in part to geography and the fact that the Soviet Union has faced shorter-range and nonnuclear air threats, and in part to vigorous U.S. efforts to maintain the ability to penetrate Soviet air defenses. But the Soviets are also heirs to a long military tradition of defending the homeland, into which strategic air defense fits naturally.[85]

Future technology trends could shake U.S. complacency on strategic air defense. The announced elimination of Soviet sea-launched cruise missiles[86] removes the main area of immediate concern,[87] but the proliferation of cruise missiles could create problems in the future. Cruise missiles could displace ballistic missiles as the weapons of choice for delivering payloads to intermediate ranges without risking aircraft and pilots.[88] They

---

[83]See the first half of James M. Eglin, *op. cit.*, for the history of early U.S. air defense debates and programs.

[84]See Arthur Charo, *Continental Air Defense: A Neglected Dimension of Strategic Defense* (Lanham, Md.: University Press of America, 1990), for a description of recent U.S. air defense efforts.

[85]See the second half of James M. Eglin, *op. cit.*, for a history of early Soviet air defense doctrines, and John W. R. Lepingwell, "Soviet Strategic Air Defense and the Stealth Challenge," *International Security*, Vol. 14, No. 2 (Fall, 1989), pp. 64–100, for a description of recent challenges to those doctrines.

[86]"Gorbachev's Remarks on Nuclear Arms Cuts," *op. cit.*

[87]Theodore A. Postol, "Banning Nuclear SLCMs: It Would Be Nice If We Could," *International Security*, Vol. 13, No. 3 (Winter, 1988–89), pp. 191–202.

[88]John C. Baker, "Program Costs and Comparisons" in Richard K. Betts, ed., *Cruise Missiles: Technology, Strategy, Politics* (Washington, D.C.: The Brookings Institution, 1981), pp. 101–133, concludes that cruise missiles are usually more cost-effective than ballistic missiles or

can also be made fairly accurate much more easily than ballistic missiles, using public signals from navigation satellites, and may be harder to intercept than ballistic missiles.

Air Defense Recommendations

Since the former Soviet Union poses the only strategic air threat to the United States, and since the United States has no existing or prospective means of defending against strategic missiles, we see no need for immediate efforts to deploy strategic air defenses. However, a U.S. move toward limited ABM defenses or the emergence of long-range aircraft or cruise missile threats from other countries could change this situation. In that case, the United States would face the great expense of purchasing surveillance radars and large numbers of SAMs and expensive interceptor aircraft in order to provide an active defense.[89]

Although arms control for air defense need not be a high priority, some approaches may be worth exploring. The United States would naturally be most interested in limiting modern Soviet SAMs and interceptor aircraft, and possibly radars as well. The main Soviet concern would be to reduce costs, but their first priority would be to retire older, less effective air defense systems. They may have also have difficulties maintaining their air defense network, which is spread across many republics with important components in the Baltic states. The Soviets have also announced the retirement of all their nuclear-tipped SAMs.[90] Given the prospect of continued unilateral actions,[91] formal arms control negotiations appear unnecessary at this point.

CONCLUSIONS AND RECOMMENDATIONS

Many factors limit the desirability of active defenses against nuclear weapons and their delivery systems:

- Defenses against nuclear weapons are not necessarily benign. Elements in the former Soviet Union could see unilateral U.S. defense

---

aircraft at intermediate ranges. Steve Fetter, *op. cit.*, p. 11, describes the possible design and cost of a rudimentary cruise missile for Third World countries.

[89]Arthur Charo, *op. cit.*, p. 131, estimates the cost of surveillance and interceptor upgrades to be $100–200 billion.

[90]"Gorbachev's Remarks on Nuclear Arms Cuts."

[91]John W. R. Lepingwell, *op. cit.*, points to indications of a potential shift in the role of Soviet air defense forces to the less demanding task of maintaining airspace sovereignty. Alexei G. Arbatov, "Blurring the Line: The Merging of Nuclear and Conventional Strategic Systems: Implications for Strategy, Politics, and Arms Control," paper presented at the IGCC Workshop on Nuclear Deterrence and Global Security in Transition, University of California at San Diego, February 21–23, 1991, has proposed air defense limits.

efforts as a threat to their ability to deter nuclear attack and could respond in a manner that would make the costs of the defense outweigh the benefits.

- The ABM Treaty, which imposes strict limits on defenses against long-range ballistic missiles, is the cornerstone of U.S.-Soviet arms control. Undermining the ABM Treaty could impede progress on strategic and nonstrategic arms control and undermine efforts to tighten control over Soviet nuclear forces.
- Cooperative measures may offer greater benefits at lower cost than limited ABM defenses as a response to the risk of accidental or unauthorized missile attack by the former Soviet Union.
- As an exception, short-range missile defenses, especially in a contingency force for rapid deployment in a crisis, may be an attractive option for responding to the proliferation of ballistic missiles and weapons of mass destruction.

These general conclusions suggest a number of specific recommendations for U.S. policy:

- To avoid undermining the ABM Treaty, the United States should adopt reasonable technical definitions for specific terms in the treaty, preferably through negotiation with the former USSR.
- The United States should continue to abide by the traditional interpretation of the ABM Treaty, which bans the testing of space-based missile defenses, implemented through reasonable technical definitions.
- To avoid the costs of premature development and testing and to facilitate compliance with the ABM Treaty, SDI should be divided into three sections:
  1. ATBMs. Point defenses (Patriot and ERINT) should be procured in limited numbers for rapid deployment in a crisis. Area defenses (THAAD and Arrow), which have yet to prove their worth, should be limited to research and development. ATBMs should not be tested in an ABM mode or given ABM capabilities.
  2. Fixed, ground-based ABM defenses. Continued development and testing serve as a hedge against possible future threats, but no deployment is warranted under current circumstances.
  3. Research on other ABM technologies. More exotic technologies, such as lasers, may offer a long-term prospect for effective ABM defense, and continued research is prudent. However, the United States should not develop or test ABM components using these technologies or space-based ABM components. The former would be premature, and the latter would violate the ABM Treaty.
- The United States should maintain vigorous efforts and give a high priority to limiting, preventing, and perhaps reversing the spread of nuclear and chemical weapons and advanced delivery systems, including ballistic missiles and cruise missiles.

APPENDIX A

ANTISATELLITE WEAPONS

No discussion of ABM defenses would be complete without some consideration of the closely related issue of antisatellite weapons. There are two connections between ABM systems and antisatellite weapons: ASATs have an extensive technological overlap with area ABM systems, and they are a potential countermeasure against ABM systems with space-based components.

Intercepting satellites in orbit is much like intercepting ballistic missile warheads above the atmosphere; both require long-range tracking and interception capabilities. But the ASAT task is generally much easier. Satellites tend to be much more fragile than reentry vehicles and to travel in predictable orbits that are known long in advance. Long-range ABM systems therefore have a significant ASAT capability.[92]

Space-based ABM components are also potentially vulnerable to ASAT attack. The added cost of launching satellites into orbit—be they ABM sensors or interceptors—gives a tremendous cost advantage to ground-based ASATs, according to Nitze's cost-exchange criterion.

As with ABMs, the end of the Cold War implies relatively little change for U.S. ASAT policy. Improved relations and disarray in the former Soviet Union make Soviet satellite and ASAT capabilities less of a concern, and no other likely U.S. adversary is close to possessing a threatening satellite or ASAT capability. We therefore describe the relevant issues in generic terms.

MILITARY SATELLITES

The war against Iraq illustrates the growing military role of satellites. The U.S.-led coalition used satellites for reconnaissance, communication, navigation, weather forecasting, and early warning of Scud missile attacks, all of which contributed to its overwhelming advantage in C^3I. Given the capability to attack them, satellites could become attractive targets in time of war.

Improvements in satellite reconnaissance capabilities, especially the trend toward real-time targeting information against mobile or relocatable targets, create the strongest incentive for ASATs. Reconnaissance satellites are generally deployed in low orbits where they are relatively vulnerable to ASAT attack. But the United States enjoys a strong advantage in space-based reconnaissance, and could gain more from a bilateral or international ASAT ban than it would lose in foregoing ASAT capabilities.[93] Simple changes in military operations could limit

[92]Ashton B. Carter, "The Relationship of ASAT and BMD Systems," in Boutwell and Long, eds., *op. cit.*, pp. 171–189.

[93]For a presentation of this argument in U.S.-Soviet Cold War terms, see Chapters 2, 3, and 4 of Paul Stares, *Space and National Security* (Washington, D.C.: The Brookings Institution, 1987).

the threat posed by an adversary's reconnaissance satellites and make a U.S. ASAT unnecessary.[94]

There are also important reasons not to attack satellites, especially those that play a role in strategic C[3]I, whose survival provides an important element of stability. These include not only early-warning satellites but also those equipped to detect nuclear explosions and those that might be used to communicate launch authorization and codes. A preemptive attack on these satellites could precipitate an escalatory response, and the capability for such attack could therefore undermine crisis stability.[95] These satellites are now deployed in much higher orbits where they are not yet vulnerable to ASAT attack, but this invulnerability could change if ABM capabilities were greatly expanded, especially if ABM interceptors were deployed in space.[96]

ASAT TECHNOLOGIES

A wide variety of technical means and operational approaches could lead to varying levels of capability for ASAT attack. Electronic jamming can disrupt communication with satellites and ground-based lasers can damage sensors, but most ASAT attacks would aim to destroy or completely disable their targets. The mechanisms for destroying satellites are much the same as those for ABM defense: nuclear explosion, conventional explosion, kinetic energy, or directed energy. The methods of delivery include direct ascent from the ground, which takes a few minutes against satellites in low orbit, or coorbital attack, in which the ASAT can take hours to maneuver into a position close enough to destroy the target satellite. Space mines, which are essentially permanently stationed coorbital ASATs, and ground-based lasers are also important possibilities.

The United States briefly deployed a nuclear direct-ascent ASAT in the 1960s.[97] In the 1980s, the United States developed and tested a direct-ascent kinetic energy ASAT, the Miniature Homing Vehicle, but Congress blocked further testing and in 1989 the Reagan administration canceled the program. U.S. ASAT development programs continue, but have been the subject of disagreement within the administration.[98] The United States has a number of other weapon systems with some ASAT capability, however, including the mothballed Spartan missiles from the Safeguard ABM system and, if properly fused to explode at high altitudes, ICBMs and SLBMs. The ERIS/GBI interceptor would also have a potent ASAT capability, and continued work on such ABM components provides the technology base for rapid ASAT deployments, should the need arise.

The Soviet Union maintains a deployed ASAT, a coorbital system that uses

---

[94]Operational countermeasures against Soviet Radar Ocean Reconnaissance Satellites (RORSATs) and Electronic Ocean Reconnaissance Satellites (EORSATs) are described in *ibid.*, pp. 131–136.

[95]Paul Stares, "Nuclear Operations and Anti-Satellites," in Carter, Steinbruner, and Zraket, eds., *op. cit.*, pp. 679–703.

[96]David C. Wright, *op. cit.*

[97]Thomas Karas, *The New High Ground: Strategies and Weapons of Space-Age War* (New York: Simon & Schuster, 1983), pp. 148–149.

[98]Philip Finnegan, "Army Again Moves to Kill Kinetic Energy ASAT," *Defense Week*, October 21, 1991, p. 2.

radar to home in on its target and destroy it with a fragmentation explosive. This system was tested with some success in the early 1970s, but a more advanced version using infrared sensors was a complete failure. Even with its limited operational capability, however, this system could pose some threat to U.S. reconnaissance satellites.[99] Soviet Galosh ABM interceptors also provide a significant ASAT capability, as do Soviet ICBMs. Many factors would inhibit the use of nuclear ASATs, however, including the prospect of collateral damage (including damage to one's own assets), the taboo against using nuclear weapons, and the risk of escalation to nuclear war.[100]

The United States and Soviet Union have taken opposite positions on ASAT arms control. The Soviet Union has proposed a treaty to outlaw the testing and deployment of ASAT systems, and the United States has expressed no interest in such agreements.[101] The United States claims that current and future Soviet satellites pose a potential threat that requires an ASAT capability, and that ASAT arms control agreements could not be verified.

The main verification challenge is distinguishing allowed ABM testing from forbidden ASAT testing; a combined ABM/ASAT test ban could be verified, but would impose severe limits on SDI testing. A ban on coorbital ASAT testing and deployment could be verified, but would affect only the Soviets. Limits on ground-based laser and interceptor testing could be verified, but would affect both ASAT and ABM activities. A compromise position would be to allow the testing of only fixed ground-based ABM interceptors, but this would not limit low-altitude ASAT capabilities.[102]

OPTIONS

The United States possesses a number of means of addressing the ASAT issue. To minimize the threat to its satellites from any country, the United States could improve their survivability and develop the ability to rapidly replace critical satellite capabilities.[103]

---

[99]Paul Stares, *Space and National Security*, pp. 85–95.

[100]Paul Stares, "Nuclear Operations and Anti-Satellites," *op. cit.*

[101]In 1983 the Soviets proposed a draft ASAT treaty, reprinted as Appendix A in Office of Technology Assessment, *Anti-Satellite Weapons, Countermeasures, and Arms Control*. Since August 20, 1985, the U.S. position has been that "no arrangements beyond those already governing military activities in outer space have been found to date that are judged to be in the overall interest of the United States . . .," quoted in U.S. Arms Control and Disarmament Agency, "U.S. Space Arms Control Policy," in Kenneth N. Loungo and W. Thomas Wander, eds., *The Search for Security in Space* (Ithaca, N.Y.: Cornell University Press, 1989), p. 237.

[102]Ashton B. Carter, "The Structure of Possible U.S.-Soviet Agreements Regarding Missile Defense," in Joseph S. Nye, ed., *On the Defensive? The Future of SDI* (Lanham, Md.: University Press of America, 1988), pp. 141–172.

[103]The simplest measures would be to put satellites in higher orbits and give them the means to maneuver and evade possible attack. For the longer term, the disaggregation of complex satellites into component pieces would make them more survivable and less attractive

The United States might also reconsider its opposition to ASAT arms control. A ban on ASAT testing and deployment, combined with satellite survivability measures, could significantly limit the threat. Additional restrictions on ABM testing and deployment could further reduce latent ASAT capabilities, but the ASAT issue would be only a minor consideration in ABM arms control. Alternatively, the United States could seek limits on ASAT capabilities to prevent the development of a high-altitude ASAT threat. Maintaining the ban on space-based ABM testing would greatly facilitate such limits.

Specific recommendations are beyond the scope of this chapter, but there is reason to reconsider past U.S. policies on ASAT development and arms control.

SUGGESTED READINGS

Boutwell, Jeffrey and F. A. Long, eds. *Weapons in Space*. New York: Norton, 1986.

Bunn, Matthew. *Foundation for the Future: The ABM Treaty and National Security*. Washington, D.C.: The Arms Control Association, 1990.

Carter, Ashton B. and David N. Schwartz, eds. *Ballistic Missile Defense*. Washington, D.C.: The Brookings Institution, 1984.

Charo, Arthur. *Continental Air Defense: A Neglected Dimension of Strategic Defense*. Lanham, Md.: University Press of America, 1990.

Chayes, Antonia H. and Paul Doty, eds. *Defending Deterrence: Managing the ABM Treaty into the 21st Century*. Elmsford, N.Y.: Pergamon-Brassey's, 1989.

Office of Technology Assessment. *Strategic Defenses: Ballistic Missile Defense Technologies; Anti-Satellite Weapons, Countermeasures, and Arms Control*. Princeton: Princeton University Press, 1986.

Stares, Paul B. *Space and National Security*. Washington, D.C.: The Brookings Institution, 1987.

---

targets, just like the deMIRVing of ICBMs. See Office of Technology Assessment, *Anti-Satellite Weapons, Countermeasures, and Arms Control* (Princeton, N.J.: Princeton University Press, 1985), pp. 75–86.

Chapter 8

The Future of U.S. Strategic Command, Control, Communications, and Intelligence

Cindy Williams

*T*he sweeping changes discussed elsewhere in this book have significant implications for U.S. strategic command, control, communications, and intelligence—the collection of systems and procedures the United States relies on to maintain control of its strategic forces and operations. Fundamental shifts in the global security environment demand a renewed assessment of the role strategic C³I will play in the future. Proposed changes in the mix and characteristics of strategic offensive forces call for a new look at the C³I systems and procedures that support them. At the same time, budget cutbacks can be expected to impose severe constraints on any plans for restructuring or modernization. Procurement opportunities will be limited, and pressure will mount to streamline operations wherever possible to save both money and manpower.

This chapter examines U.S. strategic C³I in the context of these changes and seeks a path by which the command architecture can be brought into line with the forces and missions it will support in the future. It confines itself to those C³I systems that support strategic offensive forces—the ICBMs, SLBMs, and long-range bombers discussed in Chapters 5 and 6. Strategic defenses and associated C³I are handled in Chapter 7.

The chapter begins with a brief review of existing C³I functions and capabilities. It continues with an examination of relevant changes in the world and how they can be expected to affect C³I needs. It concludes with a set of recommendations for future C³I priorities and some ideas for streamlining to provide more efficient, cost-effective control of diminishing offensive forces in the environments they are likely to face.

EXISTING C³I STRUCTURE

Strategic C³I supports the management and monitoring of strategic forces during peacetime,[1] the management and control of these forces when they are used in conventional operations, and national-level decision-making and the execution of operational plans in the event the United States or its allies come under enemy nuclear attack. With these peacetime and wartime roles, strategic C³I is of vital importance both in maintaining the safety of nuclear weapons and in deterring war by bolstering the credibility of the threat of retaliation.

Strategic C³I encompasses facilities, such as command centers; equipment, such as radars, data processing systems, and communications networks; people, including decision-makers, commanders, and the civilian and military personnel supporting them; and plans and procedures for keeping forces ready in peacetime and using them in war. This section provides a cursory overview of strategic C³I functions and current capabilities.

Specific C³I functions can be organized loosely into three categories: intelligence, warning, and assessment; command and decision; and communications. Table 8.1 summarizes some of the tasks carried out under each of these categories.

Intelligence, warning, and assessment include the gathering and interpretation of data about potential adversaries. In addition to day-to-day reporting on worldwide events and enemy forces, they encompass tactical warning and assessment of an attack—that is, warning that missiles or bombers have already been launched and estimates of their numbers, points of origin, expected times of arrival, and possible intended targets. Current systems include reconnaissance aircraft; satellite-based sensors for initial warning of ballistic missile launches (including antisatellite missiles) and confirmation of nuclear detonations; ground-based radars for confirmation of approaching missiles and for early warning of bomber and possibly cruise missile attacks[2]; ground-based stations that process infor-

---

[1]In peacetime, strategic forces require controls to ensure against unauthorized or accidental use. Such negative controls are discussed in a later section of this chapter. In addition, they engage in activities including alerts, readiness checks, training, and exercises that require management and monitoring.

[2]Sea-launched cruise missiles would probably go undetected by warning systems in place today. Although the Over-the-Horizon-Backscatter radar system has some capability to detect SLCMs, its planned coverage is not worldwide. The Airborne Warning and Control

Table 8.1   EXAMPLES OF STRATEGIC C³I TASKS

Intelligence, warning, and assessment	Command and decision	Strategic communications
Intelligence collection	Force status monitoring and assessment	Connectivity from warning sensors to command centers
Reconnaissance	Situation assessment	Connectivity among command centers
Threat surveillance	Option formulation and selection	Connectivity between commanders and forces
Combining intelligence from multiple sources	Management of force survivability	
Attack warning and confirmation	Force execution decisionmaking	
Attack sizing and characterization	Recovery of surviving forces	
	War termination	

mation from the early warning satellites; facilities like the one at Cheyenne Mountain Air Force Base in Colorado where intelligence and warning information is combined and assessed; and communications equipment for those who use the warning data, including national-level decision-makers.[3]

The command and decision function includes: monitoring and managing forces and supporting systems, such as aerial refueling tankers, during peacetime; managing and controlling bombers and tankers when they are called upon for conventional operations; maintaining force survivability during crisis or attack (for example, by moving SSBNs out of port or adjusting bomber alert postures based on information about the threat); formulating and selecting options in response to an attack; executing operational plans; recovering surviving submarines and bombers after they are used; and terminating a war. Some of the important command centers from which these functions are carried out are listed in Table 8.2. The map presented in Figure 8.1 shows the locations of several of them.

For forces intended to deter, management and direction of peacetime operations is a key function. U.S. strategic forces maintain high peacetime readiness. Bombers and tankers are engaged daily in airborne training

---

System, not generally considered a strategic C³I asset, could probably detect SLCMs, but it would have to be airborne and operating in the right location to do so.

[3]For an excellent discussion of U.S. warning and assessment systems, see John C. Toomay's chapter, "Warning and Assessment Sensors," in Ashton B. Carter, John D. Steinbruner, Charles A. Zraket, eds., *Managing Nuclear Operations* (Washington, D.C.: The Brookings Institution, 1987), pp. 282–321.

Table 8.2 EXAMPLES OF STRATEGIC COMMAND CENTERS

Command center	Location	Functions
Fixed Centers		
National Military Command Center (NMCC)	The Pentagon, Washington, DC	Command decision-making; option selection; transmission of force execution message
North American Air Defense and U.S. Space Command Warning Centers	Cheyenne Mountain, CO	Tactical warning and assessment; space operations support
Strategic Command Headquarters Command Center[a]	Strategic Command Headquarters, Offutt AFB, NE	Combining intelligence from multiple sources; war planning; nuclear force management and execution
ICBM Launch Control Centers (LCCs)	ICBM wings	ICBM launch; ICBM status monitoring
ICBM and Bomber Wing Command Posts[a]	ICBM, bomber, and tanker bases	Force status monitoring; force management; bomber and tanker launch
Ground-Mobile Centers		
Surviving Enduring Command Center (SECC)	Strategic Command Headquarters, Offutt AFB, NE	Transportable backup to STRATCOM HQ Command Center
Mobile Command and Control Center (MCCC)	Cheyenne Mountain, CO	Transportable backup to Cheyenne Mountain
Airborne Command Centers		
National Emergency Airborne Command Post (NEACP)	Offutt AFB, NE, and Grissom AFB, IN; partial airborne alert	Survivable backup to NMCC
STRATCOM Airborne Command Post (ABNCP)[a]	Offutt AFB, NE, and Ellsworth AFB, SD; partial airborne alert	Communication of execution messages; ICBM launch; limited force management
Airborne Command Posts of Atlantic Command, Pacific Command, European Command	Headquarters bases at Norfolk, VA, Honolulu, HI, and Stuttgart, Germany	Communications to submarines and theater forces; limited force management

[a]Under the air force reorganization announced in September 1991, the Strategic Air Command ceased to exist in June 1992. Its aircraft and missiles were assigned to two new air force commands, Air Combat Command and Air Mobility Command. Command responsibility and command centers were divided between these commands and the new joint Strategic Command, which is now headquartered at Offutt AFB, NE. At the wing level, major restructuring brought former Strategic Air Command and Tactical Air Command wings into common "objective wings." Thus, SAC unit command posts have become simply air force wing command posts.

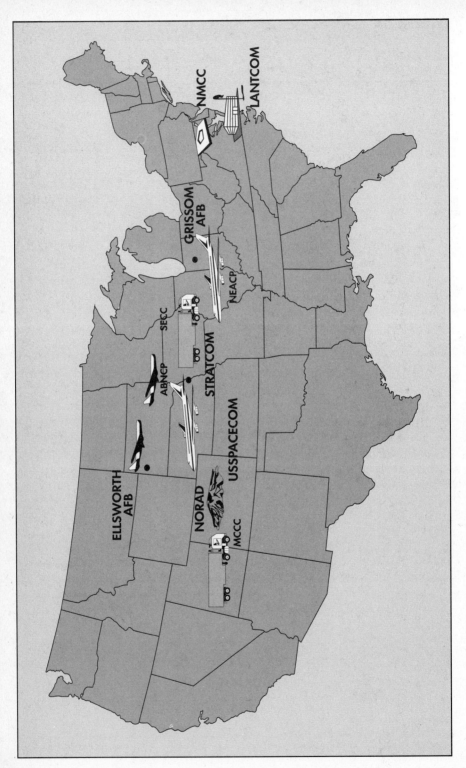

Figure 8.1 Continental U.S. locations of key Strategic Command Centers.

missions. A portion of the SSBN fleet is on patrol at any given time. ICBM launch control centers are staffed around the clock. The command structure supports the constant monitoring of safety, security, and readiness of forces and personnel; frequent tests of communications links to ensure forces remain connected to their commanders; the control of forces during scheduled exercises and training; and rapid response to accidents or threats of unauthorized takeover or use of strategic weapons.

If deterrence fails and the United States is faced with a nuclear attack, the primary command functions are to get movable forces out of harm's way to the extent possible, to decide on an appropriate retaliatory response, and to issue strike commands. Potential responses are generally based on the overall strategic war plan called the SIOP. As discussed in Chapter 3, the SIOP is actually a collection of preplanned options that allow for structured attacks against a variety of target sets. SIOP planning, once the domain of the Joint Strategic Target Planning Staff, is now carried out by the planning staff of Strategic Command. Planners from all three military services use a mix of manual and automated procedures, professional judgment, and interservice negotiation to select targets, assign weapons to them, and identify appropriate missile trajectories and bomber routes. The process takes about 18 months.[4] This extensive preplanning and the communication of the plan to force units in peacetime allow for rapid selection, communication, and execution of retaliatory options in wartime.

The strategic communications system provides links among warning sensors, warning and assessment facilities, decision-makers at all levels, and the forces themselves. The system makes use of land lines and satellites to communicate in frequencies across the spectrum.

In general, the lower-frequency bands (extremely low, very low, and low frequencies) transmit data very slowly, but they are relatively resistant to disruption by the effects of nuclear explosions. In addition, extremely low frequency signals can penetrate seawater to a depth useful for secure communications to submarines. The air force and navy have systems operating in these bands to communicate with bombers and submarines. Medium- and high-frequency communications are used by all strategic force elements in peacetime, but could be blacked out for hours by nuclear effects following an attack. The higher frequencies (very high, ultrahigh, superhigh, and extremely high) are generally limited to line-of-sight and satellite operations; they can transmit large amounts of data very rapidly and provide good communications between aircraft, between aircraft and ground-based systems, and between satellites and airborne or ground-based centers.

How capable is this overall C³I architecture of carrying out the func-

---

[4]Although the SIOP takes months to develop, it is updated regularly during the year to accommodate changes in forces, targets, or national security policy.

tions described here? The answer depends to a great extent on the circumstances. In peacetime, it is extremely well suited to its mission of monitoring and controlling forces. Through a variety of measures, it provides for what is sometimes termed "negative control," that is, control to prevent unauthorized or accidental use of nuclear weapons in peacetime.[5] If called upon to support conventional operations in theater, it is capable of adapting quickly to changing needs, although there is room for improvement, as will be discussed in the next section.

If deterrence fails, the C^3I emphasis switches from negative to positive control, that is, control to ensure that weapons use can be authorized and operations can be executed as planned. The decision to use strategic nuclear weapons rests with the National Command Authorities—the president (or his successor by law) and the secretary of defense—or presumably with those to whom the president has delegated this authority.[6] The president's actual ability to use the strategic forces depends on the level and character of the adversary's strike and the consequent survivability of the forces themselves, the C^3I apparatus, and a decision-maker with the necessary authority to use nuclear weapons. If the survival of all three of these elements were reasonably assured, the president could wait until the attack was over ("ride out" the attack) and then choose an appropriate response, based on full knowledge of the nature and source of the attack and the damage it had caused. If not, there would be pressure to use forces quickly while they and the C^3I structure were still intact. If an attack were not focused on disrupting C^3I (as for example in an accidental or third-party launch), the C^3I system would operate largely as it does in peacetime. As long as decision-makers could determine quickly that a larger attack was not on the way, they could ride out the attack, take the time to identify its source, and respond later.

Faced with a large attack directed specifically at destroying forces and

---

[5]The terms "positive control" and "negative control" are used differently in different circles. The nuclear safety community, for example, refers to the strict control of nuclear weapons at all times as positive control; the air force refers to a launch of bombers without wartime execution orders as a positive control launch. This chapter adopts the usage laid out by John Steinbruner in "Choices and Tradeoffs," in Ashton B. Carter, John D. Steinbruner, and Charles A. Zraket, eds., *op. cit.*, pp. 539–540. Negative control measures include physical protection of the weapons themselves, security screening of personnel who handle or control them, physical and procedural controls that make it necessary for two or more people to cooperate to launch weapons, and the use of physically protected codes that originate with the president and are physically or procedurally required for the weapons' release and activation. For detailed discussions, see Donald R. Cotter's chapter, "Peacetime Operations," in Ashton B. Carter, John D. Steinbruner, and Charles A. Zraket, eds., *op.cit.*, pp. 17–74; and Daniel Ford, *The Button: The Pentagon's Strategic Command and Control System* (New York: Simon and Schuster, 1985), pp. 114–121.

[6]Paul Bracken provides detailed arguments on the subject of predelegation of authority for retaliatory launch of strategic nuclear weapons in "Delegation of Nuclear Command Authority," in Ashton B. Carter, John D. Steinbruner, and Charles A. Zraket, *op. cit.*, pp. 352–372. The author does not know whether such predelegation arrangements have actually been made by any president.

disrupting command and control, the C³I structure might not fare so well. Much of the C³I literature of the 1980s argued that C³I vulnerabilities could either prevent offensive forces from being able to respond or, by forcing an immediate response to any perceived attack, pressure those in authority to act in haste, before the attack could be evaluated and a thoughtful decision made.[7] At least one analyst contended that effectiveness and survivability of the U.S. C³I under such conditions would be so poor that the United States must be planning for a preemptive first strike.[8]

A significant C³I improvement program carried out in the1980s and early 1990s actually corrected many of the deficiencies identified in the literature.[9] New warning systems were deployed and existing ones upgraded to increase confidence of timely warning. Message and data processing systems were modernized. Command centers and communications systems were hardened and protected against electromagnetic pulse effects that could damage or disrupt electronic equipment. And new systems were deployed to provide communications resistant to atmospheric and electromagnetic nuclear disturbances. As a result, U.S. strategic C³I systems are considerably more capable of assessing a situation and executing an immediate response today than they were in the last decade.

Today, most analysts seem to agree that the strategic C³I system is sufficiently flexible and redundant that, assuming the president or another individual with nuclear release authority survives, retaliatory strikes could be launched following even the most massive attack. While these retaliatory strikes might not be as well coordinated and carefully timed as planned, they would probably be large enough and certain enough to deter any enemy from attacking in the first place.[10]

CHANGING NEEDS AND DIRECTIONS FOR C³I

The dramatic security and budgetary changes affecting nuclear forces in general have specific implications for strategic C³I. Budgetary cutbacks will limit the funds available for operating and modernizing systems. Changes in the global security environment will alter both the threat

---

[7]See, for example, Bruce G. Blair, *Strategic Command and Control: Redefining the Nuclear Threat* (Washington, D.C.: The Brookings Institution, 1985).

[8]See the foreword in Daniel Ford, *op. cit.*

[9]For a running account of systems planned and procured during this period, see Secretary of Defense, *Annual Reports to the Congress* from FY1983 to FY1991 (Washington, D.C.: U.S. Government Printing Office, 1982–1990). For a summary of modernization efforts from 1981 to 1988, see Frank C. Carlucci, Fiscal Year 1990 *Annual Report to the Congress* (Washington, D.C.: U.S. Government Printing Office, January 17, 1989), pp. 185–193.

[10]Indeed, it is difficult to imagine that an enemy would believe any first strike could completely prevent a massive retaliation by the United States. For further discussion, see Daniel Ford, *op. cit.*, pp. 41–42; and Ashton B. Carter, "Assessing Command System Vulnerability," in Ashton B. Carter, John D. Steinbruner, and Charles A. Zraket, eds., *op.cit.*, pp. 555–610.

scenarios under which C³I systems are likely to have to operate and the targets against which strikes will be planned. Deep reductions and restructuring of strategic offensive forces will decrease the command burden to some extent. And new missions assigned to strategic systems will shift priorities for warning, command, and communications. This section discusses these developments.

Budget Cutbacks

As the overall defense budget declines, the pressure to fund major weapons systems at the expense of supporting programs like C³I is likely to increase. Given the choice between an airplane that can drop real bombs or a collection of relatively unknown C³I programs whose wartime utility is difficult to measure in peacetime, the military services would generally prefer the airplane. Thus, there is a real danger that C³I needs will be deferred as budgets are cut.

Historically, strategic C³I programs have accounted for about 9 percent of overall strategic spending and 1 percent of the Defense Department budget. Along with other strategic programs, they fared quite well during the last decade, increasing their share of defense spending from 0.9 percent in the 1970s to 1.3 percent in the 1980s.[11] Of course, there is no magic formula to determine a proper share for C³I in the defense budget. While C³I advocates argue that the United States has never spent enough on command and control, others insist that more spending on systems that do not destroy targets is wasted.

Whatever the eventual funding mix, we can predict with some certainty that C³I budgets will be significantly reduced from what they were in the 1980s. Thus, the need for thoughtful analysis of priorities among C³I options is greater than ever.

Changes in the Global Security Environment

As the United States heads into the twenty-first century, it faces a security environment radically altered from the one it has known since the dawn of the nuclear age, as discussed in Chapter 1. The former Soviet Union has disintegrated, and the future disposition and control of its nuclear resources have been called into question.[12] In addition, nuclear weapons

---

[11]For a year-by-year summary of strategic spending since 1962, see Benjamin F. Schemmer, "New Administration Faces Fallout over Strategic Priorities," *Armed Forces Journal International* (November 1988), pp. 72–75. For a discussion of Defense Department initiatives that resulted in increased attention, coherence, and funding for strategic C³I programs in the early 1980s, see Donald C. Latham and John J. Lane, "Management Issues: Planning, Acquisition, and Oversight," in Ashton B. Carter, John D. Steinbruner, and Charles A. Zraket, eds., *op.cit.*, pp. 641–660.

[12]Kurt M. Campbell, Ashton B. Carter, Steven E. Miller, and Charles A. Zraket, *Soviet Nuclear Fission: Control of the Nuclear Arsenal in a Disintegrating Soviet Union*, Center

8 THE FUTURE OF STRATEGIC COMMAND 245

technology and sophisticated delivery vehicles continue to spread to other countries. At the same time, regional conflicts have taken on greater importance and have even brought the United States into war. How do these political and military changes affect U.S. strategic C^3I needs and priorities?

Despite the disintegration of the former Soviet Union, the Soviet nuclear arsenal continues to pose a worst-case threat for U.S. strategic C^3I planning. The former Soviet Union (or whatever collection of states succeeds it) retains a clear capability to disrupt control of U.S. forces through direct nuclear attack, electromagnetic pulse, jamming, and other means. Although Soviet intentions toward the West appear benign today, the high degree of political instability in the former Soviet Union has fostered an environment in which intentions could shift dramatically in a short time. Thus, effective deterrence dictates that the United States retain a capability for assured nuclear retaliation after an all-out nuclear attack.

An arms reduction regime like the one offered in Chapter 6 would reduce the number of warheads in the Soviet arsenal, and thus might mitigate the degree to which an all-out attack could disrupt U.S. command and control systems. It is possible, however, that by lowering capabilities and payoffs for direct counternuclear attacks, such a regime would actually increase the likelihood of attacks on command and control assets; severing strategic forces from their commanders' control could be seen as a cheap way of rendering nuclear forces useless, an aim that could no longer be achieved via direct counterforce attacks given smaller and more survivable force structures on both sides.

While we cannot dismiss entirely the possibility of an all-out attack by the former Soviet Union whose nuclear capability remains under centralized authority, such an attack is no longer the only threat against which U.S. strategic C^3I priorities should be set. With the proliferation of nuclear and delivery vehicle technology to additional countries (potentially including several Soviet successor states), third-party nuclear attacks seem to be growing in relative plausibility. In addition, political instability in the former Soviet Union makes unauthorized or accidental attacks seem more likely than before. Thus, future U.S. strategic C^3I may have to contend with considerable uncertainty as to the source and intent of an attack.

Such uncertainty poses difficulties for a C^3I structure that was designed to deal with a single massive blow from the Soviet Union. Three areas are particularly affected: war planning, attack warning and assessment, and wartime decision-making.

War Planning When the expected adversary was a hegemon, as the Soviet Union and the Warsaw Pact were perceived to be during most of the nuclear age, an integrated operational plan like the SIOP made sense.

for Science and International Affairs Studies in International Security, No. 1 (Cambridge, Mass.: CSIA, November 1991).

Targets of retaliatory strikes could be assigned to U.S. bombers and missiles well in advance of an anticipated attack, and SIOP planners could structure a variety of strikes to be responsive to various levels of attack. If the number of potential enemies is larger and the attacker is not known before the attack takes place, however, such preplanning becomes more complicated. To ensure preplanned retaliation against any nuclear enemy, weapons would have to be assigned to targets deemed important to all attackers, and care would have to be taken to avoid striking two independent adversaries when only one was intended. An alternative would be to forgo preplanning altogether and conduct war planning "on the fly," after an attack was absorbed and the attacker identified. Such a strategy would be prudent if it were believed that any attack would leave planners, decision-makers, communications resources, and retaliatory forces intact long enough to develop operational plans and communicate them to the forces. In a massive strike directed at C^3I assets, however, this might not be the case; some degree of preplanning would be necessary to ensure retaliation.

Future war planning will probably need to combine the best of these strategies: a preplanned nuclear war plan with considerable built-in flexibility, and an increased ability to plan targets and operations in real time.

Attack Warning and Assessment   Given future uncertainties, the most important job of U.S. warning and assessment systems may shift from sizing a Soviet attack and identifying its intended targets to determining the source of the attack. In the case of land-based ballistic missiles, estimates of the location from which a missile was launched are provided by satellite-based warning sensors and permit identification of the country of origin. In the case of aircraft, which might not be sighted until they entered North American airspace, or submarine-launched ballistic missiles, which could be launched from the open ocean, the country of origin might be more difficult to trace. Better systems to identify specific missile and aircraft types would be useful in sorting things out. Sea-launched cruise missiles might not be detected at all by warning systems in place today. And the possibility that nuclear weapons could be delivered by unconventional means cannot be dismissed. Depending upon the circumstances, existing intelligence resources might or might not provide advance warning of such an attack or confirmation of its source.

Decision-making   In a world in which the possible source and intent of an attack may be unknown, the risk of responding precipitously with a potentially catastrophic decision seems even higher than when the Soviet monolith was the only nuclear-armed enemy. Reacting to an accidental or third-party attack with massive nuclear retaliation would be insane. Future strategic C^3I systems need to support delayed decision-making, allowing an attack to be fully assessed and the enemy to be identified with certainty before a retaliatory decision is made.

If fixed command centers were destroyed in an attack, the Strategic Command's transportable Surviving Enduring Command Center (SECC) would support such delayed decision-making, assuming it were deployed to a location unknown by the enemy before an attack began. To be useful in such circumstances, it would need to be outfitted with a full array of planning and decision-making tools and with survivable communications. Similar systems for national decision-makers would reduce the time pressure they face in making retaliatory decisions.

If strategic forces were made as survivable as Chapter 5 recommends for the long term, the perfect C³I architecture would be one that was sufficiently survivable to ride out any attack, including a massive one dedicated to destroying it, identify the enemy and the intent of the attack, and still support coordinated retaliation on a scale deemed by decision-makers to be appropriate to the circumstances. Such a system is probably not achievable within the bounds of future defense budgets, however. Furthermore, if forces are less than perfectly survivable, the pressure to respond quickly if faced with a massive attack will remain no matter how survivable the C³I system is made.

Short of perfection, the goal is probably a system that could very rapidly sort out a massive Soviet attack from any other. For smaller attacks, the system could then proceed under relatively little time pressure to identify the enemy, assess damage, and, if necessary, plan new operations.[13] Unless massively damaged itself, the system could support decision-making and the execution of a response as required. For a massive attack, it would support immediate retaliation if decision-makers believed ride-out was not a viable option, but would survive with enough of an intelligence, war-planning, decision-making, and communications structure intact to ensure the use of a large portion of the surviving forces, even if a retaliatory decision could not be made promptly.

Changes in Strategic Offensive Forces

Chapters 5 and 6 postulate massive reductions in U.S. strategic offensive weapons under an eventual arms control agreement with the Soviets. In addition, they make some specific recommendations for increasing overall force survivability and possibly tightening negative control through such measures as placing command destruct mechanisms on all strategic missiles and installing permissive action links on SLBM warheads. How would these offensive force changes affect C³I needs?

Because much of the warning and control system is centralized, even very deep reductions in forces would not warrant proportional cuts in C³I.

---

[13]Insurance against destruction of the C³I apparatus in such smaller attacks could conceivably be provided either by a combination of passive measures—such as mobility, redundancy, and hardening—or by a limited active defense like the GPALS described in Chapter 7.

Warning sensors and facilities provide information needed by the navy and air force to move submarines and bombers and adjust their alert postures to keep them as survivable as possible in the event that the threat of nuclear attack is deemed imminent, and by the National Command Authorities to support national decision-making. Thus, the number of sensors or facilities would not be expected to decrease simply because forces were reduced. Similarly, command centers like the National Military Command Center or the Strategic Command headquarters command center would still need to serve the same basic functions. Their roles and complexity would likely be the same regardless of force size.

Of course, reductions would be expected in the command posts supporting individual force units. For example, those air force wing command posts supporting only strategic forces could be closed as the bombers and missiles they support are removed from service. Similarly, the ICBM launch control centers that support retiring ICBMs could be closed. Under Chapter 5's recommendations to cut back in the near term to 700 ICBMs and 120 bombers, the number of wing command posts might drop from approximately 30 to 15 or fewer; the number of ICBM launch control centers could drop from 100 to 70 or fewer.

In the communications area, force structure reductions would have some effect, particularly on those assets linking individual platforms or units to commanders. For example, very low frequency receivers for B-2 bombers would obviously be needed only for the number of bombers actually built. Milstar terminals would not be needed for those B-52 bombers and Minuteman launch control centers scheduled to retire.[14] Similarly, support for both the land lines linking ICBM silos to their launch control centers and the digital transmission system that supports communications to ICBMs would be cut back in proportion to the reduction in ICBM launchers. Of course, care would have to be taken in removing such links to ensure that these systems maintained their overall integrity as networks.

A large segment of the communications architecture would not be affected by force reductions, however. For example, the navy fleet of TACAMO communications aircraft[15] is sized to keep aircraft on station over the Atlantic and the Pacific, and would probably not be reduced as long as ballistic-missile-carrying submarines continued to operate in both

[14]Milstar is a network of communications satellites being built by the air force. The new system, scheduled to be deployed during the 1990s, will be less susceptible to jamming and nuclear effects than existing satellite communications systems.

[15]TACAMO is widely held to stand for "Take Charge and Move Out." The original meaning of the acronym was evidently classified and seems to have been lost in history. The existing fleet of EC-130 aircraft is currently being replaced by a somewhat smaller fleet of longer-range, more enduring E-6As. The size of the new fleet was determined by patrol areas and communications requirements rather than by the planned size of the submarine force.

oceans.[16] Similarly, the air force's ground-wave emergency network is sized and configured to provide a redundant system with nationwide coverage, independent of the number of ICBMs and bombers it supports. These broadcast-mode systems and the central systems that support communications among sensors and command centers could not be reduced based on force structure considerations alone.

Other changes considered in Chapters 5 and 6 could have profound implications for strategic C³I. For example, a mobile ICBM force (one of the longer-term options) could not depend on land lines or fixed launch control centers, as today's fixed ICBMs do. In fact, if the underlying reason for ICBM mobility is to enhance stability by making one's forces highly survivable, then survivable C³I systems would have to be sought in parallel with survivable forces. Adding permissive action links to SLBM warheads, another change considered, would not pose significant technical problems, as PALs are already in place on ICBM warheads and bomber weapons. As discussed in Chapter 5, however, it would reduce an enemy's uncertainty regarding its ability to prevent U.S. retaliation through counterforce and counter-C³I strikes.

Another force change postulated in previous chapters is the addition of command-destruct mechanisms to ballistic and cruise missiles.[17] This change would require C³I-related alterations in the missiles themselves, in communications satellites, and in the systems and procedures at existing command centers; it might also require development of a new destruct-confirmation system for warning or other satellites. To receive, decode, and verify the command-destruct signals, missiles would require new receiver antennas and additional hardware, including a new power source. In the case of ICBMs, such equipment could be placed on missile boosters, postboost vehicles, or individual reentry vehicles. Since the boosters burn out and separate from their postboost vehicles within approximately 5

---

[16]On the other hand, both the Strategic Command's Looking Glass airborne command post and the TACAMO fleet have recently been taken off continuous airborne alert and put instead on ground alert supplemented by random airborne sorties. Most of the post-attack command and control system (PACCS), the Strategic Air Command's fleet of communications and command aircraft, of which the Looking Glass was the centerpiece, is being retired or diverted to other missions. These changes reflect a national-level judgment that a surprise strategic attack by the former Soviet Union is now extremely unlikely, rather than a reduction in force structure.

[17]See Sherman Frankel, "Stopping Accidents After They've Happened," *The Bulletin of the Atomic Scientists*, Vol. 46, No. 9 (November 1990), pp. 39–40; and "Aborting Unauthorized Launches of Nuclear-Armed Ballistic Missiles Through Post-Launch Destruction," *Science and Global Security*, Vol. 2, No. 1 (1990), pp. 1–20; and Bruce G. Blair and Henry Kendall, "Accidental Nuclear War," *Scientific American*, Vol. 263, No. 6 (December 1990), p. 58. The author is grateful to Lauren B. Di Rienzo, Thomas Ferguson, Theodore Jarvis, Robert F. Nesbit, and Carl R. Triebs of the MITRE Corporation for the analysis of command-destruct options presented here.

minutes of the total 30-minute flight time, and postboost vehicles are out of the picture within 10 minutes or so, placement on the reentry vehicle itself would offer the greatest likelihood that a destruct message would be received. Reentry vehicles are small and weight-constrained relative to boosters, however. They are also carefully balanced, so that even small weight increases at one spot require compensating increases somewhere else. Installation of the new antenna and receiver/decoder package would reduce their range of flight and would likely require redesign and remanufacture. Placement of the new equipment on the booster itself would be easier—in fact, test missiles today have command-destruct packages—but would provide only a 5-minute window for a decision-maker to receive information about an unintended launch, make the command-destruct decision, and communicate it to the missile.

To transmit the command-destruct messages to ICBMs and reentry vehicles in northbound trajectories, communications satellites would have to be supplemented or repositioned to polar or high-inclination orbits. In addition, if a unique destruct code had to be transmitted to each reentry vehicle, the power or number of satellites would have to increase substantially to handle a worst case in which most U.S. missiles were launched by accident or without authorization.

Control over the command-destruct mechanism could be exercised from an existing command center, probably the National Military Command Center and its ground-based and airborne alternates. Controllers would require access to the National Command Authorities for national-level command-destruct decisions, to the nuclear commanders-in-chief for information on errant weapons and their trajectories, to the warning centers at Cheyenne Mountain, and possibly to the warning satellites themselves. New training aids and displays would have to be developed. Finally, to provide assurance to decision-makers, allies, and targeted countries that missiles or warheads had in fact been destroyed, a satellite-based system to detect the destruction might have to be developed and deployed. (Obviously, a destruct mechanism that acted by disarming rather than destroying warheads would leave no visible evidence that it had worked. Of the proposed schemes that include actual destruction of the warheads, some would result in nuclear explosions outside the atmosphere that could be detected by sensors already developed and being installed on U.S. satellites; others would require a new family of space-based sensors.)

New Missions for Strategic Systems

One consequence of the new world situation is that strategic forces and C^3I systems will increasingly be required to support nonnuclear theater-level operations. During Operation Desert Storm, for example, the Strategic Air Command's B-52s conducted numerous conventional bombing raids over Iraq and Kuwait.[18] In addition, U.S. surveillance and C³I systems provided tactical warning and communications to help suppress the threat from Iraqi Scud missiles.[19]

Indeed, the wide use of strategic forces and C³I resources in Desert Storm cemented air force and Defense Department plans to realign command structures for improved efficiency and support of new wartime fighting arrangements. As of June 1992, Strategic Air Command (SAC), Tactical Air Command (TAC), and Military Airlift Command (MAC) ceased to exist; and two new commands, Air Combat Command and Air Mobility Command, were formed.[20] At the same time, Strategic Command was formed as a new unified command drawing together air force and navy resources; it has taken over the planning role of the Joint Strategic Target Planning Staff and some level of C³I responsibility for strategic offensive forces. At the wing level, former SAC, TAC, and MAC units were reorganized as single air force "objective wings" with the aim of improving coordination and lowering costs and manpower requirements. Under the reorganization, distinctions between strategic and tactical forces have been intentionally blurred, and theater commanders are now expected to draw as needed on long-range bombers as readily as on tactical fighters or transport aircraft. During air operations, long-range bombers will be controlled by a theater commander as an integral part of his forces.

The restructuring of commands and the planned use of strategic resources in conventional roles call for a new level of flexibility from the strategic C³I apparatus and could have profound consequences for war planning, warning and assessment, and communications.

In the war planning area, the use of strategic bombers in conventional roles could have a significant impact. While formerly only a few squadrons of B-52Gs were specially outfitted and earmarked for conventional use in theater operations, the air force now plans to outfit every bomber for dual nuclear and conventional roles.[21] Because nuclear war planning under the

---

[18]See Rick Atkinson and Dan Balz, "Allied Bombers Strike Shifting Iraqi Troops," *The Washington Post*, February 1, 1991, p. A1; Joby Warrick, "Heavyweights Called to do Close Air Support," and Sean C. Kelly, "60 Sorties Flown from Fairford," *Air Force Times*, April 22, 1991, pp. 12–13; and "Allies Shift Air Attacks to Break Ground Units," *Aviation Week & Space Technology*, January 28, 1991, pp. 20–21.

[19]U.S. Department of Defense, *Conduct of the Persian Gulf Conflict: An Interim Report to Congress, Pursuant to Title V Persian Gulf Conflict Supplemental Authorization and Personnel Benefits Act of 1991* (Washington, D.C.: Department of Defense, July 1991), p. 15-4.

[20]Department of the Air Force, *Air Force Restructure*, White Paper (Washington, D.C.: Department of the Air Force, September 1991).

[21]See the statement by Air Force General Lee Butler, commander-in-chief, Strategic Air Command, "Stealth, Strategy, and Strategic Warfare," before the House Committee on Appropriations Subcommittee on Defense, April 30, 1991. General Butler envisions a "dual triad" consisting of the traditional nuclear triad (bombers, ICBMs, and SLBMs) and of a new

SIOP is so thoroughly structured, moving several squadrons of bombers in and out of a nuclear role as world events unfold could pose difficulties. As bombers are removed, important targets in the SIOP could be left uncovered; other weapons would have to be reassigned to cover them. Reassignment of even a few bombers could easily result in ripple effects that would ultimately require the retargeting of numerous weapons, including ICBMs and SLBMs as well as bombers. Constructing a new SIOP to accommodate these changes each time a set of bombers was removed or added could take months.

Moreover, modifying the SIOP to accommodate such changes would produce ripple effects at the wing level as well. Messages to retarget ICBMs and SLBMs would be sent to missile wings and submarines, and control personnel would make the required changes. At bomber wings, the electronic cartridges that feed route data into the bombers' on-board computers would have to be reloaded, and routes would have to be redrawn on maps for the crews. In peacetime, information on such changes in plans is normally sent to missile wings at monthly intervals and bomber wings at quarterly intervals. This updating procedure (which in the case of bombers today requires couriers to carry magnetic tapes from Strategic Command headquarters to each affected unit) may prove too cumbersome to keep up with numerous changes.

Clearly, the new dual role of long-range bombers will demand some modification in U.S. nuclear war planning, from the headquarters down to the wing level. As discussed earlier in this chapter, the war planning process may need to be revamped in any case to accommodate changes in potential adversaries. Depending on the scale of force reductions (see Chapters 5 and 6) and the degree to which targeting objectives are simplified in the future (see Chapter 3), options for war planning processes less demanding and more flexible than the SIOP need to be explored.

New missions also emerged during Operation Desert Storm in the areas of warning and assessment. According to press reports, the warning and assessment system was used to identify launches of Iraqi Scud missiles and to alert Patriot batteries to launch defensive interceptors. Warning of the launches was transmitted to a ground station and simultaneously to the U.S. Space Command's missile warning center in Cheyenne Mountain, and then routed back to forces in the Persian Gulf. To ensure the efficacy of such arrangements in potential future conflicts, measures should be explored for integrating Space Command's tactical warning and assessment information with theater operations.

Such integration may require new efforts in the area of strategic communications. Clearly, to be of use in cuing defensive strikes, new tactical warning information would have to be gathered and communicated in

---

conventional triad of bombers, tankers, and reconnaissance aircraft. Bombers would shift between nuclear and conventional roles as needed.

real time. Because flight times of theater ballistic missiles like the Scud are even shorter than those of ICBMs, the time pressures on the same warning systems would be even greater than they are in a strategic nuclear scenario. On the other hand, rapid communications in these nonnuclear situations might be quite uncomplicated. Depending on the volume of competing communications traffic and the level of enemy jamming, even commercial telephone lines might suffice.

Coordinated employment of long-range bombers and air refueling tankers with theater forces would not necessarily require the specialized communications systems that support them in a nuclear role, but would require systems compatible with those already in use by other forces in-theater. During Desert Shield, SAC installed new radios on numerous KC-135 tankers to achieve such compatibility. Depending upon the degree and source of in-flight communications, bombers may need to be outfitted with new systems as well.[22]

CONCLUSIONS AND RECOMMENDATIONS

Given tight budgets, a changing threat, the prospect of dramatically reduced force levels, and shifting roles and missions for strategic systems, what recommendations can be made for future U.S. strategic C³I operations and investment?

- The first priority should be to maintain effective peacetime control and management of forces. This would include continued emphasis on safety and security of peacetime training, tests, and exercises; continued near-perfect peacetime connectivity to forces; and continued emphasis on maintaining constant awareness of force status at wings and headquarters.
- The second priority should be to improve the flexibility of warning, planning, and C³I systems and procedures to accommodate changing potential enemies and new roles and missions. A highly structured plan like the SIOP works well when there is only one enemy and the only roles of strategic forces are deterrence and assured retaliation against a known set of Soviet targets. But as enemies change and missions widen to include an emphasis on conventional roles, a more flexible planning environment may be warranted. In addition, warning sensors need the flexibility to focus on emerging

---

[22]Two-way in-flight communications with other aircraft or command posts would be especially useful in "Scud-busting" or other missions against relocatable targets. One can envision scenarios in which bombers outfitted with precision weapons would be used cooperatively with airborne tactical reconnaissance systems like Joint Surveillance/Target Attack Radar System (Joint STARS) to conduct attacks on mobile enemy targets. Such cooperation would require bombers to be outfitted with communications gear compatible with the tactical systems.

threats as well as existing ones. If warning assistance is to be provided to theater-level defenses against ballistic missiles, improvements in survivable communications and coordination mechanisms might be needed. These changes would, of course, need to be accompanied by changes in training across the board for commanders, planners, and other C³I personnel.

- Because the risk of all-out nuclear attack today seems remote, the ability of U.S. C³I to cope with such an attack should probably take third priority. In this area, considerable improvements have already been made in the capabilities that support prompt retaliation. Although of lower priority than enhancements in the other two categories, improvements in survivability against nuclear threats should still be considered to reduce the danger of miscalculation under pressure. Measures that would increase national confidence in the ability of decision-makers and commanders to ride out an attack before retaliating would go a long way toward increasing stability by decreasing pressure to launch first or quickly. Various combinations of mobility, redundancy, and hardening should be examined. Possible improvements include upgrades of the truck-transportable mobile command and control system operated by U.S. Space Command to provide survivable tactical warning and assessment, and Strategic Command's surviving enduring command center.

- In planning to meet these priorities, particular attention should be paid to aligning C³I programs with force structure plans. Obviously, Milstar terminals should not be procured for bombers likely to be retired in five years anyway. Wing-level command posts and launch control centers should not be upgraded if their associated weapons platforms will not be retained in the force.

- Finally, every effort should be made to streamline operations where possible and to adopt acquisition approaches that reduce overall investment and operations costs. One such measure would be to delete redundant systems that are not big contributors to overall C³I effectiveness. For example, SAC's Numbered Air Force command centers at March Air Force Base in California and Barksdale Air Force Base in Louisiana contribute to peacetime force management, but add little to wartime operational C³I effectiveness. In the context of a reduced force, even the peacetime role could probably be handled just as well by headquarters and wing command posts. The air force has plans to eliminate these intermediate command centers as part of its reorganization and to replace them with new Numbered Air Forces with minimal staffing and a strong operational role. The new structure is expected to save money and staff and to streamline operations.

Another source of potential savings is to replace some of the C³I system's outmoded, expensive, one-of-a-kind systems with modern commercial equipment. SAC's Primary Alerting System, the principal voice communications link for transmission of emergency action messages, is a good example. A dedicated, high-speed commercial link would provide better capability at significantly reduced operating cost.

Opportunities for such replacements are particularly ripe in the electronics world, where old-technology systems have high failure rates and require increasingly costly maintenance. For example, the Klaxon system that alerts bomber crews to rush to their aircraft in the event of war currently depends on electromechanical relay devices with high failure rates. Replacement of these devices with modern circuitry has recently begun and will save both maintenance costs and the bomber operating costs associated with failure-driven false alarms. Similarly, the computers, software, and display systems formerly developed and built specifically for individual command centers can now largely be provided off-the-shelf from civilian commercial sources. The savings in acquisition and operations costs are expected to be substantial.

In summary, future C^3I choices will have to be made carefully given the limited funding likely to be available. The United States should set priorities to maintain effective peacetime control over its strategic nuclear forces, increase the flexibility of the C^3I system to accommodate potentially changing enemies and missions, and improve its ability to ride out any nuclear attack. In working within this priority scheme, particular care should be given to reducing unnecessary redundancy, aligning C^3I systems with likely force structures, and taking advantage of the new commercial marketplace for applicable electronics and software.

SUGGESTED READINGS

Ball, Desmond. *Can Nuclear War Be Controlled?* Adelphi Paper 169. London: International Institute for Strategic Studies, Autumn 1981.

Ball, Desmond, Hans A. Bethe, Bruce G. Blair, Paul Bracken, Ashton B. Carter, Hillman Dickenson, Richard L. Garwin, Kurt Gottfried, David Holloway, Henry W. Kendall, Lloyd R. Leavitt, Jr., Richard Ned Lebow, Condolleezza Rice, Peter C. Stein, John D. Steinbruner, Lucja U. Swiatkowski, and Paul D. Tomb. *Crisis Stability and Nuclear War*. Ithaca, N.Y.: American Academy of Arts and Sciences and Cornell University Peace Studies Program, 1987.

Blair, Bruce G. *Strategic Command and Control: Redefining the Nuclear Threat*. Washington, D.C.: The Brookings Institution, 1985.

Bracken, Paul. *The Command and Control of Nuclear Forces*. New Haven: Yale University Press, 1983.

Carter, Ashton B., John D. Steinbruner, and Charles A. Zraket, eds. *Managing Nuclear Operations*. Washington, D.C.: The Brookings Institution, 1987.

Ford, Daniel. *The Button: The Pentagon's Strategic Command and Control System*. New York: Simon and Schuster, 1985.

van Creveld, Martin. *Command in War*. Cambridge, Mass.: Harvard University Press, 1985.

Zraket, Charles A. "Strategic Command, Control, Communications, and Intelligence." *Science*, Vol. 224 (June 22, 1984), pp. 1306–1311.

Chapter
9

Improving the Arms Control Process

Joel S. Wit

*F*or more than three decades, the United States and former Soviet Union have been engaged in nuclear arms control negotiations. These negotiations have involved complicated issues—including weapons technology and verification—critical to prospective agreements. But, for the United States, they have also been a political process whose success has depended on building coalitions at home and abroad in support of its arms control positions. Thus, the "arms control process" has required not just negotiating with the former Soviet Union, but also extensive consultations and negotiations within the United States—between the White House, key bureaucratic actors, and Congress—and with important allies in Europe and the Far East. This process has often proven to be time-consuming and frustrating.

Previous chapters in this book recommend a broad new agenda for nuclear arms control over the next decade. Items on this agenda include: (1) reducing strategic nuclear forces to 3,600 deployed (or 3,000 accountable) warheads on missiles and bombers; (2) withdrawing all air-delivered nonstrategic nuclear weapons to secure storage sites in the United States and the former Soviet Union; (3) banning all naval nonstrategic nuclear weapons; (4) halting the production of fissile materials for weapons; (5) reaffirming the traditional interpretation of the ABM Treaty, and (6) clarifying permitted and prohibited activities for the development of ABM systems.

Achieving this agenda requires the establishment of a flexible, effective arms control process, responsive to opportunities for progress but also able to build coalitions at home and abroad. This will not be easy. The existing arms control process is a laborious enterprise in need of basic institutional reform in the United States, in dealings with key allies, and in negotiating with the former Soviet Union. A process capable of implementing the ambitious agenda we outline must be better managed, conducted in closer cooperation with Congress and our allies, able to sustain a variety of forms of agreement and negotiations, and more effective in handling compliance and implementation issues.

The changing domestic and international environment of the 1990s may present new opportunities for establishing such a process. For example, the receding Soviet threat and the declining relevance of nuclear weapons, aside from creating new arms control opportunities, might allow the United States to seek agreements other than comprehensive, legally binding treaties. But change may also present new challenges. Uncertainties about the direction and speed of change in the former Soviet Union may require an arms control policy able to rely on multiple forms of agreement and negotiation to keep the relationship on an even keel.

In an effort to delineate guidelines for improving the arms control process, this chapter will: (1) examine the political process of formulating arms control proposals and agreements, identifying problems that need to be remedied; (2) analyze the potential implications of the changing environment for the arms control process; and (3) recommend measures to correct existing problems and avoid new ones.

THE EXISTING PROCESS

The political process through which arms control proposals are made and agreements reached is one of formulation, consultation, and negotiation. This process involves critical elements of the U.S. government—the president, the bureaucracy, and Congress—important U.S. allies (usually but not always in NATO), and potential negotiating partners. Because the process deals with basic issues of national security, it takes time and effort to build consensus. Much of this effort has been devoted to navigating treacherous domestic political waters. While the danger of nuclear war created pressures for political accommodation, distrust of Soviet motives created strong constituencies in favor of unilateral military measures. Bridging these positions was often difficult. Moreover, building consensus required reaching common ground with an archadversary, the Soviet Union. In addition to these built-in difficulties, the process has suffered from self-inflicted wounds. This section examines the various components of the arms control process and identifies existing problems.

The White House

Central management can make or break the success of the arms control process. Weak central management invites stalemate and encourages inertia, the result of diverging bureaucratic interests. Strong central management can help minimize difficulties by charting a course through the political mine field. White House leadership is critical. Only the president and the National Security Council (NSC) can integrate the broad range of considerations—the international and domestic environment, arms control policy goals, the workings of the bureaucracy, dealings with adversaries—important to the arms control process.

Two styles of strong central management have emerged, neither of which guarantees success.[1] In the first, presidents are deeply involved. For example, President Kennedy consummated the Limited Test Ban by personally dealing with the bureaucracy, running negotiations with the Soviets, and tending to the political needs of the legislative branch.[2] In contrast, President Carter became engrossed in minor details of the SALT II treaty to resolve tactical disputes among his advisors. While these interventions worked, the resulting delays may have doomed SALT II to failure.[3] In the second, a strong national security advisor, supported by the president, imposes order on the bureaucracy. Henry Kissinger during the first Nixon administration is the prime example of this style. However, while Kissinger successfully negotiated the ABM Treaty and SALT I agreements through a secret back-channel, even he has admitted that this approach demoralized the bureaucracy and made it difficult to build domestic consensus. Others have emphasized this latter point, noting a general perception that the United States was "out negotiated" in SALT I and the resulting Jackson Amendment, which required equal limits on the ballistic missiles of both sides in the future arms agreements and was a thorn in the side of subsequent administrations.[4]

---

[1]For a good concise summary of the importance of strong central management, see Robert C. Gray, "The Internal Dynamics of U.S. Nuclear Arms Control Policymaking," in *Fundamentals of Nuclear Arms Control*, Report Prepared for the Committee on Foreign Affairs, U.S. House of Representatives (Washington, D.C.: U.S. Government Printing Office, 1987), pp. 199–247.

[2]For authoritative firsthand accounts of Kennedy's test ban policy, see Glenn T. Seaborg, *Kennedy, Khrushchev and the Test Ban* (Los Angeles: University of California Press, 1981); Arthur M. Schlesinger, Jr., *A Thousand Days: John F. Kennedy in the White House* (Boston: Houghton Mifflin, 1965), pp. 454–461, 495–97, 893–898. Excellent academic studies include Harold Karan Jacobson and Eric Stein, *Diplomats, Scientists and Politicians: The United States and its Nuclear Test Ban Negotiations* (Ann Arbor: University of Michigan Press, 1966), pp. 444–495, and Ronald J. Terchek, *The Making of the Test Ban Treaty* (The Hague: Martinus Nyhoff, 1970).

[3]Gray, *op. cit.*, pp. 239–236, provides an excellent summary of Carter's role and bureaucratic politics. The best overview of the Carter administration's arms control policy is Strobe Talbott, *Endgame: The Inside Story of SALT II* (New York: Harper & Row, 1979). Also see Jimmy Carter, *Keeping the Faith: Memoirs of a President* (New York: Bantam Books, 1982); Zbigniew Brzezinski, *Power and Principle: Memoirs of the National Security Adviser 1977–1981* (New York: Farrar, Straus and Giroux, 1983); and Cyrus Vance, *Hard Choices: Critical Years in America's Foreign Policy* (New York: Simon and Shuster, 1983).

[4]For accounts of the Nixon administration's arms control policy, see John Newhouse, *Cold Dawn: The Story of SALT* (New York: Holt, Rinehart and Winston, 1973); Gerard Smith,

Other administrations have been hamstrung by weak central management. Such systems have been characterized by strong policy differences between key bureaucratic actors, decisions required by consensus, and sometimes poor implementation since agencies are able to continue to pursue their own agendas with impunity. The early Eisenhower administration's efforts to shape a nuclear test ban policy were hampered by continuous, unresolved interagency disagreements.[5] Likewise, decision-making in the early Reagan administration, which was decentralized and controlled by competing bureaucracies, the State and Defense departments, was a laborious process requiring consensus.[6] The Bush administration has been plagued by the same problems. Although the NSC chairs the decision-making process, it has not exerted a strong influence. The process has at times been ad hoc, decisions have required universal agreement, and implementation has been uneven.

Historically, as arms control has become a higher priority, successive administrations have created strong, informal decision-making processes in parallel to still existing formal systems. The informal process is usually restricted to a few individuals; it can involve the president and a few top aides or a group of senior officials run by the White House. It is also characterized by compartmentalized channels of communication, both within the bureaucracy and with delegations abroad. Very early in its first term, the Reagan administration established the "Dam Group," chaired by Deputy Secretary of State Kenneth Dam, in an unsuccessful attempt to exclude hard-line Assistant Secretary of Defense Richard Perle from INF policy-making.[7] Later, in Reagan's second term, informal groups

---

Doubletalk: The Story of SALT I (Garden City, N.Y.: Doubleday, 1980); Henry Kissinger, *The White House Years* (Boston: Little, Brown, 1979); and Seymour M. Hersh, *The Price of Power: Kissinger in the Nixon White House* (New York: Summit Books, 1983).

For more on the SALT I back-channel, see Thomas Wolfe, *The SALT Experience* (Cambridge, Mass.: Ballinger Publishing Company, 1979), pp. 80–84; Raymond L. Garthoff, "Negotiating with the Russians: Some Lessons from SALT," *International Security*, Vol. 1, No. 4 (Spring 1977), pp. 8–10, 15–16; Newhouse, *op. cit.*, pp. 203–206, 214–243; and Kenneth A. Myers and Dimitri Simes, *Soviet Decision Making, Strategic Policy and SALT* (Washington D.C.: Georgetown Center for Strategic and International Studies, December 1974), p. 25.

[5]For the best accounts of Eisenhower's test ban policy, see Robert A. Divine, *Blowing on the Wind: The Nuclear Test Ban Debate, 1954–1960* (New York: Oxford University Press, 1978); and Harold Karan Jacobson and Eric Stein, *op. cit.*

[6]The most authoritative account of the Reagan administration's arms control policy is Strobe Talbott, *Deadly Gambits: The Reagan Administration and the Stalemate in Nuclear Arms Control* (New York: Alfred A. Knopf, 1984). On the Reagan decision-making structure for foreign policy, see Leslie H. Gelb, "Is Washington Big Enough for Two State Departments?" *New York Times*, February 21, 1982 (Section 4), p. E1; Leslie H. Gelb, "Foreign Policy System Criticized by U.S. Aides," *New York Times*, October 19, 1981, pp. A1, A8; Statement by President Ronald Reagan, "National Security Council Structure," *Public Papers of the President*, January 12, 1982, pp. 18–22; and *The Tower Commission Report* (New York: Bantam and Times Books, 1987).

[7]Strobe Talbott, *op. cit.*, pp. 154–155.

were established to speed START deliberations. The Bush administration is reported to have established a restricted body that initially communicated with the START delegation through a special back-channel.

Informal processes may alleviate some of the problems of weak central management but, as Leslie Gelb, a former State Department official, has pointed out, "to the extent that the informal system deviates from the formal system, we have a corrupt and inefficient operation."[8] An informal system chokes off input from the lower levels of the bureaucracy where most of the corporate memory, expertise, and technical know-how resides. It can also complicate the implementation of decisions, since those responsible for implementation are frequently unaware that decisions have been made or of their content.

The Bureaucracy

Because arms control is intricately tied to U.S. foreign, defense, and intelligence policy, proposals are formulated taking into account the views of a large number of government organizations. Given the many actors and differing organizational perspectives, the bureaucratic process of working out a common position can be complicated and often time-consuming. The twin dangers of inflexibility and inertia are always present.

The bureaucratic process, consisting of two steps, has become increasingly difficult to manage. First, individual agencies devise their own positions. The number of intra-agency groups and personnel involved in this process has naturally expanded with the growing importance of arms control in U.S. foreign policy. For example, in the 1950s, there were never more than four officers in the State Department working on disarmament issues, all located in the uninfluential Office of United Nations Affairs.[9] By the time of the Bush administration, some 30 officers were working on a broad range of arms control issues in the Bureau of Politico-Military Affairs, the Bureau of Intelligence and Research, the Bureau of European Affairs, the Policy Planning staff and the Office of the Undersecretary of State for Security Affairs. This ongoing process of government-wide diversification has been supplemented during recent administrations by the creation of specialized offices within each agency to deal with verification, compliance, and treaty implementation.

Views on arms control issues often vary within agencies. For example, one agency may have separate offices dedicated to verification and negotiation matters respectively, and their perspectives on issues such as verifi-

---

[8]"Remarks by Leslie Gelb" in Lawrence J. Korb and Keith D. Hahn, eds., *National Security Policy Organization in Perspective* (Washington, D.C.: American Enterprise Institute, 1981), pp. 19–21.

[9]Duncan L. Clarke, *Politics of Arms Control: The Role and Effectiveness of the U.S. Arms Control and Disarmament Agency* (New York: The Free Press, 1979), pp. 10–11.

cation standards may clash. In other circumstances, particularly in the Pentagon, verification measures can conflict with established military procedures. For example, movement restrictions on treaty-limited systems, such as submarines or mobile missiles, prior to the conduct of on-site inspections are essential. Otherwise, potential "cheaters" could be relocated after an inspection is announced, but before it takes place. But, such restrictions could hamper normal military operations. Finally, within the intelligence community, methodological or philosophical differences must be hammered out. In general, because internal consensus is hard-won, flexibility is limited; changing positions often requires decisions by high-level agency officials.

The second step, creating a government position, can also be difficult. While the key players have remained essentially the same, the cast of characters has evolved since the Eisenhower administration. The Committee of Principals, established in 1958, was attended by the secretaries of State and Defense, the directors of the CIA and U.S. Information Agency (USIA), the chairmen of the Joint Chiefs of Staff (JCS) and Atomic Energy Commission (AEC), and the President's Science Advisory Committee (PSAC).[10] (The PSAC, a key source of technical advice and an active player in defense and arms control issues, was later abolished by President Nixon.) In 1961, the Arms Control and Disarmament Agency (ACDA) was established by the Kennedy administration as an advocate for arms control whose roles ranged from dissemination of public information to "management" of U.S. participation in international arms control negotiations.[11] In 1988, the On-Site Inspection Agency was created to handle the growing burden of treaty implementation resulting from new verification regimes, which emphasized on-site inspections.

Agencies have differing perspectives given the "where you sit is where you stand" syndrome and prevailing political winds. The Department of State, because of its central interest in diplomacy, has a positive view of arms control negotiations and sometimes seeks to incorporate broader political objectives—such as improving U.S.-Soviet relations—into its approach. The JCS supports arms control to build certainty into future U.S. military planning but also seeks to limit changes in U.S. weapons programs or military operations. The office of the secretary of defense (OSD), while sympathetic to protecting U.S. military options, has, according to one author, "lacked enduring organizational interests."[12] Its attitudes tend to change with administrations; OSD was a vocal opponent of the nuclear test ban under President Eisenhower but under President Kennedy and Secretary of Defense Robert McNamara, it was a supporter.

---

[10]*Ibid.*, p. 13.

[11]*Ibid.*, pp. 20–28.

[12]Gray, *op. cit.*, p. 209. Gray's chapter also provides a good historical summary of the bureaucratic players and their views.

The same is true for ACDA; during the Kennedy and Johnson administrations, and the first term of both the Nixon and Carter administrations, it actively supported arms control initiatives. Under other administrations—particularly those of Presidents Ford, Reagan, and Bush—it has adopted a more skeptical attitude. Finally, the intelligence community seeks to shape treaty provisions to maximize its ability to monitor Soviet forces regardless of whether unacceptable reciprocal restrictions will be required on U.S. forces. Reconciling all these perspectives is rarely easy.

In fact, in recent years, this process of reconciliation has become increasingly difficult. First, the eight years of the Reagan administration polarized bureaucratic perspectives. The administration's skeptical, if not hostile, attitude toward nuclear arms control infused some agencies while others, the State Department and the JCS, tried to moderate administration policy. The arms control views of high-level officials changed over time but those of the bureaucracy did not. Hence, only a restricted, informal decision-making process could exclude bureaucratic opponents and minimize difficulties. The Bush administration has continued to be plagued by this polarization.

Second, the potential for bureaucratic gridlock has been increased by an ever more complicated arms control agenda. Not only has the number of simultaneous, major arms control negotiations reached a new height, but emphasis on cooperative measures of verification and on drafting lengthy, precise treaty texts has grown. Crafting treaty documents hundreds of pages long requires bureaucratic agreement on thousands of issues, many minor, others of secondary importance, and still others of major importance. Moreover, issues are addressed and readdressed as U.S. negotiating positions evolve. The bureaucracy can cope with this deluge by creating the necessary interagency groups to hammer out options and decisions and adjusting the pace of its deliberations. But such a process can easily get bogged down in a politically polarized system and, as suggested in the previous section, without strong central management.

The bureaucratic system has also been dysfunctional in a number of other areas. The arms control process has long been plagued by a disconnect between defense and arms control policy. This has had two practical effects. First, arms control players have not been sufficiently involved in defense decision-making to insure that nonmilitary considerations are aired, or to influence final decisions. Historical examples include preliminary studies of MX basing and the development of MIRVs and long-range cruise missiles.[13] Second, arms control officials have been uninvolved in or unaware of weapons developments with important implications for ongoing negotiations. For example, from 1969 to 1971, the Nixon administration flip-flopped between ABM arms control positions because "the White

---

[13]These examples are cited in Philip A. Odeen, "Organizing for National Security," *International Security*, Vol. 5, No. 1 (Summer 1980), pp. 122–123; and Clarke, *op. cit.*, p. 198.

House had not matched its control over SALT policy-making with suffi-cient awareness, watchfulness, or control over incremental Safeguard de-velopment choices."[14] More recently, U.S. officials were surprised during INF ratification proceedings by a debate over the treaty's implications for future weapons development programs of which they were unaware.[15]

Past efforts to rectify this disconnect have proven unsuccessful. Presi-dent Nixon's Defense Program Review Committee, an interagency group to review the defense budget, fell into disuse by 1971 in the face of DOD opposition.[16] Congressionally mandated "Arms Control Impact State-ments," to assess the arms control implications of U.S. weapons systems, were first produced by ACDA in 1976. ACDA continues to perform this task but the statements have only been burdensome and have not suc-ceeded in giving the agency a voice in weapons decisions. A Carter admin-istration study, the Odeen Report, recommended early access for the NSC, State Department, and ACDA to DOD's basic defense planning document and weapons acquisitions cycle, and greater participation in DOD studies with implications for foreign policy and defense issues. Inter-agency reviews of weapons acquisition decisions were instituted but dropped by the incoming Reagan administration, which saw little need to consider the arms control implications of its defense buildup.[17]

Finally, the bureaucratic process has also been plagued by a narrow base of technical advice on key national security issues, particularly arms control policy. Arms control issues, as a rule, are highly technical, cover-ing, for example, the intricacies of weapons systems and verification tech-nologies. Those agencies where technical expertise naturally resides, such

[14]Burton R. Rosenthal, "Formulating Negotiating Positions for SALT: 1968, 1969-22" in *Commission on the Organization of the Government for the Conduct of Foreign Policy*, Vol. 4 (Washington, D.C.: U.S. Government Printing Office, June 1975), p. 339.

[15]For more on this debate, see *Article-by-Article Review of the INF Treaty*, American Enter-prise Institute, February 1988, p. 3; Peter Adams, "Senate Committees Clear Way for the INF Ratification," *Defense News*, April, 4, 1985, p. 5; "Nunn Seeks Weapon Definition," *Defense News*, April, 4, 1988, p. 2; Warren Strobel, "INF Impact on Arms of Future Ques-tioned," *Washington Times*, April 27, 1988, p. 10; Susan F. Rasky, "Nunn Says Arms Treaty May Need Amendment on Future Weapons," *New York Times*, April 20, 1988, p. A10; Pat Towell, "Futuristics Debate Clouds INF Floor Schedule," *Congressional Quarterly*, April 16, 1988, p. 1000; and Michael Mecham, "Futuristic Technology Issue May Delay Senate Action on INF," *Aviation Week & Space Technology*, April, 11, 1988, p. 105.

[16]Clarke, *op. cit.*, pp. 97–99.

[17]See *National Security Policy Integration*, President's Reorganization Project, September 1979; Philip A. Odeen, *Organizing for National Security*, Vol. 5 (Summer 1980), pp. 111–129; and "Remarks by Philip Odeen," in *National Security Policy Organization*, pp. 4–7. A good discussion of the Odeen report and policy integration is Duncan L. Clarke, "Integrating Arms Control, Defense and Foreign Policy in the Executive Branch of the U.S. Govern-ment," Hans Guenter Brauch and Duncan L. Clarke, eds., *Decisionmaking for Arms Limita-tion: Assessments and Prospects* (Cambridge, Mass.: Ballinger, 1983), pp. 3–36. Past recom-mendations for reform also include *Commission on the Organization of the Government for the Conduct of Foreign Policy*, pp. 344–345.

as the Department of Defense and the Atomic Energy Commission (now the Department of Energy [DOE]), have been the most skeptical about arms control. The difficulties presented by this potential conflict of interest were recognized three decades ago by Dr. James B. Fisk, a prominent scientist and government advisor, when he stated that the DOD and the AEC "should not be expected to carry the burden both of maximizing and, simultaneously, minimizing arms."[18]

Institutions were created in the past to provide alternative technical advice. By 1962, the United States had established a scientific advisory system in the White House including the Special Assistant to the President for Science and Technology, the President's Science Advisory Council, and the Office of Science and Technology. These organizations acted as a counterbalance to the Pentagon and AEC on nuclear test ban policy, supervised the development of intelligence systems for national technical means of verification, facilitated conclusion of the 1968 Nuclear Non-Proliferation Treaty, and persuaded President Nixon to renounce biological weapons in 1969. However, in 1973, President Nixon effectively dismantled the system because of his distrust of the scientific community's opposition to his Vietnam policy and plans to build an ABM system. Over the next two decades, the scientific mechanisms were gradually restored. But, with the exception of scientific panels on the Comprehensive Test Ban run by President Carter's science advisor, Frank Press, they have played little or no role in providing alternative technical advice.[19]

The need for multiple sources of technical advice may become more urgent in the future. First, arms control issues are becoming more technically complex. This trend has become abundantly clear with the recently revised Threshold Test Ban Treaty, whose details are intricately related to seismology and nuclear weapons technology, and with deliberations for START, which have included detailed discussions of telemetry encryption, tagging, and warhead elimination. Second, the concentration of tech-

---

[18]This quotation appears in Hubert H. Humphrey, "Government Organization for Arms Control," in Donald G. Brennan, ed., *Arms Control, Disarmament and National Security* (New York: George Braziller, 1961), p. 398.

[19]The literature on the science advisory apparatus in the White House is extensive. Personal memoirs by science advisers include James R. Killian, Jr., *Sputnik, Scientists and Eisenhower* (Cambridge, Mass.: The MIT Press, 1977); and George B. Kistiakowsky, *A Scientist at the White House* (Cambridge, Mass.: Harvard University Press, 1976). An excellent compilation of articles by science advisers and experts is William T. Golden, ed., *Science Advice to the President* (New York: Pergamon Press, 1980). Also see National Academy of Sciences, *Science and Technology in Presidential Policymaking: A Proposal* (Washington, D.C.: National Academy of Sciences, June 1974); Forrest R. Frank, "CBW: 1962–67; 1967–68; 1969–72," in *Commission on the Organization*, pp. 305–324; D. Allan Bromly, "Science and Technology: From Eisenhower to Bush," Center for the Study of the Presidency, Austin, Texas, October 27, 1990; and G. Allen Greb, *Science Advice to Presidents: From Test Bans to the Strategic Defense Initiative*, IGCC Research Paper No. 3 (La Jolla, Calif.: Institute on Global Conflict and Cooperation, 1987).

nical advice in DOD and DOE may hamper the ability of the policy community to make balanced technical judgments. Both agencies still have vested interests and organizational perspectives that may influence their technical advice. For example, DOE and DOD have always been skeptical about nuclear testing limits, which is bound to influence technical input into any Bush administration studies on future testing limits. Moreover, the concentration of expertise makes it difficult for some agencies, particularly the State Department, to be full participants in interagency deliberations on important but technically complex issues. Finally, future negotiations may require reopening old technical issues, such as SLCM verification or warhead elimination, but a fresh reexamination may be next to impossible without new sources of information.

The Legislative Branch

Congress's relationship with the executive branch on arms control has been characterized by tension, sometimes hidden and sometimes overt. The legislative branch has a number of levers at its disposal to influence the arms control process, including the approval of treaties, the funding of major weapons systems, and the holding of hearings. Nevertheless, until treaty ratification, the executive branch spends much of its time trying to minimize congressional involvement in order to preserve its freedom of action. On rare occasions, it has attempted to coopt the legislative branch by allowing greater involvement in the arms control process.[20]

Until the 1970s, Congress's influence was exercised only sporadically, out of deference to the president's preeminent role in making foreign policy. Occasional hearings, periodic consultations, and infrequent ratification debates were the order of the day. However, Watergate and Vietnam eroded executive branch authority and Congress, "egged on" by public concerns, actively sought a greater voice in defense and arms control policy. It was aided in this effort by a rapid expansion during the 1970s of congressional staff expertise on defense and arms control issues.[21] The Carter administration, reacting to this upswing in congressional interest, attempted to coopt key legislators. For example, Senator Henry Jackson's views helped shape the unsuccessful March 1977 proposal for greater reductions in SALT II. Members of Congress were also included on the SALT II delegation. However, judging from the difficulties SALT II en-

---

[20]An excellent overview of Congress's role in the arms control process can be found in Ellen C. Collier, "The Congressional Role in Nuclear Arms Control," in *Fundamentals of Nuclear Arms Control*, pp. 379–424.

[21]For good summaries of Congress's role in arms control policy prior to the Carter administration, see Alan Platt and Lawrence D. Weiler, eds., *Congress and Arms Control* (Boulder, Colo.: Westview Press, 1978); and Alan Platt, *The U.S. Senate and Strategic Arms Policy, 1969–1977* (Boulder, Colo.: Westview, 1978).

countered during the ratification debate, the administration's efforts clearly did not guarantee success.[22]

Congress's role in the arms control process reached its zenith during the Reagan years. The administration's attempts to exclude the legislative branch from the process failed because of growing public qualms about its hard-line policy toward the Soviet Union. Congress used its power to deny money for weapons systems that would have exceeded the numerical limits of the unratified but observed SALT II Treaty, to impose a moratorium on antisatellite testing, and to limit strategic defense tests to those allowed under the traditional interpretation of the ABM Treaty. Ratification of the INF Treaty, while an overwhelming success for the executive branch, was used to force the administration to back away from its reinterpretation of the ABM Treaty, viewed by Congress as an unacceptable attempt to circumvent its constitutional prerogatives.[23]

At the same time, during its second term, the Reagan administration gradually became more adroit in handling the legislative branch and in finding a new equilibrium, one that has continued under President Bush. Established in 1985, the Senate Observers Group, through frequent consultations with U.S. officials and visits to a variety of negotiations overseas, including the INF discussions and START, has served as an informal information channel for the Senate and as a potential source of assistance for the executive branch in lobbying for ratification of agreements.[24] While members do not serve on U.S. delegations, they have underscored U.S. concerns, for example about the SS-18 missile force, in meetings with Soviet negotiators. These roles have continued under the Bush administration, but Congress, distracted by other international issues, has focused primarily on maintaining its legislative prerogatives. Thus, aside from a cursory examination of substantive issues, key concerns during the Threshold Test Ban Treaty (TTBT) ratification debate were the authoritativeness of executive branch testimony and the executive branch's right to amend certain provisions of implementing agreements without congressional approval.[25]

---

[22]Strobe Talbott, *Endgame: The Inside Story of SALT II* (New York: Harper & Row, 1979), pp. 52–54, 66, 207–208. Also see Alan Platt, "The Politics of Arms Control and the Strategic Balance," in Barry M. Blechman, ed., *Rethinking the U.S. Strategic Posture* (Cambridge, Mass.: Ballinger Publishing Company, 1982), pp. 155–179.

[23]Barry M. Blechman, *The Politics of National Security: Congress and U.S. Defense Policy* (New York: Oxford University Press, 1990), pp. 63–112. An additional account of congressional interest in arms control during the Reagan years is Douglas C. Walker, *Congress and the Nuclear Freeze* (Amherst, Mass.: University of Massachusetts Press, 1987).

[24]Blechman, *op. cit.*, pp. 76–77. Interviews with Senate Observer Group staff, April 1991.

[25]U.S. Senate, *Threshold Test Ban and Peaceful Nuclear Explosions Treaties*, Ex. Rept. 101-31, 101st Congress, 2nd Session (September 14, 1990), pp. 17, 19. Interview with Bush administration official, April 1991.

The Allies

The allies have been sensitive to anything in the arms control process that might affect the credibility of the U.S. nuclear guarantee to NATO or the viability of national nuclear programs. The United States has had the task of reassuring them without compromising control over its nuclear policy or nuclear weapons. American leadership on nuclear security issues has been critical in successfully managing alliance policy. But success or failure of U.S.-allied arms control relations has also depended on gauging the level of allied interest and allowing an appropriate degree of allied involvement. This can require periodic consultations and allied participation in shaping broad policy goals or in crafting specific negotiating positions.

The process of gauging allied interest in strategic arms control has been successful since, for the most part, this interest has been minimal. Periodic briefings and consultations on SALT and START have been sufficient. However, on special occasions greater involvement has been warranted. Britain participated in CTB negotiations three decades ago because of its nuclear weapons program, close relationship with the United States, and serious interest in controlling nuclear testing. It also participated in CTB negotiations during the Carter administration for all of these reasons plus the fact that all British nuclear tests were conducted at the U.S. nuclear test site in Nevada. Britain's participation complicated the policy process since the United States had to consider the views of its ally in formulating test ban policy. However, this complication was counterbalanced by Britain's more moderate approach and its continuous efforts to influence the United States to be moderate as well. More recently, because British Trident missiles will be stored at the American submarine base at Kings Bay, Georgia, the United States consulted closely with Britain on excluding those weapons from START inspections.[26]

Theater nuclear issues have clearly been more central to allied interests and therefore more fraught with pitfalls for American policy-makers. Lack of consultations with the allies on possible SALT limits on theater GLCMs and SLCMs threatened the Carter administration's arms control policy in 1977 and led to a presidential pledge to "increasingly draw NATO" into administration counsels.[27]

On the other hand, NATO's 1979 "dual track" decision to deploy INF weapons and hold parallel arms control discussions was heavily influenced by the allies and successfully managed by the United States. The sugges-

---

[26]For an excellent study of Britain's role in the test ban negotiations, see J.P.G. Freeman, *Britain's Nuclear Arms Control Policy in the Context of Anglo-American Relations 1957–68* (New York: St. Martin's Press, 1986), pp. 71–155.

[27]Simon Lunn, "Policy Preparation and Consultation Within NATO: Decisionmaking for SALT and LRTNF," in Hans Guenter Brauch and Duncan L. Clarke, eds., *Decisionmaking for Arms Limitation: Assessments and Prospects* (Cambridge, Mass.: Ballinger, 1983), pp. 262–266.

tion for an arms control track was first made by then French President Valery Giscard d'Estaing in January of 1979 and eagerly adopted by the Carter administration.[28] Through a newly established consultative mechanism, the Special Consultative Group, the allies helped establish broad objectives for the pending negotiations. The allied role receded as negotiations began, in part because of Reagan administration efforts to exclude them. Periodic consultations were held in the North Atlantic Council and a temporary group, the Quint, consisting of the five countries in which INF missiles were deployed. As the treaty neared completion, the role of the basing countries grew. They helped draft on-site inspection provisions and West Germany helped resolve the issue of limits on its Pershing IA missiles.[29]

Alliance management has also involved other key allies whose core security interests have been affected by U.S. arms control policy. Beginning in 1979, America's Asian allies were continuously concerned that an INF arms control agreement focusing on Europe might encourage the Soviets to shift missiles to the Far East. The U.S. position throughout seven years of negotiations that any limit on Soviet SS-20 missiles would have to be global was directly attributable to Asian concerns, particularly those of Japan. Consultations were conducted through normal diplomatic channels, supplemented by periodic trips by Ambassador Edward Rowny to meet with high-level Foreign and Defense Ministry officials.[30]

The Soviets

In the past, arms control diplomacy has been essential for the Soviet Union to demonstrate its superpower status, promote the relaxation of tensions, influence U.S. weapons programs, and simplify planning for its own. Many of the same goals have applied to the United States. But the diplomatic process has proven difficult for both countries. Adversarial relations have complicated matters. And, for the United States, accommodating the views of allies and powerful domestic constituencies has required constant attention. For its part, the Soviet Union has had its own arms control process to contend with, a process whose difficulty has no doubt depended on the level of U.S.-Soviet tensions, the role of the general secretary, and the diversity of views and influence of different groups. For both countries, successful management of arms control diplomacy has required a political juggling act.[31]

---

[28]Talbott, *Deadly Gambits*, pp. 36–37.

[29]Interview with former Reagan administration official, April 1991.

[30]Talbott, *Ibid.*, p. 38; Communication with Japanese Embassy, May 1991; interview with former Reagan administration official, April 1991.

[31]For an excellent historical examination of Soviet arms control diplomacy from Khrushchev to Brezhnev, see Michael Mandelbaum, ed., *The Other Side of the Table: The Soviet Approach to Arms Control* (New York: The Council on Foreign Relations Press, 1990). Also, for

Negotiations   Traditionally, the U.S.-Soviet arms control experience has been characterized by protracted negotiations periodically prodded by high-level meetings of foreign ministers or even summits. Arms control negotiations carried out by permanent delegations in neutral cities have served a variety of roles: to illuminate carefully the two sides' positions on important issues, provide an ongoing forum for treaty drafting and resolving differences, and demonstrate political commitment to interested publics. Periodic high-level meetings, summits, and ministerials have been used to resolve major issues and to force progress in the negotiating process. Occasionally, this pattern has been short-circuited by restricted negotiations between high-level officials, for example Kissinger's conduct of the SALT I/ABM Treaty negotiations without the knowledge of the U.S. delegation.

Over the past decade, bureaucratic stalemate at home, pressures for more comprehensive agreements, and the increasing complexity of issues on the table have imposed new burdens on the negotiating process. High-level meetings have been used not only as a means of stimulating progress but also, since the mid-1980s, as a substitute for negotiations in Geneva.[32] This reflects a growing emphasis on a top-down approach, forcing bureaucratic decisions on issues that might otherwise languish for months. Such meetings have sought to resolve even the most minor issues, more fitting for working-level officials than foreign ministers. However, in some cases they have been just as ineffective as negotiations. Witness the U.S.-Soviet ministerials in the months following the resignation of Soviet Foreign Minister Eduard Shevardnadze, where neither side, but particularly the Soviets, was willing to compromise due to encroaching bureaucratic realities.[33]

This overreliance on high-level meetings has distorted the negotiating process. Given the expanding U.S.-Soviet arms control agenda, the complexity of the many issues involved, and the limited amount of time for these meetings, limited progress at high-level meetings has hardly made up for the weeks or months many delegations spent treading water.

Form of Agreement   In the past, the adversarial U.S.-Soviet relationship has pushed both sides to seek maximalist forms of agreement. First, most U.S.-Soviet arrangements have been treaties. Since treaties are legally binding international obligations, they provide both sides with the greatest assurance that the other will abide by them. Second, most agreements

---

a more detailed study, see Christer Jonsson, *Soviet Bargaining Behavior: The Nuclear Test Ban Case* (New York: Columbia University Press, 1979).

[32]In 1990 alone, the United States and Soviet Union held 20 ministerials to deal with arms control and other issues. See "The True Believer," *U.S. News & World Report*, July 1, 1991, p. 36.

[33]Interviews with former Reagan administration officials, April 1991.

have been comprehensive. Both sides have attempted to create "complete, self-contained regimes" of limits on weapons and verification measures that reduce the risks of circumvention.[34] During the first two decades of the nuclear age, comprehensive packages found their ultimate expression in plans for General and Complete Disarmament.[35] But since the late 1960s, the two sides have been able to focus on more discrete packages, for example, focusing on strategic offensive weapons. Nevertheless, within these boundaries, agreements have grown more all-encompassing. Limits have become more detailed, verification procedures more intrusive, and language more specific. Thus, the START Treaty is hundreds of pages long.

However, the United States and the Soviet Union have also resorted to other forms of agreement. Political commitments, which are not legally binding, have been used to deal with politically or technically contentious issues. For example, the SALT II declaration limiting Soviet Backfire bombers, a unilateral Soviet political commitment, was kept outside the treaty text because the Soviets insisted that the Backfire was not a strategic weapon.[36] The START SLCM declaration, a parallel political commitment by both parties, was essentially a compromise between the Soviet position that SLCMs must be limited by START and U.S. insistence that limits are not verifiable. Finally, executive agreements not requiring congressional approval, such as the Ballistic Missile Launch Agreement, have served as confidence-building measures that increase transparency but do not limit weapons.

On rare occasions, both sides have advanced proposals for unilateral measures. Many have failed, largely because they were put forward for propaganda purposes. For example, in 1964 the United States proposed to destroy B-47 bombers, which were being retired in any case, in exchange for Soviet dismantlement of TU-16 aircraft, the backbone of the Soviet bomber force. In contrast, unilateral initiatives have produced results when costs and benefits were roughly equal for both sides and when political conditions were ripe for accommodation. The 1962 U.S. pledge not to deploy nuclear weapons in space was reciprocated by the Soviet Union and followed five years later by the Outer Space Treaty (1967).[37] More recently, in the fall of 1991, Presidents Bush and Gorbachev put

---

[34]This term is borrowed from Robert Einhorn, "Revising the START Process," *Survival*, Vol. XXXII, No. 6 (November-December 1990), pp. 497–507.

[35]For a brief summary of those proposals see Jerome B. Wiesner, "Comprehensive Arms Limitation Systems," in Donald G. Brennan, ed., *Arms Control, Disarmament and National Security* (New York: George Braziller, 1961), pp. 198–233.

[36]Talbott, *Endgame*, p. 14.

[37]A thorough study of U.S. unilateral initiatives is William Rose, *U.S. Unilateral Arms Control Initiatives: When Do They Work?* (New York: Greenwood Press, 1988). For an examination of the Kennedy Outer Space Initiative, see Raymond L. Garthoff, "Banning the Bomb in Outer Space," *International Security*, Vol. 5 (Winter 1980/81), pp. 25–34.

forward sweeping reciprocal initiatives that drastically reduced nonstrategic nuclear weapons on both sides, canceled several nuclear modernization programs, and reduced the day-to-day readiness of many strategic forces.[38]

Compliance During the Cold War, arms control treaty compliance was highly controversial because of the largely adversarial nature of the U.S.-Soviet relationship and a basic American distrust of Soviet motives. U.S. accusations of Soviet noncompliance with arms control treaties date back to the 1960s and the alleged venting of radioactivity from Soviet nuclear tests across national boundaries, a violation of the Limited Test Ban Treaty. Nevertheless, the first compliance forum, the Standing Consultative Commission (SCC) created by the ABM Treaty, proved fairly effective through the use of low-key, confidential diplomacy to clear up "ambiguities" in compliance behavior.[39]

Compliance issues have become increasingly politicized over the past decade. President Reagan scuttled the approach of the Nixon, Ford, and Carter administrations and adopted a policy of publicly accusing the Soviet Union of misbehavior and then turning to diplomacy to resolve differences. Although major compliance issues have been resolved—in particular the Soviets are dismantling the Krasnoyarsk radar, which was built in violation of the ABM Treaty—this was more the result of new Soviet leadership than the Reagan administration's compliance diplomacy. In contrast, the Bush administration has sought to restore some balance to this process; for example, the administration's 1990 report on Soviet noncompliance with arms control agreements tried to place potential differences in perspective by assessing their military significance.[40]

In addition, as the range of U.S.-Soviet negotiations expanded, the

---

[38]See "Remarks by President on Reducing U.S. and Soviet Nuclear Weapons," *New York Times*, September 28, 1991, p. A4; and "Gorbachev's Remarks on Nuclear Arms Cuts," *New York Times*, October 6, 1991, p. A12. Chapter 4 offers a more detailed description and analysis of both initiatives.

[39]An excellent study on these issues is Michael Krepon and Mary Umberger, eds., *Verification and Compliance: A Problem-Solving Approach* (London: Macmillan, 1988). In particular, see Sidney N. Graybeal and Michael Krepon, "Improving the Vitality and Effectiveness of the Standing Consultative Commission," pp. 239–259. Also see Gloria Duffy, *Compliance and the Future of Arms Control* (Stanford: Stanford University and Global Outlook, 1988), pp. 163–184; Robert W. Buckheim and Dan Caldwell, *The US-USSR Standing Consultative Commission: Description and Appraisal*, Working Paper #2, The Center for Foreign Policy Development, Brown University, May 1, 1983; and United States Arms Control and Disarmament Agency. "More Effective Use of the SCC to Resolve Arms Control Compliance Questions," January 13, 1989, as it appears in *United States Arms Control and Disarmament Agency, 1988 Annual Report*, 101st Congress, 1st Session, S. PRT. 101-67, December 1989, pp. 313–328.

[40]The White House, *Annual Report on Soviet Non-Compliance with Arms Control Agreements*, Feb. 6, 1991, pp. 8–9.

breadth of compliance diplomacy also dramatically increased. During the 1970s, the SCC was the sole forum for compliance issues. But the Reagan administration, to emphasize its distaste for the SCC, began a pattern of creating a separate forum for each new agreement.[41] Thus, the INF Treaty has a Special Verification Commission (SVC), the TTBT a Bilateral Consultative Commission (BCC), and the START agreement a Joint Compliance and Implementation Commission (JCIC). New forums are being created for conventional arms control agreements and perhaps future arrangements covering tactical nuclear weapons.

Finally, the potential number of future compliance problems may grow. The number of completed agreements is increasing. At the same time, the Reagan administration's arms control policy, characterized by comprehensive agreements and extensive verification measures, has resulted in increasingly complex, lengthy treaties, often accompanied by similarly long implementing agreements. The prevailing view is that crafting very specific treaty language will help avoid imprecisely worded provisions that have given rise to ambiguous Soviet behavior in the past. While this may be true, attempts to draft precise treaty language can prove difficult given a bilateral negotiating process that often requires compromise and the sheer length of new treaties. Moreover, the length and technical complexity of arms control agreements begun under Reagan seem, at the very least, to create a larger number of potential areas where each side's interpretation may differ. At the same time, as will be discussed in the following, positive changes in U.S.-Soviet relations may facilitate the depoliticization of compliance issues.

Implementation   Treaty implementation has been an important but little recognized component of U.S.-Soviet arms control diplomacy. In 1974, the first implementing agreements for a nuclear arms control treaty were negotiated for the SALT I agreement by the Standing Consultative Commission. They included procedures for notification and for replacement, dismantlement, and destruction of strategic systems.[42] Since SALT I depended on national technical means of verification (NTM), these procedures were fairly straightforward.[43] Implementing agreements were also negotiated for the ABM Treaty and the 1971 Accidental Nuclear War Agreement.

Over the past decade, treaty implementation has become an increasingly burdensome, but important, task. The number of implementing agreements has grown with each new treaty, and there has been an enor-

---

[41]Interview with former Reagan administration official, May 1991.

[42]Thomas W. Wolfe, *op cit.*, p. 35. For a list of SCC agreements, see *More Effective Use of the SCC*, p. 327.

[43]The procedures remain classified. The author bases this conclusion on discussions with a former Nixon/Ford administration official, May 1991.

mous growth in their length and complexity due to new cooperative verification measures and continued distrust of the Soviet Union. For example, the 1987 INF Treaty, the first nuclear arms control agreement to include a variety of on-site inspections, is accompanied by an implementing Memorandum of Agreement (MOA) that took four more years to negotiate. The MOA is extremely long and even includes a provision governing hotel accommodations for inspectors. It reflects not only new inspection procedures but also a perception that even the smallest details must be spelled out when dealing with the Soviet Union.

In summary, this brief examination of the arms control process yields the following conclusions. First, strong White House management is critical to an effective process but reliance on informal decision-making is inefficient. Second, the bureaucratic process, by nature inflexible and inertia-prone, has become even more so in recent years. Also, it continues to be plagued by a disconnect between arms control and defense planning and a lack of multiple sources of technical advice. Third, executive-legislative relations are often adversarial but this can be minimized through selectively involving Congress in the process and respecting congressional prerogatives. Fourth, U.S.-allied arms control diplomacy can be successfully conducted provided that the level of allied involvement equals the intensity of allied interests. Fifth, arms control diplomacy has focused on long, careful negotiations and comprehensive treaties but, over the past decade, has relied too much on high-level meetings to resolve even the most minor issues. Sixth, the conduct of compliance diplomacy has become more difficult, the result of politicization under the Reagan administration, the growing number of forums established by new treaties, and a bow wave of ambiguities likely to arise from complicated agreements. Finally, treaty implementation is becoming an increasingly burdensome, although critical, task to insuring an effective arms control process.

ENVIRONMENT AND PROCESS IN THE 1990S

As described in Chapter 1, the end of the Cold War has triggered a number of important changes in the international security environment confronting the United States. If these trends—political, military, and economic—continue, they should provide the United States with new opportunities in its arms control dialogue with the former Soviet Union. However, taking advantage of these opportunities will require correcting existing problems in the arms control process and making adjustments to avoid new problems that may arise as a result of environmental changes.

First, the intellectual basis for arms control diplomacy in the post–Cold War world will have to be firmly established. Arms control policy is clearly a component of broader national security policy. As U.S. security policy adjusts to the changing environment, arms control diplomacy will also have to adjust in order to continue to be relevant. Furthermore, a realistic intellectual basis for arms control initiatives will be critical to building political coalitions at home and abroad in support of arms control diplomacy.

Future nuclear arms control policy should serve a broad spectrum of objectives. Politically, arms control can provide a measure of reassurance that changes in the military deployments of the former Soviet Union (or its successor states) are irreversible, bolster Soviet leaders by demonstrating their successful management of relations with the United States, and enhance transparency through a broader range of negotiations or contacts. In Europe, arms control can play a positive role in managing the transition to a new regional security system by codifying the end of the Cold War, defining any new roles for nuclear weapons and integrating Eastern Europe into the regional system. Militarily, arms control may help further insure against the accidental or unauthorized use of nuclear weapons, particularly by an unstable former Soviet Union. In the longer term, it may also provide an important diplomatic tool for shaping an emerging multilateral nuclear balance.

Second, and even more important, the arms control process will have to be able to respond effectively to the emerging realities of the 1990s. The political process of building coalitions at home and abroad and negotiating with the former Soviet Union has been a difficult, time consuming effort. This is, in part, the natural result of any complicated political undertaking. But the process has also been conditioned by environmental realities: the adversarial U.S.-Soviet relationship, the central role of nuclear weapons in deterring Soviet aggression, and active nuclear modernization programs. Integrating these realities with diplomacy designed to limit nuclear weapons has been difficult; changes in these realities should help ease the way for reforms in the arms control process.

At the same time, adjusting to the environment will also require taking full measure not only of broad trends but also the pace of evolution, which may be haphazard. The 1990s is likely to be a decade of adjustment, consolidation, and uncertainty. Major actors—the United States, Europe, and the former Soviet Union—adjusting to evolving international and domestic realities, will be groping for new foreign and defense policies. When the course is clear, change may be rapid and irreversible. However, periods of adjustment may be followed by periods of consolidation when change is digested. And there may also be periods of uncertainty when change will be glacial.

Developments in the former Soviet Union will be especially important. The failed August coup, while pushing hard-liners into the background and allowing reformers to seize control, also accelerated the centrifugal forces pulling the union apart. The final outcome is as yet unclear. Continued domestic political and economic turmoil can, however, be expected to detract attention from international issues, including arms control, making a sustained relationship difficult. The disintegration of the central government and the devolution of greater influence, even in foreign policy, to the republics will complicate matters further. And, at least in the short term, given the presence of nuclear weapons in many republics, the latter will play an important role in reaching and implementing arms control arrangements.

Third, structuring an arms control process for the 1990s will depend on reshaping its individual components. As noted in the previous section, the process currently suffers from a number of problems, the result of maladjustment to the past decade of nuclear arms control and perennial afflictions that have never been remedied. In other areas, such as U.S.-allied and executive-legislative branch consultations, potential difficulties always lurk beneath the surface and could emerge in the absence of adept political management. Existing problems with the process may only get worse and new tensions may be created where problems do not exist unless the process adjusts to the changing environment.

However, reforming the process is not likely to be easy. For example, just as it has been difficult for countries to adjust to changes in the international system, bureaucracies weaned on old realities may well resist change. However, without reform, the arms control process risks becoming increasingly unreliable, and achieving the prescribed menu of arms control measures risks becoming even more difficult, if not impossible.

RECOMMENDATIONS FOR THE FUTURE

The task for the 1990s is to build an arms control process that corrects existing problems; is structured to avoid new difficulties; is responsive to the changing political, military, and economic landscape; and is effective in building consensus at home and abroad. Key criteria for judging this process are:

- Relevance to the national agenda. The process must insure an effective link between arms control efforts and the broader dictates of U.S. foreign and defense policy goals.
- Timeliness of decision-making. Bureaucratic inertia should be minimized through reforming existing structures and, when absolutely necessary, creating new bureaucratic mechanisms.
- Access to advice and information. Bottom-up input, advice from sources outside the bureaucracy, and thinking about long-range issues should be valued to enhance policy formulation, provide a range of options, and reduce the risks of bureaucratic stalemate.
- Outreach to key constituencies. Consultation and cooperation, particularly with Congress and the allies, should help lay the foundation for a politically viable process.
- Insulation against shock. Early warning of potential shocks, particularly force planning and technology development, should facilitate

an agile policy process and a relevant and coherent arms control
policy.

- Coordination and cross-fertilization. A broad arms control agenda
  will require efficient coordination, as issues might cut across different discussions; to make the best use of ideas, management should
  encourage policy cross-fertilization.
- Flexibility of diplomacy. Dealing with the Soviets or leaders in the
  republics in the next decade could be rewarding or frustrating or
  both; flexible use of a broad range of diplomatic tools will be required.

With these criteria in mind, the following recommendations are designed to shape an arms control process for the next decade.

Strong Central Management

Presidential leadership will be important but could be limited by realities.
The arms control agenda has expanded since the 1960s when President
Kennedy was able to focus on one major negotiation, the Limited Test
Ban. Moreover, that agreement was fairly straightforward, requiring only
ten days of negotiation. In contrast, the Bush administration's arms control
agenda included a broad range of complicated nuclear and conventional
negotiations on treaty documents hundreds of pages long. In the future,
close presidential involvement, except in setting broad policy goals and
resolving issues periodically, will be burdensome. This burden may ease
somewhat if mechanisms other than major treaties are more effectively
utilized.

A strong National Security Council could act as the president's surro-
gate in managing the interagency process. Under such a system, the NSC
would chair all interagency working groups up to the cabinet level. It
would communicate overall administration arms control goals and policy,
as well as lead and direct the decision-making process. The NSC would
supervise the formulation of policy options for decision by the White
House, poll key agencies for their views, and guarantee that decisions are
properly implemented. Such a system would be characterized not by
consensus but by timely framing of options, perhaps by recording majority
and minority views, and sending paper up the line to high-level officials
for decision.

Such central management would have a number of advantages. First,
it would avoid the institutional problems of informal decision-making by
"harnessing the talents of the system and its professionals."[44] Second,
strong central management would coordinate a broad-ranging arms control agenda more efficiently and facilitate cross-fertilization of ideas.
Third, such a system would be more sensitive to overall policy goals, for

---

[44]Gelb, *op. cit.*, p. 20.

example in U.S.-Soviet relations, insuring that decision-making takes place in a timely fashion. Fourth, strong central management would minimize bureaucratic inertia. Fifth, it would encourage an arms control policy more consistent with overall defense policy. Finally, an activist NSC might infuse the system with greater flexibility in considering innovative policy options, for example, arrangements other than formal agreements.

The Kissinger years illustrate the major drawback of strong central management: possible abuse of too much authority, which could damage domestic political consensus. However, one author has argued that, given the enhanced role of Congress and the growing reach of the media, such abuses may no longer be possible.[45] In any case, the potential benefits of strong central management for a coherent policy process certainly seem to outweigh the potential risk of abuse.

Integration of Arms Control and Defense Policy

Better integration of modernization and arms control policy will be especially important in the future. As Chapter 6 argues, modernization and arms control should reflect careful assessments of needs, available resources, and applicable restraints and their net effect on stability in light of likely Soviet reactions. They should also be synergistic, viewed not as independent endeavors but rather as mutually reinforcing means of achieving a common goal. These considerations will be particularly critical in the future since the process of building a stable nuclear balance at lower force levels, as well as the balance itself, may be more easily upset by technological developments and force modernization.

Institutional reform can help insure that foreign policy and arms control considerations are better integrated into the defense policy process and that defense plans that may have arms control implications are disseminated in a timely manner. As in the past, the Department of Defense is likely to resist strongly the participation of other departments, such as the State Department and ACDA, in its deliberations. Therefore, as a general rule, DOD should remain in charge and care should be taken to avoid complicating the defense budget process. Nevertheless, consideration of foreign policy and arms control implications must take place early in the process otherwise adjustments will be costly in terms of time, money, and diplomatic ramifications.

Specifically, dealing with technology development will require wider participation in the weapons acquisition process supervised by the Defense Acquisition Board (DAB). Currently, this process consists of four steps: concept exploration, demonstration and validation, full-scale devel-

---

[45]Alan Platt, "The Anti-Ballistic Missile Treaty," in Michael Krepon and Dan Caldwell, eds., *The Politics of Arms Control Treaty Ratification* (New York: St. Martin's Press, 1991).

opment and preliminary production, and full-scale production.[46] Insuring arms control considerations receive full consideration at the appropriate time will require State Department and ACDA participation in concept exploration and demonstration and validation. This might be done through a process similar to that instituted under the Carter administration, whereby a separate committee chaired by DOD would examine foreign policy and arms control considerations prior to major milestone decisions.[47]

In addition, steps should be taken to facilitate interagency participation in the defense budget process to allow full consideration of foreign policy and arms control issues. For example, the State Department and ACDA could be permitted to attend meetings of the Defense Planning and Resources Board (DPRB), chaired by the deputy secretary of defense, with members from key civilian and military organizations in the Pentagon. The DPRB is responsible for shaping key documents in the defense budget process, including the Defense Planning Guide and program reviews, which are issued every two years, and the Future Year Defense Program, which gives six-year projections for the defense budget. Participants could be as observers (the DPRB already invites nonmember specialists from the Pentagon to its meetings as observers) and, if important issues arose, they could be discussed in separate channels by agency officials. Alternatively, key defense budget documents could be provided to officials from other agencies for comment early in the budget process.[48]

Multiple Sources of Technical Advice

Creating multiple sources of technical advice on arms control policy may be vital to an effective political process over the next decade. Additional sources of technical advice outside the existing DOD/DOE framework would help disseminate such information throughout the arms control bureaucracy, encourage fuller participation by all concerned agencies, and, it is hoped, facilitate better-informed decisions. Moreover, information may be more "bias-free." Also, multiple sources of technical advice may reduce the risks of bureaucratic stalemate by stimulating a broader

[46]The weapons acquisition process under the Defense Acquisition Board has been modified in recent years. Milestone II decisions now include a tentative production decision. For a useful, if somewhat dated description, see *Fiscal & Life Cycles of Defense Systems*, General Dynamics, 9th ed., May 1983, p. 79. Also see DOD Directive 5000.1, "Mayor System Acquisitions," and DOD Directive 5000.2, "Mayor System Acquisition Process."

[47]Clarke, "Integrating Arms Control, Defense and Foreign Policy," p. 14.

[48]Statutory members of the Defense Planning and Resources Board are the undersecretary for acquisition, undersecretary for policy, chairman of the JCS, secretaries of the army, navy, and air force, the assistant secretary of defense for programs and analysis, and the DOD comptroller.

range of policy options. Finally, establishing multiple sources of technical information might be important in sustaining a wide-ranging arms control relationship with the former Soviet Union, which may encompass a variety of technical discussions, assistance programs, and maybe even technology cooperation.

Establishing additional sources of technical expertise may be possible through making better use of the science advisory system in the White House. Future administrations could use the Office of Science and Technology Policy (OSTP) to coordinate ad hoc studies by panels of scientific experts, both inside and outside the government. These might be short-term or long-term studies and could focus on major issues (such as next steps in nuclear test limitations), secondary issues (such as warhead elimination, verification of nonstrategic nuclear arms reductions, or specific verification technologies), and other topics (such as technical assistance or cooperation with the former Soviet Union). This approach would have the flexibility to deal with many arms control issues, some time-urgent and some not, and to match scientific expertise and subject matter. On the other hand, like all science advisory bodies, OSTP has been perceived in the past as "indulging in special interest pleading and ax grinding, and as unwilling to respect the sensitive and privileged nature of White House interests."[49] One possible solution, which would also encourage greater coordination with the national security bureaucracy, would be to give key OSTP staff members joint appointments on the NSC.[50]

The White House might also reinvigorate the national security role of the Bush administration's PSAC look-alike, the President's Council of Advisors on Science and Technology (PCAST). This group already has a number of subpanels dealing with domestic policy issues, such as education, competitiveness, and biotechnology. An additional panel might be established to cover national security issues, including arms control. It could function in much the same manner as the Defense Science Board, which is responsible for providing independent technical advice to OSD and JCS and conducts research projects on key defense issues.[51] Such a group would probably be better suited to dealing with broader arms control issues than more narrow topics or those with a short-time fuse. Nevertheless, it could work in conjunction with OSTP-coordinated studies on micro arms control issues and might also provide quality control for such studies.

---

[49]James Everett Katz, "Organizational Structure and Advisory Effectiveness: The Office of Science and Technology Policy," William T. Golden, ed., in G. Allen Greb, *op. cit.*, p. 241.

[50]Both the Johnson and Carter administrations followed this practice.

[51]The Defense Science Board currently has 44 members including former military officers, industrial leaders, and academics. It is conducting research in 29 areas with 12 projects in active preparation. The current head of the board is Dr. John S. Foster, former director of defense research and engineering for the Department of Defense.

Closer Executive-Legislative Branch Consultations

A closer consultative process may be required over the next decade for several reasons. First, far-reaching measures may require frequent executive-legislative interaction to insure consideration of Congress's views on national security requirements. Second, using forms of agreement short of treaties would, in effect, circumvent Congress's role in treaty ratification. At the same time, Congress will still play a key role in appropriating money for any arrangements short of ratifiable agreements, and its power of the purse will continue to expand in the areas of arms control verification and implementation. Finally, there has been a growing focus in Congress on the interconnection between strategy, weapons procurement, and arms control, particularly for strategic nuclear forces, because of force reductions and resource limitations.[52] This may further enhance Congress's ability to influence the course of arms control efforts.

It is not clear whether new institutional arrangements will be needed to support the consultative process. Existing mechanisms are already complex and may prove sufficient to achieve this goal. Clearly, reliance on forms of agreement other than treaties will require greater House involvement. And, in any process leading to informal agreements, relevant committees will have to be kept more closely apprised of policy as it develops. Congress should eventually be allowed to bless outcomes, for example, through Senate resolutions or language in authorization bills. Finally, House and Senate Observer Groups can provide an important executive-legislative channel for information sharing, a corporate memory, and a cross-section of foreign policy, military, and intelligence expertise. But given their ideological diversity and representative membership, these may also play an increasingly useful role in mediating between warring factions on Capitol Hill.

If these mechanisms prove insufficient, it may be necessary to institutionalize further a formal role for Congress in the arms control process. One alternative might be to establish a Senate, and perhaps congressional, National Security Consultative Group. Such a group would consist of the chairpersons and ranking members of all relevant committees that deal with national security and foreign policy. Its purpose would be to coordinate congressional policy on national security issues and to meet periodically with high-level executive branch officials on arms control policy.[53] Such a group could provide an institutional forum for consultations, both within the Congress and between the executive and legislative branches. On the other hand, it could add an additional

---

[52]Symptomatic of this have been pressures on Capitol Hill to learn more about U.S. targeting policy resulting from the B-2 bomber debate.

[53]This recommendation is made by a number of authors including Blechman, *op. cit.*, p. 216; and Lori Esposito Murray, *SALT I and Congress: Building a Consensus on Nuclear Arms Control* (Unpublished Ph.D. Dissertation, Johns Hopkins University, 1989), p. 453.

layer of unnecessary bureaucracy and engender conflicts with existing congressional committees.

Evolving U.S.-Allied Consultative Mechanisms

The changing U.S.-European relationship will have important implications for the nature and setting of future consultations. First, trends toward a common European foreign policy will probably complicate the conduct of American arms control diplomacy. Arms control may be one of the first issues on which the Europeans seek to forge a common front. If they are successful, the United States will be confronted by one common European position rather than a number of national positions. The U.S. ability to influence European thinking through traditional consultative machinery may be limited in this case, but this need not hinder the consultative process. Rather, creative American diplomacy should seek to influence national decision-making before a common European policy is formed, much the same way Europe seeks to influence American decision-making in Washington before an American position is presented at NATO.

Even more important, existing mechanisms for arms control consultations may eventually prove inadequate or outdated. In the short term, NATO's North Atlantic Council and Special Consultative Group should continue to be the primary mechanisms for consultations, although more regular discussions will have to be conducted with East European states, particularly on nonstrategic nuclear forces issues. In the long term, these institutions may become increasingly obsolete if Europe is denuclearized and/or NATO is superseded by a new all-European security structure, for example, a beefed-up Western European Union (WEU). In the latter case, consultative mechanisms would obviously have to be established within the new security organization. However, there might be less need for U.S.-European consultations, particularly if key nonstrategic nuclear forces issues are resolved.

Finally, a continuing strategic arms control process could create new management problems in the trans-Atlantic relationship. Under one scenario, the former Soviet Union might insist on including Britain and France in the strategic arms control process, through confidence-building talks or discussions covering limits on weapons. At the same time, both countries' reluctance to participate could increase, due to uncertainties in Europe, concerns about the U.S. security commitment, or latent fears about German acquisition of nuclear weapons. Under these circumstances, the United States would face a delicate diplomatic task which could strain its relationship with key allies unless properly managed. On the other hand, this scenario may not materialize in the next decade. In any case, the quickening pace of strategic arms reduction efforts and the increasing relevance of third country nuclear forces suggest the need to pay greater attention to bilateral or trilateral consultations with key allies on strategic issues.

Multiple Forms of Agreement

Over the next decade, the pace of political and technological change, lessening tensions between the West and the former Soviet Union, cutbacks in defense establishments, and a broadening arms control agenda will both require and allow greater flexibility in forms of agreement. Flexibility could be particularly important if change is haphazard; at different times, some forms of agreement may be more fitting than others. For example, confidence-building measures may be more possible than treaties in periods of consolidation.

Treaties   There is a growing sense that comprehensive arms control treaties like START are increasingly ill-suited to cope with the changing world of the 1990s. However, they may still play an important, if diminished, role. Treaties might help codify reductions achieved through other means, such as political declarations or reciprocal unilateral initiatives. Also, treaties may have some utility in areas where no arrangements have been reached and where preventing circumvention may be important. For example, as suggested in Chapter 4, it might be in the interests of both the United States and the former Soviet Union to negotiate a multilateral treaty banning naval nonstrategic nuclear weapons.

Amendments   Amending existing treaties could be a growth industry in the 1990s. There has been an expanding foundation of comprehensive agreements—the recent START and INF agreements and the older ABM Treaty—which provide greater opportunities for further limitations through amendment. Building on existing agreements would lessen bureaucratic and negotiating burdens and, in general, could prove to be a simple, flexible diplomatic instrument.

Nevertheless, the benefits of agreement through amendment may be limited by practical considerations. Package deals involving two or more issues may still prove necessary given potentially different U.S. and Soviet negotiating agendas. And a narrowly focused amendment approach may also cause difficulties at home, since negotiations not only require trade-offs among the negotiating parties but also among bureaucratic participants. Finally, this approach presumes a broad political consensus in support of the original agreement. It may be subject to the vagaries of future administrations' desires to make their own arms control mark rather than build on the past achievements of others.

Any number of existing agreements might be amended in the future. Changes to permitted numbers of ABM interceptors or clarifications of ABM Treaty provisions should be concluded within the framework of the existing agreement. And START's existing limits could be progressively lowered through amendment to achieve further reductions in strategic weapons. Chapter 6 recommends several provisions, such as cutting the existing START throwweight limit in half, which might be achieved through such an amendment process.

Political Commitments Whereas political commitments have been made in the past as part of treaty negotiations, they may have greater utility in the future as stand-alone arrangements. A more cooperative U.S.-Soviet relationship may ease past pressures for legally binding agreements. Moreover, such commitments would seem to be a simple, more responsive diplomatic tool that could help both sides to derive some political benefit from unilateral defense adjustments likely to take place anyway. Political commitments may best apply in cases where partial verification is deemed adequate. For example, in the wake of unilateral but reciprocal nuclear reductions, the United States and the former Soviet Union might consider reenforcing these actions by making explicit political commitments not to redeploy weapons that have been withdrawn and placed in storage.

Unilateral Initiatives There may be wider latitude for both countries to frame unilateral initiatives in the future. Continued unilateral adjustments in force levels and operational practices might set the stage for packaging changes to solicit reciprocal responses. Moreover, continued improvements in the U.S.-Soviet relationship and corresponding reductions in international tensions could increase the chances that such efforts will be successful.

Unilateral initiatives dominated President Bush's September 1991 nuclear arms speech and President Gorbachev's positive response. Many, if not all, of the proposals were based on mutual recognition of evolving international and domestic political realities. For the United States, it had become increasingly clear that tactical nuclear weapons were of diminishing utility in the post–Cold War world. Moreover, it was recognized that the withdrawal and elimination of U.S. weapons could provide the former Soviet Union both an incentive and an opportunity to take similar steps and thereby reduce the risk of the accidental or unauthorized use of its nuclear weapons amid growing political instability. President Bush's cancellation of some U.S. strategic modernization programs, particularly ICBM modernization, was a response to both domestic budgetary pressures and the widespread perception that the requirements of strategic deterrence have diminished as the U.S.-Soviet relationship has become more cooperative. In the future, additional measures might include the withdrawal of air-delivered nonstrategic nuclear weapons to secure storage sites, reductions in the yields and numbers of nuclear tests, and a cutoff in the production of fissile materials for weapons. (See Chapter 4.)

Joint Projects As the arms control dialogue between the United States and the former Soviet Union broadens and their relationship improves, the scope for joint projects—seminars, research, technical assistance, or joint technology development—will dramatically expand. The main goal would be to increase transparency and foster improved communication, particularly with new regional and key military industrial elites. Joint projects would establish an important additional channel of communication at a time when the Soviet system is devolving into something new and unknown. Indeed, this rationale appears to have been behind those portions of the 1991 Bush-Gorbachev initiatives that called for cooperation in dismantling nuclear warheads, improving the safety and security of nuclear weapons, and insuring tight command and control.

First, bilateral seminars could be held, not to reach agreements but rather to enhance transparency, establish bilateral working relationships, and impart useful information. The "seminar" format has been used before: The January 1990 Vienna meeting between all participants in the CSCE process included presentations on conventional military doctrine. Future meetings on nuclear issues could focus on a variety of strategic and nonstrategic weapons issues. Topics could range from doctrinal issues, such as strategic doctrine and the relationship of strategic offense and defense, to technical issues, such as on-site verification technologies, warhead safety, command and control, and technologies for dismantling and destroying treaty-limited items. Chapter 6 recommends several such efforts.

Second, technical issues related to nuclear arms control might lend themselves to joint studies and research.[54] Such studies, building on previously held joint seminars or representing new initiatives, might lay the groundwork for further technical work and encourage future cooperation. For example, during the Bush administration, as part of an effort to agree on tagging for missiles under START, each country demonstrated to the other its proposed technology. Tagging was eventually dropped because of technical misgivings. But joint studies of tagging technology in the future might help ease the way for their incorporation into agreements. Likewise, the Joint Verification Experiment conducted prior to the conclusion of the TTBT involved U.S.-Soviet cooperation in gathering data on determining the yield of two nuclear tests.[55] Future cooperation might involve a sustained joint effort. Other potential areas of cooperation in-

---

[54]The author has based this section on discussions with scientists at the Lawrence Livermore Laboratory, May 1991. Official technical cooperation on nuclear issues could build on already increasing scientific exchanges and the "Memorandum of Cooperation in the Field of Environmental Protection and Waste Management Between the United States of America and the Union of Soviet Socialist Republics" signed in late 1990.

[55]See Lynn R. Skykes and Goran Ekstrom, "Comparison of Seismic and Hydrodynamic Yield Determinations for the Soviet Joint Verification Experiment of 1988," *Proceedings of the National Academy of Science*, May 1989, pp. 3456–3460; "U.S., Soviet Union Agree on Joint Nuclear Tests," *Arms Control Today*, Vol. 17, No. 10, December 1987, p. 26; Warren Strobel, "Early Joint Nuclear Tests Foreseen," *Washington Times*, Feb. 1, 1988, p. 12; Philip Taubman, "U.S. Aides Witness Soviet Nuclear Test for First Time," *New York Times*, September 15, 1988, p. A8.

clude improving warhead safety and developing techniques for weapon dismantlement and destruction.

More extensive cooperation might build on initial technical discussions. Technical assistance could be provided in cleaning up radioactive waste at weapon production facilities, developing insensitive high explosives to enhance nuclear warhead safety, or facilitating disposal of nuclear reactors from decommissioned submarines. Or, the United States and the former Soviet Union could cooperate in joint technology programs. Such programs have been discussed in the past. For example, during the Comprehensive Test Ban negotiations in the late 1970s, the two countries considered joint development of in-country seismic stations to monitor a cessation of nuclear testing.[56] Similar programs could be initiated in the future covering verification techniques such as tags and seals or weapons disposal.

Multiple Forms of Negotiation

Multiple forms of negotiation will be required to pursue this wide-ranging agenda expeditiously. Forms of negotiation should be tailored to the subject matter, the form of agreement, and the prevailing environment in U.S.-Soviet relations. Different forms of negotiation can emphasize the traditional model of permanent delegations conducting ongoing negotiations, high-level meetings, or periodic experts' discussions.

Permanent delegations may become less prevalent, particularly with fewer negotiations for comprehensive treaties. However, they may continue to be necessary, punctuated by high-level meetings, when treaties are deemed necessary. Also, amending existing agreements may prove so complicated and time-consuming that ongoing discussions through delegations are needed to complete the task. For example, such discussions may be needed to delineate permitted and prohibited activities through ABM Treaty amendments. Finally, delegations may play the important role of providing political reassurance if U.S.-Soviet relations enter a period of consolidation characterized by little progress in arms control discussions.

The "top-down approach" to concluding agreements may be more attractive in the future. Agreements would be negotiated at high-level meetings and any remaining details would be quickly wrapped up by experts from both sides. There would be no permanent delegations or ongoing discussions of any duration. Such an approach would seem to hold the greatest promise in reaching simple arrangements and when U.S.-Soviet relations are harmonious. For example, under the right conditions, parallel political commitments to establish nominal limits on U.S. and

---

[56]Interview with former Carter administration official, March 1991.

Soviet air-delivered nuclear weapons in Europe might be quickly concluded at a ministerial meeting. This approach may have less utility when relations enter periods of consolidation when little progress is possible, or in negotiating complicated arms control arrangements.

Finally, periodic, short-duration meetings to discuss specific issues on the arms control agenda, the third approach, may prove extremely useful. Special delegations composed of appropriate experts could attend seminars on a wide variety of doctrinal or other issues, join in technical discussions, or meet to reach quick agreements on technical assistance and cooperation. This approach may prove particularly helpful in fostering transparency by establishing multiple contacts with key elites in the former Soviet Union, such as the military and military industrialists. It may also prove less susceptible to fluctuations in relations because delegations could be composed predominately of technicians, not political representatives, and discussions might not require agreement.

More Balanced Compliance Policy

There are compelling reasons for reforming the U.S. approach to treaty compliance. Already existing problems—an impending bow wave of new issues arising from recently completed agreements and lingering politicization of the process—warrant attention. But, solving these problems becomes even more critical in an environment characterized by U.S.-Soviet cooperation, rather than confrontation, since they could derail improving relations. Moreover, a broader arms control dialogue might include nontreaty arrangements sensitive to disruption by ill-considered diplomacy. The goal of reform should be a balanced, low-key, depoliticized compliance policy.

One important step would be to overhaul the bureaucratic process for judging treaty compliance. U.S. compliance is determined solely by a compliance review board in the Department of Defense.[57] Efforts to involve other government agencies have heretofore been thwarted. For example, in the mid-1980s, the State Department attempted unsuccessfully to participate in deliberations on the compliance implications of SDI testing.[58] By contrast, Soviet compliance is determined by a separate interagency group without reference to U.S. weapons programs. As a result, the process is skewed; all U.S. programs by definition are compliant while Soviet activities are considered without reference to similar U.S. programs. The impact on compliance diplomacy is striking; for example,

---

[57]This process was established in 1972 by direction of President Nixon. Department of Defense Directive 5100.70, *Implementation of Strategic Arms Limitation (SAL) Agreements*, January 9, 1973.

[58]Interview with former Reagan administration official, March 1991.

the United States views the Patriot upgrade as compliant with the ABM Treaty but has criticized the less-capable Soviet SA-12 air defense missile as a potential violation of the same treaty.[59]

An interagency review board to determine both U.S. and Soviet treaty compliance with existing agreements should be created. Such a board would provide all relevant agencies with an opportunity to examine new U.S. programs, raise questions, and further integrate information on U.S. and Soviet activities into compliance deliberations. It would serve as a mechanism through which disputed cases would go forward for higher-level consideration. The board would also provide the arms control community with information on U.S. military programs that might affect the arms control process or U.S. compliance diplomacy. Overall, creating greater bureaucratic cross-fertilization would help insure a more balanced, even-handed compliance policy.

Better Management of Compliance/ Implementation Policy

Management of compliance and implementation issues is becoming critical given their growing importance and the need to maintain the viability of increasing numbers of new arrangements.[60] The multiplication of compliance forums and implementation agreements has made it exceedingly difficult to shape a coherent, coordinated U.S. policy through ad hoc bureaucratic arrangements. The policy-making process in the future should be structured to encourage coordination and coherence, both to insure that the pursuit of these policies is in line with overall national objectives vis-à-vis the Soviets and to improve policy-making through cross-fertilization of ideas. Management should not only be across the spectrum of compliance forums but should also be cross-cutting since compliance and implementation arrangements are intimately related.

First, the United States should consolidate proliferating treaty compliance and implementation forums. Proliferation only complicates policy management and hampers cross-fertilization. However, returning to the pre-Reagan model of one forum might prove unmanageable given the large number of complex agreements and the addition of multilateral discussions with their own particular dynamics. Alternatively, the United States could seek to establish two separate forums, one for multilateral agreements and one for bilateral agreements. Countries would be represented by ambassadors, supported by delegations able to participate in treaty-specific working groups. (Nuclear working groups would be bilat-

---

[59]This disconnect has been noted in the past. See Michael Krepon, "U.S. Government Organization for Arms Control Verification and Compliance," in Michael Krepon and Mary Umberger, eds., *op. cit.*, pp. 282–308.

[60]The author would like to thank Sidney Graybeal for many of the suggestions in this section.

eral but could become multilateral over the next decade.) This would facilitate greater policy coordination, encourage cross-fertilization, and allow specialization. On the down side, consolidation might encourage linkage even though individual compliance issues should be considered on their own merits. However, this tendency could be avoided with proper management.

Second, compliance and implementation should be centrally managed by a senior NSC official responsible for arms control in the postnegotiations phase. Strong central management of these issues would insure that U.S. policy remains coherent and well-coordinated. Presumably, the NSC would establish a uniform set of standards for judging and handling compliance and implementation issues across the board. In addition, strong central management would minimize bureaucratic mischiefmaking which, during the Reagan years, reached an all-time high. Deadlines in making decisions should be enforced and implementation of decisions closely monitored. Furthermore, NSC management would encourage cross-fertilization between treaty-specific groups, both helping to maintain policy coherence and disseminate cross-cutting ideas. Finally, strong central management would help insure that postnegotiation policy, particularly compliance, is in sync with U.S. national objectives. For example, the tone of any accusations of Soviet misbehavior may have to change if U.S.-Soviet relations become more cooperative. One further measure that would reinforce this concept would be to have U.S. ambassadors in charge of compliance and implementation delegations report directly to the NSC rather than to the director of ACDA.

Third, efforts should be made to integrate more fully compliance and implementation policy into overall U.S. arms control efforts. Since the Carter administration, organizations concerned with these issues have been effectively segregated from others concerned with negotiating agreements. Under the Bush administration, these issues are not joined until the deputy assistant secretary level. The result has been to perpetuate largely isolated bureaucracies focused on uncovering noncompliance. Establishing closer ties between those responsible for these issues and those involved in negotiations would insure more efficient policy-making. It might help negotiators avoid potential compliance problems, encourage compliance bureaucracies to see the big arms control picture, and facilitate the learning of lessons from previous negotiations.

CONCLUSIONS AND RECOMMENDATIONS

This chapter makes the following recommendations for an arms control process in the 1990s:

- The United States should adopt a system of strong central management for arms control policy, with the National Security Council managing the process and chairing all interagency groups. Such a system would ensure the timely consideration of important issues, be able to coordinate a broad-ranging policy agenda, encourage an arms control policy more consistent with larger U.S. defense and foreign policy goals, and help the bureaucratic process overcome stalemate and achieve greater flexibility in considering innovative policy options.

- The United States should seek a greater degree of integration in defense and arms control policy-making. The goal of such institutional reform should be to encourage wider participation in the weapons acquisition and defense budget process. The State Department and the Arms Control and Disarmament Agency should be allowed to participate in the Defense Acquisition Board's deliberations on new weapons systems and the Defense Planning and Resources Board's discussions of the defense budget. Such integration would facilitate early warning of technological developments and force modernization programs that could have important implications for efforts to build a stable nuclear balance with fewer weapons.

- The United States should cultivate and utilize multiple sources of technical advice on arms control matters rather than relying solely on the Department of Defense, the Department of Energy, and their contractors. As the arms control agenda becomes increasingly crowded with technical issues, the United States should avoid turning exclusively to those with vested interests and organizational biases for technical analysis. Greater use should be made of the Office of Science and Technology Policy to run ad hoc arms control panels and of the President's Council of Advisors on Science and Technology to examine broader arms control issues. Diversifying sources of technical advice on arms control could stimulate a broader range of policy options, reduce the risk of bureaucratic stalemate, disseminate information more broadly, and insure the fuller participation of other interested agencies in policy debates.

- The executive branch should seek closer consultations with the legislative branch on arms control matters. The goal of such consultations should be to sustain a domestic consensus for a new and far-reaching arms control agenda. Although Congress will retain important levers for shaping policy in the future, it may become concerned about its constitutional prerogatives if the United States pursues arms control arrangements that need not be ratified by the Senate. To avoid potential problems, Congress should be consulted early and often in the arms control process, preferably through existing mechanisms such as the relevant committees and the congressional observers groups. If this proves insufficient, a National Security Consultative Group, comprised of key members of Congress, could provide a new institutional forum for executive-congressional cooperation.

- The nature of U.S. arms control consultations with its European allies should evolve with changing European security structures. As U.S. arms control diplomacy confronts greater European cohesion, it should place increased emphasis on influencing national policies before common positions are formed. In the near term, existing consultative mechanisms—NATO's North Atlantic Council and Special Consultative Group—appear sufficient. But over the next decade, if NATO's role in European security diminishes, consultative mechanisms should be established in new defense organizations. Greater efforts should also be made to consult those outside of NATO, particularly East European countries. Finally, the United States should pay greater attention to bilateral or trilateral consultations with Britain and France if the pace of strategic arms reductions quickens.

- The United States should consider using multiple forms of agreement in pursuing its arms control objectives. As the security environment evolves and new arms control opportunities arise, different forms of agreement may be appropriate in different circumstances. For example, comprehensive, legally binding treaties may remain the most appropriate form of agreement for codifying reductions achieved through other means and for establishing arms control regimes in new areas. But overall, their utility can be expected to decline. Amendments to existing agreements may be a desirable alternative in situations where the bureaucratic and negotiating burdens of starting from scratch would prohibit progress toward a desired goal. In addition, if U.S.-Soviet cooperation continues to increase, domestic political pressure for legally binding agreements may ease and the utility and acceptability of political commitments as a form of arms control may rise. As the Bush initiative of September 1991 demonstrates, there may also be more room for unilateral initiatives; continued adjustments in force levels and operational practices could be presented in a way that emphasizes their arms control benefits. Finally, joint projects—seminars, research, technical assistance, or technology development—should expand dramatically to increase transparency, foster improved communication, and pave the way for future arms control arrangements.

- The United States should also consider using multiple forms of negotiations tailored to the form of agreement being sought and prevailing trends in its relations with the former Soviet Union. Permanent arms control delegations will prove increasingly unnecessary and inappropriate if the utility of comprehensive treaties declines. Nevertheless, they could be useful in negotiating complicated treaty amendments or in providing political reassurance to domestic publics during periods when little arms control progress appears possible. The "top down" approach, emphasizing high-level meetings, should be utilized to negotiate quick political commitments, when U.S.-Soviet relations permit. Finally, periodic meetings of short duration would be extremely useful, particularly for joint projects.

- The United States should seek to establish a more balanced arms control compliance policy by integrating the groups that review U.S. and Soviet compliance. In order to make progress on its arms control agenda and in order not to derail U.S.-Soviet relations as they move forward, the United States will have to deal with compliance problems more effectively than in the past. This will require a more balanced, less politicized approach. However, the current system for evaluating compliance—a Department of Defense group that considers U.S. compliance and a separate interagency group that judges Soviet compliance—is skewed. As a result, U.S. activities are always deemed compliant while similar Soviet activities are often deemed suspicious. To remedy this situation, the United States should establish an interagency compliance board to examine both U.S. and Soviet compliance. Such a board would encourage bureaucratic cross-fertilization and help insure a more balanced, even-handed compliance policy.
- The United States should improve its management of arms control compliance and implementation policy. As compliance and implementation issues become not only more complicated but also more critical, the United States must move from existing ad hoc bureaucratic arrangements to a more integrated structure. First, proliferating diplomatic forums for discussing these issues should be consolidated into two separate bodies, one for bilateral issues and another for multilateral issues. This would facilitate greater policy coordination and encourage cross-fertilization, yet allow specialization through subordinate working groups. Second, compliance and implementation should be centrally managed by a senior NSC official with direct responsibility for arms control in the postnegotiations phase. This would help ensure that U.S. policy is coherent, well-coordinated, and less vulnerable to bureaucratic mischief-making. Third, compliance and implementation policy should be more fully integrated into U.S. arms control efforts overall. Such integration could help negotiators avoid potential compliance problems, encourage compliance bureaucracies to see the big arms control picture, and facilitate the learning of lessons from previous negotiations.

SUGGESTED READINGS

Clarke, Duncan L. "Integrating Arms Control, Defense and Foreign Policy into the Executive Branch of the U.S. Government." In Hans Guenter Brauch and Duncan L. Clarke, eds. *Decisionmaking for Arms Limitation: Assessments and Prospects*. Cambridge, Mass.: Ballinger, 1983.

Collier, Ellen C. "The Congressional Role in Nuclear Arms Control." In *Fundamentals of Nuclear Arms Control*. Report prepared for the Committee on Foreign Affairs, U.S. House of Representatives. Washington, D.C.: U.S. Government Printing Office, 1987.

Divine, Robert A. *Blowing in the Wind: The Nuclear Test Ban Debate, 1954–1960*. New York: Oxford University Press, 1978.

Greb, G. Allen. *Science Advice to Presidents: From Test Bans to the Strategic Defense Initiative*. IGCC Research Paper, No. 3. La Jolla, Calif.: Institute on Global Conflict and Cooperation, 1987.

Lunn, Simon. "Policy Preparation and Consultation Within NATO: Decisionmaking for SALT and LRTNF." In Hans Guenter Brauch and Duncan L. Clarke, eds. *Decisionmaking for Arms Limitation: Assessments and Prospects*. Cambridge, Mass.: Ballinger, 1983.

Rose, William. *U.S. Unilateral Arms Control Initiatives: When Do They Work?* New York: Greenwood Press, 1988.

Seabourg, Glenn T. *Kennedy, Khrushchev and the Test Ban*. Los Angeles: University of California Press, 1981.

Smith, Gerard. *Doubletalk: The Story of SALT I*. Garden City, N.Y.: Doubleday, 1980.

Talbott, Strobe. *Endgame: The Inside Story of SALT II*. New York: Harper & Row, 1979.

———. *Deadly Gambits: The Reagan Administration and the Stalemate in Nuclear Arms Control*. New York: Alfred A. Knopf, 1984.

Conclusion

*A*s the United States contemplates reshaping its nuclear weapons policies in light of the new realities of the post–Cold War era, it needs a vision and a blueprint for doing so. The following compilation of recommendations seeks to answer this need. Drawing together the main recommendations of the preceding chapters, it seeks to define an action plan for the United States—a set of clear and consistent guidelines for seven key areas of nuclear weapons policy. These include: appropriate and inappropriate roles for nuclear weapons; nuclear strategy and targeting doctrine; nonstrategic nuclear forces; strategic offensive forces; defenses; command, control, communications, and intelligence; and the arms control process.

APPROPRIATE AND INAPPROPRIATE ROLES FOR U.S. NUCLEAR WEAPONS

1. The United States should rely on nuclear weapons only to deter or respond to the use of nuclear weapons. While nuclear weapons may have the additional effect of deterring conventional aggression between two nuclear-armed adversaries, this should not serve as the basis of policy. The fuse between conventional and nuclear war should be lengthened as much as possible, particularly as nuclear weapons are no longer needed to deter conventional aggression in Europe. Operationally, this "deterrence-of-use-only" policy should decrease the emphasis placed on nuclear weapons and increase U.S. reliance on conventional capabilities for planning purposes.

2. Basic deterrence (deterrence of nuclear attack on the U.S. homeland) should remain the primary role of U.S. nuclear weapons. With the fading of the Soviet threat, however, the requirements of deterrence will be lessened.

3. Extended deterrence (protection of U.S. troops or allies) should not rely on nuclear weapons to deter conventional attacks against U.S. troops or allies. The United States should continue to make explicit security guarantees to important allies—NATO members, Japan, South Korea—but should reserve nuclear guarantees for countering nuclear threats. In the absence of nuclear threats, the United States should rely on conventional capabilities to deter or respond to aggression.

4. The United States should not rely on nuclear forces to deter or respond to the use of chemical and biological weapons. It is doubtful whether a U.S. threat of nuclear retaliation in response to such attacks would credibly deter them. Moreover, the United States possesses sufficient conventional capabilities to respond in such contingencies. It should, therefore, base its plans for dealing with chemical and biological threats on nonnuclear means. While all weapons of mass destruction should ideally remain unused, it is most important that nuclear weapons remain unused.

5. While deterrence of nuclear use by new nuclear states constitutes a valid role for U.S. nuclear weapons, the possible unreliability of deterrence may require the United States to consider other measures. Nuclear use by the United States in response to an Nth country nuclear attack should be a highly contingent option. Even if another country uses nuclear weapons, it may be in the United States' long-term interest to refrain from using its own nuclear weapons in response. The United States should ensure that it possesses adequate nonnuclear capabilities and options for such contingencies. It should also champion measures that promote deterrence and stability in regions where nuclear weapons have spread.

NUCLEAR STRATEGY AND TARGETING DOCTRINE

1. U.S. targeting doctrine should stop placing the highest priority on Soviet strategic forces and strategic command and control systems and should eliminate leadership targeting. The primary objective of counternuclear targeting—damage limitation—is infeasible at current force levels and is becoming increasingly so as Soviet nuclear forces go mobile and become more difficult to target. Targeting strategic command and control lessens the likelihood of escalation control and war termination. Targeting Soviet leadership is difficult, if not impossible, to accomplish effectively, and massive attacks on these targets would virtually eliminate any chance of negotiated war termination. Because maintaining leadership targets in the SIOP as a withhold would create requirements for weapons that could be destabilizing in crisis, they should be removed altogether.

2. Instead, U.S. strategy should be based on targeting those Soviet conventional forces and command and control systems needed for power projection as well as war-supporting industry. Targeting policy should be designed to threaten primarily the former Soviet Union's ability to project power in a sustained fashion beyond its borders. Such a policy would have the advantages of being credible, sensible from a military perspective, and not as challenging technologically as counterleadership or counternuclear targeting. In addition, it would not require capabilities that would threaten Soviet nuclear forces and strategic command and control with prompt destruction. Targeting of war-supporting industry should be restricted to facilities whose military significance is clear.

3. The United States need hold at risk in retaliation no more than 1,100–1,900 Soviet targets. A notional target base of about 1,500 targets is adequate for determining weapons requirements. If the United States were able to strike targets above this upper bound, the marginal contribution to deterrence would probably be small.

4. The United States should continue to develop and refine flexible, limited attack options involving up to a few dozen weapons, preferably of relatively low yield. Such options are most important for the purposes of war termination and escalation control, and would be intended primarily to show U.S. resolve or to accomplish highly circumscribed military objectives. Having adequate limited options available is crucial to the credibility of extended deterrence and would provide a hedge against the unlikely prospect of limited nuclear attacks by the former Soviet Union or other countries.

5. The United States should take steps, wherever possible, to improve the ability of its strategic forces and associated command and control systems to ride out a substantial nuclear attack and delay retaliation for up to hours or days. The United States should seek to be able to wait until the brunt of a nuclear attack has been absorbed before ordering retaliation. This approach would give the United States more time to weigh its options, resulting perhaps in a more restrained response, and would virtually eliminate the chance that war might be started because of false or incomplete information.

NONSTRATEGIC NUCLEAR FORCES

1. Nonstrategic nuclear weapons have been rendered largely obsolete by changes in technology and the global political situation. The United States and the former Soviet Union should seek to eliminate most or all of these weapons.

2. The Bush-Gorbachev initiatives of September–October 1991 constituted a breakthrough in efforts to limit NSNWs and should be implemented as quickly as possible consistent with safety and security considerations.

3. The United States should accept the Soviet proposal to destroy all naval NSNWs. Further, the two countries should consider formalizing a ban on naval NSNWs and urge other nations to subscribe to such an agreement. Destroying all naval NSNWs would reduce each country's breakout potential, eliminate the unnecessary burdens associated with keeping increasingly irrelevant military capabilities in secure storage, and close the door on redeployment.

4. U.S. air-delivered weapons based in Western Europe should eventually be withdrawn to the United States. This withdrawal should occur on a time scale determined in consultation with the United States' NATO allies.

5. The United States and the former Soviet Union should agree, as proposed by Soviet President Gorbachev, to withdraw all air-delivered NSNWs to a small number of highly secure storage areas. At least on an interim basis, some of the U.S. storage sites could be in Western Europe. Such a withdrawal could contribute significantly to the security of both U.S. and Soviet nuclear weapons and would create a significant political barrier to their redeployment. The two countries should also consider denuclearizing a large portion of their tactical air forces. The United States should ultimately consider merging its remaining air-delivered weapons and nuclear-capable aircraft with its strategic bomber force to form a single integrated force.

6. Arms control efforts for any remaining tactical air-delivered nuclear weapons should eventually be combined with those for the strategic forces. This would avoid the problem of having to distinguish between strategic and nonstrategic bombs.

7. Enhancing the safety and security of Soviet nuclear weapons and minimizing the impact of the breakup of the former Soviet Union on nuclear proliferation should be central objectives of U.S. national security policy. There are many steps the United States could take to help reduce the nuclear dangers inherent in Soviet disintegration, including: pursuing discussions on cooperation on nuclear safety issues; conducting with the former Soviet Union a comprehensive data exchange on all nuclear weapons; urging individual republics to renounce nuclear weapons and to commit themselves to either the prompt destruction or removal, under U.S. or international observation, of all nuclear weapons on their territory; conditioning aid to and diplomatic recognition of individual republics on their signing the Nuclear Non-Proliferation Treaty and accepting full-scope safeguards on all their nuclear facilities; negotiating an agreement to subject all nuclear weapons storage sites to continuous monitoring or joint or international inspection; and negotiating additional reductions beyond START aimed at eliminating those strategic weapons still outside the Russian Republic.

8. The United States and the former Soviet Union should agree to halt the production of fissile materials for weapons. Further, since both countries have far more fissile material than is needed to maintain the arsenals

that will result from START and the unilateral initiatives, they should also agree to remove some of this fissile material from weapons stockpiles and either convert it to civilian use or place it in secure, monitored storage. An initial 50-percent cut in fissile material stockpiles is suggested here.

9. The United States and the former Soviet Union also should consider destroying in a cooperative, verified manner some of the warheads they plan to eliminate. At a minimum, this would ensure that intact plutonium-containing pits of reduced nuclear weapons would not be recycled into new nuclear weapons or stockpiled for future use. They should also investigate the potential role that a program of verified warhead elimination and fissile material limits could play in directly limiting nuclear warheads.

STRATEGIC OFFENSIVE FORCES

1. U.S. strategic forces should be designed to maximize deterrence while minimizing the risk of accidental, unauthorized, or inadvertent nuclear weapons use. The United States should seek to meet these objectives at the lowest possible force levels consistent with stability and within anticipated constraints. Deploying forces in excess of what is required for deterrence is a waste of national resources. In the long term, deep cuts in the U.S. strategic arsenal would likely save money; and in the near term, such cuts would facilitate U.S. efforts to restructure its strategic forces to be more survivable and could reduce the risk of accident or loss of control. In addition, such reductions would encourage U.S.-Soviet cooperation and signal the willingness of both countries to decrease their reliance on nuclear weapons, both of which could advance nuclear nonproliferation efforts. In order to safeguard stability at lower force levels, the United States should seek to minimize the risk of breakout and to deploy forces that are robust against changing strategic conditions. Finally, the United States must field a strategic force that is consistent with the constraints imposed by declining defense budgets, a troubled nuclear weapons production complex, possible future restrictions on nuclear testing, and domestic and international political trends.

2. As a next step in the context of a U.S.-Soviet agreement beyond START I, the United States should seek to reduce its strategic nuclear forces to approximately 3,600 deployed warheads. Such an arsenal, properly configured, would enable the United States to threaten, in retaliation for a Soviet nuclear attack, the former Soviet Union's ability to project power beyond its borders. This force size is based on the notional target set presented in Chapter 3, several estimated measures of weapons performance, and the assumption that the former Soviet Union will not deploy a nationwide ballistic missile defense.

3. As the United States reduces and restructures its strategic offensive forces, it should emphasize the following force characteristics: survivability (to enhance crisis stability), control (to reduce the risk of accidental,

inadvertent, or unauthorized nuclear weapons use), and flexibility (to ensure that a reduced force can still accomplish a broad range of missions).

4. At the same time, the United States should seek to eliminate, or at least deemphasize: extensive MIRVing, especially of silo-based missiles; hair-trigger postures; excess throwweight on ballistic missiles, if the Soviets agree to do the same; and weapons systems that pose new threats to survivability. Doing so could reduce incentives to use nuclear weapons early in a crisis, the capability for breakout, the damage that would result from unintentional missile launches, and the chances of inadvertent nuclear war.

5. In the near term, the United States should maintain a strategic triad as its forces are reduced, deploying 700 warheads on ICBMs, 1,440 on SLBMs, and 1,440 on heavy bombers. Deploying a diversity of forces complicates an adversary's attack planning, increases the overall survivability of U.S. strategic forces, reduces the risk of a technological breakthrough in countermeasures against any one type of weapon, and complicates the task of defending against a U.S. retaliatory strike. In structuring a triad, the United States must pay particular attention to making each leg of the triad a serious concern to an adversary and to weighing the relative costs of different systems in determining the appropriate distribution of warheads.

6. The U.S. ICBM force should consist of 700 single-warhead ICBMs in silos: 500 downloaded Minuteman IIIs and 200 refurbished Minuteman IIs. The United States should complete research and development on road-mobile and carry-hard basing for a small ICBM. Such a force would enhance crisis stability. In the context of strictly limited strategic forces, the former Soviet Union would have little incentive to attack single-warhead missiles in silos, as it would have to expend at least twice the number of warheads it could hope to destroy. The least expensive way for the United States to field such a force would be to download 500 Minuteman III missiles and to refurbish 200 of the 450 Minuteman IIs currently slated for retirement. (Because downloading missiles, when matched by the Soviets, creates a capability for breakout, we would have preferred banning it in the START I Treaty; but given that a limited right to download is allowed under START, there is no additional harm in the United States exercising that right.) Shifting to mobile or deceptive basing schemes would, of course, do even more to enhance ICBM survivability, but the added expense seems neither necessary, given the survivability of the triad, nor affordable, given budgetary constraints, at the present time. Nevertheless, the United States would be wise to preserve more survivable basing options through research and development as a hedge against threats to survivability that may arise in the future.

7. The options of launching ICBMs on warning or under attack should be abandoned in order to reduce the risk of inadvertent nuclear war. Such prompt launch procedures compress decision-making into just a few minutes, increasing the risk that nuclear weapons could be used as a result of

false warning or miscalculation. Rather than focusing on being able to launch its ICBMs quickly, the United States should instead seek the strategic forces and C^3I capabilities necessary to ride out a large-scale nuclear attack, for a period of a few hours to days, and respond only after having had time to determine the origin, scope, and nature of an attack and an appropriate response.

8. The U.S. SLBM force should consist of 1,440 warheads on Trident I/II missiles on 18 ballistic missile submarines, each with 14 of its 24 tubes disabled. The United States should also research and develop a low-MIRV SLBM and a small sub for the longer term. There is widespread consensus that a U.S. fleet of 18 SSBNs would be survivable in the context of anticipated ASW developments. In order for the United States to retain this fleet size as the number of SLBM warheads is reduced, it must deploy only 80 warheads per sub—about 60 percent less than it does today. Although downloading SLBMs would have several advantages, not the least of which would be low cost, the United States should seek to minimize the Soviet capability for breakout by holding the line on downloading at one missile type (the Minuteman III). Although disabling missile tubes, if duplicated by the Soviets, would also create some breakout capability, the United States and the former Soviet Union should be able to settle on disablement techniques whose reversal would require a visible and fairly slow process that would give each side time to respond and would make a breakout attempt less likely in the first place. Deploying either a less fractionated SLBM or a smaller sub would be prohibitively expensive in the near term, but research and development on these options make sense as a means of keeping them open for the longer term.

9. The United States should install PALs on all SLBM warheads to reduce the risk of unauthorized SLBM use. Although the risk of the unauthorized use of SLBMs may indeed be low, the size of the nuclear firepower aboard a single submarine makes this risk worth reducing still further. It is of the utmost importance that the means of enabling the actual use of nuclear weapons remain in the hands of the highest civilian and military authorities—and in their hands alone. In order not to overburden the existing system with unworkable complexity, the United States should design a PAL system for SLBM warheads under which unlocking the PAL and giving a missile its instructions are one and the same action.

10. The United States should deploy a force of 120 heavy bombers: 105 B-52Hs and B-1Bs equipped as cruise-missile carriers and 15 B-2s equipped as penetrators. Because there is no foreseeable mission for penetrating bombers that is feasible, necessary, and able to be performed only by such bombers, the United States need not maintain a substantial force of them. Given the high cost of penetrating bombers, it should emphasize bombers that carry air-launched cruise missiles instead. The United States should, however, retain a residual penetration capability for unforeseen missions that may arise in the future. Given that the B-1B bomber's ability to penetrate air defenses, particularly Soviet air defenses, is expected to decline over time, the more stealthy B-2 bomber is a better long-term

investment. Although the additional cost of buying the small number of B-2s currently in the production pipeline is substantial, the advantage for future research and development of gaining experience with operational stealth bombers is probably worth this cost.

11. The United States should research command destruct systems and, if viable, develop and deploy them on all strategic offensive missiles. Such systems would mitigate the consequences of accidental, inadvertent, or unauthorized missile launches. They would provide the United States with the capability to disarm or destroy a missile and its warheads after launch, or to help the potential victim to do so through the transmission of a code to the system. In order to be viable, these systems would have to preclude the possibility that an adversary could use them to foil an intentional attack.

12. In seeking to reduce and restructure its strategic offensive forces, the United States should seek arms control arrangements with the former Soviet Union that build on the START I regime to the extent possible rather than starting from scratch. These arrangements, whether formal agreements or unilateral measures, should include the following provisions:

- Central limits of 3,000 accountable warheads and 1,200 SNDVs
- Complete freedom to mix among the legs of the triad
- A sublimit of 500 warheads on fixed, MIRVed ICBMs
- A ban on future production of MIRVed ICBMs and, if necessary to gain Soviet acceptance, future production of SLBMs with more than 4 warheads
- A sublimit of 750 warheads on mobile ICBMs
- A ban or reduced sublimit on Soviet heavy ICBMs
- A 50-percent reduction in throwweight below the START I ceiling
- The destruction of one missile of the same type and its warheads for every missile launcher eliminated to comply with limits or converted to a new type
- A ban on the testing of MaRVs and earth-penetrating warheads, if effective verification is possible
- A limit on short-time-of-flight SLBMs, if a meaningful constraint can be defined

13. The United States should pursue as many cooperative measures as possible with the former Soviet Union to enhance verification, transparency, predictability, weapons safety and control, communication in crisis, and greater mutual understanding on a range of nuclear issues.

DEFENSES

1. The United States should continue to abide by the traditional interpretation of the ABM Treaty, which bans the testing of space-based missile defenses. The primary reason for abiding by the traditional interpretation

is the Soviet response that failing to do so would likely evoke. Such a response could take the form of offensive countermeasures, defensive deployments, or a withdrawal from other arms control agreements. Unilateral actions that threaten the ABM Treaty could undermine U.S.-Soviet relations and complicate the delicate and important process of encouraging tighter control over and reductions in Soviet nuclear forces. Furthermore, the restructuring of the SDI program proposed in the following would leave the United States with little to gain from the new interpretation.

2. The United States should seek discussions with the former Soviet Union to clarify ambiguous restrictions in the ABM Treaty. As a treaty of unlimited duration, the ABM Treaty must be able to adapt to changes in technology and the world. The United States should, therefore, seek to resolve important ambiguities in the treaty. Specifically, it should negotiate with the Soviets rational definitions of the terms "ABM capability," "testing in an ABM mode," and "component," among others, in the form of verifiable threshold limits on specific technologies. It should also seek to establish thresholds to distinguish ATBMs and SAMs from ABMs. The United States would also be wise to conduct open-ended discussions on the strategic roles of ABM defenses, as in the future it may wish to reconsider the specific deployment restrictions in the ABM Treaty.

3. To avoid the costs of premature development and testing and to facilitate compliance with the ABM Treaty, the United States should divide SDI into three sections:

- ATBMs. Point defenses (Patriot and ERINT) should be procured in small numbers for rapid deployment in a crisis. Area defenses (THAAD and Arrow), which have yet to prove their worth, should be kept in research and development. ATBMs should not be tested in an ABM mode or given ABM capabilities.
- Fixed, ground-based ABM defenses. Development and testing should be continued as a hedge against possible future threats, but no deployment is warranted under current circumstances.
- Research on other ABM technologies. More exotic technologies like lasers may offer a long-term prospect for effective ABM defense, and continued research and development is prudent. The United States should not develop or test either ABM components using these technologies or any space-based ABM components.

4. The United States should give greater emphasis to research and development on ABM countermeasures. Such research and development would provide another means, beyond maintaining the ABM Treaty, of discouraging and limiting the danger of Soviet ABM deployments. It would provide an effective hedge against Soviet breakout. In addition, a strong research program in this area would provide the United States with an essential foil against which to test ABM systems and concepts. Because of its contrasting purpose, however, this effort should be kept administratively separate from SDI.

5. The United States should maintain vigorous efforts and give a high priority to limiting, preventing, and perhaps reversing the spread of nuclear and chemical weapons and advanced delivery systems, including ballistic missiles and cruise missiles. Such efforts, if successful, could greatly reduce the need for defenses.

STRATEGIC C³I

1. The United States' first priority in C³I should be to maintain effective peacetime control and management of strategic nuclear forces. Maintaining tight negative control over strategic forces in peacetime is crucial to avoiding accidents and unauthorized weapons use.

2. The United States' second priority should be to improve the flexibility of intelligence, planning and C³ systems, and procedures to accommodate changing potential enemies and new roles and missions. A highly structured plan like the SIOP might have been appropriate when the United States had only one clear nuclear-armed enemy. But as enemies change and missions widen to include a broader range of contingencies, planning must be made more flexible. In addition, warning sensors must have the flexibility to focus on emerging threats as well as existing ones, as determining the source of a nuclear attack may be a growing challenge in the future. Improvements in survivable communications and coordination mechanisms might also be needed if warning assistance is to be provided to theater defenses against ballistic missiles.

3. As a third priority, the United States should enhance its C³I capabilities to be able to ride out any nuclear attack. Measures that would increase national confidence in the ability of decision-makers and commanders to ride out an attack before ordering retaliation would go a long way toward enhancing nuclear stability by reducing pressure to launch first or quickly. Improvements in survivability—through mobility, redundancy, and hardening—should be stressed.

4. The United States should make every effort to streamline C³I operations where possible and to adopt acquisition approaches that reduce overall investment and operations costs. The United States should scrap redundant systems that are not significant contributors to overall C³I effectiveness and replace some of the system's outmoded, expensive, one-of-a-kind systems with modern commercial equipment.

THE ARMS CONTROL PROCESS

1. The United States should adopt a system of strong central management for arms control policy, with the National Security Council managing the process and chairing all interagency groups. Such a system would ensure the timely consideration of important issues, be able to coordinate a broad-ranging policy agenda, encourage an arms control policy more consistent

with larger U.S. defense and foreign policy goals, and help the bureaucratic process overcome stalemate and achieve greater flexibility in considering innovative policy options.

2. The United States should seek a greater degree of integration in defense and arms control policy-making. The goal of such institutional reform should be to encourage wider participation in the weapons acquisition and defense budget process. Such integration would facilitate early warning of technological developments and force modernization programs that could have important implications for efforts to build a stable nuclear balance with fewer weapons.

3. The United States should cultivate and utilize multiple sources of technical advice on arms control matters rather than relying solely on the Department of Defense and the Department of Energy and their contractors. As the arms control agenda becomes increasingly crowded with technical issues, the United States should avoid turning exclusively to those with vested interests and organizational biases for technical analysis. Diversifying sources of technical advice on arms control could stimulate a broader range of policy options, reduce the risk of bureaucratic stalemate, disseminate information more broadly, and insure the fuller participation of other interested agencies in policy debates.

4. The executive branch should seek closer consultations with the legislative branch on arms control matters. Such consultations should aim to sustain a domestic consensus for a new and far-reaching arms control agenda. Given that Congress may become concerned about its constitutional prerogatives if the United States pursues arms control arrangements that need not be ratified by the Senate, it should be consulted early and often in the policy process, preferably through existing mechanisms but, if necessary, through new channels.

5. The nature of U.S. arms control consultations with its European allies should evolve with changing European security structures. As U.S. arms control diplomacy confronts greater European cohesion, it should place increased emphasis on influencing national policies before common positions are formed. In addition, new consultative mechanisms should be established as European security structures are formed. Greater efforts should also be made to consult those outside of NATO, particularly Eastern European countries. Finally, the United States should pay more attention to bilateral or trilateral consultations with Britain and France if the pace of strategic arms reductions quickens.

6. The United States should consider using multiple forms of agreement in pursuing its arms control objectives. As the security environment evolves and new arms control opportunities arise, different forms of agreement may be appropriate in different circumstances. Possibilities include: comprehensive, legally binding treaties; amendments to existing agreements; political commitments; unilateral initiatives; and joint projects such as seminars, research, technical assistance, or technology development.

7. The United States should also consider using multiple forms of negotiations—permanent delegations, high-level meetings, and periodic short meetings—tailored to the form of agreement being sought and prevailing trends in U.S.-Soviet relations.

8. The United States should seek to establish a more balanced arms control compliance policy by integrating the groups that review U.S. and Soviet compliance. The creation of such an interagency board would encourage bureaucratic cross-fertilization and help insure a more balanced and effective compliance policy.

9. The United States should improve its management of arms control compliance and implementation policy. As compliance and implementation issues become not only more complicated but also more critical, the United States must move from existing ad hoc bureaucratic arrangements to a more integrated structure.

Index